Francis Allston Channing

The Truth about Agricultural Depression

An Economic Study of the Evidence of the Royal Commission

Francis Allston Channing

The Truth about Agricultural Depression
An Economic Study of the Evidence of the Royal Commission

ISBN/EAN: 9783337039080

Printed in Europe, USA, Canada, Australia, Japan

Cover: Foto ©ninafisch / pixelio.de

More available books at **www.hansebooks.com**

THE TRUTH ABOUT
AGRICULTURAL DEPRESSION

A

THE TRUTH ABOUT AGRICULTURAL DEPRESSION

AN ECONOMIC STUDY OF THE
EVIDENCE OF THE ROYAL
COMMISSION

BY

FRANCIS ALLSTON CHANNING, M.P.

ONE OF THE COMMISSION

LONGMANS, GREEN, AND CO.
39 PATERNOSTER ROW, LONDON
NEW YORK AND BOMBAY

1897

NOTE.

To meet a wish conveyed to me from several quarters, the present volume is now issued with the view of laying before the general reader, in a more accessible and convenient shape, the Report which I felt it to be my duty to present as a Member of the recent Royal Commission on Agricultural Depression. The revision has been mainly verbal, and such as the recasting of its form necessitated. The statement of reasons for dissent from the Main Report is now placed in an Appendix.

F. A. C.

CONTENTS

PAGE

PREFACE xi

CHAPTER I

THE DECLINE OF BRITISH AGRICULTURE

The depression continuous—1882 and now—Results in different districts— Essex — Suffolk — Norfolk — Hampshire — Berks, Oxon, Bucks, Herts, Wilts, Gloucester—South Midlands—Lincolnshire, Cambridgeshire—North Midlands—Yorkshire and Durham—Lancashire, Northumberland—Other English counties—Wales—Scotland, arable districts—Scotland, south-western grazing and dairy counties—The General Situation   1

CHAPTER II

EVIDENCE OF SUCCESSFUL FARMING DURING THE DEPRESSION, AND OF PROFITABLE READJUSTMENTS OF FARMING METHODS

Even in distressed districts—Farming large areas under one management—Instances of success from Lincolnshire, Lancashire, etc.—Stockfarming in Yorkshire, etc.—Self-supporting farming—Special experiments, market gardening, etc.—Poultry farming—Dairy Farming—Scotch farmers in Essex, etc.—Dairying in other English counties—Prospects of butter trade—Jersey dairies—Other evidence—Laying down to grass; Permanent and temporary pasture—Conditions of success   29

CHAPTER III

THE FALL OF PRICES

Sir Robert Giffen's estimates—Corn prices—Wool prices—Meat prices—Fall in dairy produce prices—Potatoes—Notes as to the present position   53

CHAPTER IV

PROTECTION AND CURRENCY CHANGES

Raise prices or lower expenses—Protective duties; evidence for and against—Currency changes—Bimetallism not an immediate issue   60

CONTENTS

CHAPTER V

THE ECONOMIC POSITION OF FARMING IN COMBATING LOW PRICES

PAGE

The outgoings of farming—Cost of farming—Cost of growing corn crops—The four-course system—The cost of labour—The efficiency of labour—The position of the labourer—Fertilisers and feeding stuffs—Does high farming pay?—What items must be cut down to get a true balance . . . 64

CHAPTER VI

THE FARM ACCOUNTS

The balance is generally wrong—Illustrations—Too narrow margin—Instances of better equilibrium—Position nearly hopeless—A fair commercial return—Summary of whole of the accounts put in—The tenant's share—The landlord's share . . 76

CHAPTER VII

RENTS AS A CAUSE OF DEPRESSION

Excessive rents a chief cause of depression—Reduction of rents insufficient—Abatements and remissions—Rents not reduced soon enough—Conclusion—Reductions to bad and new tenants more than to good and old tenants—Scotch evidence—Confiscation of tenants' improvements 93

CHAPTER VIII

COMPETITION AND RENT

Competition in its relation to rent—Causes of competition—Results of competition. Rack-renting by competition—Not the fault of the tenant—Disclaimed by many landlords—Mr Gilbert Murray's suggestions—Rents by valuation . . . 111

CHAPTER IX

THE RELATION OF RENTS TO LANDLORDS' IMPROVEMENTS AND CAPITAL VALUE OF LAND, AND TO MORTGAGES, ETC.

Landlords' improvements—Causes of expenditure since depression—Figures as to some large estates—Improvements on Crown and other corporate estates—Expenditure charged under Improvements Act—Exceptional efforts on large and small estates—Neglect of improvements—Heavy expenditure on mansion houses—The farmers' demand for improvements—Landlords' improvements as a justification for rent—Fallacies of some assumptions—Landlords' improvements really paid for by tenants—Tenant has no similar rights—Rents in relation to capital value of land—Some high rents confiscate wages—Mortgages and other encumbrances—Consequences of overcharging estates—Insecurity of tenants—suggestions, conclusions, and recommendations 119

CONTENTS

CHAPTER X

THE GENERAL RELATIONS OF LANDLORD AND TENANT

Friendly relations—Tenants not satisfied with rents, but disinclined to speak out—Existing rents in distressed districts—Conclusions—Urgency of this question 147

CHAPTER XI

THE AGRICULTURAL HOLDINGS ACT (1883)

Principle of Act—Essential defects: (i.) no machinery; (ii.) no protection to best tenants—Largely inoperative—Costly and uncertain—Dread of counter claims—Restrictive covenants, etc.—Remedies.—Simultaneous claims—Scheduling dilapidations—Limit of claim for waste—Record of condition—Freedom of cultivation and sale of produce—Limitation of counter-claims and penal rents—Freedom to make improvements—Market Gardeners' Compensation Act, 1895—Scotch demands—English suggestions—The law should encourage improvements—Cumulative fertility—Continuous good farming—Laying down of pasture—Other improvements, etc.—Retrospective compensation—Compensation for sitting tenant—Compensation for disturbance—Law of distress—One award for payments under Act and under custom—Existing valuers—Demands of agriculturists—Scotch suggestions—English suggestions—Conclusion as to arbitrators . . . 154

CHAPTER XII

ARBITRATION AS TO RENT

How far reforms suggested really protect tenant—Nature of evidence—The demand for fair rents—Arbitration rather than land courts—The "three F's" policy—Objections discussed—Unfavourable evidence—Conclusions—How far arbitration as to rents is possible—The national importance of such a policy 231

CHAPTER XIII

LEGISLATIVE PROPOSALS

Bills brought before Parliament . . . 256

CONTENTS

CHAPTER XIV

RAILWAY RATES

Character of evidence and complaints—Prohibitive and unequal rates—Preferential rates on imported produce—Helpless position of agriculturists and traders—Recent concessions by companies—Recent history of questions. Report of Select Committee — Legislation—Recent decisions as to undue preference, &c.—Right of associations to complain—Right to analyse rate—Indirect increase of rate, &c—Observations and recommendations 260

CHAPTER XV

SMALL HOLDINGS

Small holdings and the future re-organisation of labour—Isle of Axholme, etc.—The New Forest—Cumberland "Satesmen" and other small holders—South Lincolnshire smallholders—The good side of small holdings—Conclusions—Economic difficulties—Co-operative credit banks—Summary of other evidence—Lord Wantage's experiments, etc.—Sir Arthur Arnold's suggestions—Recommendations . . . 282

CHAPTER XVI

TUBERCULOSIS

Contagious diseases (Animals) Acts—Tuberculosis—Danish experience and Policy—Sir T. D. Gibson Carmichael's experiment at Castle Craig—The probable money gain from stamping out tuberculosis—Mr Speir's suggestions—Action of France and the French Shorthorn Society—Summary and recommendations 300

CHAPTER XVII

GENERAL SUMMARY OF CONCLUSIONS AND RECOMMENDATIONS 311

APPENDIX—

I. Reasons for dissenting from the Report of the Majority . 321
II. Summary of Farm Accounts 347
III. Agricultural Holdings Bill (1897) 356

PREFACE

THE Agricultural Commission may have disappointed those who put their faith in revolutions or panaceas; but the materials it has brought together must inevitably shape and guide public opinion. Whatever else it has done, this inquiry has swept away some delusions, and has helped to crystallise and group in their true relations the inferences which men of sense have long been drawing from the plain facts before them.

Opinions will vary as to the adequacy or practical value of the Final Report of the Majority. To some the Majority Report will appear to lack cohesion, to shrink from thinking out the issues raised, and to keep out of sight many important facts and arguments advanced in evidence. It strikes no definite note, and points to no positive policy. It is vigorous and uncompromising only in its defence of the existing land system. If it has a real policy anywhere, it is that things must be left to take care of themselves.

But this is not the lesson which will be drawn by any impartial reader from the comprehensive evidence of the Commission, or from the vivid records of the local inquiries of our Sub-Commissioners.

So far from telling us nothing, and leading us nowhere, this vast accumulation of facts and figures, of life-long struggles with difficulty, of the decay of land values and crumbling away of the human happiness that has rested on them, of economic injustice and unwisdom, crushing out the hopes of the honest, and stimulating the recklessness of the unscrupulous, of skilful adaptation and patient industry winning success, and of loyal work and kindly consideration, has opened a mine of suggestions for practical statesmanship in dealing with the future of agriculture.

The evidence supplies, as no previous body of evidence has ever done, full materials for an exhaustive analysis of the real mischiefs which have paralysed agriculture, and aggravated the loss and the suffering inevitable from great economic changes.

The long strain of having to make ends meet in bad times has made a good many things more certain. Many truths have been driven home by stern necessity, strong men have thought out the conditions of their work more clearly, and are more ready to say what they think.

In the following pages an attempt—doubtless imperfect in many aspects—has been made by one of the Commission to analyse and sum up with precision what is the real outcome of the evidence as to the economic position of the working agriculturist.

No policy for agriculture would seem worth considering which does not face the facts and the whole of the facts, and which does not supply some real solution for the mischiefs which have intensified the economic breakdown, and stood in the way of economic recovery.

The wider causes of agricultural loss and trouble are beyond our reach.

Protection is dead; bimetallism an academic theory.

What we have to do is to try to clearly understand and deal practically with what is within our reach. And this is exactly where the definite and matter-of-fact evidence of the Commission is a help.

The problem is simple—so simple indeed, that many people seem to miss its point.

We have to keep things going under conditions which we cannot materially alter. The value of the produce of a given area is half—or at most three-quarters—of what it used to be, while the cost of production is not less than it used to be, but possibly more. We have got to make it possible for those who till the land either to produce more, or to produce what will command the higher range of price. That means that our more and more limited resources must, on the one hand, be used with more freedom, and on the other hand, must be concentrated in the most effective methods.

In other words, the narrower the margin of the gross profits over the cost of production, the larger must be the proportion of gross profits left with the working partner to keep him going. But this is just what our evidence proves has not been done. In this great depression, the whole economic loss has been, in general, thrown on the working partner, while the margin has been eaten away by the sleeping partner. It is the sleeping and not the working partner who has been kept going. Hence the sweeping destruction in those districts where the margin has dwindled most.

If the vigilant and open-minded scrutiny, which is applied to scientific questions, be only applied with equal effect to the evidence of the Commission, many misconceptions would be quickly brushed aside which too often have clouded the vision of ordinarily just men.

The gravity and reality of agricultural depression becomes clear to any one who has grasped the fact that, taking the produce and the prices of 1872 as a starting-point, the diminution since then of the gross profits, annually divisible among those who own and work the land, has probably amounted to an aggregate loss of not less than £1,000,000,000, or nearly the freehold value of the land itself.

So, too, most of the economic collapse of farming should be intelligible enough, when it is seen from the evidence that these diminished returns from the land, have, under our present system of tenure, been so unequally divided, that in many cases during the depression, the landlords' share in rent, instead of being double the tenants' profit, as is assumed in Income Tax assessment, has been from seven to as much as fifty times the share of the tenant.

Agriculture has been the weaker to resist the strain of hard times, because of the short-sighted policy of the owner who has in general pushed the loss from himself to his tenant as long as he could.

Again, the evidence of this Commission has thrown a flood of light over the defects and perversions of the law, and the fallacies—wilful or unconscious—which have led to the economic robbery of the men who should be rewarded for enriching their landlords as well as themselves. Instead of a clear line being drawn between the money interests of each party in the current value of the holding, as equity demands, the greater the investment of the improving tenant, the more surely he has been creating a fixity of tenure in his landlord's favour and not his own, and is compelled to go on paying a rent which merges his interest wholly in the landlord's.

In view of the uniform evidence on these points from the ablest and most experienced farming witnesses, the assumption of the Majority Report that things must be all right, because there has been and is absolute freedom of contract, is as indefensible as their assumption that competition is the only fair test of value, is absurd, in the face of the statement of a wise landlord like the Duke of Richmond, that it would be fatal to set men bidding against each other, or of the speech of Lord Londonderry at Darlington in December 1894, when he said "that the root of the present evil was to be found in the offering of competition rents which the land was unable to bear."[1] If the Duke and the Marquis are right, as we have every reason to believe, so far from competition being a fair measure of rents, it is obviously an instrument for enabling the landlord to put up to auction his tenant's property as well as his own.

Again, when it is realised that in agriculture changes of cultivation, the development of less unprofitable methods, the building up of a paying stock, the opening and organisation of new markets, all the operations and processes of re-adjustment, take a long time, and mean investments which do not at once begin to pay, the urgent need for ampler elbow-room and greater elasticity of action is manifest. The evidence of success is even more eloquent than that of failure. Men of judgment and energy have pushed their way everywhere, through the worst of these bad times, where they have had a free hand and unimpaired capital, and reasonable chances.

Whether we examine these central and essential topics, or study the possibilities of organisation in production, handling, and distribution, winning back and keeping the control of home markets for butter, poultry, eggs or other products, for which the British farmer has so many natural advantages ; or again, the future supply of the most skilled and competent labour, which in the opinion of the present writer, would be the result of a

[1] Quoted by Mr John Clay. "Memorandum on Rent, Final Report," p. 183.

bolder development of small holdings on economic lines; or, further, the completion of the triumphs of science in stamping out the last and worst of cattle diseases, tuberculosis; or turn to other well-known fields for useful reform, either by legislation, or administration, or organisation, the evidence of this Commission will be found helpful. It has opened wide the door and pointed out many paths.

All the materials for a bold constructive and restorative policy, to build up and expand the future of agriculture, are ready to hand.

Such a policy has its justification even more in the national welfare than in the relief of a particular class. And in so far as it touches questions on which the interests of the owner and of the worker on the land appear to conflict, there is no fallacy which the evidence of the Commission more clearly sweeps away than the fallacy that tenant right must mean landlord wrong. On the contrary, where improvements are encouraged by absolute security, the value of the landlord's property is the more certainly maintained and increased.

The history of the depression, and of the working of its contributory causes, establishes the fundamental unity of interests, and the law that justice means the best, injustice the worst, economic result to both sides.

FRANCIS ALLSTON CHANNING.

Oct. 12th 1897.

THE TRUTH ABOUT AGRICULTURAL DEPRESSION.

CHAPTER I.

The Decline of British Agriculture.

THE Commission, presided over by the Duke of Richmond, brought together an immense volume of evidence illustrating the initial stages of the great decline in British agriculture, which has been in progress now for nearly twenty years, in the parts of the country worst affected. The reports of the Assistant Commissioners appended to the evidence of the Richmond Commission gave a systematic review of the position of agriculture in typical sections of the country, which is of the utmost value for purposes of comparison with the state of things disclosed by our own inquiry, and by the reports of the present Assistant Commissioners as to the same sections of the country in 1894 and 1895.

In the main it will be found that the tendencies at work from 1875 to 1882 and the results, either general in all parts of the country, or locally limited, which are noted in the earlier inquiry are, broadly speaking, identical in character with what has been brought before us in the present inquiry. The general symptoms of depression in the years 1892 to 1895 were but the more acute development of what was recognised in the years 1879 to 1882.

But there are some essential differences between the agricultural situation now and the agricultural situation fifteen years ago. At the former period farmers were, some of them, swept off their legs, and many of them getting into difficulties, from a succession of cold, wet, and ungenial seasons. These culminated in the worst season ever known, that of 1879. There was for some years a deficiency of crops, and a deterioration of their quality. And the persistence of bad seasons got the land into a more or less unworkable condition, or at any rate very much diminished the productive powers and qualities of the soil. These results were, of course, more marked and decisive in the case of the heavy clays, and generally of arable land, but it may be affirmed that no class of farm really escaped, unless it were the pasture and upland farms of Cumberland and some districts in the north, including large portions of Scotland, where the season of 1879 especially was not so disastrous as in England. But, in the later period, the decay of agriculture has not been marked so much by physical deterioration of the soil from unseasonable weather as by a dwindling alike of the returns and the resources of agriculturists of all classes, showing itself in the inferior working of the soil, and the loss alike in the quantity and the quality of the produce. The physical and economic difficulties of agriculture have not been due so much to Nature as to the increasing poverty of resources and the decreasing margin between returns and cost of production. It is true that the cold summers of 1891 and 1892 and the great drought of 1893 have contributed largely to this impoverishment. But in many parts of the country the continuous heat of 1893 had a specific restorative power on arable land of high quality, like the warp lands of North Lincolnshire, and in its after effects on pasture land. In the opinion of many experts, so far as Nature is concerned, though few of the seasons since 1882 have been exceptionally good, the average of seasons since 1883 has been such as to gradually restore the tone of the land.

In the words of Mr Huskinson, who speaks of large estates in several counties, "There has been a progressive improvement;" "the grass has come round in quality, and arable land never was better." "We were never in a better state with regard to the quality of the land than we are now." But, in spite of this natural restoration, there can be no reasonable doubt from the mass of evidence before us that taking the country as a whole the land is, in many districts, not farmed so well as twenty years ago, that its productive power has been lessened, and that, in some parts of the country, much of the land has virtually passed out of cultivation altogether, in the sense understood for a generation back.

One of the points which merits closest attention in the results of the economic struggle we are tracing is, that, while agriculturists have had an uphill fight everywhere, which has left few unscathed, the results of the struggle have been so disproportionate in different parts of Great Britain. Taking rent as one of the measures of depression, on the excellently managed estates of the Duke of Richmond, there has been a fall of 37 per cent. on the Goodwood property, while on his Scotch property, in spite of heavy occasional remissions, land values have not seriously fallen. Lord Aberdeen, on his Haddo estate, stands where he did about ten years ago, and his agent could relet farms at a 10 per cent. advance. Lord Wantage, in Northamptonshire, gets only half the net receipts he did ten years ago, and but a third of what he got in 1875. The contrast is still more striking when we find on cold clay land a Yorkshire farmer, near a moderately big town, can keep going and pay a rent of 36s an acre, and all the successive increases of local rating in addition, while on hundreds of farms, with a soil not wholly dissimilar, in Essex, a rent of from 10s down to 1s an acre has not meant a livelihood, within an hour by rail of the largest concentrated population in the whole world.

The north, on the whole, has been and still is far better off than the south. This may be roughly illustrated by the net rental of the agricultural portion of the Crown lands. In the northern counties of England, 21,503 acres are let, a rent of £26,747, with only £470 of remissions, and none of the land is in hand; while in the southern and midland counties £8191 has to be remitted on a rental of £53,251 for 46,317 acres, and 1676 acres are in hand.[1]

It is obviously, therefore, of importance in elucidating the causes of the depression, both fundamental and contributory, and in arriving at suggestions which may help the future position of agriculture, to summarise the evidence as to the special characteristics and stages of the depression in the several parts of the country.

Using for convenience the divisions adopted in the agricultural returns, it is plain that the great tract of arable land in Divisions 1 and 2, the chief corn-producing area, in which scientific agriculture has had its most striking triumphs, has suffered most. And within this vast area, it has been in the eastern and some of the southern counties, that agriculture has been longest in decay, and has sunk to the lowest stage of exhaustion. To a large extent, the nature of the soil has been the measure of the acuteness of the depression. The very heavy clays which are hardest and most costly to work, and the light lands which were artificially brought into high cultivation under the stimulus of high prices for corn have naturally been worst hit. This has been the general result in Essex, Suffolk, and Norfolk, Wilts, Hants, Berks, Beds, Northants, Hunts, and other counties. Where, on the other hand, there is a rich and fertile soil, which can be easily and cheaply worked, as in parts of Lincolnshire and Cambridgeshire, and in some districts of Northamptonshire, or where the nature of the soil has led to mixed farming, there the losses and deterioration of agriculture have been materially lessened.

In Essex, within twenty years whole tracts of land, previously yielding heavy crops and paying high rents, have passed almost out of cultivation, while hundreds of the men who have spent their lives in earning those rents have been ruined and obliged to give up farming.

"No one can well conceive, who has not seen it, the condition to which a large part of the land, which has been allowed to tumble down to grass, has been reduced.

[1] Appendix A. II., Vol. I.

A real calamity has fallen upon a wide district. The farmers and labourers have gone. The farms, where let, have been taken rather as ranches for cattle than for serious cultivation. The farmers who have survived have lost heart."[1]

The stages of this process are clearly indicated in Mr Pringle's report. Essex farmers began to break as soon as wheat went below 50s a quarter, from 1875 onwards. The season of 1879 crippled the remaining old tenants, ruined many new tenants, and threw a large number of farms upon the hands of owners, who cultivated them for some years with heavy losses. "Farmers continued struggling along as best they could, paying rent in driblets, getting involved in various ways, and gradually allowing their stiffest fields to drift out of cultivation."

Between 1880 and 1889 there were an enormous number of changes of tenancy. Everywhere farms have been falling from old rents of 40s to 25s down to a shilling or two, or the tithe, or absolutely nothing. One witness says, "In this parish more than half the land has gone out of cultivation. I am the only old tenant left. On many farms, tenants, two or three deep, have come and gone within the last ten years, the greater part either completely ruined or nearly so." "Landlords will accept any rent rather than take exhausted land into their own hands." There are fewer unoccupied farms in Essex now than ten years ago, largely because the land which has tumbled down to rough herbage is now capable of being used for temporary sheep runs, and is let for that purpose at a nominal rent.

The soil and subsoil in most of the Essex corn area have been as responsible for these disasters as the great fall in prices. The Essex farm has always and will always be costly to work. It is costly even where the blue clay has a porous, gravelly subsoil. It is still more costly when the subsoil is, in the words of one of Mr Pringle's witnesses, "stiff, tough, numb, dumb, and impervious, so that during heavy rains the vegetable

---

[1] Notes of visit of Mr Shaw Lefevre, p. 5.

mould and manures are washed off the surface on to the great mud beds of the rivers. The plants are at once waterlogged and starved." "When once the strong, three-horse, clay land is let lie untended for twelve months, the probability is that it will pass out of cultivation altogether."

And recovery, in these cases, is economically impossible. This heavy land would require two years' fallowing and a good dressing of lime, and in many cases thorough redraining to restore it to cultivation. But this description of land is now not worth more than £5 or £6 an acre, and the process of restoration would cost from twice to three, or, even in some cases, four times the freehold.

The situation is the less hopeful for this class of land, because it will not naturally bear really good grass.

The heavy land is hopeless for arable purposes if present prices continue.

Mr Darby's evidence does not materially qualify the general results stated. His contention is that most of the land is earning some small rent, and although he does not deny that the cost of restoring the workable condition of the heavy clays, under present circumstances, is prohibitive, he thinks that the "tumbled-down" deteriorated fields could be made much more of than they are now. He does not attempt to disprove the general disappearance of high cultivation, or the enormous depreciation of values, and his evidence rather turns on the definition of the word "derelict" land.

Mr Matthews, who farms nearly 1600 acres on the Dunmow side of Chelmsford at a rent of £1 an acre—land more easily worked, and suitable for heavy manuring with fertilisers—states that selling off all roots, clover, hay, and straw, feeding bullocks, and going in also for poultry and pigs, he has done fairly well, and "keeps even now on the right side of the line." Others are in the same position. Farmers even on this better soil cannot save money. Mr Matthews wholly confirms Mr Pringle's views of the worst districts.

Turning to Suffolk, the heavy lands which form

two-thirds of the agricultural area, have had much the same history as in Essex.

Things began to go down from 1875, and went from bad to worse, unpropitious seasons and progressive impoverishment of tenants deteriorating the soil, and making recovery more and more economically impossible.

The losses on the light land, which only high prices brought under cultivation, are only less heavy. Mr Fox gives particulars of 38 farms, comprising 4741 acres, which were totally abandoned at the close of 1894, and thinks there may be many more.

He adds, " Many predict that a considerable quantity of the very heavy and very light land must go out of cultivation after Michaelmas 1895. Even where farms are let, much of such land is practically uncultivated, and used as rough sheep runs. Its value is put at 1s an acre or less. The deterioration has been progressive, less labour being employed, the land getting foul, and, less stock being kept, fertility has been decreasing.

" There has been an enormous depreciation, both in the letting and selling value of land, especially the latter. Rents have fallen anywhere from 50 per cent. to nothing at all. Land, where saleable at all, has sold at nominal value, less than the cost of the buildings in some cases.

" Again, things have gone badly with Suffolk, mainly because, with rare exceptions, the Suffolk soil is not suited for producing, at any rate, the best quality of pasture. It is difficult to grow anything else but cereals on a considerable proportion of it." On many estates there is practically no return at all, on most it would be impossible for owners to keep up buildings and repairs unless they have other resources than the rents, while among tenant farmers there is widespread despair, and even on liberally managed estates there have been practically no applications for farms.

In Norfolk, as in Suffolk, there has been disastrous and persistent falling away from a high standard of productivity, and of prosperity ever since 1875. The features of the decay are also similar. With the exception of the naturally rich soil of the north-eastern part of the county, the splendid results of arable farming in Norfolk were due to the triumph of science and capital over the "niggardliness of Nature," and there has been a steady tendency to revert to the poorer condition of things a century ago, a tendency accompanied by widespread ruin to both landowner and farmer.[1]

Mr Read, whose lengthened experience and authority is of exceptional value, describes the condition of the farmers of Norfolk as "verging on absolute ruin and wholesale bankruptcy."

"*Almost all the land that has been improved during my lifetime has now gone back to its original condition.*" The light lands are not now worth as much as they were before they were broken up; the heavy land which steam cultivation and high farming has made so productive, and the light fens, which were drained fifty years ago, have now all gone back. Bad seasons began the troubles, persistent fall in prices deepened them, and the impoverishment of both owner and tenant have helped to complete the work. The land has either drifted out of the old cultivation altogether, or production is less, because the land can neither be properly stocked nor farmed.

Mr Rew describes the position at the close of the year 1894 as one of acute panic. The long process, which had begun in the bad seasons from 1876 to 1883, was brought almost to a close by the unpropitious harvests of 1892 and 1894, and the drought of 1893, coupled with the great fall in prices of corn, wool, cattle, and sheep. The Report of the Committee of the Norfolk Chamber of Agriculture estimates that the depreciation of the freehold value of agricultural land has been £25 an acre, or £30,000,000, in the whole county, while the tenant farmers have lost £5 an acre of their capital, or over £6,000,000.[2] On Lord Leicester's estate, where no tenant had ever before thrown up a farm, eight farms were vacated from Michaelmas 1894. As in Suffolk, even on excellent estates, there have been few, if any, applicants

---

[1] Rew, Norfolk, p. 3.   [2] Norfolk, p. 25.

for vacated farms. In one district it was stated that 3000 acres might be had rent free.¹

Dealing further with the great corn-growing belt of country where depression has been most severe, we find that in Hampshire much of the land which formerly yielded large returns with turnips, oats, and rotation grasses, is now worth nothing, and has gone out of cultivation. Mr James Stratton estimates this area as " about one-eight of the whole county."

Dr Fream, in his report on the Andover side of the county at the close of 1893, gives a deplorable picture of despairing farmers, asking for " prairie rents," and at their wits' end to find any profitable or economical substitute for wheat, which can no longer be grown without heavy and constant loss.

North of Andover there is much land letting at 2s 6d an acre, upon which the tithe is 6s, and yet with " rents down to nothing," not even a fair interest on the cost of buildings, much less enough to enable landlords to carry out repairs, the majority of tenants seem to be losing money.

The average fall of rents has been 50 per cent., but, in Mr Stratton's opinion, rents must go down 25 per cent. more to enable tenants to make ends meet. Mr Stratton himself was able to hire a square mile of arable land for a sovereign, in other words for the rates and taxes and cost of cultivation.²

Mr Eyre's interesting evidence as to small holdings in the New Forest district is dealt with in the chapter on small holdings.

Although the position has probably improved not a little since the disastrous drought of 1893, Mr Stratton's opinion that landlords who had no other resources than agricultural land could not maintain their estates, and that tenants are on the verge of ruin, cannot be treated as an exaggerated view of the position in many such districts.

In adjacent districts of Berkshire and Oxfordshire,

¹ App. B. 1. p. 19.
² This farm has since been relet by the owner.

on the line of the downs, large tracts of land which have in past years grown fair wheat and barley, excellent turnip crops, and have produced some of the finest sheep in the country, are now out of cultivation and practically worthless. The freehold value has enormously depreciated throughout this district. On the Duchy of Cornwall farms in Berkshire rents have fallen from 35s in 1880 to 4s 5d in 1893.

In districts like the Vale of Aylesbury, the rich pastures have not suffered though the price of milk has fallen, but even there land values are shown to be depreciated by sales. Hertfordshire has seen many changes of tenancy on the poor and heavy lands; tenants are impoverished, land worse cultivated.[1] But the condition of this county is altogether better than the adjacent districts of Essex, and farms near railways have by catering for the London markets secured a degree of profit where worked with skill and capital.

As to Wiltshire, on the great chalk tableland of Salisbury Plain, where 57 per cent. of the total cultivated area is still under the plough, there have been reduction of rent from 30 to 75 per cent., while farmers have lost heavily, the large holdings of this district requiring the constant application of a considerable capital. Sir Michael Hicks Beach vividly illustrates the depression in Wiltshire by his evidence that, with the heavy reductions of rent, tenants were neither gaining or losing money, but just holding on, and, on the other hand, the rents were not "living rents" for the landlord. Some witnesses doubted whether any reduction of rent could keep the land in cultivation, but the course of events has led rather to the abandonment of farms. The poor and thin downlands were broken up between the forties and the seventies, and are now "tumbling back" to their former condition, but deteriorated so that the old grasses will take many years to get back to what they were forty years ago. To some extent agriculture has been helped by the careful system of water meadows adopted. Where dairy farming is possible, and has been well

[1] A. Spencer, Aylesbury and Herts, pp. 21, 22.

developed as in North Wiltshire, the conditions are much more favourable.

In the hill districts of Gloucestershire, farms which rented from 20s to 31s 9d an acre in the seventies, now stand at from 12s to 8s.

Mr Spencer says of this stretch of country, "The poorest arable land has suffered most of all. The cold, bleak soil of the Cotswold Hills, and the thin chalk land on the Berkshire Downs and Chiltern Hills, when prices fall below a certain level, can no longer be cultivated at a profit, and as they cannot be laid down, must economically drop out of cultivation."[1]

Turning to the South Midlands, Mr Pringle has given a vivid sketch of the decline of agriculture in Bedfordshire, Northamptonshire, and Huntingdonshire.

The cold, wet seasons from 1875 to 1880 gradually put the heaviest clays out of workable condition, and started the ruin of the rest. And the mischief was not confined to arable land. The finest pastures of Northamptonshire were deteriorated by the icy rains of 1879; the grasses became coarse and fell to the level of store grazing, while "fluke" destroyed flocks by the thousand, and swept away farmers' capital. And since 1879 there have been continually falling markets, and the farmer has been unable to recover his capital.

"Serious loss, if not ruin," he says, "threatens everybody whose capital is represented by or invested in land. I much doubt whether half of the arable farmers of the three counties could pay 20s. in the £. Were I to accept the evidence given to me without qualification, I would be compelled to report that over a large proportion of these counties, farming has assumed all the features of a bankrupt industry."[2]

Up to 1890 graziers had done fairly well, but since that year the fall in the value of fat stock, and the scarcity and dearness of store cattle, have pulled them down too.

In these, as in the eastern counties, the heavy clays and the light lands have suffered most, while there is, in all of them, a residuum of exceptionally good and well

---

[1] Spencer, Oxford, etc., p. 29.   [2] Pringle, Beds, etc., p. 54.

placed land that has escaped—sometimes rich pastures, in other districts the deep loam of the fens.

Lincolnshire and Cambridgeshire show, except locally, a less serious phase of the distress. Mr Fox in 1895 reports of Lincolnshire, "Owing in the first instance to bad seasons, commencing in 1874, and then to the rapid and continuous fall in all prices from 1882 and 1883, coming at a time when there had been great losses, through decreased yields and sheep rot, and also when the land was much deteriorated, the farming industry has suffered blow after blow, until the present time, when the situation is extremely critical and the future outlook of the gloomiest character."

During the wet seasons "grass was deteriorated, manure washed out of the soil, and there was no opportunity of getting the farms clean." "The strong land felt the effect of the wet first, and that suffered more than any other, as it became perfectly sodden and almost incapable of being worked," while the warp and marsh lands were seriously affected also. In mere physical condition, the hot seasons of 1887 and 1893 had a distinctly restorative value. But this county has, from the quality of its several types of soil, and from the high standard of cultivation maintained for generations, and the large amount of capital in the hands of farmers, held out better than East Anglia.

The letting and selling value of land, where there is any demand, has gone down practically nearly one half.

The best farms are said on good authority to have depreciated 20 per cent., the average farms 33 per cent., and the heavy clays from 60 to 75 per cent.[1]

Much of the land, especially in North Lincolnshire, is still well farmed and in a high state of cultivation, and the rich potato and market gardening lands in the south and east are still productive, though rents have fallen. There is a striking absence of the "tumbled-down" and "twitched-down" land of several other counties, and there has been so far little, if any, of the starving off of stock, especially sheep, which has helped

[1] Messrs Thompson & Sons, quoted by W. F., p. 48.

to ruin the fertility of other counties. But the last ten years have made tremendous inroads on tenants' capital, and the bad seasons of 1892 and 1894 have still further weakened the corn farmers, as the drought of 1893 struck down the grazing men.

The position of the small freeholders in the Isle of Axholme and elsewhere is dealt with in the chapter on small holdings.

In Cambridgeshire, while much of the fen land in the Wisbech district (used largely for fruit growing) and some of the medium turnip and barley land in the Newmarket district has pulled through without much loss, the heavy land has followed much the course of Suffolk and Bedfordshire, has been allowed to seed itself down, and "is on the verge of abandonment," while rents have fallen from 50 to 80 per cent. Changes of tenancy have been frequent, celebrated flocks of sheep have been broken up, and farmers are on the brink of bankruptcy. But the economical position is not everywhere unsatisfactory. Mr Pell, farming 1034 acres of good land in the Isle of Ely, had, up to 1892, been able to pay himself a rent of 47s an acre, though he lost money in 1893 and 1894. Such an experience cannot be unique, and obviously leaves a margin for a moderate rent for owners, and a small profit for occupiers.

Mr Turner, Assistant Commissioner, reporting at the end of 1893, gave a gloomy account of the position of the heavy, and formerly most productive, wheat and bean land in Warwickshire, and of the decay and abandonment of land and buildings in these districts. Rents have fallen from 25 to 60 per cent. Other evidence puts a more favourable light on the condition of other parts of Warwickshire. Staffordshire has suffered less, rents having fallen from 10 to 20 per cent. ,but in Mr Carrington-Smith's opinion, the tenant farmer has borne most of the loss. On the other hand, landlords have a smaller margin, as the increase of stock and dairy farming demands outlay on buildings. The spread of dairy work and stock feeding has mitigated the depression.

The milk, butter, and cheese districts in Cheshire, Derbyshire, and in the Melton division of Leicestershire, have fairly weathered the times, though prices have fallen heavily for cheese, and about 20 per cent. for milk. Professor Sheldon says of these North Midland districts that twenty-five years ago farmers were making good profits, now they are just paying their way. Here, as in all the dairy and stock-feeding counties, the low price of imported grain and feeding-stuffs has helped some farmers, while it has been ruin to others. There is in these districts an active competition for all farms in fair condition, and no difficulty in letting land, at any rate for dairy farming.

In Yorkshire it took the porous, shallow soils of the wolds six years to recover from the "washing out" of their fertility in 1879. The depletion of capital thinned the stock and impoverished the land, but the main body of farmers managed to hold on, and the last three years have not been as unfavourable in Yorkshire as further south.[1] But the enormous fall in the price of wool has crippled these sheep-breeding lands, meaning by itself a loss of 10s an acre. The career of the heavy clay land in the Darlington and Cleveland districts was much the same as in other counties. A large proportion went out of cultivation before 1885, and much of it has fallen two-thirds in value, and where, as is not infrequent, redraining is necessary the clays cannot be let at all. On the mixed soil the depression has been only less marked. Where there has been "a fair proportion of old grass things have been helped by sheep breeding." Till the exceptional drop in the prices of sheep and lambs in 1891 and 1892, the pastoral farms in the Yorkshire dales did well. On the whole, though there have been heavy losses to all classes concerned with the land, the high standard of cultivation has been kept up, and grass land shows signs of liberal treatment, and there is a keen competition for farms in fair condition, and no farms are derelict.

Mr S. Rowlandson, in the Darlington district, states

[1] Pringle, Yorkshire, p. 9.

that for some years he has "been hard set to make a balance, and has had heavy losses," and Mr Christopher Middleton, near Middlesborough, says, "profits have vanished," and that he cannot "understand how rents are kept so high. They must be paid out of capital. He would not like to say any farmer is making a profit beyond living." "Not half the farmers in the country have sufficient capital employed on their farms."

The evidence of Mr Riley, Mr Harrison, and others was generally to similar effect.

In the grazing districts near Skipton the position of farmers has been extremely precarious.

Lancashire farmers have hitherto held their own through periods of depression by their remarkable industry and thrift. But in the last few years it is clear that the heavy fall in prices, especially of stock, has swept away the whole or most of their margin, and there have been no sufficient reductions of rent to restore it.

"Most of the farmers are nearly ruined, and many are farming on borrowed capital. Some large farmers state that, after feeding and clothing themselves and their families, and paying no wages to their sons and daughters, they have made nothing for the last year or two, and some have had to draw on capital."[1] Some witnesses think there has been deterioration of farming and of the soil, but Mr Fox thinks that in many cases the land is farmed even better than formerly.

The economic loss of the last few years has not fallen exclusively on the tenant, although remissions of rent have fallen far short of a fair proportion to depreciation of produce. On many estates a heavy outlay has been maintained to keep tenants going.

In Northumberland, agriculture seems to have been kept in a somewhat more stable position. Security of tenure, by long leases, concentrated the capital and enterprise of improving tenants on the land in the good times, and even in the bad times the heavy expenditure of landlords in improvements has helped to mitigate loss. But Mr Scott, farming nearly 10,000 acres, and

[1] Mr Wilkinson, quoted by Wilson Fox, Garstang, p. 13.

speaking from long experience, states that at present prices profits are unattainable.

"I happen to keep books, and last year I showed that I had made no money on all this land of mine, and paid no income tax at all." Farmers are poorer, and farming has deteriorated. More farmers would throw up their farms, but the poorer they get the more reluctant they are to lose their homes and realise their losses. And although rents have not fallen in any proportion to prices there is a keen competition for farms, mainly from those "who have not yet burned their fingers."

There is no doubt that the fall in prices of cattle and sheep, etc. in recent years has pinched agriculture most, and that the reason why things are not as bad as farther south is that there is a considerable reserve force to draw upon in the thorough farming of the past. "The land has for many years been exceedingly well farmed, and hence is more able to bear economy of labour, manure, and feeding stuffs."[1]

Cumberland, one of the few districts reported by the Richmond Commission to be in a prosperous condition, has suffered little, except from the contracted corn prices, and their inevitable effect on some of the heavy land. But cattle and sheep, which have fallen least, have been the staple products, and the patient industry and economy of the northern farmers has kept things fairly straight.

Turning to the south-western and western counties, farming has had more channels to work through, and has not fared so badly.

Dorset, with nearly 300,000 acres of permanent pasture, and less than 200,000 of arable land, and of that only 89,000 in corn crops, and being more a breeding than a grazing county, has suffered chiefly from the fluctuations in the price of stock and the heavy fall in the price of wool. There has been an inevitable depression in the letting and selling value of land; tenants have lost capital, and here and there are examples of ruin and acute depression.

[1] Wilson Fox, Glendale, p. 10.

Devonshire, whose position was favourable at the time of the Richmond Commission, has not generally sunk beyond the stage of 10 to 20 per cent. remission of rent. " In many cases there has been no reduction of rent at all." The economic loss so far, of the fall of prices, has been left on the shoulders of the tenants. The drought of 1893, coming on top of the bad prices of previous years for stock and everything else, has undoubtedly reduced many farmers to financial straits. Farms are less well kept up, in the opinion of some witnesses, but the management of stock has improved, and the use of manures and feeding stuffs greatly increased. There is also an increase in the number of live stock.

Cornwall is, on the whole, even better off than Devonshire. This is partly because so little corn is grown, and stock farming is the main feature, partly because where the farming is arable the rotation has some time ago been lengthened by laying down grasses, and by a full use of labour-saving machinery.

In Herefordshire and Worcestershire, there is no serious depression more than the economic narrowing of the margin between outgoings and incomings for owner and tenant. Good stock, and fruit growing have lessened the difficulties of agriculture. Nor does distress appear to be extensive in Shropshire.

In Kent, part of which has been reported upon by Dr Fream, hops and fruit have tided many men over, and made some prosperous. But where there are no hops or fruit, rents are in some cases down to a nominal figure, and much land has been passing out of cultivation, as in Hampshire and Essex.

WALES.

The evidence from Wales shows that, while Wales generally escaped the earlier stages of the depression, in which many parts of the arable districts in England suffered so severely from the effects of bad seasons, the course of events in the later stages has been much the same as in

England. Arable districts, such as parts of Denbighshire, Flintshire, Glamorganshire, Cardiganshire, Carmarthenshire, and Monmouthshire, have suffered severely, and there have been many changes of tenancy. The larger farmers seem everywhere to have suffered most, though this is mainly a question of adequate capital.

Mr R. Stratton, who farms over 3000 acres in Monmouthshire, says that for the last ten or fifteen years he has just made a living, without interest on his capital.

"Farmers are just living from hand to mouth."

Mr Jones, Merioneth, says, "Taking the last ten years, there is not a penny of profit, and I am doing my best."

Depression seems to have reached the upland and grazing districts about 1884.

The heavy fall of prices of all the staple produce of Wales, especially the drop of fully 50 per cent. in wool, and the exceptional depreciation of all stock in the disastrous seasons of 1892 and 1893, have inflicted severe losses everywhere through the hill and grazing districts, which had, before 1884, been moderately prosperous. The fall in dairy produce has also hit many districts.

The position of farmers in many districts is described as serious, and involving great hardship and uncertainty. The small occupying owners have largely lost their capital, and are in some districts anxious to sell their land. The capital of tenant farmers has been heavily reduced where it has not been completely swept away.

Mr Fisher states that farmers can only meet the increased cost of production and fall in prices by cutting down the chances of their children.

"The great majority of farmers are gradually getting poorer."

There are essential points to be borne in mind in estimating the position of agriculture in Wales, and the real effects of the depression in the Welsh counties.

In the first place, there has been a relatively exceptional rise in the price of labour. It is perfectly true, as pointed out by several witnesses, that many of the small "mixed" and dairy farms of Wales have good markets in neighbouring large towns and collieries. But this very advantage has raised wages more rapidly than in most rural districts in England. Thus the cost of production has been rapidly rising, while prices have been steadily falling.

In the second place, in no part of Great Britain have landlords left the main, and, in some cases, practically the whole, burden of loss on the tenants so obviously and completely as in Wales. The insufficient reduction of rent is the universal complaint made, and, in my opinion, proved by the tenant farmers whom we have examined. Further, Colonel Hughes, the agent of the Wynnstay estate, admitted that rents were not reduced in proportion to prices, and that a serious economic injustice had been done by the raising of many rents in good times.

"The tenants have to live so hard to make up a sum of money. I think there is a great deal one has to do in adjusting rents, because they are very unfair in many places compared with others."

Mr T. Roberts complained that while wool and sheep had fallen one-half, and other produce 35 per cent., farmers only received abatements of 10 to 15 per cent.

Hill farms had actually risen in rent in spite of the fall in prices.

Mr Williams, in the Vale of Clwyd, said that the real causes of the depression were high rents and low prices with increased cost of labour. Abatements were only 10 to 15 per cent., with rare exceptions.

Mr Jones said reductions were small, or none at all, except for vacated farms, or on a few generously managed estates.

From Merioneth we hear that farmers are kept in suspense till rent day, and then perhaps get 10 or 15 per cent.

Mr Davies (Denbighshire) says that, although wheat sold for half what it did when he took his farm, and other produce had fallen heavily, rents were not materially reduced. Cultivation was necessarily deteriorated.

Mr O. Price (Brecon) says the larger landlords have given 10 to 25 per cent.

Mr Drummond, agent to Lord Cawdor, admits that rents are partly paid out of capital, and in some cases from children's wages.

In conclusion, I feel it to be my duty to state, as regards Wales, and after considering the Report of the Welsh Land Commission, as well as the evidence laid before our own Commission by Welsh witnesses on the subject of agricultural depression, its causes and its possible remedies, that I am of opinion that the economic position of agriculturists in Wales deserves the immediate attention of Parliament, and that, so far as our own evidence covers the ground, I concur in the conclusions and the recommendations made on these subjects by the Welsh Land Commission.

Scotland.

In estimating the character of agricultural depression in Scotland, it must be borne in mind that the nineteen years' lease has been practically universal. These leases have led to high and thorough cultivation, the results of which have enabled the soil and the occupier to hold out better. On the other hand, in times of rapidly falling prices, rents fixed years before, under different circumstances, become an intolerable burden, and lead to the impoverishment and ruin of tenants, if the letter of the agreement is insisted on.

Again, the security of a long lease has raised rents and increased competition, so that relatively Scotch rents have been and are somewhat higher than English rents generally.

Further, the standard of wages has been rising more rapidly in Scotland than in England, except in the most northern counties of England.

Thus the facts that Scotland escaped one or two of the bad seasons which have most severely crippled the east and south of England, and that Scotch farmers have had, in their thoroughly cultivated farms, a better weapon with which to battle against hard times, are counterbalanced by excessive renting of the great majority of farms, and by a relatively greater increase of the cost of production.

The rise in the labour item would have been greater but for the more rapid adoption of changes of rotation and cultivation, and especially in the extensive development of the temporary pasture system, which has slightly lessened the numbers of men and horses employed. Expenses under the head of labour have also been somewhat kept down by the increasing use of machinery.

Mr Hope, in his two reports, covers the whole of the eastern counties, or the mainly arable districts of Scotland. The general result of his inquiries was that depression has been present in all the districts in varying degrees, and that at no time had the difficulties been greater, and the struggle more keen to meet them than in the last few years.

"In the case of old leases, many proprietors granted abatements of rent; but in some cases proprietors were slow or unwilling to recognise the fight which their tenants were having against adverse times, and held them firmly to their obligations, and exacted the rents contracted for without any allowance for the great alteration in the position of things." In other cases tenants were saved from bankruptcy by timely reductions and by allowances for manures, etc.

Protection being out of the question, and unsound in argument, Mr Hope holds that "the real solution of the difficulty created by low prices is to be found in the reasonable reduction of rent." "The question of rent lies at the root of the whole matter, and is the main factor which ultimately determines the margin of profit."

The whole of the eminently practical evidence from Scotland turns on these economic issues, and the main purport of suggestions of the Scotch witnesses is to protect the tenant in the enjoyment of the profit his outlay and skill enables him to gain.

The fall in rents has varied greatly. In the south of Scotland, Mr Hope mentions estates where the rental has fallen from £6949 in 1882 to £4806 in 1893, from

£3290 in 1882 to £2693 in 1893, and from £2256 to £1415 But on estates in the north the fall has been trifling. An instance quoted gives a drop from £37,877 to £35,584.

"Some farmers who kept accounts plainly said that these accounts showed such a bad result that they were indisposed to produce them, and many others gave the general answer that each year had shown a loss."[1]

Farm accounts obtained by Mr Hope show serious losses. Thus, on a farm in the Lothians, 400 acres, while an average annual profit of £677 had been earned up to 1882, for the next ten years the average was only £121, and in 1893 there was a loss of £174, although rent had been reduced 25 per cent.; on a Berwickshire farm, 400 acres, there was a net loss of £373 on ten years; on five other farms in the Lothians, Roxburgh, and the north, a loss of capital; while there was about 3 per cent. interest on capital earned in one case, and "a fair profit over a twenty-three years' lease" in another.

The loss of capital by farmers is further shown by numerous instances in which their stock is really owned by auctioneers and dealers.

Taking them all over, rents have fallen 25 to 30 per cent., but the fall is insufficient.

On a Roxburghshire farm of 541 acres, the tenant says "the farm left double the profit in 1877 at a rent of £1865 that it does now at £1000."

"The farmers consider that the proper adjustment of the rent lies at the root of the present agricultural question."

The heavy loss from low price of potatoes is illustrated by Mr Hope's own evidence. With potatoes at 30s a ton, and rent at £4 10s per acre, Mr Hope says he was losing in 1893 about £10 an acre.

In the Lothians, Mr Riddell, whose highly worked farm kept up its value while other similar farms fell from 30 to 40 per cent. in annual value, stated that there had been a great number of farmers who became bankrupt, and have retired during the depression.[2]

[1] Roxburgh, &c., p. 17. pp. 23-28.   [2] *See* pp. 47, 48, 193, 194.

Mr Smith, Longniddry, East Lothian, said that the land of medium or inferior quality was being half-starved and insufficiently farmed. The fall of 20 to 40 per cent. in rents did not meet the fall of prices and greater cost of production.

Mr Dun, from the Galashiels district, states that where there have been fair reductions men with ample capital have held on fairly, but the high rents under old leases have ruined many and reduced capital. " Lower rents are the first remedy."

Mr Gibb, Berwickshire, says that losses have come year by year now on crops, now on stock. The capital of farmers has been much reduced.

Mr Elliott thinks that with rents only down 20 to 40 per cent. it is impossible to make money, and tenants are losing capital.

Mr Rutherford, speaking of Roxburghshire, thinks the land is being deteriorated and farms run out owing to depression of prices and insecurity of tenants' capital.

In Perthshire, Mr Ferguson, a large farmer of experience, states that few farms are paying their way.

The highest rented of the three farms he holds is the only one of the three that makes money, and that only because everything is sold off at Perth, which is near, and manure cheap and easy to bring back.

The new men who come in and take farms at the old rents are not making a profit, but "are living on hope." "I shall be very glad if I get out without loss, without counting any interest on my capital." The increases in the wages of labourers makes the poorer land less remunerative even at lower rents.

The reductions of rent represent nothing like the reduction in prices of produce.

"If I had not made some money in the good times, I could not have stood the bad."

"Not one farmer that I know is making his present rent."

"The men who have very little capital are in a very bad way indeed." "Those who have let their farms down have got deeper in the water, and cannot get out."

In Forfarshire, though rents are reduced about 22½ per cent. on Lord Strathmore's estate, his agent states that the tenants may be "making two ends meet, but are not making money; they have a fair comfortable living, but not more than that. The farmers are getting their living for their labour; and probably some of them with £10,000 invested are getting very little interest, whereas in former days they got a good profit."

In the important arable and stock-farming districts of Fife, large numbers of farmers have succumbed, after their capital was almost exhausted. Many farmers were submitting to severe losses from year to year in the hope of better times.

Mr Fyshe says farms were too dear, and there have been many changes of tenancy through farmers failing. Farmers were losing money now, because prices had fallen more than rents.

Mr Ballingall "could not say that, even with present reductions, farmers were holding their own." His own farm of 1200 acres, with rent reduced from £2400 to £1500, has not been paying interest on capital. Farmers had at first thought depression was chiefly a matter of bad seasons, but then it became chronic, and they found their capital rapidly slipping out of their hands. Rents must ultimately fall to what can be taken out of the land.

In the arable districts of the northern counties, the farmers of the highly cultivated and fertile county of Elgin are just able to make a living at the reduced rents, and in many places are losing capital, while the advantages to their children have had to be greatly curtailed. Fair reductions have been made only in the case of one tenant out of four or five. The large reductions have been confined to new tenants, and many old tenants are still paying the higher rents.

A statement of what fair rents should be was drawn up by the Morayshire Farmers' Club in 1882, on a basis arrived at by extending the principle of the fiars prices. The average reduction of 33 per cent. on rent then demanded had been more than justified.

Mr Stuart, from Banffshire, stated that the larger farms had changed tenants three or four times within nineteen years. Reductions were made to the new tenants which had been refused to the old tenants. The average reduction to the new tenants on fourteen of these farms after the old tenants left was 30 per cent. Six of the old tenants of these fourteen farms had gone bankrupt. Tenant farmers had lost much capital and can no longer make the improvements they did before, as they have no margin of profit, and no security. Mr Stuart himself has been losing money for several years on his farm, and has only received an abatement of 5 per cent. The value of his own permanent improvements was completely covered by the rent. Land which had been reclaimed was reverting, and about 9000 acres in Banff have sunk back to their natural condition.

The position on liberally managed estates, like those of the Duke of Richmond and the Earl of Aberdeen, is obviously more prosperous.

The Duke of Richmond says that, except higher prices, there is no other way in which a tenant can be helped to meet these times than to lower his rent:—

> "I have reduced the rent, and therefore I have given practical reason for thinking that if things remain as they are at present, a reduction of rent is necessary. If prices fall, I certainly shall not be able to put them back to the old rent before the remission." "A landlord ought to be beforehand to make remissions, and not to wait until he is asked to do so."

If a liberal policy of this nature had been universal, much of the severity of the depression in Scotland would have been mitigated, a very large number of tenants, who have been crushed out between high rents and low prices, would have been saved, and much of the economic loss to both landlords and tenants would have been prevented.

Mr Speir, in his report on the south-western counties of Scotland, which are mainly given up to dairying, stock farming, and also have arable districts, makes it clear, that, although there has been no wholesale collapse of agriculture, and there is undoubtedly a keen competition for farms, the depression has made itself felt everywhere.

"Bankers," he reports, "had no hesitation in saying that farmers were going steadily backward."

All through the inland districts of Ayr, Wigtown, Kirkcudbright, and Dumfries, evidence was continually cropping up to show that tenants' capital was gradually being lessened.

Rents here, as everywhere in Scotland, had played a principal part in increasing difficulties.

"The majority thought that if only rents were made proportionate to the value of farm produce, and the cost of growing it, there was no reason why farmers might not yet do very well. Nearly everybody was, however, of opinion that few farmers seemed even yet to realise that present prices were not likely to alter much for a considerable time, or to base their calculations on present values." "Next to low prices, the most potent cause was generally considered to be the unwarrantable competition which exists among farmers themselves."

"Even in the best of times, farmers' profits are never great, and when low prices set in, it is rare that anything remains after expenses are paid." Mr Speir adds: "The balance sheets in the Appendix show that, notwithstanding the capital invested, the remuneration of the average farmer of moderate means is no greater than that of a first-class artisan."

Some of the most painful evidence from Scotland is given in the figures as to changes of tenancy in Mr Speir's report. He obtained returns of the changes on about 200 farms, comprising about 100,000 acres in Ayrshire. "During the past fourteen years" there have been thirty-eight changes in the arable and dairy, and fourteen changes in the sheep-grazing farms.

The rents of all North Ayrshire are very high, the farms are comparatively small, and the farmers frugal and industrious, yet their lot is anything but an easy one. Many are complaining now who previously said little, preferring to work away rather than be turned out in their old age. Hard as the farmers work themselves, their wives and families do often more, and in many cases two of them perform the work of three hired servants for little over half the remuneration.

From Wigtownshire, out of 457 farms in the Rhins district there have been eighty-three changes, and on twenty-five of these changes of tenancy the farmers who left were bankrupt, or left without means. In the Machars district, out of 607 farms there have been two hundred and forty-five changes, and, from the examination of several parishes, it appears that about every third change means a tenant leaving his farm without means.

In certain districts of Dumfriesshire, of 245 farms, during fifteen years past, 131 farms have changed hands, several of the farms having had two or three tenants successively. "About 31 per cent. of the farmers who removed are said to have done so on account of rent, and 26 per cent. of them are said to have been bankrupt when they left."

Such a record speaks for itself, and is a convincing proof that the havoc worked by the depression among an industrious and specially skilled tenantry, such as is usually found in most districts of Scotland, has necessarily been largely due to the faulty system of tenure, and the impracticability of readjusting the item of rent in time to prevent disaster.

In the immediately succeeding chapter, an attempt is made to draw lessons from evidence laid before the Commission as to the more profitable types of farming, and the success of individual farmers, and thus to bring out more clearly the lines of readjustment.

But it is impossible to conclude this concise summary of the agricultural situation in various parts of Great Britain, during the period of our inquiry, without indicating at once that the situation in many districts is extremely grave, that readjustments are, in general, so slow and inadequate that, whatever may be the ultimate outlook for agriculture, the position of the existing farmers in the depressed areas is extremely precarious, and deserves the prompt and careful attention of Parliament.

It would seem, therefore, a plain duty to probe the causes of depression to the utmost, and to initiate in any direction which may prove practicable, such legislative and administrative changes as will quicken the transition to a better state of equilibrium, and promptly check, so far as may be, the operation of the forces which have been pulling down agricultural enterprise. If this can be done so as to save from ruin the largest possible number of those upon whom the full force of the economic loss of the last twenty years has fallen, every effort should be made to attain this result.

CHAPTER II.

Evidence of Successful Farming during the Depression, and of Profitable Readjustments of Farming Methods.

The evidence and the reports of Assistant Commissioners give many instances of successful farming during the period of depression in all parts of the country, even in those counties where depression has been most acute, and on the old lines of farming. From every county there are striking illustrations of what results may be obtained by more economic methods and by changes of cultivation suited to the times.

This class of evidence deserves careful consideration. The signs of distress and the course of decline are more obvious, and may be more easily and fully traced. The indications of recovery or reconstruction are harder to define, whether as to time or as to method.

It is important to determine as far as possible whether such instances of relative success are individual, whether they are due wholly to special local advantages or circumstances, whether they merely indicate a stage of endurance or resistance, which really means that resources got together in better times are being drawn upon, or whether there is any true economic readjustment from which continued success is to be anticipated. And, lastly, it is of the utmost importance to ascertain the conditions, the presence or absence of which is found to accompany such cases of doing well in bad times. A selection of instances from the evidence is appended.

Taking first cases of farming on existing lines and in the most depressed districts, Essex itself furnishes several striking instances.

Thus:—A mixed soil farm, of 950 acres, some of it stiff land, and two-thirds of it arable, excellently managed by an exceptionally good farmer and judge of stock, with a capital of nearly £13,000, brought an average annual profit between 1879 and 1893 of close on £400 a year, or over 3 per cent. on capital. Profits began with the starting of dairy work, and, since the rent was reduced from 25s to 16s, have averaged for the last six years 6 per cent. on capital. These results have been obtained by mixed farming, without any material alteration of cultivation, by the sale of corn as well as milk, and live stock, and with the liberal expenditure of £2 an acre on labour, and £3 5s 8d on feeding stuffs and manures.[1]

An instance like this shows what may be accomplished on land which has not been allowed to get out of order, by energy and capacity with adequate capital, and sufficiently reduced rents.

Again, in Huntingdonshire, on stiff clay, a farm of 462 acres, two-thirds arable, has been farmed since 1880 with an average profit of nearly 5 per cent. on a capital of £4000, or 8s 5d per acre a year, without any material change of cultivation, but with a reduction of rent from £400 to £262. The proceeds have been from corn and stock in nearly equal proportions.[2]

A Northamptonshire farm of 324 acres, chiefly strong land, has made in the past seven years an average profit of about 6 per cent. on capital, even allowing for the bad seasons of 1892 and 1893, when profits did not exceed 1¼ per cent.[3]

In the county of Berks, where the depreciation of land has been exceptionally great, Lord Wantage, in 1893, gave as the result of farming 4427 acres, a fourth part of his Berkshire estates, an average net profit of £800 to £1000 a year, after paying 5 per cent. interest on his very large outlay of capital in buildings, roads, and other improvements, and a rent reduced in the same pro-

---

[1] Pringle, Essex, App. C. I.
[2] Do., Beds, Hunts, and Northants, App. C. VII.
[3] Ibid., App. C. X.

portion as to his tenants, about 40 per cent. This success in working a large area on one uniform system, with vigilant economy, but with a full expenditure, leads Lord Wantage to recommend farming on a large scale by syndicates.[1]

This view gets some support from what Mr Clare Sewell Read says of the success, in Norfolk, of a few men of large capital, and business capacity, who have hired vast tracts of land, and worked them thoroughly well with a large head of stock. One of them, who had taken seven farms, thus puts the economy of his attempt to readjust agriculture: " If there were seven farmers on these seven farms, they would all want to make a living; it is a hard thing if I cannot make one living out of seven farms."

Again, in Essex, an estate of 3555 acres, in five farms, worked under one management with a capital of £10 an acre, has over the whole, good and bad soils together, earned a net annual profit of over 7 per cent., besides paying what in these days is a full rent. Two of these farms are of good mixed soil, with one-third old grass, and carry dairy cows. These farms pay in rents and rates about 25s a year, and earn a profit of over 10 per cent. The remainder are heavy clays without much grass. Yet even these pay in rent and rates over 16s an acre, and still make a profit of over 1 per cent. on capital.[2]

Mr Strutt, as agent for his brother, Lord Rayleigh, farming about 4000 acres in hand, has found that, with the exception of 1893, when there was a loss, the seven years gave a return of about 6 per cent, on a capital of £8 an acre, after paying himself a rent of about 18s an acre, including tithe 4s, or a net rent of 14s an acre. This result has been obtained by dairying for the London market.

---

[1] In a letter to Mr Shaw Lefevre, November 15, 1895, Lord Wantage writes that the land in hand has increased to 10,076 acres, and that on the Down lands, comprising nearly 6000 acres, the adverse seasons of 1894-5 operated most prejudicially.
[2] Pringle, Essex, App. C. X., p. 75.

Mr Dewar, in North-west Norfolk, makes mixed farming pay "with two or three strings to his bow," such as poultry, which "has paid better than any other branch of stock this last year or two." He has not altered the method of cultivation, as the land is not suited for permanent pasture, but saves by machinery, and sells off straw.

Mr Jabez Turner instances a farm in the heavy clay district of Stratford-on-Avon, where potato-growing, combined with bullock fattening, succeeds well. The tenant has capital, farms high, and sells or consumes at discretion.

Scotch farmers are doing well in Hertfordshire, near the railways, by a seven-course system, including two years of potatoes, somewhat on the Lothian system. They work hard, and manure from London helps. They even pay increased rents.[1].

In the Sleaford union of Lincolnshire a holding of 790 acres, one-fourth pasture, farmed on the four-course, in excellent order, and in good hands, has made an average of nearly 3 per cent. on capital between 1889 and 1894.

Another four-course, turnip and barley farm in the Grantham Union, in the owner's hands has made for same period about 1½ per cent. on capital.[2]

Mr E. Turnor, who owns 21,000 acres in Lincolnshire, has made off an excellent barley farm, now in hand, an interest of 3½ per cent. on capital, besides the same rent as the old tenant—16s an acre. Four other farms, heavy land, taken in hand in bad condition, have paid 3½ per cent. interest, but scarcely any rent.

An arable four-course farm in North-east Norfolk of 425 acres, half of it good mixed soil, half light land, uniformly worked and well kept up, shows on fourteen years an average net return of £246 or over 7 per cent. on capital, but taking the last six years, from 1887 to 1893, there is an average net profit of £391 or over 11 per cent.

[1] A. Spencer, Herts, pp. 14, 40.
[2] Wilson Fox, Lincolnshire, App. A. I. F.

on capital. There are no restrictions; and apparently only a very moderate reduction in rent.[1]

Another farm, two-thirds arable, in Mid Norfolk, has yielded for seven years about 3 per cent. on capital.[2]

A farm in South-west Norfolk described as a "fair average," two-thirds arable, gives 3½ to 4 per cent. on capital.

Mr. Johnson, of Ixworth, says that on mixed soils, adapted for stock and vegetables, some Suffolk farmers make ends meet at reduced rents.

Mr Riley gives in the Wolds of Yorkshire striking instances of very high farming, command of capital, and keeping up of first-class stock, enabling energetic and capable men, by the splendid condition of their land, to get through bad years. They will succeed unless over-rented.

Similarly in Northumberland, Mr Wilson Fox infers, from the information supplied him, that the comparative prosperity of farmers was due to the fact that "the majority of them are farming on a large scale, and have had capital; that the land has for many years been exceedingly well farmed, and hence is more able to bear economies practised in labour, manure, and feeding stuffs; and that, when the depression just began to show itself, liberal permanent reductions were made in rents." And it is important to note that the high condition of the land in many districts of this county is directly attributed to the encouragement given to continuous good farming by long and favourable leases.

Mr Wilson Fox in North Lancashire gives striking instances of farming success:

Thus on a farm of 245 acres in the Fylde, three-fourths arable, rented at 28s an acre, an energetic farmer, who keeps accounts, estimates his expenditure beforehand under every head, and has spent in labour nearly twice, and manures and cake nearly three times his rent, has made a net profit of 12s an acre, after paying himself 5 per cent. interest on his capital—about £12 an acre. And all this on the four-course system.[3]

[1] Rew, Norfolk, p. 25, and App. E. 1.   [2] Rew, Norfolk, App. E., 4.
[3] Wilson Fox, Garstang, Appendix. C. 1.

Another thrifty, hardworking man, who has been farming thirty years, has done all the drainage and roads and other permanent improvements, lived hard and farmed high, and has taken a prize in North Lancashire for the best managed farm of mixed husbandry, has made farming pay well every year, and has made an independence out of nothing.[1]

What can be done by such men is shown in his statement. He bought, in 1892, a water-logged and wrecked farm of 120 acres for £2640, sold it at once for £200 more, and took it on lease at 14s an acre. He has already expended £1,200 in improvements, has grown a heavy crop of potatoes, and expects to recoup his outlay in two years. He says emphatically, "High farming pays. What we have to do is to produce."[2]

Again, a small farmer with sixty-three acres, which he and his father have worked for thirty-six years, says, "Throughout all this agricultural depression I have farmed on lines which have proved successful." He, too, favours high farming. "It is far better to have a small farm and farm it really well, than a big one and to farm it indifferently." He attributes his success to prompt laying down to grass when he found crops did not pay the cost of production.[3]

But it is plain that this man and a large proportion of the Lancashire farmers have been holding their own partly because their children work on the farms without wages, and so effect a considerable economy in labour.

The comparative immunity from the worst features of depression noted in North Yorkshire is largely attributed by Mr Pringle to scientific stock farming and to the economy as regards food, manure and labour, effected by covered yards, concentrated buildings, and manure tanks. The southern farmer, "with his cold, wet, wasteful, open yards, cannot compete with" this practical and effective equipment of stock farming in the north. Corn is now wholly subordinated to stock, much of the barley and wheat being "fed," and oats largely supplanting

---

[1] Wilson Fox, Garstang, p. 60.
[2] W. Fox, II, 436.   [3] II, 440.

wheat. The steam plough for heavy land is disused. The old proportion, before 1879, of one-third in grass is being rapidly expanded by temporary pastures and laying down of the strong clays.

Sir Gabriel Goldney seems to have had a fair balance of profit in working a dairy farm absolutely on self-supporting lines, all feeding stuffs and manure being made on the farm. The yards and buildings are concentrated, and large manure tanks enable the land to be irrigated like water meadows. The farm carries nearly three times as many cows as it did before these methods were adopted, and has paid a high rent.

Mr Pringle's experience in the South Midlands is that farmers, with fair turnip and barley land with useful grass, " have escaped tolerably well." Where breeding of sheep or cattle has been made a feature, and the heavier land is laid down, and the rotation on mixed soils has been lengthened, agriculture has become more self-supporting and independent of the dangers of fluctuation of prices.

Mr Pringle is probably correct in reporting that besides the graziers and dairymen, the only farmers who have weathered the storm and kept up a show of prosperity, are those who could draw on private means, or had some other paying business in addition to farming, or occupied land near towns and sell vegetables, hay and straw, and who have not put everything into corn growing. But the first two of these classes cannot be said to be making farming pay.

Mr Ferguson's farm near Perth, where he gets good profits though paying 50s an acre, because he can sell everything off and "drive back manure," and Mr Mercer who can pay a rent of over 40s close to Liverpool, growing wheat, oats, and potatoes and hay, and selling everything off, are good illustrations of the effect of nearness to a large town.

Mr Worthington, near Wigan, makes a profit by high farming, special scientific feeding of cattle, and the sale of milk. He has absolute freedom as to cultivation and sale of produce.

Some men of exceptional enterprise and intelligence and of large capital have made farming pay even in the worst times on special lines.

Thus Mr Prout's well-known experiment in continuous corn growing, with large applications of artificial manures, though much less profitable, is found by Mr Spencer to still yield some profit.

Two farms in owners' hands in Hunts, worked on much Mr Prout's plan, and kept in garden-like order, seem to pay their way after a fashion, in spite of distance from railway, which strikes off some profit from straw and hay selling.[1] In these cases it is clear that success has largely been due to an absolutely free hand as regards cultivation, ample capital, and considerable knowledge and skill.

Again, farmers in many counties who have acquired a reputation for special types of stock, pedigree cattle, or sheep, or in horse breeding, have had advantages which no fall in prices could quite take away. They have been the recognised purveyors of the best articles of their kind. And in bad times, the tendency of the more capable farmer is to save himself by keeping the best quality of everything whether in stock or seeds. The greatest fall in values has invariably been with the inferior grades of stock and of produce.

Where the soil and other circumstances are suitable, market gardening and fruit growing has been found highly profitable, and has greatly raised both the capital and the letting value of land. In the Vale of Evesham and surrounding district, land of the best quality for fruit growing has sold at £300 an acre, and lets at from £3 to £14, and in some cases up to £18 an acre. The value of the tenant right of well-established market gardens in this district has ranged from £30 to £100 an acre, and it is said, sometimes, to even higher rates. Naturally, when farms fall vacant they are at once turned into market gardens, and there has been a rapid and very wide extension. The highest rents and profits depend on special quality, such as the "black

[1] Pringle, Beds, Hunts, Northants, p. 42.

soil," which grows exceptional plums. Market gardeners can pay from £12 to £20 an acre for the preliminary clearing of the land before planting; wait for maturing of trees and plants; spend "quite £38 per acre per annum in rates, manure, and labour," besides the high rents, and yet make a considerable profit. The profit would be still greater but for the arbitrary imposition of railway charges.

On the easily-worked and productive "warp" lands in the north of the Isle of Axholme, near the Humber, men of capital and energy, who have in the last few years taken, as tenants at fair rents, a number of small farms together, are making excellent profit by substituting celery and asparagus for wheat and potatoes.

Poultry Farming.

Mr Rew's interesting report on the poultry industry in Sussex shows that its special success depends not on local advantages, but on organisation and skill, which could be applied with similar results in other districts. Poultry farming as a specialty is generally a failure, but as an adjunct to other farming pays. Cows, chickens, and oats go together. Fowls' manure as a dressing rapidly ripens laid down grass, and skim milk and oats are used in large quantities both in rearing and fattening poultry. Owing to the great demand for young fowls for fattening, rearers get full prices, and, latterly, large quantities are brought from Ireland. The fatteners collect from a large area, fowls being reared in great numbers by farmers and labourers. The marketing is thoroughly organised, carriers collecting throughout the district, and delivering in London at 1s a dozen, and about 1s 6d a dozen charged as commission by the salesmen. The profits are considerable, and the system especially tends to help intelligent labourers to rise. The expenditure and receipts are relatively very high. Thus, from the accounts of poultry rearing and fattening only on a 200-acre farm, for 1891, as are supplied by Mr

Rew, the outgoings for twelve months were £1749 1s 9d, and the receipts £2058 19s 1d; and in addition to paying 5 per cent. on the capital invested in poultry, the net returns gave the farmer a profit more than double this interest, and paid the rent of the whole farm besides. The cheapness of corn and other feeding stuffs has been a help, and rents do not seem to have been raised unduly. On the other hand, the great increase in the imports of Russian chickens, and railway rates, both on young chickens and on consignments, have been drawbacks.

A successful trade in poultry and eggs is also carried on from South Lincolnshire and Cumberland.[1]

In the Aylesbury district, the ducks are collected by the London and North Western Railway Company's carts and forwarded in bulk to London at 1d a bird. A similar arrangement has been made by a successful duck farmer near Fleetwood, who makes a good profit by sending to Manchester.

The want of organisation deprives the English farmer of the egg market, where there is an enormous unsupplied demand, and this although English eggs fetch 10s to 11s per "long" hundred as compared with 8s for French, down to 5s·8d for Russian. Now, more than half the eggs sold are foreign. In spite of the importations having more than doubled in the last twelve years, prices have materially improved. Organisation of collection and delivery, and the provision of winter eggs, would make great profits. The demand for high class poultry is increasing and would grow with the supply; for "well fatted" poultry we are only at the beginning of the demand in many parts of the country.

Dairy Farming.

Dairy farming has generally, but by no means universally, brought moderate but steady profits during the years of depression; but it is essentially a localised branch of farming. In several counties where distress has prevailed, notably in Norfolk, there is too little

[1] E. Brown, 62,284, etc.

pasture owing to the lightness of the soil for dairy work, and no sensible relief to agriculturists from this source. Similarly Suffolk is badly supplied with good pasture, and much of the soil appears unsuitable. But it is shown from Arthur Young that 100 years ago Suffolk was famed for its dairies, and was then "essentially a dairy county." "One very great object of their ploughing," says Arthur Young, "is the culture of turnips and cabbages for their cows." Milk selling is spreading steadily, especially where Scotch immigrant farmers have settled, and on the whole successfully.

In Essex, the extension of dairy farming has been more general, the increase in dairy stock between 1882 and 1892 having been as much as 52 per cent. The Scotch dairy farmers from Ayrshire, who came early in the period of depression to Essex, seem to have been successful men in their own country, who anticipated better profits from dairy farming, within easy reach of London, when the wheat began to fail, and the rents of Essex farms in consequence began to fall much lower than rents in Scotland. Others who came later were in some instances half broken men, and some of them have barely held their own, while others have failed in Essex also.

They have succeeded in laying down some of the land, and have tried to lay down less favourable soils with varying results, but at any rate, by leaving rotation grasses down for two or three years and grazing them, and by using the "tumbled-down land" for rough pasture, they have managed to make, most of them, a tolerable thing of dairying work. The results, in our opinion, tend to show that much greater extension and diffusion of a moderate prosperity is quite possible if the area of really sound and useful pasture can be increased. But the key to the success of these Scotch settlers in Essex and Suffolk, such as it has been, or rather to their escape from the losses of other agriculturists in the same neighbourhoods, has been their vigilant economy and patient industry.

"They live hard, they work hard, and they spend nothing except on their cows."

In general they have brought their Ayrshire cows, which thrive well, and are good milkers, and have to some extent replaced them year by year from Ayrshire, though latterly they are taking to crossing with short-horns to improve the returns from cow beef.

And those who have succeeded have brought with them sufficient capital for exactly the type of farming they aimed at, and have not been tempted to lay out a farthing without seeing a chance of a prompt though small return of profit.

Mr Pringle gives some instances in which this type of farming pays well.

Thus the balance sheets of a farm of 636 acres, worked by a Scotchman in Essex, composed of 318 acres of old grass, 247 of temporary pasture, and 71 acres arable, between the years 1884 and 1893 inclusive, with a capital of only £3450, and at a rent of £600, reduced afterwards to £500, shows an average annual profit of about $12\frac{1}{2}$ per cent. The labour bill was kept between 15s and 20s an acre. Hay and straw were sold off. The rotation on this and similar Scotch managed farms would be: (1) oats after grass; (2) roots; (3) wheat or oats with grass seeds. Such success is not achieved by many. Mr Pringle does not think that most of the Scotch farmers are more than holding their own by extreme industry and frugality, and by cutting down expenses to an irreducible minimum. Some "have had to succumb to the bad times."[1]

Besides the extension of temporary pasture, the low price of corn has to some extent increased, and helped dairy farming, as the second-class wheats and barleys have brought more, when fed to cows, in the production of milk than in the markets.

But the relief to agriculture from the sale of milk has its limits. Mr Pringle is of opinion that "this branch of husbandry has in Essex already assumed dimensions sufficiently large for the welfare of those engaged in it, and to still further add to the output of milk for London, would be not only to cripple the affairs of those already

[1] Notes of Chairman on visit to Essex, p. 1.

engaged therein, but ultimately to destroy the future prospects of milk sellers." The profit, as it is, has been very narrow. A marked increase in the supply would bring profits to the vanishing point. There is, however, room for the profitable making of cheese.

In Lincolnshire, dairy farming does not seem in favour, owing to restricted markets, heavy railway rates, and distance from stations. But remarkable instances of success are given. Thus, on 1000 acres in the Lincoln Union, two-thirds grass, the occupier lost £701 9s 6d between 1889 and 1885, but starting a dairy in that year had made a profit of £968 18s. 2d. between 1886 and 1893. Another farmer, near Gainsborough, who has laid some land down to grass, and uses machinery for cutting and crushing and pulping chaff, cake, turnips, linseed and corn, cooking potatoes also with the exhaust steam, and who apparently puts everything to his cows, says he has done much better than sticking to the old course.

Another farmer finds milk, even with the heavy railway charges, "pays him much better than beef."

Mr Wilson Fox states that where good butter was turned out in uniform quality, there was plenty of competition for it, but there is a general want of technical knowledge and of proper equipments for dairy work; while one butter factory has done well, and has raised the price and increased the sale of butter, other experiments carried out with skill and capital have failed, and the Lincolnshire towns are full of Danish and New Zealand butter.

Mr J. Stratton thinks dairying "the best branch of the business. I dairy 200 cows, and rear all the stock. I keep the young stock upon the poor lands I have laid down to grass, and keep the dairy cows on the better land at home. It is much better to sell the milk than to make cheese or butter," but he complains that the railway company take an eighth of the value of his milk, which is "very exorbitant." And he holds that although milk prices have gone down some 17 per cent. and the value of 700 or 800 head of cattle of his own breeding has greatly depreciated, there is a substantial profit in the dairy industry.

In parts of Somersetshire and Dorsetshire, it is found a workable and profitable system for the farmer to let his cows and buildings to dairymen, the dairyman, in addition to all the dairy produce, taking the calves, and the pigs fed on the buttermilk and other waste. The farmer has to find sufficient pasture, or to buy artificial food, and the payments range from £10 to £12 a cow; while milk, butter and cheese had fallen in price considerably, pigs and calves have not materially fallen. The hire of the cows has fallen about £3 a head.

In Lancashire, Mr Wilson Fox reports that there has been a great increase in dairying, especially in milk, and adds: "no doubt those who are exclusively engaged in the sale of milk have felt the depression far the least."

But their success depends largely on an adequate reduction of rent. Mr Barlow is of opinion that many dairy farmers in the Blackburn neighbourhood have had to leave their farms because of the refusal to reduce rents in proportion to the fall of prices.

If there is scepticism as to the future of the milk trade, there is also great diversity of opinion as to the future of English butter. Mr Sheldon and other witnesses consider that the general butter trade is practically lost to the British farmer, while many witnesses look hopefully both to the perfecting of processes by technical education, and to the development of the factory system, which has been worked successfully by Lord Vernon and others in England, and has had, according to Mr Anderson, Secretary to the Irish Agricultural Organisation Society, still greater success in Ireland. There can be no doubt that there is to the ordinary farmer a slight gain in price of milk, owing to the higher price obtained by the butter being turned out in large quantities of uniform quality and appearance.

Mr Lovell, who has great experience in the wholesale butter trade, has no doubt that a large portion of the butter trade could be recovered by the British farmer if production and distribution were rationally expanded, so as to enable wholesale dealers to obtain promptly supplies of the best grades of guaranteed and uniform excellence.

Mr Treadwell has given up butter-making; at the lowered prices it would not pay for labour; milk he has found profitable.

Mr J. F. Hall strongly recommends dairy farming with Jersey cows. Butter profits depend on the economical production of the greatest quantity, of the highest quality of milk. With Jerseys he obtains 1 lb of butter from seven quarts of milk, while the ordinary rate is 1 lb of butter from ten or twelve quarts of milk. On his farm of 180 acres he obtains a rent of 25s an acre, 5 per cent. interest on his capital as tenant, and also interest on his outlay on permanent improvements.

Mr Hall argues that butter from shorthorn cows cannot pay at 1s a pound, because 4d to 4¾d a gallon for the milk required is an impossible price; with Jerseys Mr Hall was realising 10d a gallon, selling his butter at 15d a lb; but by breeding from the best Jersey butter cows he is confident of getting milk which will produce 1 lb of butter to six quarts. The breed is far more important than the feeding. Two shorthorn cows require as much land as three Jerseys. But the three Jerseys would produce 1500 gallons in the year as compared with 1200 from the two shorthorns, and this means that the Jersey milk would be 1d a gallon cheaper to produce. Three Jerseys will thus produce in butter and skim milk £15 a year more than two shorthorns, and that for a number of years. On the other hand, the two shorthorns when sold to the butcher will, he estimates, bring £12 more. On these grounds Mr Hall argues for a large extension of Jersey dairies. But it may be objected that not only the question of beef supply puts a limit to such extension, but also any great increase in the supply of high class butter would probably lower prices so as to eat away profits.

In Derbyshire, dairy farms are, as a rule, small—

from 40 to 100 acres, are often combined with some other trade, and after the reductions of rent made, still are rented at the high average of 30s. Those farmers who have ability and capital have not suffered much.

The best pastures in the Vale of Aylesbury are used for fattening stock ; the next best land for dairy work, of which milk pays best.

The evidence from the South-Western Counties of Scotland shows that throughout these counties dairying is gradually supplanting other systems of farming. Coupled with stock farming, and with sheep grazing, it has been the mainstay of these districts. While there cannot be said to have been anything "like a total collapse of farming," there are unmistakeable signs of mischief in the frequent and sweeping changes of tenancy, and in the depletion of tenant's capital. If Mr Speir's report fairly represents the position, there can be no doubt that these unfavourable results in a district admirably suited for this class of farming, among men thoroughly experienced, are largely due to the fact that too great a proportion of the returns are absorbed in rents, and that the sitting tenants, owing partly to the action of the owners and agents, partly to the extreme competition of outsiders, are unable to obtain fair reductions of rent, though this is not universal.

The conversion of arable into dairy farming has tended to raise or rather to uphold rents.

There is also keen apprehension as to the increase of foreign competition, facilitated by milking machines as well as by cheap freights, and as to the whole trade being overdone in Great Britain itself.

The evidence from Wales shows that dairying pays where milk and butter can be sent to the slate and mining districts, and that the grass districts have greatly escaped loss, as in Cheshire. The butter trade has been depressed by foreign competition, but the best qualities have maintained their prices.

Many drawbacks and obstacles to success are indicated here and there. The competition of foreign countries and the colonies has undoubtedly lowered the range of profits, especially as regards butter, the price of which practically regulates the price of milk and of cheese. Foreign butter gets the market partly from cheapness, but still more from uniformity of quality and appearance.

Thus, in Berkshire village stores, Italian butter holds the field at 1¾d lower price.[1]

"It is not so much quality as uniformity which is required, because the large dealers will not look at people who merely sell butter, but not of uniform quality."

This competition may, to a certain extent, be met by a thorough practical and scientific organisation of the dairy industry.

Then there are the physical, and to some extent legal, difficulties in the way of laying down land profitably to grass, dealt with fully elsewhere.[2]

One of the most serious of all the difficulties is the prevalence of tuberculosis and the great losses therefrom, which is separately discussed in Chapter XVI.

In several districts buildings are most defective. In spite of the efforts of some landowners, the equipment for dairy work is very imperfect in Essex. In Lancashire, cowsheds are cramped and unhealthy, and promote the spread of tuberculosis. "The buildings have not been changed or increased with the change in the system of farming from corn growing to dairying." In one district an inspection disclosed the fact that only one out of twelve farmers had satisfactory premises. Butter has often to be made in kitchens, and butter and cheese kept in sleeping rooms. There is also much complaint of unsatisfactory and unhealthy water supply.

Other difficulties are the scarcity and dearness of skilled labour, which retards the development of dairying, especially in districts hitherto mainly arable.

There is also a frequent complaint that land is deteriorated by constant use for milk or cheese production. Possibly a certain proportion of farmers in these hard times try to lessen loss, or increase profit, by starving

[1] Lord Wantage, Letter to Mr Shaw Lefevre, November 1895.
[2] Pages 48, 49 and 199, etc.

the soil, but the evidence tends to show that success in dairy farming, as in other branches, depends in the long run on careful feeding of the soil, whether by cake, or by occasional boning or liming, and that this is recognised by the successful farmers.

The general result of the evidence on this head, is that, where there are good markets at hand, dairy farming does and must succeed, and that it succeeds in proportion to the quality and condition of the land, and to the degree in which production is made most scientific and most economical, and in which distribution is best organised and facilitated. The remarkable success attained by the co-operative organisations in Ireland, under the guidance of Mr Horace Plunkett, should be followed up in Great Britain with confident expectation of similar results. A well-judged expenditure on the improvement of dairy stock, on buildings, equipment, on the technical training of those employed, and on scientific appliances and methods of preparation, handling, and packing of butter, will probably be a highly reproductive investment. On the whole, this branch of farming seems the most hopeful in the near future for the country at large, and it is certainly, in my opinion, advisable that any administrative or legislative proposals, which can be shown to be necessary for its development, and for the removal of obstacles to its success, should be promptly initiated.

In this connection it seems probable, that in the interests of health, some legal restriction should be put on the abuse of so-called preservatives, which enable importers to put on the market, milk, cream, and butter from abroad, which are only kept in consumable condition by a liberal infusion of boracic and salicylic acid, and even of lime, in such quantities as to be highly injurious to health.

LAYING DOWN TO GRASS.

Sir John Lawes, the strongest advocate before the Richmond Commission of the policy of meeting the fall of corn prices by prompt laying down to grass, is still more emphatic now. Hopes of a change for the better and the cost and delay of making good pasture, caused postponement. Now it is imperative. And his view is distinctly encouraging. He does not believe in heavy outlay, in cleaning and fallowing, and other preparation of the land. "If you manure the land well, the best grasses will drive out all the weeds and bad grasses." "I have had a field, with a thick bed of couch grass, and I have destroyed it all by manure. The grasses have come of themselves and driven it out. It is a longer process, but it does it." Even the worst Essex clays "will by degrees come into grass—manure is the great thing." And pasture is constantly accumulating fertility which may be drawn out again, if times improve and land is broken up. His own method has usually been to sow the grass seed with a barley crop, and "after that I have entirely depended upon feeding with cotton cake" —sheep being the best manurers.

To select one or two illustrations from a mass of evidence on this point from all parts of the country:— Mr J. Stratton states that in Hampshire he has "laid down 2000 acres of poor arable land to grass, and instead of losing money, as that land did before, I consider it pays its way." It may pay occasionally to take a crop of oats, and break up some of it when a large accumulation of stock is sold off at a favourable moment, "but if I were farming my own land, I would never plough it out of grass." Careful feeding of cattle with cotton cake will make pasture of almost any land. Mr Pringle gives an instance of a farm rescued by scientific laying down, and now in excellent condition and paying well. Furthermore, the saving in labour on 879 acres has been £659 a year.

Mr Riddell, on a large mixed and grazing farm[1] in the hilly part of Midlothian, converted 775 acres of land, previously in rotation, to permanent pasture at an outlay of £20,000 during his nineteen years' lease, and states that his system resulted in multiplying the stock-

---

[1] Corsehope; see pp. 193, etc.

carrying power of the farm about four times, giving him a good profit and also maintaining the rent of the farm, which was high at his entry, at practically the same amount. His view is that the land would have been exhausted by cropping, and the farm would gradually have sunk in value, like other farms in the same neighbourhood. But by very liberal feeding on the young grass, and never breaking up again, the land became more and more fertile, and after it was "fairly established, I found I had most power over it to improve it. According to my experience I can improve it far more after I have been ten years at it."

Mr Gibb, a Berwickshire farmer, says about the permanent pasture he laid down that "it was paying the rent all through as well as it could have done as if it had been in ordinary cropping rotation, but before it came to be a distinct advantage it would be ten or twelve years old. It is always necessary to keep under crop a certain proportion of land for wintering cattle and sheep."

Much of the evidence, and some of the Assistant Commissioner's reports, show a widespread belief that "the eastern side of England will not grow grass like the western." The typical Lincolnshire farmer, "on the Wolds, the Heath, and the Cliff," (reclaimed from waste at the beginning of the century, but now some of the finest arable farms in England), says that grass is no remedy: "if we cannot make our present system pay, the land must go out of cultivation."

The still lighter lands of Norfolk, broken up from rough sheep walks when corn prices were highest, cannot now, Mr Read says, be got back to their old state. "The soil is so light, and the climate so dry, that the grass will not last, and has to be ploughed up, cropped and laid down to grass again."

These views as to the lighter soils are possibly just, but the general impression that the clays will not carry grass in Lincolnshire probably arises from want of experience in laying down and subsequent treatment. Thus a large landowner, who has spent £2 an acre on seeds for his tenants, finds in about five years they wish to plough them up, and adds: " As no farmyard manure has been put on the seeds they are worn out in our East Coast climate." Messrs Sutton also point out that, instead of top dressing and caking pastures more liberally, the Lincolnshire farmers keep their manure for their arable land.

Mr Pringle says as to the heavy Essex clays that much of land laid down with good seeds was indistinguishable from " tumbled-down " land. Failure is due partly to the land having been allowed to get thoroughly out of condition before the attempted change, much of it being waterlogged, partly owing to ignorance of the best methods, the heavy land generally being left flat instead of in ridge and furrow, partly to the practical bankruptcy of the farming class before it was attempted.

In Mr Pringle's opinion, the Essex solution is in well-managed temporary pastures, under which even the heaviest lands may be turned to some profit. " The formation of a really good old pasture is a tedious, costly, and uncertain business, and is generally a commercial loss during the years of transition." Among native Essex farmers there is little knowledge either of laying down, or of the management of temporary pastures in the first year or two. Bad management and inexperience have involved them in additional losses.[1]

Even in Essex there has been some success in permanent pasture. A successful Scotch farmer, who came from Ayrshire fourteen years ago, and has gone in both for temporary and permanent pasture, thinks "there is no reason why heavy clays should not be laid down." But, even allowing for some superfluities in Mr Pringle's estimate for bringing the abandoned clays back into a state of cultivation, which with draining and liming he puts at nearly three times the present value of the freehold, laying down with any kind of preparation of the soil which would give the new seeds a chance, must in most cases cost too much money. And half measures to introduce good grass by harrowing, sowing among the

[1] Pringle, Essex, pp. 49, 27. Appendix on grass question, p. 4.

twitch, and manuring, have only resulted in final mastery by the weeds. Parts of the derelict heavy clays are rapidly lapsing into scrub and bushes, and waste.[1]

Some clays, though stiff and costly to work, have a natural tendency to grass, and do better. Thus in a bad district in Hunts very heavy clay land, which had gone to grass of itself, is now letting at £1 an acre, after lying twelve to fourteen years.

The lengthening of rotation by keeping grasses down two, three, or four years is at once the cheapest and most effective expedient everywhere, but especially on heavy and mixed land, where the latter is not still profitable on old lines.[2] But lack of experience, and still more lack of capital for additional stock, and other incidents of a change of cultivation, are grave obstacles to the extension of this system.

The practical results of the temporary pasture system are well given by Mr Ferguson, a Perthshire farmer. The saving in labour and manure on a 300 acre farm would be about £200, and the land would produce more when ploughed up the third year. There is a great increase in fertility. It is a remarkable and not very satisfactory feature of the past few years, that while permanent pasture increased between 1885 and 1895 by 1,268,085 acres, temporary grass land, clover, sainfoin and rotation grasses increased only by 75,000 acres.

The suggestion frequently recurring of experimental farms belongs properly to the topic of agricultural education. Its value is more apparent as a permanent part of the equipment of British agriculture than as an immediate help to agriculturists.

More attention should be given to the removal of restrictions and discouragements to the effective conversion of arable into pasture land. It is plain from much of the evidence that, if there had been a more general freedom to cultivate in whatever way, a profit was obtainable, and if the laying down of permanent and temporary pastures had been made matter for full

[1] Pringle, Essex, p. 2.
[2] Nunneley, 55,035. Pringle, Beds, Hants, Northants, p. 43.

compensation, whether the landlord's consent had been given or not, the transition from unprofitable corn to partially profitable stock and dairy and other farming would have been quicker and more general.

Conclusions.

To sum up briefly the results from this type of evidence, it is hard to take, as regards the country at large, quite the sanguine view of Mr Wilkinson, a Northumbrian witness, who thinks, "We have got out of the trough of bad times, and are adapting ourselves to new conditions." But some progress has certainly been made in carrying out Mr Stratton's excellent advice to "keep down the expenditure upon unprofitable land, and do your better land as well as possible." But the starting of remedial lines has been too much delayed. In all probability some of the worst land should have been abandoned sooner. It is certain that a prompt and careful laying down of much of the heavier land years ago would have saved enormous losses. In too many districts the land had got out of condition, and the farmers had lost their capital before the true policy was seen. Even where it was grasped in time, the stereotyped rules or estate agreements, the habits and traditions of the English land system, the charges and burdens under which too many landlords have lost initiative power, or again the liabilities of the farmers themselves limiting their command of capital, have made it difficult, if not impossible, to effect promptly the indispensable revolution in the order of things.

Where any degree of success has been obtained, which is not obviously due to special or local circumstances, its conditions have been (1) a high degree of capacity, energy, and industry; (2) free scope of action; and, most indispensable of all, (3) adequate capital.

The exceptions establish clearly the general rule. The essential factor in the struggle with low prices is the capital of the working farmer. Unless the tenant's capital is kept together, and made fully and freely and safely applicable for the everyday work of the farm, agriculture must come to a standstill. Where money and brains have free scope, even bad soils can be made to earn something. Where the tenant is tied down to unprofitable systems, or where his capital is nibbled away by rents which are not made out of the land, and which more than absorb profits, the best land must soon deteriorate, and the position become hopeless. And if one man breaks and goes in the bad times, his successor has to expend what capital he has in trying to get the land in condition again, and then has no more to go on with. That appears to be the obvious lesson to be drawn both from the history of the decay of agriculture in the depressed districts, and still more from the examination of the causes and conditions of the instances of more or less profitable farming that have been brought before the Commission.

CHAPTER III.

THE FALL OF PRICES.

THE most potent factor in bringing about the present situation has been the heavy and continuous fall in the prices of corn, and the fluctuating and recurrent fall in the prices of other staple articles of agricultural produce. The other causes of weakness and failure would have kept agriculture back even if prices had not fallen, but those causes severally and collectively could not have had such disastrous results had it not been that prices have been tending to sink to the level or below the level of the cost of production.

Sir Robert Giffen holds that up to 1891 the general change in agricultural prices ranged to about a fall of 25 per cent., that in many manufactured articles there has been a greater fall, and that the fall in agricultural produce has not been greater than the fall in general prices, except in the one article of wheat. But the heavy fall of agricultural prices is felt more keenly because readjustments are slower.

Sir Robert's estimate rests on the figures of 1891. The evidence of many witnesses would make the general average fall of agricultural prices considerably greater, and when the period of 1892 to 1894 is taken, including months in which the lowest recorded prices of wheat and barley, and some of the most exceptionally low prices of stock occurred, it would be safe to estimate the general fall at not less than 40 per cent since about 1872-74.

The fall in agricultural prices is illustrated by Sir R. Giffen's tables.

Thus the money value of the total amounts of agricultural produce in 1891, at the current prices of 1891, is given as £222,915,000. But if prices had remained at the figures of 1874 the money value of the total produce of 1891 would have been £298,997,000.[1]

Corn Prices.

Since 1891 prices have fallen considerably. The later position is strikingly shown in a report of the Norfolk Chamber of Agriculture. Taking the whole production of wheat and barley together, the value of the two crops in 1874 was £4,033,666, from 379,790 acres, and in 1894 was only £1,279,261 from 336,767 acres, taking the prices of October 1894, and allowing for half the barley being unfit for malting, and only used for stock feeding. The value per acre of the two crops averaged in 1874, £10 2s; in 1894, £3 16s. This is a drop in gross produce of £6 6s per acre, and a "loss of nearly £6 per head for every man, woman, and child in Norfolk."[2]

A similar calculation made for Lincolnshire, by Mr Roberts, shows that the average annual value of the total wheat crop in that county, taking the ten years 1874-84, was £2,443,590, while the average for the years 1884-94 was only £1,406,463, a decrease of 42·21 per cent. The corresponding fall for barley alone was 14·06 per cent. Taking the total wheat and barley crops together, the average annual values were for 1874-84 £3,769,538, and for 1884-94, £2,554,635, a fall of 32·2 per cent. Again, taking separately the years 1874 and 1894, and the average produce of those years, viz., in 1874, 4½ quarters of wheat per acre and 5 quarters of barley, and in 1894 3½ quarters of wheat and 3 quarters of saleable barley, and 1 quarter of "hinderends" at 10s; the value of the total crops of wheat and barley together at the prices of the two years was in 1874, £4,815,951, and in 1894 no more than £1,350,929. This shows a

[1] Vol. II., Appendix VI.
[2] Rew, Norfolk, Appendix, B. 1, p. 78.

decrease in the value of the crop of 1894 as compared with that of 1874 of no less than 66·46 per cent. The average value of the two crops per acre in 1874 was £10 4s 4½d, and in 1894 only £3 8s 6½d.[1]

Taking some of the separate farm accounts put in, we find, in one case, the value of wheat per acre given as £12 10s 9d in 1873, and as £2 18s 11d in 1893, a difference of 76·4 per cent., and comparing the average of the years 1873-77 with the average of 1888-92, there is a drop in the value of the wheat crop of £4 17s 6d, or 47.3 per cent., and comparing the same figures with the average of 1893-94, there is a drop of £7 1s 10¼d, or 68·4 per cent. In another instance the corresponding decreases of value are 43 and 67·5 per cent. Again, barley sank from £9 13s 1d per acre in 1873 to £5 6s 4d in 1892, to £4 4s, in 1893, and in the unfavourable season of 1894 to £2 14s, a fall between 1873 and 1894 of £6 19s 1d, or 72 per cent.[2]

Oats averaged 15·7 per cent. less in value in the years 1884-94 than in the years 1874-84, while in 1874 the average price was 29s 2d, and in 1894 14s 6d, a decrease between those two years of 50·3 per cent.

On one of the best farms in Cambridgeshire, 565 acres, the receipts for corn in 1874 were £4222, in 1894 were £1585, a difference of £2636, the land being farmed on the same lines.[3]

There runs through all these calculations a very natural disposition to take the bottom figures which have been reached, perhaps at exceptional moments (such as the autumn markets of 1894), and compare them with the top figures which have also been in some sense exceptional. It is plain, however, that, with ample discount for this natural tendency, there has been an enormous depreciation in the values of cereal crops, and that to enable agriculturists to continue growing them some corresponding diminution of the cost of production is absolutely necessary, if prices remain at anything like their recent level.

---

[1] Wilson Fox, Lincolnshire, Appendix A. 3 (*a*), pp. 42, 43.
[2] Ibid., p. 42.   [3] Ibid., Cambridge, p. 41.

WOOL PRICES.

As to wool, the total value of the wool produced in 1891 is put by Sir Robert Giffen at £6,000,000, assuming the average price to be 9·6d per lb. The same quantities at 1s 6¼d per lb., the average price of 1874, would have made £11,406,000.[1]

With the later price of 7d down to 5½d, the total loss to the wool grower is still more striking.

This closely agrees with the results from farm accounts. Wool seems to have averaged about 40s per "tod" between 1873 and 1878, and the fall to 1893-94 has been about 20s per "tod."[2]

In Cumberland, the Teviotdale Farmers' Club supply figures showing a drop in values of wool between the averages of 1870-74 and 1890-94 of about 50 per cent. In Devonshire and Dorset, the fall has been nearly 50 per cent.

Mr Pringle gives startling figures from a farm on the Wolds of the North Riding of Yorkshire, where the clips of 1500 fleeces in 1864 made £1925, and of 1260 fleeces in 1894 made only £507 11s.

In Scotland the fall in "black-faced" wool is put at from 1s a lb. in 1872 to 5½d or 6d now.

MEAT PRICES.

By Sir Robert Giffen's tables the value of meat in 1891 is given at £75,000,000, while the same quantities at the prices of 1874 would have brought £98,000,000, a decrease in value of £23,000,000, or of about 23·47 per cent.[3]

Mr Fox's inquiry into the Garstang district of Lancashire in the autumn of 1893 shows heavy falls in price of cattle:—"Bullocks worth £15 to £16 eight years ago, now worth from £10 to £11. The autumn cattle have sold 40 per cent. less than five years ago." Calving cows and heifers sell at a fall of from 25 to 50 per cent.

[1] Vol. II., Appendix A. Tables XI. and XII.
[2] Wilson Fox, Lincolnshire, Appendix A 4. A.
[3] Vol. II., Appendix A., Tables XI. and XII.

Taking the average prices realised at Lincoln beast fair in 1882-3 and in 1893-4, the fall in the prices of all classes of cattle between the two periods is from 28·68 per cent. to 33·90 per cent.[1]

In Essex, Mr Pringle says farmers complain that fattening no longer pays. Buying a beast of 9 cwt. in October, and putting on 4 cwt. by feeding, "the extra price made did not cover the cost of food consumed and labour."

In Banffshire in the "seventies" a cwt. of prime beef was worth 84s. It has frequently sold since for 54s, and in June 1895 was worth 60s.

Store cattle in Suffolk have fallen from an average of £11 14s per head in 1889, to £9 16s in 1894, partly because farmers have not now capital enough to stock their farms.

With regard to sheep, though there has been a recent recovery of prices in 1894 and 1895, and though it can be shown that the average prices thirty and forty years ago were, on the whole, lower than present prices, there were very heavy declines of value since ten and fifteen years ago. Thus Mr Hope puts the fall in store sheep between 1882 and 1892, as from 40s to 30s, and in fat stock from 70s to 50s.

The average price of sheep at Lincoln Fair from 1877 to 1894 was about 62s, for the first nine years, and about 52s 7d for the last nine years, a fall of 15 per cent. The prices shown in the evidence and accounts of individual farmers confirm the approximate accuracy of these figures.

There is of course more difficulty in getting at the fall in prices of meat in the same way as in the case of cereals. It may be affirmed generally, as regards the values realised by stock, that although the tendency downwards has been marked, it has not been nearly so sweeping and decisive as with corn. The losses to agriculturists under this head have been largely due to sudden and sharp fluctuations, to combined dearness of "stores," and cheapness of fat stock, and to one or two

[1] Wilson Fox, Lincolnshire, p. 45.

specially unfavourable seasons, such as the drought of 1893, and the cold summer of 1892.

Dairy Produce.

But even in the direction where most hope is felt of successful re-adjustment, in dairy products, there has been recently a striking fall of values.

The price of butter usually regulates the price of milk, and the enormous importations of cheap butter from the colonies, as well as from Denmark and France, has lowered the price of milk as well as of butter.

Mr Drew, in Galloway, says, "We make the very best butter. We have the largest creameries in the country, but the fall in butter has been so great," that the creameries can "only offer 4d a gallon for milk, and it has also to bear the cost of transport."

Some witnesses put the fall in dairy products at from 10 to 25 per cent.

In Sir Robert Giffen's tables dairy products in 1891 are estimated at £35,000,000, while at the prices of 1874 the same quantities of milk, butter, and cheese would have been worth £52,500,000, a fall of 33 per cent.

Mr Finney and Mr Osborne, of the Derbyshire Dairy Farming Association, state that cheese has gone down from 60s to 80s to 40s to 50s, butter from 1s 2d summer, and 1s 10d winter price, to about 9d or 10d and 1s 4d.

In Dorsetshire, where the larger farmers usually let their cows to dairymen, dairies are now let at £2 to £3 less per cow than ten or twelve years ago, a rough measure of the fall.

The fall in the price of potatoes from £4 and £5 a ton down to 35s, and even 30s a ton, has caused heavy losses in many districts. On farms in the Lothians, Mr Hope has estimated the crop at about 8 tons an acre, though it is frequently much heavier. Taking that estimate, the value of the crop per acre in 1874 was nearly £40, in 1895 between £12 and £18.

NOTE AS TO THE PRESENT POSITION.

At the present moment,[1] owing to the delay in the issue of the Report, these figures may be held not to represent the actual state of affairs. The wheat area of 1896 was 1,693,957, and the produce 57,053,000 bushels, whereas in 1895, the corresponding area was 1,417,483, and produce 37,176,000 bushels. The value of the crop of 1896 at an average price of 26s per quarter was £9,271,112, while in 1895 it was at 23s only £5,056,550. Allowing for the value of displaced crops on the area taken from those crops in 1896 and restored to wheat, an area of 276,474 acres, there would remain a very substantial increase to the assets of corn growers on the year, placing them obviously in a different position from the terrible despair of 1892 to 1894, when English wheat was being fed to cattle or pigs in more than one district.

But the tendency of wheat has been again to fall, and as there is also a downward or at any rate a stagnant tendency in the prices of meat (the triennial average of beef for 1894-6, is the lowest recorded, while mutton showed but a minute improvement) and other produce, we cannot think that the record of the position as given in our evidence, and condensed in the reports, is in any true sense out of date.

* * * * * *

Since the completion of the Report of the Commission there has been a remarkable rise in wheat, but this is clearly due to temporary causes, and the careful analysis of the prospects of foreign competition in the Main Report of the Commission, makes it more rather than less probable that competition will further increase and inevitably lower prices.

[1] May, 1897.

CHAPTER IV.

Protection and Currency Changes.

In times of depression it has always been the first impulse of a majority of agriculturists to demand direct or indirect protection. The desire to keep up prices and receipts naturally comes before the patient and rational procedure of cutting down expenses.

This desire to artificially keep up prices was brought before us in the two demands for currency reform and for protective duties.

To take the question of protective duties first, it is most satisfactory, in the interests of agriculture as well as of the whole community, to note that our evidence shows, conclusively, that protection has practically sunk to the position of a "pious opinion."

A small number of our farmer witnesses, and one or two landowners, favoured protection in one form or another, some advocating the taxation of manufactured goods coupled with relief to agriculture, others the taxation of foreign barley, others the re-imposition of a registration duty on wheat, etc.

Mr Harris, who alone argued the question out, would place a moderate duty on all imported corn or flour, except from India and the Colonies, and also on all manufactured articles. With the proceeds he would pay bounties for wheat growing and take off the burdens on agricultural land.

In their local inquiries, our Assistant Commissioners naturally came in contact with the undoubtedly widespread protectionist feeling of many farmers, but even in the rural districts, opinions in favour of protective duties were freely qualified by the comment that, however desirable, it was hopeless to expect to get them.

Among witnesses not hostile to protection as a principle, the prevalent opinion was probably expressed by Mr Punchard, who thought protection might be a remedy for depression, but that it was wholly out of the question.

Other strong witnesses think protection would be no remedy as well as impossible, and that it would not better the condition of agriculture.

Mr Albert Pell and Mr Squarey see no reason whatever to depart in any degree from the principles of free trade.

Mr Turnbull thinks an import duty on wheat might raise the price of home wheat, but it would depress the price of home cattle and stock. In the long run it would benefit neither owner nor tenant.

Mr Gilbert Murray says Derbyshire farmers do not want protection, it would be against their interests.

The evidence generally as to the branches of agriculture which have held out best during the depression, dairy farming, and stock-breeding and fattening, show that everywhere things would have gone much worse for the farmers in these branches were it not for the cheap feeding stuffs imported from abroad.

Mr Turnor, a large Lincolnshire landowner, said: "I would sooner have the cheap foreign barley for fattening stock."

Mr Stratton recommends farmers to sell their hay and other crops, and buy for feeding Russian barley at 84s a ton.

A Lancashire farmer who has got on says: "I am a free trader; I say we all buy our feeding stuffs cheaper, and we all live cheaper because of free trade."

Alike among the sheep farmers in the Western Highlands, and in the south-western dairying counties of Scotland, the protection theory is wholly out of favour with many.

As to the bimetallic solution of the difficulties of agriculture, the case for these proposals was laid before us with ability and completeness by Professor Foxwell,

Mr Everett, and others, and the theories and arguments of its supporters were rebutted very fully by Sir Robert Giffen, Lord Farrer, and other experts.

It is unnecessary to attempt, in this report, to sum up the contentions and illustrations for and against bimetallism presented to us.

It will be sufficient to say that I am unable to agree with many of the views expressed by some of my colleagues in their memorandum on this subject, and that a consideration of the evidence leads me to generally support the views laid before us by Sir Robert Giffen, both as regards the relation of the fall of prices to contraction or expansion of standard money, and as to the impracticability and undesirability of a double standard.

While grave doubt attaches to most of the bimetallic interpretation of past events, still graver doubt seems to me to rest on the view bimetallists take of the probable course of events in case their proposal was carried out. I cannot be satisfied by the evidence of Professor Foxwell and others that there would be a better equilibrium and more stability of prices under the new system, even if a ratio of the metals could be definitely fixed.

And when it is admitted that the period of transition may lead to so much confusion and perturbation of business that it may be advisable to adopt what is called a "climbing ratio," and to make the transition by successive and periodic revisions of the ratio of the two metals, each such revision necessarily involving the modification of millions of contracts, such an undertaking would seem not unlikely to disturb and harass commerce, and the commerce of agriculturists as well as of others, and to introduce anarchy and confusion and panic into business relations. Such results could not fail to be ruinous to agriculture, even if at the outset there was a temporary rise of prices, just as inflated paper currency, in America and elsewhere, has usually developed a feverish expansion of spurious prosperity, inevitably followed by disastrous reaction and widespread bankruptcies.

Further, Professor Foxwell and the ablest advocates of bimetallism obviously think it either impracticable, or hazardous, or both, to start a bimetallic system without concerted action by the great commercial nations.

If this is a sound view the whole question is at once relegated to the metaphysics of the agricultural future, and has no practical or immediate bearing on the problem of dealing here and now with the present phases of agricultural depression.

What the present inquiry is concerned with, and what our reference invites us to deal with, is to ascertain what are the immediate readjustments and remedial measures which can be applied at the present moment to the wants of agriculture, to minimise economic loss and friction, and to restore such prosperity to farming as is humanly possible under conditions which practical men admit cannot be altered by a stroke of a wand.

We have, therefore, to see what can be done now for agriculture without attempting to raise prices artificially by protection or bimetallism.

CHAPTER V.

THE ECONOMIC POSITION OF FARMING IN COMBATING LOW PRICES.

THE general position resulting from the fall of prices is necessarily before us in a clearer and more precise form than the degree and manner in which the outgoings of farming have been, or can be, re-adjusted so as to leave some profit on the working. Though exact accounts are not generally kept by farmers, a considerable number of accounts which appear to be fairly trustworthy have been obtained. And it may be taken that where accounts are kept, in those cases generally there will have been more organised and persistent effort to make ends meet. So that, though the number of accounts is not large, they may be taken as fair illustrations of how far outgoings have been brought into line with incomings under present circumstances.

Estimates of the cost of growing cereals vary considerably according to local conditions, and to the allocation, in farm accounts, of various items of outgoings to the several crops. A Lincolnshire farmer of experience puts the cost of an acre of wheat at £7 0s 10d; barley, £5 11s 2½d; oats, £7 3s 6½d. In 1894, seed costing less, wheat took £6 18s to grow; barley, £5 10s. At the autumn prices of 1894 the cost of producing wheat exceeded the returns by £3 17s 4¾d an acre, while barley cost £2 16s 10d per acre more than it fetched.[1]

Taking a five years' average of yield and price, 1889-93, an acre of wheat made £5 3s 4d, an average loss of £1 17s 6d an acre. For barley the average return was £5 2s 11¾d, and the loss 3s 2¼d per acre. This esti-

[1] Wilson Fox, Lincoln, p. 46.

mate allows nothing for interest on capital or depreciation, and rent is put at 18s 8d an acre.[1]

Another calculation, based on a six-course rotation—fallows, oats, wheat, seeds, wheat, barley—and allowing interest and depreciation at 15s an acre, gives the cost of growing the corn crops at £7 1s 10½d on the six years, and the loss on the six years taking wheat at 25s, barley at 30s, and oats at 20s, is put at 17s 11d, an acre.[2]

On a four-course system, the cost of the corn crops is found to be £6 18s 3d, and the loss, at 25s for wheat and 30s for barley, is put at £1 0s 4½d an acre.[3]

In both cases rent is put at 26s an acre.

On medium soil in South Lincolnshire, a six-course system gives cost of corn crops at £7 5s 6d an acre. The low prices of 1894 make the loss no less than £2 0s 3d per acre, though this land is very productive (wheat, 4½; barley, 5; oats, 7 quarters). Rent is put at 26s, and interest and depreciation at 15s per acre.

On fair light land, the four-course gives the two corn crops at £8, and the loss at £2 0s 6d, taking rent at 16s and 1894 prices for wheat and barley.

It is to be noted in all these estimates that the straw is supposed to be consumed. In most instances, if the straw were sold off, a small margin of profit would be found, and the land would retain its fertility if the full manurial equivalents were returned, which can of course be done much more cheaply at recent prices than by using all the straw at home. In 1893 oat straw was sold in Lincolnshire at £3 5s, and wheat straw at about £4 a ton.

The accounts of Mr Prout's farm in Herts, where the system of continuous corn growing and sale of straw, with return of artificial manures, has been followed for many years, with undiminished productiveness of the soil, give a fair measure of the margin of profit thus obtainable on heavy land well farmed.[4]

The cost of growing an acre of wheat, taking rent at

[1] Wilson Fox, Lincoln, Appendix, A. 8—A., p. 142.
[2] Ibid. App. A. 8—B., pp. 143-4.   [3] Ibid, p. 145.
[4] Spencer, Aylesbury, and Herts, p. 11.

25s, tithes, rates, and taxes at 7s 6d, interest on capital at 10s, is put at £7 2s 6d.

The average market value of an acre of wheat, during the fourteen years from 1880 to 1893 inclusive, has been found to be £7 2s 4d, and of barley £7 13s 9d. The aveage value of straw of all kinds has been £1 19s 3d. For 1892 and 1893 the acre of wheat fetched only £3 14s and £4 19s, and the straw of all kinds for those years fetched £2 12s 6d, and £2 8s 4d. In 1892 there would therefore be a loss of 16s, even with the straw sold off, and in 1893 the profit would be only 4s 10d per acre. In 1894 there would be a loss on wheat of over 30s, and probably a slight loss on barley.

A Wiltshire farmer of experience gives the cost of a four-course rotation as follows; Roots, £5 10s 3d, clover, £2 9s 3d, wheat or oats, £6 0s 3d, barley, £4 6s 9d. This is taking rent at 12s 6d and making no allowing for tenants' interest or depreciation.[1]

In Dorsetshire, the cost of the four courses is put by a competent farmer at £18; the returns, taking straw at consuming value, are only £16 13s. This works out at a loss of 6s 9d an acre per annum on average arable land without allowing for rent.[2]

Three estimates in Dorset for an acre of wheat are— £5 9s, with rent at 30s, and no interest on tenant's capital; £7 19s, rent at 25s; and "after two years lay," £5 10s, with rent at 15s.

In Norfolk the estimate of experienced agents and valuers is £5 8s for an acre of wheat—rent, tithe, rates and taxes taken at 25s; while two "of the best known farmers" put it at £6, rent, etc., being put at £1 7s 6d. Estimates collected by the Norfolk Chamber of Agriculture, put the cost of wheat or barley at £4 8s 4d, exclusive of rent, tithe, rates and taxes, and also excluding, as the two estimates above do, allowance for interest on tenants' capital.

Returns were obtained by the same chamber for 1894 from 47,000 acres of land, producing wheat and oats rather over the average, and barley just under average,

---

[1] Rew, Salisbury Plain, p. 8. [2] Rew, Dorset, p. 10.

"the best farmed land in the county."[1] Of the crops, 58 per cent were sold, making a return for wheat of £2 6s 11d, barley, £2 19s 10d, and oats £1 14s 2d per acre. The 42 per cent. of corn used at home is put at—wheat, £1 15s 4d, barley at £1 0s 10d, oats at £3 7s. The total money returns from each crop are—wheat, £4 12s 3d, barley, £4 0s 9d, oats, £5 3s 3d, or an average on all of £4 5s 2d.

According to these figures, on the best farmed land of a county where scientific farming has worked wonders, the returns in 1894 left nothing or less than nothing over working expenses either in the way of rent for landlord, or tithe, rates and taxes, or interest for tenant. If all the straw were sold at a fair price, ends would not be made to meet.

Mr Nunneley, a Northamptonshire farmer, who has farmed heavy land successfully, holds that wheat costs just under £5 an acre, plus rent. At 30s a quarter, four quarters would just repay expenses, and pay 20s rent, and you would have the straw for the profit.

Mr W. J. Harris, who thinks that the average advantage the foreign producer has, in cost of production and expenses, till his wheat is marketed in England, is about 40s an acre, says, "There is a fair acreage throughout England that is so fine that it would compete (with imports) even under present conditions, especially if you allow the sale of the straw, or a portion of it."

With a liberal allowance for exaggeration consequent on a state of panic, such as Mr Rew describes in Norfolk in 1894, it must be admitted that, even with the small rise in prices in the present year, the staple crops of arable farming have ceased to pay any return which can keep up their cultivation. If a narrow margin can be got, it must be by the sale of straw at full market, and not at consuming, prices. It is true that a certain relief comes from the low price of seed corn and of fertilisers to replace the farmyard manure, if straw is sold off. But any such "set-off" is trifling, and unless prices rise above at least a minimum of 30s for wheat and barley, it will

[1] Rew, Norfolk, pp. 30, 25.

only be in exceptional circumstances and positions that corn growing can be persisted in, except at much longer intervals of seasons, or so far as it may be an indispensable adjunct of stock farming.

In the face of such testimony from all districts, the four-course system, so long the mainstay of English arable farming is, naturally, condemned in the letter of Lord Leicester to Mr Shaw Lefevre when Chairman, and by many witnesses who have come before us.[1]

If the estimates of the cost of the four-course system and of the returns from roots and seeds are approximately correct, to make ends meet a return from the two corn crops is demanded, which is impossible at present prices. For instance, in two careful estimates the cost of the four years is put at £19 16s 6d, and £19 15s, and the value of roots and seeds at £6 in one case, and £3 15s in the other. In the former case wheat and barley have to make up £13 16s 6d, in the latter £16 per acre, between them, an insoluble problem at the prices of the last few years.

The only chance of economic recovery lies in the direction of reducing expenses by throwing land into grass, and occasionally breaking up. Lord Leicester is able to reduce his horses from thirty-four to eighteen, and the labourers employed on his home farm from twenty-two to twelve. He also finds the land so full of nitrogen after temporary pastures that two corn and two root crops may be taken without manuring.[2]

The Cost of Labour.

The most important element in the cost of production economically, as well as socially, is the cost of labour. Sir Robert Giffen has shown that in the progressive changes of values during the past twenty years, the wages of labour have been fairly maintained, while the general fall in the prices of all the articles consumed by the workers represents a real improvement in the condition of labour. Taking the two facts together,

[1] Vol. IV, App. D.   [2] Wilson Fox, Suffolk, § 81, p. 62.

wages not having fallen with prices, labour, he thinks, is at least 20 per cent. better off than in 1874. Again, where labour has become more efficient, there may have been some adjustment of the labour item in the cost of production, but where things have remained as they were, or where labour has become less efficient, it means that out of the depreciated produce of the soil, a larger portion than before has to be set aside to pay for labour.[1]

This general law is amply supported and illustrated by evidence and farm accounts supplied to us.

Thus, on a typical arable farm in North Lincolnshire, comparing the years 1873 to 1877, with the years 1893-94, while the decrease in the values of the wheat and barley produced has been 63 and 61·6 per cent. respectively, and in wool 49 per cent., the decrease in the labour bill has been only 9·4 per cent.[2]

Mr Read's labour bill is practically the same as twenty years ago. "Rent used to be double labour; now labour is twice the rent."

Sir John Lawes thinks labour is the chief item in the increase of the cost of production.

Mr H. H. Scott thinks labour has become a 10 per cent. larger item.

In Scotland, Mr Hope thinks the rise in the item of labour has been about 15 per cent., Mr Ferguson puts it at 25 per cent., and "even this rise does not prevent the best men from going off to the towns."

Generally speaking, the evidence is uniform that where farming is proceeding on the old lines, and is kept up to anything like the old standards, the cost of labour is either about the same, or has materially increased.

And, even in the case of a changed system of farming, there is not always a saving. Where dairy work is taken up, there is often an increase in the item of labour, as skilled men and women are wanted, and in stock farming also.

The same is stated even as regards machinery. Machinery makes production easier and saves time, but higher wages are paid to skilled labour. Mr Dewar, on

[1] Giffen, 18,084, 18,118, 18,156. [2] Wilson Fox, Linc., p. 46.

the other hand, a successful farmer, says he saves the harvest wages of seven men, £49, by binding. And "in Cornwall," says Mr Collins, "our farmers have adopted mechanical power, and effected an immense saving in labour. The work is now done with American reapers and binders."

Lord Wantage, on the other hand, thinks that, while changes in cultivation and the introduction of machinery are lessening employment, "social reasons and moral obligations prevent the agriculturist from farming his land to the best advantage, and preclude him from freely using labour-saving machinery," as does also the fear of throwing men upon the rates.[1]

On his own estates, as on Lord Leicester's estate, the men displaced by changes of cultivation are found employment in estate work, such as road-making, planting, etc.

That tenant farmers share in this feeling and give it effect, seems to be confirmed by evidence from the eastern counties, that wages have, to a certain extent, been paid out of capital in the past few years.

There is a difference of opinion as to whether labour now is less efficient or not. Some farmers emphatically state this to be the case. Others take a decidedly more favourable view.

Mr Read thinks the young labourers of to-day take little interest in their work. Mr Cocks says there is a great difficulty in getting efficient men. Mr Watson thinks "the labour quite as good as it was." Mr Worthington: "You can get first-class men; there is no doubt about the quality."

Lord Wantage, who has studied the position of the labourer and small holder, and has special experience, says, "the labourers are quite as good as they were. I do not think that there is any deterioration among them. A good cottage and a good garden is a great inducement to a married man to stay."

Mr Ralston, Lord Strathmore's agent, says: "Labour is very good. The quality has been quite maintained."

Mr Latham thinks the men earn as much as

---

[1] Letter to Chairman, November 1895.

formerly in summer, except during harvest, "when the machinery does not give them as good a chance of earning high wages as they used to have." "All through the winter time in my early days, the labourers were always on piecework, and earning much larger wages than they do now." "We have a good supply of labour. The actual labour has not deteriorated. Where men have had good masters they are pretty good now. I wish I could think it was not the other way, but I do think the masters have deteriorated, and not the men."

The advantages of the labourer consist, in Mr Latham's opinion, in their greater spending power, and their improved cottages and allotment gardens.

In Scotland, Mr Black thinks the position and advantages of labourers greatly improved—"half as well off again." "A larger share of the produce goes to the labourer and less to the landlord and tenant; but the labourers deserve it, and work well for it."

Mr Dickie: "Their condition has very materially improved."

Mr Lockhart: "They are more attentive and keep things in better order than they used to do."

Mr Dun, on the other hand, doubts whether the work is as good as it was. The best men go away.

On the whole, there can be no doubt that the general cost of labour has materially risen, and that where the scale of wages is highest and advantages greatest, as in the north of England and in Scotland, and on well equipped and generously managed estates everywhere, the efficiency of labour is as great, if not greater than ever. Where the scale of pay has sunk, as in some counties, the best men naturally seek employment elsewhere.

The Cost of Maintaining Fertility.

As to the other main item in farming outgoings, the expenditure on fertilisers and feeding stuffs, the facts disclosed are highly significant. It is plain that where the capital of farmers has been drained away to a low point, and the stage of ruin, both of the farmer and of the land is near at hand, as in some of the worst districts, this expenditure has fallen. But even in these districts, so long as it was possible, the energetic farmer has clearly worked on the plan of trying to beat low prices by full production, and the evidence of proportionately heavy outlay on feeding stuffs and manures is very striking. In the case of nearly all the successful farmers, the expenditure has been considerable and generally maintained continuously. Where a change of cultivation has taken place, with the increase of stock, there has been also a considerable increase in the outlay on cake.

There is very naturally some difference of opinion as to the financial results of this type of expenditure.

Thus, Mr H. H. Scott thinks "high farming does not pay so well as it did. . . . I expend about £1800 to £2000 in artificial foods alone. At one time, when prices of stock were good, I do not think there was any expenditure I made that yielded me more profit than that expenditure on artificial foods; but now there is no direct profit from it, and last year I made out that there was a loss from it." But Mr Scott is speaking under the pressure of the great drop in prices of stock in 1893, and he admits that there is "an indirect profit by the benefit the consumption is to the farm," and that it cannot be "in the end good policy to reduce the condition of the soil, even though it does not pay for a year or two at present. I believe in good and liberal cultivation."

Mr Wilkinson, also from Northumberland, holds strongly that, even on secondary land, wise outlay in feeding stuffs and artificial manures might help farmers to get over their difficulties. "You can go beyond justifiable expenditure, but with careful attention to your business, and careful spending, cakes and manures still pay."

Mr Pell, though he condemns as reckless many of the later forms of expenditure, still believes that the farmer who goes in for thorough clean farming and the best of everything has more chance of holding his own.

Mr Treadwell, on the other hand, though he admits that nothing will make or restore a pasture so quickly as a liberal use of cake by sheep or cattle, and has proved that "to the hilt" by his own experience, is convinced that, at the present price of produce, the higher you farm the more money you lose.

Sir John Lawes says "the last bushel always costs more than all the others." With low prices, you cannot force the produce of the land remuneratively beyond what he calls the average of the seasons. He fears that farmers who have farmed very highly have lost money. But his view is rather a condemnation of extreme forcing of the soil, than what people ordinarily understand by liberal treatment of the land. "It would be equally bad economy to farm too low." The natural produce of the soil would not pay a man to cultivate now.

In every case, when closely questioned, there came the admission that the chances of success in these times were increased by having the best stock, the best seeds, the best cake and manures, the best equipment, and the best labour.

It is the letting down of land which is the sure and unfailing precursor of the ruin of the farmer. The higher fertility created by doing everything well, not only makes the best bid for a profit now, but is continually adding to the savings bank for the future. The only qualification is that the cultivation must be appropriate to the land, and that on many of the heaviest and lightest of lands, irrespective of their having been let down, the chance of a margin of profit is too slender now to justify outlay. These types of land must, in some cases, for the present disappear from cultivation, and their owners and occupiers must be content with the lowest return from these either as rough temporary grazings, or for the still humbler function of rabbit warrens.

One unanswerable proof that liberal outlay in farming still pays is that the testimony of almost every witness is practically unanimous that there is a striking competition for farms where this policy has been pursued, and that this eagerness of the outsider to come in and reap the advantages of good farming, is the greatest peril of the good farmer at the present day, and actually leads to the absorption of his possible margin of profit, either by enhanced rent, or by the refusal of a moderate and reasonable reduction in consideration of depression of prices.

Another fact which shows that farmers have been alive to the benefit of high farming is that the prices of cakes and manures have considerably fallen, and yet we have in a large proportion of farming accounts handed in, undeniable proof that the money outlay in this direction is, if anything, increasing, and, therefore, the quantities must be still more increasing. Further, economy has been effected by the more careful analysis and selection of feeding stuffs and manures.

It is most satisfactory to note that a considerable protection and pecuniary advantage has been conferred by Parliament on agriculturists by the passing of the Fertilisers and Feeding Stuffs Act in 1893. That Act, where effectively administered, has been of the greatest service.

What Items must be Cut Down.

Whether this tendency to maintain and to concentrate outlay on adequate working, and adequate fertilising of the land is viewed in the interest of the production of food, or the provision of employment, we are bound to consider it as a sound economic instinct, and, in fact, the only rational method of readjusting the outgoings of farming to present returns which is consistent with the permanent interests of agriculture. Even supposing that the large proportion of money returned from rents to the land, in the shape of drainage, buildings, and other improvements, and in repairs, which we have noted on certain large and liberally-managed estates, were more general than it appears to be, it is plainly necessary that rent should be subordinated, as an outgoing, to the payments for labour and fertilising, that in the farmers' expenditure the reproductive items should in bad times be kept up, or, if necessary, increased, and the balance obtained by cutting down the non-reproductive items, rent, and through rent, rates, and taxes, to the lowest point possible. This policy is also obviously to the interest of the owner in the long run. The heaviest losses to owners have been from the breaking down of old tenants, the deterioration of the land, and the heavy cost of getting things going again with new tenants.

CHAPTER VI.

THE FARM ACCOUNTS.

BUT this is just what we find, from analysis of the farm accounts handed in, is not being done, or is being done in a most inadequate fashion.

To take a few instances :—Mr Rew gives the accounts of a large and well-managed farm on Salisbury Plain (827 acres) for a quarter of a century between 1868 and 1893. Labour has averaged £774, and for the last two years stands at £745 and £767, showing no diminution. For manures, feeding stuffs and seeds, the average of 1868-78 was £714; from 1878-93 these items averaged £1236, and the last two years were £1118, and £1193 respectively. For the period 1868-78 rent averaged £956; for 1879-85, £845; for 1886-88, £740; and from 1889 rent has been £536. The total profits were, from 1868-78, £2655 11s 7d, and from 1886-88 inclusive, £675 2s 3d; losses, from 1879-85 were £1777 8s 6d, and from 1889-93, £279 8s 9d. Profit and loss were calculated after allowing 5 per cent. interest—£350 on the average capital of £7000.[1]

To what extent this farm has been over-rented is shown by the following figures :—From 1879-93—the period of depression—£10,814 was paid in rents, and a loss of £1381 15s incurred by tenant. In the last five years, £2679 was paid in rents, and the loss was £279 8s 9d. It is plain that a further reduction of rent of about 13 per cent. through the whole period would have enabled the tenant to make ends meet (without any reward for management and skill), and a similar

---

[1] Rew, Salisbury Plain, p. 14, App. C. V. Farm Accounts, p. 184.

reduction of about 11 per cent. on the reduced rent of £536 would have made ends meet on the last five years; in other words, would have left the clear interest of 5 per cent. on tenants' capital intact. A very small additional fall in rent would have given the tenant a small working profit. These accounts amply illustrate the insufficiency and tardiness of reductions, and how the best type of farmer is gradually brought to ruin. In this case, the tenant could not have held out without private resources of his own. "But for the private means which my father and I possessed we could not have lived on the returns of the farm." Yet in the twenty-five years the owner has received in all £21,339 from this father and son in rents.

Mr Wilson Fox says of the admirable series of farm accounts in his Lincolnshire Report: "All these accounts come from representative farmers who are at the present time farming high. Consequently these accounts can only be regarded as the best samples, and do not represent those of a more struggling class, handicapped by want of capital." Taking one instance:

On a farm of 474 acres, heavy loam, half arable and half pasture, accounts from 1883 to 1893 inclusive, 11 years, show that labour averaged £452, nearly £1 per acre, and in the last two years stood at £467 14s, and £480 7s, while manures, feeding stuffs, and seeds averaged £400, and were in the last two years £378 13s, and £410.

The rent has averaged £478, or about £1 an acre; but the farmer's profits, taking the balance of profits over losses for the eleven years, have only averaged £15 1s 9d over the whole 474 acres, or under 8d an acre per annum. In such a case as this the economics of farming are obviously upset in favour of the landlord in most outrageous fashion. This tenant has been doing his land well, and has had as his reward the right to use about £185 worth of produce per annum from the farm, the use of the farmhouse, and £15 a year as interest on £3055 capital and payment for his own skill and exertions. If 5 per cent. interest on tenant's capital and

2s 6d an acre for management were also charged, the deficit would be about £200 a year. But the owner has in the eleven years drawn no less than £5236 from this farm. A reduction of about 26 per cent. would have left the tenant with a profit equal to 5 per cent. interest on his capital.[1]

A Bedfordshire farm of 922 acres, one-third pasture, well worked with plenty of capital and excellent buildings, shows over twelve years—1882 to 1893—and comparing the averages of 1891-2-3 with 1882, a drop in the total outgoings from £4967 in 1882 to £3430, or 30 per cent., while labour has fallen from £1000 in 1882 to an average of £854, or 14½ per cent., and cake and manures have risen from £272 to an average of £352, an increase of 29 per cent. Rent at the same time has fallen from £1256 to £1069, or 11 per cent., and in the last year to £944, or 24 per cent. The balance of profits over losses for the twelve years has been £1811 16s, an annual average of £150 19s, or 3s 3¼d an acre, as the total return for interest on capital, and for management and personal work; whereas, worked commercially, with interest on capital and something for management, the tenant should have been getting £400 more. But the owner has drawn in the twelve years in rent £13,241 or, about £1120 a year, or over 24s an acre.[2]

A farm in the Lincoln Union of 320 acres, nearly all arable, shows over the nine years from 1885 to 1894 a total loss of £464 19s 5d, or average loss of £51 15s 3d, or 2·2 per cent. on average capital of £2309, without charging interest on capital or for management. Labour has averaged £434, and in last two years stands at £480 and £487. Manures, feeding stuffs, and seeds have averaged £229, and for last two years are £237 0s 6d, and £271 2s 4d, an increase in the essential outgoings. The rent has averaged £235, and has not been sensibly reduced in these years. A reduction of rent by about £100 a year would have changed the tenant's loss of £464 into a profit of the same amount, or about 2 per

[1] Wilson Fox, Linc., p. 63, App. A. I A., p. 117. Farm Accounts, p. 127.
[2] Pringle, Beds, &c. p. 112, App. C. III. Farm Accounts, p. 64.

cent. on his capital, and would have left the owner with a rent of 8s an acre.[1]

A strong "wold" farm in Louth Union, 491 acres,[2] of which 99 are grass, shows since 1888 averages—labour, £499; manures, feeding stuffs, etc., £532; rent with rates, tithe and taxes, £645. Without charging interest on capital or for management, the tenant has lost £51 13s 8½d a year. But here, as in several other Lincolnshire accounts, there is an ample margin in the rent out of which to construct a small profit for the tenant.

The result of the six years' farming is that the owner has drawn in rents £3871, out of which it appears only £121 4s, has been remitted in 1893, and 1894—while the occupier has lost nearly 10 per cent. of his working capital, £3400, and has had as his share the use of the farmhouse, and an average of £175 worth of produce for his housekeeping.[3]

The accounts of a large "middle marsh" farm in the same district, 1200 acres, one third grass, show average outlay on labour, £1249, and on feeding stuffs and manures, £535. The loss between 1884 and 1894 has averaged £38 9s 6d a year, without interest on capital or charge for management, or even taking anything from the farm for housekeeping. But the rent has averaged no less than £1579, and even now stands at £1250, or a little over 20s an acre. The owner has drawn in the ten years no less than £15,793, while the accounts prove that the tenant has employed a capital of £7407, in keeping up the farm at a good and uniform level of labour and manuring, and has not only received nothing, but has lost nearly £400 of his capital. A reduction of the rent to 10s an acre would have left the tenant in 1893-4 with a profit of about £300, or about 4 per cent. It may be added, too, that this tenant's rates stand at the high figure of £298, which would have been materially reduced if the rent had been adequately reduced a few years ago.[4]

---

[1] Wilson Fox, Linc., App. A. I. B., p. 118. Farm Accounts, p. 128.
[2] Ibid., App. A. I. C., p. 119. [3] Farm Accounts, p. 129. [4] Ibid., p. 131.

Such instances as these of the complete transfer of the economic loss of these bad times to the shoulders of the tenant, placing him in the position of a man who sacrifices his whole time and energies and capital to produce wealth in which he is allowed no share whatever, are clearly inconsistent with common sense, and ruinous to the interests of agriculture, to say nothing of their injustice.

A splendid "wold" farm of 837 acres, 90 per cent. arable in North Yorkshire, "ably managed and in prime condition," shows in the fifteen years from 1879 to 1893, profits of £2052 in seven years, and losses of £1997 in eight years. The net profit of fifteen years' working is £55 5s 8½d, or £3 13s 8d per annum, without charging interest on £12 an acre capital. Labour has averaged £1009, and last two years are £1069 11s 9d and £1084 19s 2d. Manures and feeding stuffs were in 1892, £816, and in 1893, £866. Thus the farm has been thoroughly well kept up by the tenant, with the result that the use of over £10,000 of capital, and the whole skill and energy of an expert farmer, has been given for nothing. But in the fifteen years the owner has drawn in rent[1] no less than £13,887 10s, and the rent in 1893 still stands at £735, 15s. Such an absolute transfer of the whole economic loss to the tenant seems to us wholly incompatible with the interests of agriculture and with common fairness.[2]

A grass farm of 431 acres in Northants, where labour has since 1889 averaged £270, and cakes and manures £380, has made a loss of £112 a year, or nearly 3 per cent. on capital, while paying an average rent of £708, which left an ample margin to allow the tenant a small working profit. In five years the owner has drawn £3357 15s, while the occupier has lost £561 or a seventh part of his capital.[3]

A farm of 750 acres, nearly all arable, in Mid Norfolk,

---

[1] In these accounts insurance is not separated from rent.
[2] Pringle, North Yorkshire, App. C. II., p. 47, *See* par. 52. Farm Accounts, p. 192.
[3] Pringle, Beds, &c., App. C. IX., p. 125. Farm Accounts, p. 130.

for nine years from 1884 to 1893, shows averages: for labour, £1065; for manures and feeding stuffs, etc., £753; and profit, £25, without allowing anything for interest or management. Rent, with which tithe is counted, averaged £1128 from 1884 to 1889, and since then £580. There was, therefore, a large margin for allowing a reasonable profit to the tenant, who only received £225, while the owner took in rent £7964 13s.[1]

Accounts are given from North Cambridgeshire by Mr Wilson Fox.[2] Thus, twenty-one years of a well-worked fen farm of 565 acres, one fourth pasture, give average outgoings—for labour, £912; manures, etc., £1665, and an average profit of £363, or 6·6 per cent. on capital, while the rent paid to landlord has averaged £1117, or £2 an acre. These accounts clearly show the different position of tenants in the last few years. The total profit on this farm from 1874 to 1885 was £6819, or £620 a year, or 11·3 per cent. interest on capital. From 1885 to 1895 the profit has been only £798, or £79 17s a year, or only 1·5 per cent. on capital. For the last five years the tenant has lost £335 a year, or 6 per cent. on his capital, and this with a return of half the agreed rent. A further reduction is essential if bad times continue. According to the tenant, profit is no longer obtainable, even on this splendidly kept up farm, without seriously curtailing the most essential outgoings. The net rent received by the landlord from this farm from 1890 to 1895—five years—was £3690 11s 4d, while the net loss to the tenant for the same period was £1676 18s 11½d.

Accounts showing how a very high rent prevents ends meeting when the pinch comes, such as the following :—

A farm of 869 acres, two-thirds arable, most of it good sound black land, and about one-fifth heavy clay, shows a profit of £112 on 1892-93, and a loss of £195 13s 11d on 1893-94. In 1892-93 labour stood at £1494 and fertilising at £711; in 1893-94 the two items

---
[1] Rew, Norfolk, App. E. 2, p. 112. Farm Accounts, p. 142.
[2] Wilson Fox, Cambs, App. A. 1 A. Farm Accounts, p. 74.

F

were £1339 and £1048. The rent paid in the former year was £1372, in the latter, £1257. The net loss to tenant on the two years, £83, was about 0·66 per cent. on his capital, no allowance being made for interest or management. Interest at 5 per cent. on capital would have been £325. A reduction of 20 to 25 per cent. would have done something to share the loss of the two years fairly between landlord and tenant.[1]

On a farm of 1600 acres in the Caistor Union the outlay on labour in 1892-93 was £1523, and on manures and feeding stuffs £270, while rent was £1700. The loss in that unfavourable year was £232, which might have been converted into a profit of 3 per cent. on tenant's capital by a reduction in rent of 28 per cent., leaving the owner 15s an acre.[2]

A strong soil farm in the Spilsby Union of 812 acres, two-thirds arable, shows in 1893-94 outlay for labour £885, for manures and feeding stuffs £407, and a loss of £302 for the year, or 6 per cent. on capital—£5000. But the rent is £1017, or 25s an acre. This certainly leaves an ample margin to protect the tenant from the wasting away of capital.[3]

Seven years' accounts of a 490 acre farm (300 acres arable) in the same district show net profits averaging £420 from 1887 to 1890, and net losses averaging £192 from 1891 to 1893-4, or a net profit over the whole seven years at the rate of £157 a year. In 1893 labour was £682; manures, feeding stuffs, etc., £633; and rent, including tithe, £523. To make ends meet, and give the tenant even 3 per cent. on his capital during the last three years, rent should have been reduced nearly 70 per cent., which, as tithe is included, would be nearly impossible.[4]

Mr Pringle gives the results of the balance sheets of a grass farm in Yorkshire, where sheep-breeding and dairy farming are carried on, for two good years, 1880 to 1883,

---

[1] Wilson Fox, Linc., App. A. 1. M., p. 126. Farm Accounts, p. 136.
[2] Ibid., App. A. 1. N. Farm Accounts, p. 136.
[3] Ibid., App. A. 1. P. Farm Accounts, p. 126.
[4] Rew, Norfolk, p. 26, App. E. 4, p. 115. Farm Accounts, p. 146.

and two bad years, 1891 to 1893. In the former there was a profit of £226 10s 11d, in the latter a loss of £142 7s 10d, while the rents paid were £883 5s in the former and £616 in the latter, tithe, rates, and taxes being £64 16s 2d and £58 3s 10d. The average net profit then was thus £21 0s 9d, while the average rent was £749 12s 6d, or 35 times the average net profit.

But it must be admitted that, with the exception of two or three cases quoted above, even these more favourable balance sheets do not give the farmer anything like a fair commercial return. At most they show that there is a margin in some cases out of which a profit could be made, and that in some cases the balance between owner and occupier in sharing the produce of the farm has been made more approximately fair.

On the other hand, some accounts show a not unfair distribution of the economic pressure. A heavy clay farm of 540 acres in Bedfordshire, where nearly half the land has been laid down, still shows a labour bill in 1893 of £790, and for manures, feeding stuffs, etc., of £826. From 1886 to 1893, seven years, the average net profit was £198, or 7s 4d an acre, or nearly 4 per cent. on capital, including the bad year 1893, when £322 was lost. Rent and tithe stood at £350.[1]

Five years' accounts of a well worked farm on the "Heath," near Sleaford, 790 acres, one-fourth pasture, show average outlays, on labour, £786 (last two years £823 and £817); manures, feeding stuffs, etc., £1311; and a total profit of £844 3s 2d on the five years, and £168 16s 7d average profit, or nearly 8 per cent. on capital. The rent, rates, and taxes together have averaged £603. This would seem to give the owner a fair return, considering the times, and enable the tenant to scrape along without any return for his skill and work, but with enough margin to prevent loss of capital.[2]

On a very strong clay farm in Hunts, 462 acres, two-thirds arable, thirteen years' working from 1881 to 1893 inclusive, gives averages of labour £390, manures, etc.

---

[1] Pringle, Beds., &c., App. C. VI.
[2] Wilson Fox, Linc., App. A. I. F., p. 122. Farm Accounts, p. 132.

£380, and profits £194, or 4·9 per cent. on capital, or 8s 5d an acre. Rent has averaged £344, was reduced from £400 to £300 in 1886, and in 1893 was £262 10s. The owner has taken about 11s 6d an acre as his share, and left his skilful tenant to draw 8s 5d an acre—a fair adjustment, which has had excellent results.[1]

A Northants farm of 324 acres, three-fourths arable, well worked by a tenant who has private means, shows averages over seven years for labour, £466 15s, in 1893 £478 11s; for manures and feeding stuffs, etc. £347, in 1893 £402 13s, and an average profit of £241 16s 1d or 14s 10¾d an acre, or 6 per cent. on £4000 capital. Rent and rates together were, in 1887 £474, and in 1893 £324 15s, a reduction in these items of about 28 per cent. Here, again, is shown a favourable economic result from a fair sharing of profit and loss between owner and occupier.[2]

A heavy clay farm of 316 acres, in the same county, two-thirds grass, shows a slightly diminishing labour bill, £243 17s in 1885, and £168 8s in 1893, and a slightly increasing outlay in feeding stuffs and manures. The average annual profit has been about £100 or a little over 4 per cent. Rent has averaged £333.[3]

A "four-course system" farm in Norfolk, of 425 acres, nearly all arable, shows over thirteen years, averages of £544 for labour (in last three years £586, £587, and £598) of £856 for manures, feeding stuffs, etc., and a profit of £280 for interest on capital and remuneration for management. The average for rent, tithes, rates and taxes has been £465. This shows a fair distribution as between owner and occupier.[4]

A three years' average of accounts on a farm of 640 acres (two-thirds arable) in West Norfolk shows a balance for tenant's interest and remuneration of £185, after outgoings for labour of £621, manures, etc. £147, and rent, tithe, rates and taxes of £555 14s. The

[1] Wilson Fox, Linc., App. C. VII., p. 119. Farm Accounts, p. 119.
[2] Ibid., App. C. X., p. 126. Farm Accounts, p. 151.
[3] Ibid., App. C. XL. Farm Accounts, p. 152.
[4] Rew, Norfolk App. E. I., p. 112; also para. 45, p. 25. Farm Accounts, p. 142.

capital of tenant has gradually shrunk from £5000 to £3000.

Accounts for four years—1882, 1886, 1890, 1893—of a strong clay farm in Beds of 260 acres, three-fourths arable, show the labour item stationary at about £306, cake and manures going up from £69 to £103, and an average profit of £82, or 6s 4½d an acre, or a little over 3 per cent. on capital. Rent has been reduced about 25 per cent., from £484 to £356. But in 1893, while the rent secures to the owner a return of 27s 5d an acre, the tenant has a loss of over 19s 6d an acre. And over the four years the owner gets an average of 33s an acre, and the tenant only 6s 4d.[1] These are very moderate returns, but show an attempt on the part of owners to meet the times, but there is clearly a margin to make the tenants' returns more satisfactory.[2]

A farm of 840 acres in Dorset, excellently worked for thirty-six years by a business-like farmer, shows, over twenty years, average outgoings for labour £878; manures, feeding stuffs, etc., £510; and rent £505. The average profit has been £279. Rent was reduced to £505 in 1886, to £411 in 1890, and to £357 for 1893. The last two years give:—1892, rent, £411; labour, £949; manures, etc., £724; and profit, £223; for 1893, labour, £956; manures, etc., £684; rent, £357; and profit, £193. Considering the times such an account is a record of good sense and good management and fair play.[3]

A light and sandy farm in East Suffolk of 260 acres, more than half arable,[1] "in the hands of a first-rate farmer," and near a good market, shows from 1874 to 1894 an average profit of £168, or 8½ per cent. on capital, while rent has averaged £245, and has been reduced from 23s an acre in 1877 to 13s an acre in 1894, over 40 per cent. Labour and fertilising have been kept up to a high uniform level, averaging £331 and £614 respectively.[4]

---

[1] Pringle, Beds., &c., App. C. II. Farm Accounts, p. 63.
[2] Ibid., App. E. 8, p. 118. Farm Accounts, p. 148.
[3] Rew, Dorset, App. B. 6, p. 61, see p. 18. Farm Accounts, p. 86.
[4] Wilson Fox, Suffolk, App. A. 1. D. Farm Accounts, p. 174.

Accounts from 1883 to 1892 of a grass farm of 494 acres, only 96 arable, in Northumberland, show that labour costs practically £1 an acre even on such a farm. With a rent of about 18s an acre the tenant has made an average profit of £126 a year, or 4 per cent. on his capital.[1]

Some of the accounts show an almost hopeless position. Thus a strong clay farm in Beds, of 800 acres, from 1885 to 1890 inclusive, shows an average labour bill of about £1 an acre, and amounting to £826 in 1890. Feeding stuffs and manures averaged 21s 3d an acre up to 1890, when this item fell below labour. The losses of the tenant averaged £152, and the rent £543 up to 1890. To cover this tenant's loss, and to secure him even 3 per cent. on his capital, a reduction of over 60 per cent. in rent would be necessary; and the rent would sink to 5s an acre. Such farms would seem almost unworkable at present prices, unless the labour item as well as rent can be materially reduced.[2]

Another Bedfordshire clay farm of 275 acres averages, from 1888 to 1893 inclusive, £411 for labour, £289 for manures, etc. Rent, rates, taxes, and insurance have averaged £184 7s, and allowing 5 per cent. interest on capital, the tenant's losses have averaged £290 14s, or more than double the rent. If no interest on capital is allowed for, the losses still are £188, so that under present circumstances the tenant would lose about 3 per cent. on his capital if he held the farm rent free. Unless a material alteration can be made in the labour item this farm seems unworkable.[3]

The following account also shows complete economic breakdown :—

The balance of profit on a farm of 1080 acres, on only one-third of which rent is paid, was for fourteen years from 1880, only £1284. In other words, the profits of farming 1080 acres amounted, after paying a rent, which spread over the whole is from 3s to 4s an acre, to about

---

[1] Wilson Fox, Glendale, App. A. 8, p. 32. Farm Accounts, p. 163.
[2] Pringle, Beds, App. C. IV. Farm Accounts, p. 66.
[3] Ibid., App. C. V. Farm Accounts, p. 66.

£90 a year for interest on capital and living for the tenant. The labour item has been fairly maintained at from 22s to 19s 6d an acre.[1]

Various estimates may be given of the minimum return for which it may be to the interest of a capable farmer to go on working his farm.

Ten per cent. on capital, taking one year with another, is assumed by many to be a fair return for a farmer to count upon. And, in general, a farmer expects, in addition to interest on capital, about 2s 6d an acre return for management, and it is only after these two heads are provided for that "profits" are supposed to begin. But, if 5 per cent. is taken as about the minimum which would keep a man going, and enable him to prevent his capital from melting away, it is plain from this survey of typical accounts—all presumably from farmers of more than average prudence and capacity—that nothing like even this modest standard is being attained. On the other hand, it seems plain from the accounts that, except in the cases of complete collapse where no available margin any longer exists, landlords are still drawing rents, out of which a reasonable though small profit might be made for the tenant. In the worst cases the landlord continues to place the entire loss upon the tenant, and is obviously living upon the capital and the labour of the tenant, who receives no return whatever. In the best cases the larger share of economic loss is being borne by the tenant, and in nearly every instance, while the tenant is clearly trying to secure the best returns by keeping up a high standard, both of labour and manuring, a rent is being drawn which completely excludes any possibility of the tenant obtaining, as the result of his loyal work and ample expenditure, anything like a reasonable commercial return.

So far as the accounts collected can be depended on to illustrate the general position, they indicate that it is indispensable for the future of agriculture that rents not already reduced to an equitable figure should be further reduced without delay, so as to secure, where

[1] Rew, Dorset, App. B.16, p. 60. See pp. 17, 18. Farm Accounts, p. 84.

possible, a moderate return for farmer's capital and skill.

The position of some of the farmers whose accounts are analysed in this chapter is only intelligible in view of many statements in evidence that farmers are universally reluctant to realise by selling out in these times of bad prices, and that the more embarrassed they are the more they cling at all hazards to their farms.

These accounts should also be considered in their bearing on the general evidence, that many farmers in most districts have been paying rents out of capital till they break down and their farms are taken at great reductions by new tenants.

The analyses of the accounts seem to establish a strong probability that the two tendencies disclosed—the tendency on the part of the best farmers to keep up the high cultivation and fertility of their farms to the utmost, in the hope of better prices and results, and the tendency of owners and agents to maintain the item of rent, irrespective of the necessity of establishing some sort of equilibrium in the farmer's outgoings by subordinating non-reproductive to reproductive items of outgoings—these two tendencies have probably been largely responsible for the ruin of many deserving and capable and hardworking men, and for the wholesale deterioration of the soil in the districts most affected.

SUMMARY OF ACCOUNTS.

The facts and figures brought before us in the farm accounts are tabulated in the Appendix to this Report. Of the ninety-seven [1] English farm accounts set forth in the "Particulars of Expenditures and Outgoings on Estates and Farm Accounts reprinted from the Reports of the Assistant Commissioners," [2] twenty-one are omitted from consideration as being accounts of owners farming land in hand, or as being imperfect in details. They do not illustrate the relations of landlord and tenant in the

[1] Accounts VI and X refer to the same farm.
[2] Parliamentary Paper (C.—8125), 1896.

THE TENANT'S SHARE   89

economics of farming. The remaining seventy-six are accounts of tenant farmers for various periods of years, from twenty-six down to one year.

As has been already indicated, these accounts include a large percentage of accounts from men who have had exceptional advantages in farming, so that a strong presumption may fairly exist, that they put the relations of farmers' profits to rents in a much more favourable light than if we had before us the accounts of the unfortunate men who have broken and gone, or are still in occupation, but reported to be on the verge of insolvency in many districts. In any case it cannot be held that the accounts sent in represent an exceptional or unfavourable sample of the present position.

These 76 farm accounts cover an area in all of 42,966 acres. Five of these accounts, covering 4025 acres, only give profits and losses, and do not give detailed items of outgoings. The accounts for 38,941 acres give the details of the outgoings with sufficient precision, except that, in two accounts, the value of produce taken from the farm and used in the farmer's house is set down on the side of expenditure, and not on the side of receipts, where it should appear. Correcting this error, we find that the whole area of 42,966 acres has been farmed with the result that while the total average profits on some of the farms amounted to £6553, the total average losses on other of these farms amounted to £6452, or a net average profit over the whole area of £101.

Taking the 71 accounts which give detailed items, it is found that over the area of 38,941 acres, the average total outgoings per annum were £214,964, or about £5 14s per acre.

Of these outgoings, the average annual amount paid for labour was £47,009, or 21·9 per cent., or about £1 4s 6d per acre; for feeding stuffs, manures and seeds, £47,548, or 22·5 per cent., or about £1 5s per acre. Rents took up, on the average, £39,530 per annum, or 18·5 per cent. of the outgoings, or about £1 0s 7½d per acre. The total average annual profits over the 38,941 acres were £6468, and the total average annual losses were £5616. Deducting losses from profits, we have over the whole 38,941 acres an average annual profit of £852.

In other words, 71 tenants, employing in their business probably a capital of not less than £350,000, and throwing in their experience, skill, energy, and physical labour, have only had the average annual return of £852 profit, or about 5·25d an acre, to divide among them. This result of the analysis of these accounts is still more striking, when it is noted that in only four of these 71 accounts, does the tenant charge interest on his capital, as he certainly ought to do, if his accounts are to keep him going on reasonably commercial lines. If the total capital of the 71 tenants is taken at £350,000, and the capital on which interest is charged in four accounts, viz. £31,800, is deducted, the interest at 4 per cent. on the remaining £318,200 would be £12,730 per annum, and the modest profit of £852 would at once be converted into the heavy loss of £11,878, or an average annual loss of 6s 1¼d per acre. It is thus seen that the whole return to the tenant for interest on capital employed as well as for profit has been just over 5d per acre, so far as these accounts throw light on this problem.

To arrive at the landlord's share a slight correction must be made in the figures.

In twelve of these accounts the rent has not been separated from rates and taxes. These twelve accounts cover 6344 acres. But it appears from the accounts in which rents are separately stated from rates and taxes, that the average annual amount of rates and taxes has been almost precisely 3s an acre. It is probable, therefore, that the total average rents of £39,530 include about 3s an acre on 6344 acres, which goes, not to the landlord, but to rates and taxes. We have, therefore, to deduct about £950 from the total average rents, leaving the net average rent £38,580, or a return of £1 0s 4¾d.

Treating, then, the whole 38,941 acres as if they formed one estate, for the purposes of argument, it thus appears that the share taken by the owner of the gross returns has been at the rate of a little over 20s an acre, while the share left to the tenant has been only 5·25d an acre.

It must, of course, be borne in mind that twenty-one of these accounts are for one year only, and most of these for the very bad year of 1893.

It may also be urged, with some force, that in a considerable majority of the accounts a certain portion of the farm produce is consumed in the farmhouse, and has not been entered among the receipts.

On the other hand, in all but four accounts no charge whatever is made for interest on capital, or for management, and the amount which should have been estimated for these two heads would certainly be much greater than the value of produce consumed in the house.

The "Estates Accounts"[1] confirm this reasoning. On thirty great estates or groups of estates in England, the total cultivated area is shown to amount to 440,490 acres; the total amount of rents actually received in the year 1892 (the last of the series given) was £535,436, and the net income of the owners, after paying outgoings of all kinds, including outlay on new buildings, drainage, and various allowances, is £243,724 1s 8d.

The outgoings, as is pointed out in the chapter on landlords' improvements, are, if anything, too comprehensive, but, taking them as they stand, they take up over 54 per cent. of the gross income. This leaves rather over 45 per cent as the net rent received by the landlord.

It will be noted that these estates include two or three well-known estates belonging to the Duke of Westminster and the Duke of Bedford, *where the outlay on repairs, new buildings, and other items, has considerably exceeded the gross rent.* So that the remaining owners are clearly receiving a higher net income than 45 per cent. of the gross rents.

In view of figures of this nature, if these accounts can be taken as representative, it is impossible to admit that there has been any sweeping reduction of rent in this country, in any degree commensurate with the heavy fall

[1] Parliamentary Paper (C.—8125), 1896.

in the values of the produce of the soil. As contrasted with the enormously enhanced rents of twenty years ago, the present rents undoubtedly represent a considerable drop in the income of owners. But the farm accounts, and the almost unvaried testimony to the persistent losses, or the very restricted profits obtained by tenants, makes it practically certain that tenants cannot conceivably, even in the most favoured districts, be drawing from their holdings any sum which is not a mere fraction of the net incomes derived from the same land by their landlords, and (as compared with the average gross rents paid by them to their landlords) must be the smallest possible fraction.

These figures can only be treated as creating a strong presumption that rents are still at a level far above the economic value of the land, in view of possible returns at present prices. But it must be remembered that this is substantially the only area occupied by tenant farmers, for which we have any exact accounts.

It is only reasonable, therefore, that considerable weight should attach to such evidence as a *primâ facie* proof that the economic pressure of low prices has not as yet been fairly adjusted as between owner and occupier. And, the very general unanimity in the evidence of farming witnesses as to the critical position of their class in nearly every district has not in my opinion been rebutted. The two classes of evidence—the figures of the accounts, and the evidence of the farmers, appear to confirm each other, and make it an imperative duty to advise that such a state of things deserves the fullest and most prompt attention of Parliament.

CHAPTER VII.

Rents as a Cause of Depression.

The evidence goes to show that over-renting (1) has been a chief cause of depression, in bringing farmers to ruin, and in deteriorating the condition of the land; (2) is even now very general; and (3) that the opinion that further reductions are necessary and inevitable, is, among farming witnesses, practically universal.

Colonel Hughes, agent to Sir W. W. Wynn, says: "The men who put things wrong were those who raised rents in the prosperous times; there never was a more unwise step."

Mr Fyshe puts "high rents" before low prices as a cause of depression.

Mr Kidner places second in the list of causes of depression "the great increase in rents in times of inflated prices, with too slow reduction under the subsequent depression." Rents are made up "by good cultivation, and by drawing upon capital."

Mr Harrison, who says "rent is the first remedy" for depression, and thinks rent may be fairly defined as "the profit that is made after the farmer has been able to live and pay the outgoings on the farm," states that "for the last twenty years tenants have been paying a large amount of rent out of capital."

Mr Middleton, taking the same view, says: "More relief could be got by reduction of rent than in any other way."

Mr Rolleston, a land agent, thinks that from hoping for a change for the better, "farmers paid more rent than they ought to have paid." "Their capital has completely melted away."

Mr Cooke thinks "many men are now paying rents which the products of the farm will not justify."

Mr Latham says "tenants have been paying their rents out of capital for such a length of time, that they are much reduced in their method of farming, and in their capacity of farming." The deterioration of the production of the soil is very general.

Mr Looker, an agent, admits that "tenants are not satisfied that the land is worth any rent at all." "They continue to fulfil their obligations; occasionally one drops out, and somebody else comes in at a less rent."

Mr Lander: "Farmers are very short of capital through paying rent out of it."

Professor Long thinks that excessive rents paid out of capital, and therefore reducing the capital of the farmers, have contributed to the depression.

Mr James Hope, Mr C. S. Read, Mr Reynolds, Mr Wyatt, and many other witnesses are generally of opinion that rents have largely been paid out of capital, and that this has caused numerous changes of tenancy, and deterioration of farming. Mr Rankin, as a landlord, generally assented to that view.

Mr Herman Biddell, speaking of the distressed districts of Suffolk, says that "if they had had a reduction of rent, the same as they have got now, when wheat was selling at 38s and barley at 34s, they would have been able to go on, and admits that even present reductions have not been sufficient to prevent tenants from paying rent out of capital."

Mr Pringle says of the South Midland districts, "I believe, of those who still remain as the remnant of the old stock of farmers, a very large proportion have done so, because they had some private means to fall back upon. As was said in the great depression in 1836, so now the evidence given to me in Bedford, Huntingdon, and Northampton (and I think it is thoroughly supported by the balance sheets from farmers), all points to a repetition of that feature of depression from 1879 to 1894, that rent has been paid not out of profits but out of capital, and that farmers are getting worse from year to year. There has been either a melting away of the working capital represented by live stock, accompanied by necessary indebtedness to tradesmen, dependence on dealers, and all-round deterioration in farming, and ending in bankruptcy or abandonment, or the private banking account and investments have been drawn upon to meet liabilities."

Mr Foster, a Northumberland farmer, whose rent stood at £750 for a farm of 500 acres in 1875, and at £525 in 1893, puts his expenses in 1875, including rent, at £2056. His savings on labour, manures, and feeding stuffs, and rent, amount to £381. But, owing to the fall in prices (taken at 30 per cent.), the same amount of produce which would have paid his expenses in 1875, would now bring only £1439, while the expenses now, after deducting the various savings, would still be £1675. Thus "a reduction in rent of 61 per cent. instead of 30 per cent. would be required to recoup losses through fall in prices."

Mr Epton, a large Lincolnshire farmer, who gave remarkable evidence as to farming expenditure and losses, showed that his receipts are £2600 less than twenty years ago, while his rent is only £1000 less. While avowedly reluctant to press his landlord and considerate of his interests, he says: "all my profit is gone, and I am losing money besides." "If prices do not rise, the ultimate remedy must be a further reduction of rent." "The tenants are losing a deal more than the landlords now." In the previous reduction of rent, the landlord took over the tithe, and interest on loan for improvements, together £615. But as Mr Epton, paying the rent of £1900 in 1893, lost £800, both those burdens, and still more of the economic losses, rest on his shoulders.

Mr Bowen Jones (Shropshire) says: "In the last twenty years my returns have fallen £1800 a year, and my rent and rates have fallen only £300. I cannot go on making losses at the same rate as I am doing now, or I shall be bankrupt in a few years. If the rent was all taken off I should have done no good, that is the real position we are in now."

Mr Squarey, whose experience is extensive, and who has made heavy reductions on properties under his charge, states that "as a rule, with the reductions that have been made, the tenants are not doing themselves any good, and are not adequately remunerated for their labour and energy."

Mr Wyatt states "the reduction—40 per cent.—in Somersetshire is certainly not in fair proportion to the fall in prices. Some of the farmers have had to take the rent out of their banking account, and out of money invested, and a great many have taken it out of the land, deteriorating it in value."

Mr Middleton says, there must be large arrears of rents—"It is a marvel to me how rents are paid at all in some cases."

Mr Ferguson says, "If I had not made some money in the good times, I could not have stood the bad."

As to the insufficiency of existing reductions, even those witnesses who expressed their appreciation of the manner they had been met by their landlords, stated that others were rented too high, and could not make their rents.[1] Thus, among others, Mr Baker states that, even with reductions ranging from 20 to 60 per cent, further reductions of 25 to 30 per cent. are desired by tenants in Northamptonshire. Even, apart from the bad seasons of 1893 and 1894, they cannot make ends meet. Rents have not been sufficiently reduced, or reduced in time.

Other striking evidence on this point may be quoted. Thus Mr J. Stratton says, "Rents will still have to come down, as we tenant farmers will not go on occupying land and investing capital in it, unless we get something like a fair return."

Mr R. Brown, who has received 50 per cent. remission on the Duke of Bedford's estate, takes the same view.

So does Mr Treadwell, who says "the present rents cannot be made anywhere this year" (1893-94).

---

[1] Rowlandson, 17,573; Noakes, 3365; Parton, 26,225, 26,229; R. Britten, 56,468, 56,568-7; T. Carrington Smith, 9678-82; 9744; Scott, 30,042; 30,016; Baker, 47,176, 47,250-5, 47,284-91; Riley, 36,458, etc., 36,511, etc.

Mr Clare Sewell Read says that you must now make six or seven rents to live, in consequence of the relatively increased expenses that we have in these days of high farming. Though nothing, in his opinion, can now save most of the Norfolk farmers from ruin, he holds that rents must be further reduced.

Mr Rew reports from North Devon general protests against the present rents as excessive, and that landlords ought to reduce them.

Mr Rankin admits that reductions of rent, in such proportion to fall in prices as would enable farmers to meet their outgoings, "would in most cases sweep away the rent altogether."

Mr Albert Pell says, "A further reduction of rent would improve the farmers' position, and if I was a farmer I would go very strongly in for that, and I think I should be justified."

Mr R. Stratton says that Monmouth and Gloucestershire farmers are paying too much. "It is difficult to understand how land can be worth anything at all, if you are to judge of the value of the land by the value of its produce."

Mr Wilkinson says, "You cannot get a sufficient reduction of rent so as to enable you to meet the requirements of the times."

Mr Forster, who has received a reduction of 40 per cent. where most tenants have had only 25 per cent., says, "It would take on an arable mixed farm 60 per cent. to meet the difficulty."

Mr James Hope: "I cannot see how the men are to live at all, unless it comes off the rent. It cannot come off the labour bill, or off the manure and feeding stuffs, or else the fertility is let down."

Mr Lander says that the first remedy suggested by the Shropshire farmers for the depression is the reduction of rents.

Mr Ferguson (Perthshire): "A further reduction of rents is the only thing we have in our own hands—labour and taxes cannot be touched—we used to draw more out of the land, and the only apparent way to get it is from the landlord." "The reductions represent nothing like the fall in prices, not one farmer I know is making his rent."

Even Mr Mercer, who thinks rents have little to do with depression, admits, "We are not making any money at the present time, and that is why the man without capital is bound now to go."

A Hampshire farmer, quoted by Dr Fream, gives as one of the causes "of the present ruinous condition of our industry, the disinclination and refusal of landlords in most cases to meet their tenants. Some, not all, are now offering 15 or 20 per cent. abatements. When, as in the last two years, more than the rent has been lost, this is too little. In seasons like the last two, 50 per cent. should be allowed to tenants of a few years' standing, to enable them to hold on." This man, whose family had been tenants for two centuries on the same estate, has since sold off, being unable to make the farm pay.

There is much evidence to show that reductions are by no means universal, and that in many districts and on many estates the system of temporary remissions or abatements, sometimes wholly insufficient to meet the times, is still common. In many cases, even in districts where depression is general, there would seem to have been neither reductions, nor abatements of any kind.

Mr Albert Pell points out the hardship of the abatement system to tenants who are thus deprived of any reduction of the assessment of their farms to local rates, and are kept under unfair pressure from excessive rates. The same complaint comes from North Wales.

Other witnesses condemn the abatement system as keeping tenants in a disheartening uncertainty in bad times, as tending to demoralise them, and to check outlay or effort in improving farms, and as inducing men who have been losing money to hang on and lose more. Again, the tenant, it is pointed out, is left wholly at the mercy of his landlord, who may, if occasion or wish arises, reimpose upon him without notice the old rent, however excessive or unjust. This power has, it is alleged, been used in the case of tenants who made use of the Ground Game Act, or in other ways put themselves in conflict with the owner or agent.

The relative advantage to agriculture of a permanent reduction of rent is roughly shown in the case of Lord Sefton's tenants, who preferred a 5 per cent. reduction to 10 per cent. remissions.

In the last six or seven years, as depression has deepened, the obvious advantage to landlords as well as tenants of obtaining a reduction in the assessments of farms has greatly stimulated owners and agents to turn abatements into permanent reductions. But this process has developed slowly, and cannot as yet be said to be general.

The evidence is practically unanimous that rents did not go down soon enough. There were in many counties large remissions of rent in 1879 and 1880, but the heavy remissions and reductions everywhere range in date from 1882 to 1887, and even later. Essex farmers were in trouble several years before 1879, but from estate accounts given in Mr Pringle's report the gross rent, and, even with the remissions, the net rent does not go down substantially in most cases till 1884, while from the farm accounts of tenants the first heavy drop in rents would seem to have been in 1886 and 1887. And it appears from his report that great numbers of tenants had been ruined, and frequent and sweeping changes of tenancy had occurred before the heavy reductions were made. The estates held in Essex by Guy's Hospital have dropped in rental from £12,883 to £6771, but the drop in 1879-80 was trifling, and it was not till 1885 and 1886 that a substantial fall came. On their Lincolnshire estates, rents of 49s an acre in 1879 did not fall below 40s till 1883, and had not in 1893 fallen below 33s 6d, a higher rent for the same land than before the corn laws.

A Scotch witness gives the probable explanation of this:—" Many farmers submitted to severe losses on the faith that possibly better times might come, and a large number were obliged to succumb after their capital was almost exhausted."

Mr Huskinson says of a Lincolnshire estate:— "Matters continued steadily there up to 1887, and the reason was that the tenants were all men of substance and capital, and they bore the loss for some considerable period without troubling the proprietor." In 1887 there had to be a reduction of 40 per cent., and "since then it has been rather a serious case all through."

Lord Wantage thinks that the hope of times changing and the help of bankers kept tenants going on at the old rents.

Mr Boyd Kinnear says, "The depression fell in the first instance upon the tenants. Undoubtedly, until rents were reduced, they lost heavily."

Mr Bamford:—"Reductions were not made soon enough, and thus the farmers as a class lost their capital in a great measure."

Mr Turner reports of the Frome District complaints that reductions did not come soon enough to save the original tenants.

One of the farmers quoted by Dr Fream says: "Good farmers have not been sufficiently well treated and met by the landlord, and so long as any balance was thought to be at the bankers, no reduction was made, and even after, not considering whether or no the farm paid any interest on tenant's money."

Mr Clare Sewell Read says: "Some of the larger landlords hardly reduced the rents in time. I got into a terrible row some years ago, when I was a Member of Parliament, because I advised the landlords to make those concessions to the old tenants that they were forced to make to the new ones; but some of them did not take my kindly hint, and on those estates there has been a considerable change of tenancy; but upon the others, I am happy to say, that timely reductions have kept the tenantry there."

Mr Johnson (Suffolk) says that in many cases the application of old tenants for a reduction of rent to meet fall of prices has been refused, the landlords thinking the land worth more, or that the tenants could tide over, or being unwilling or unable, with the consequence that the old tenants have to go and a much less rent is taken from new men.

Mr Bear says: "Many of the old tenants were not allowed any reductions in rent till they were ruined, and then the reductions were given to new men. It has been a great complaint in many counties that the reductions were not made soon enough, and that the farmers lost their capital before the reductions came to help them."

In Banffshire, Mr Stuart mentions an estate where the old tenants were refused a reduction, and six out of fourteen became bankrupt, while the farms had to be relet at over 30 per cent. fall in rent.

In Wigtownshire, many farms are said to have been relet at heavy reductions, which were refused to old tenants, some of whom were then ruined.

Mr Spencer quotes the opinion of a Gloucester witness that, "if reductions had been made, as they ought to have been made, many tenants would have been able to continue their holdings." The course of events is vividly indicated: "Unfortunately, for many years, no reduction was made, the landlord being of opinion that the depression was only temporary, but as prices continued to fall abatements were made. The farmers, thinking times would improve, continued on at the old rents, got into debt, borrowed money. Still times did not mend. The land became depreciated in consequence of dismissed labourers, the produce became less, and at last the only alternative was to become bankrupt, and give up. This is the case in many instances."[1]

Dr Fream reports complaints that "the tenants had borne the brunt of the bad years, and now, when too late, the landlords were offering reductions, which at an earlier stage might have saved tenants from collapse."[2]

The consideration of evidence of this nature taken by the Commission, and of the results of the local inquiries by Assistant Commissioners, makes it clear that, while some landlords probably met the depression from the

[1] Oxfordshire, Gloucestershire, etc., p. 20.   [2] Andover, p. 5.

first in a generous and enlightened way, and while, on a small number of great estates, reductions were not immediately necessary because the rents had not been raised in the time of highest prices, in a large proportion of cases, especially in the counties most severely hit by depression, substantial reductions only began when considerable numbers of the old tenants were either broken and had to leave, or reduced to such a position that the reductions were unavoidable, and were generally too late to keep the old tenants going.[1]

It may not have been possible to forecast the consequences. Still, we have Mr Read's and other evidence to show that fair warning was given by some sagacious agriculturists.

The complaint is very general, both in the evidence and in the reports of Assistant Commissioners, that the farmer who farms his land liberally and well, does not obtain a reduction of rent to the same extent that the farmer with little capital who farms badly does, and this acts as a premium on bad farming.[2]

The only weapon a tenant has to obtain a reduction of rent is the notice to quit. There is much evidence to show that this has been ineffective to obtain adequate reductions for old tenants in time, and that it has been found more than useless in the case of men who have expended much money and skill, and labour, in maintaining or increasing the productiveness of their farms.

The farmer who has run down his farm and exhausted its fertility can lose nothing by quitting, and therefore serves his notice. The farmer who has farmed well has a continually increasing stake invested in his holding, and has formed business connections which it would take him years to build up in a new neighbourhood. In general, all he has is in the farm. His losses in removing, even in good times, would be a deterrent, in bad times, when everything is sold off at the worst, are absolutely

---

[1] Pringle, Beds, Northants, pp. 8, 9-19, 20.
[2] A. Spencer, Oxfordshire, Gloucestershire, etc., p. 20; Rew, Dorset, p. 28; Wilson Fox, Garstang, p. 17; Rolleston, 13,654; Hope, 12,233; Carrington-Smith, 9705.

prohibitive. The compensation for his improvements, which he might receive under the existing Agricultural Holdings Act, or custom of the country, would cover but a fraction of the loss. His motives, therefore, for abstaining from giving notice for a reduction are overwhelming, and it is clear from the evidence that in most cases these motives have made tenants acquiesce in rents which deprived them of profits, and in many cases gradually elbowed them out of their farms, if not actually ruined them.

To take a few of many illustrations. Mr Rowlandson says:—"Tenants who have farmed highly have suffered more than those who have not, because in many cases they have not got that proportion of reduction of rent, which some of those who farm badly have received." "Advantage has been taken when the farm is in a good state, where the tenant will not leave if he can come to any reasonable terms."

Mr Hutchinson (North Riding), who won the first prize for the best managed farm at the Royal Agricultural Show, 1883, says:—"I know that the men who farm the best get the least. In the case of the estate I am on, I get the least reduction of any tenant, because I farm my place well. I have invested a lot of money in it. Because I farm my land well, I dare not give it up in order to try to get the rent reduced, because there are plenty of men who would take it at my rent. They would take it to get money out of it."

Mr Riley:—"The good tenants are suffering more than the bad ones, for if a good tenant, who has been farming very high, gives notice for a reduction of rent of his farm there would be no end of applications for it; so that he dare not give up a farm now, he would rather lose a little more capital than give it up."

Mr Lander:—"Agents do not sufficiently consider the case of old tenants. In many cases they let the old tenant go, and put men in without sufficient capital, or other qualifications to farm in the best way. This is often done to keep up a standard of rent, which they can quote to other tenants."

Mr Wilkinson:—"What we complain of in Northumberland is this—that the sitting tenant, perhaps, has farmed his farm well and cannot get as fair a bargain for that as does the man who farms his farm badly." In his opinion, tenants who have large interests at stake in their land are at the mercy of the agents, both as regards rents and agreements as to mode of cultivation. He was told "to sign an agreement, or leave the farm." He gives, as an instance of the position in which the tenant stands, his own case as a sheep farmer.

"It takes a number of years to get a proper stock together, and I do not consider it fair to have my stock forced upon the market at an inopportune moment. My own agent said to me once, 'You cannot afford to sell your stock in these bad times,' and I say he has no right to exact rent from me under these conditions." "The sitting tenant cannot get the same reduction, if he has his farm well stocked, as the man can who farms his farm badly."

Mr Olver (Cornwall)—" If the tenant farmer improves his farm and wants a reduction, the landlord replies ' I can make no reduction, your farm will always make its money.' But if he racks his farm and goes to his landlord, the landlord sees that he cannot make the rent and makes the reduction; this hardship to the improving farmer is strongly felt all through our county, that the good farmer is not properly secured." The same witness points out that the improving tenant has also to pay higher rates in consequence of the refusal of a reduction.

Mr Kidner, who himself felt compelled by his interests at stake in the holding to renew his father's lease at a greatly increased rent, and with conditions which made it difficult to work the farm at a profit, thinks that considerations of this kind, and the losses by removal, prevent tenants from being free agents in bargaining.

Mr Pringle, as the result of his inquiry in Beds, Hunts, and Northants, believes that "since 1879 there have been very many examples of cruel injustice accidentally inflicted on tenants who were apparently hardworking and conscientious." The tenant who has worked a farm for years, and paid rent for years, is a better judge of what is a fair rent than the landlord. When bad times come and grow worse, such a tenant asks for a moderate reduction and is refused. He goes on—"during the last fourteen years on encumbered and badly managed estates, old tenants have been got rid of because the rent which they considered fair was not so regarded by the landlord or his agent. Others have been leant upon because they were known to be well to do, attached to their farms, and accordingly likely to pay excessive rents rather than leave." Farms so vacated have been worked by the owner at a loss, or let to some new man, with the result that the rent promised was not paid in full, and the farm deteriorated. Again "so many cases were related to me of big reductions having been made to new tenants, and even to sitting tenants who had let their farms down, but either refused *in toto*, or extended in lesser quantity to the better class of tenant, that it is clear the latter is helpless. Under present conditions, the landlord is at the mercy of the unscrupulous tenant, but has the honest, upright man in his clutches. At present there is, on many estates, a distinct penalty attached to good farming, and a clear incentive to bad farming."

Mr Rew reports a striking case from Devonshire. An occupier of 500 acres for thirty-five years had his farm on lease till five years ago. It was then re-valued by a well-known valuer at £520. But the agent compelled the tenant to pay £570 on renewal (yearly agreement). The last three years an abatement of 10 per cent. has been granted, but a permanent reduction of 15 to 20 per cent. is refused and the tenant told he may go.

Mr Cooke gives the case of two farms in Cheshire. In one the old tenant left and two successive new tenants have got reductions and heavy outlay by landlord in improvements. On the adjoining farm, where the tenant has been improving all the while, he cannot get a reduction at all.

In a case like this, it is plain that the good tenant has not only been paying too much, but has been paying for the losses caused by the bad farming of his neighbours.

"The new tenant need not come unless he likes, but the sitting tenant is not in the same position, because it costs him so much to move."[1] "Between 1879 and 1882 landlords did not like reducing to sitting tenants, but they soon began to find it cheaper to make reductions, as new tenants want so much new building."

From much of the evidence it appears probable that this lesson has been widely learned by landlords and agents, especially in the worst districts, and further that on some estates a wiser policy has been consistently pursued, while there seems no reason to doubt that, in intention, the best landlords have wished to deal impartially with tenants on the merits of the case.

Mr Tindall says of Lord Yarborough's estate in Lincolnshire, "Nothing is ever done on this estate for a new tenant which is not done for an old one. I should think it a lasting disgrace to let an old tenant go and take a less rent from a new one."

But, from the dates of reductions, and from the evidence as to sweeping changes of tenancy, this wiser and more equitable view of things seems to have been arrived at in most cases far too late to help the majority of the old tenants.

The Scotch witnesses, who generally deal with the system of nineteen year leases, are equally emphatic on these points.

Thus, Mr Dun :—"A tenant with his farm run down has no difficulty in taking it again, but the tenant with his farm in a high state of cultivation was not able to renew his lease till within a few months of its expiry."

Mr Guild, a land agent: "I have known of cases where the rent was raised on the sitting tenant because of the extra condition of the farm; he is told that if he cannot pay such and such a rent, they can get another man who will. 'Pay the rent or go' are the terms."

Mr G. Riddell says a good landlord may be willing to agree on fresh terms some time before end of lease. "But if a landlord is keen, and wants to get all he can get, the chances are, if the farm is in very high condition,

[1] W. Fox, Lincoln, p. 18.

he will take advantage of the fact. At least that has largely been done in Scotland."

The inclusion of the value of tenants' improvements in the rent demanded for farms is necessarily part of the same subject. Withholding such a reduction from the full rent of a farm as will leave the tenant a fair return from his outlay is clearly appropriating the tenant's improvements just as effectually as a direct raising of the rent upon those improvements would be.

This grievance is complained of by many witnesses, both in the form of raising the rent on tenants' improvements—now relatively infrequent—and in the form of refusing the reduction which would protect the tenant's interest.

The best type of tenant has been the man who has treated his "land as his bank; as a rule, when he makes money he puts it into his land, thinking he is going to get it out again." Or, as Mr Punchard puts it: "In the old times when they made any profit they spent it on the farm in improving it, and so they gradually got their farms up to a higher condition."

This is exactly the type of tenant who most needed protection in the view of Sir James Caird, urged in 1883,[1] and this is exactly the type of tenant that, according to the uniform tenour of the evidence, has had, in this worst stage of depression, no security whatever, except the spontaneous goodwill of those landlords who understand and sympathise with their claims, and are themselves in a position to give them full protection.

Mr Sheldon gives the case of an old tenant in Derbyshire, who doubled the carrying capacity of his dairy and stock farm by repeated applications of bones and other manures during thirty years, with the result that his rent was raised in spite of promises that it should not be raised.

Mr Forster, who had by heavy outlay raised his farm to a high state of cultivation, complains that he could not get the return he was entitled to. That is why I

[1] Letter to the Times, May 17, 1883.

had to leave that farm. They wanted me to pay on my own improvements. They would not bring the rent down to the rent it would have been if I had not had the farm in that high state."

Mr Nunneley points out that where tenants' improvements prevent rent falling—" say a farm is let at £1 an acre, which otherwise would come down to 10s but for the tenant's improvements "—he is entitled to have their value considered in fixing a new rent on renewal of a tenancy.

Mr Black holds that " much of the injustice that tenants have suffered has been by putting a rent upon the tenant at the renewal of a lease, based upon improvements carried out with his own labour and his own money." . . . " The rent should be fixed not upon the farm as it is improved by the tenant's labour and outlay, but upon the farm as it would have been without these improvements." This is justice, but " the practice has been, as a rule, that the proprietor, either through his factor, or through a professional valuator, has put a rent upon his farm, and the sitting tenant has just the option of taking it at that rent or leaving."

Mr Wilkinson puts the case of tenant farmers very clearly. While he repudiates the landlord's claim to sell the use of his land to the tenant for the best price he can get, the market price, he equally repudiates the Irish notion of joint ownership ; " but," he adds, " I hold that the landlord should not have my improvements or live on my capital any longer. . . I want to have our landlords deal more fairly with sitting tenants, and sitting tenants should not pay rental upon what they have done upon their farms." " What belongs to the landlord let him sell at the best price, but he has no right to sell what belongs to the tenant."

Mr Scott: " Men do not farm as high as they would if they had more security. At present their everlasting fear is that the landlords will reap the benefit of their expenditure. What we want to do is to prevent men feeling that others may reap what they sow."

Many other illustrations are to be found in the

evidence and reports, but these sufficiently indicate the vitally important issue raised by many of the most energetic and capable agriculturists now occupying farms.

That issue is that when the terms of a new letting of a holding are considered, and the new rent fixed, the new rent ought not to include that portion of the letting value which is due to the tenant's improvements, unless the landlord has paid for the improvements. The injustice of including in the rent the tenant's interest in his improvements, where the improvements were of a permanent character like buildings or drainage, would be obvious, and such improvements, where made by the tenant, are sometimes protected by agreement. But it would appear from the evidence that in the case of high continuous cultivation increasing the fertility of the soil, the improvements are usually ignored, when the rent is reconsidered on a renewal of the tenancy, and the tenant is too frequently charged the full sum his farm would fetch in the market.

This complaint is usually met with the arguments—(1) that the tenant, if he remains on the holding, has the enjoyment of the improvements, and thus reaps their full remaining value in the operations of farming, and (2) that in these times of depression, and of approximate bankruptcy among agriculturists, landlords are obliged to accept any terms in order to retain old or get new tenants, and that therefore the farmers are masters of the situation.

But if the landlord, in re-adjusting the rent on renewal, charges the tenant the full annual value, including the annual value added by the tenant himself, without paying some equivalent for the latter, it is absurd to contend that the tenant is left in the enjoyment of that annual value. On the contrary, the tenant has first paid out of his own pocket the cost of the improvements, and is then asked to pay a second time in the rent for the improvements. His reward for improving his farm is, that his natural disinclination to leave is made the screw by which to force him to pay interest on his own outlay to the landlord instead of receiving, as he justly ought to receive, a fair return for his own money.

The second reply to this complaint is beside the point, because it assumes that what is quite true as to deteriorated farms is also true as to farms which have been kept in high condition. No evidence has been brought before us, to show that, in regard to farms of this class even in the worst districts, the old tenant is in a position to dictate terms. The only perfect freedom of contract exists in the case of practically worthless farms, which have been thrown up in despair. Even in Essex there have been as to farms in high or good condition some tight bargains both as regards rents and conditions. For farms in high condition even a new tenant is not able to make his own terms anywhere. "There is strong competition for good farms even in these days of depression." Even in the case of a new tenant before he starts, "a man is not in a position to make a fair bargain. A man who wants to make a strong bargain is often kicked out of our county." (Wilkinson.)

But in the case of an old tenant and a highly-improved farm there is not a shadow of freedom of contract. He, probably enough, on many estates managed on just and liberal lines, is perfectly safe so long as the policy of the estate remains the same; but he has no security, and is in no position to bargain. The more capital he has sunk, the more he dreads being turned out, and the more he is disposed to acquiesce in a rent which, in practice, transfers his interest in the holding to the landlord's pocket. The better tenant he has been, the less strong is his position. If he serves a notice to quit, the higher the condition of the farm, the more certain he is to be cornered by the fact that others are eager to reap the fruits of his efforts.

CHAPTER VIII.

COMPETITION AND RENT.

This leads naturally to the consideration of the evidence as to the bearing of competition upon rent. There can be no doubt from the facts before us that, except in a few of the very worst districts, there is competition—in most districts considerable competition—for farms, and that even in the very worst districts there is competition for good farms.[1] It would, in our opinion, be misleading to take the degree of competition as a measure of depression, and to assume that keen competition necessarily shows that farmers have overcome the difficulty of making ends meet. The evidence from Scotland shows that while on the one hand prices are much lower than they were five or six years ago, and profits have practically disappeared, competition has greatly increased.[2] The same state of affairs is reported by Mr Wilson Fox from Lancashire, where plenty of men compete for farms and bid the old rents, even when the outgoing tenant has failed to make farming pay.

"Notwithstanding that farms will fetch as much in the market, and in many cases more, than is being paid, it is almost the universal opinion among the farmers that, if prices continue as they are, and rents are not further reduced, farmers cannot keep their heads above water."[3]

Though part of the competition may be due to a con-

---

[1] Strutt, 13,841; Matthews, 61,460; Pringle, Beds, Hunts, Northants, p. 23; Riley, 36,509.

[2] Riddell, 54,668; Guild, 53,565; Mitchell, 54,283; Speir, Ayrshire, etc., p. 5; Ferguson, 23,108, etc.; Hutchinson, 23,505-11, 24,397; M'Connell, 55,334.

[3] Garstang, p. 17.

viction that things are in process of readjustment, and that chances are on the whole more favourable, there are other obvious causes.

One reason must be satisfactory in the interest of agriculture. There clearly are still many men about who have been brought up to agriculture, and wish to pursue it. We have not exhausted the stock of the well-trained sons of good farmers. The emigration of farmers from Scotland and Devonshire to the depressed districts in England, and the fact that even in Essex there are fewer unoccupied farms now than six years ago, proves that there is an ample supply of working farmers.

Further, there have been, and still are, all over England, and notably in Scotland, considerable numbers of men, some of whom know something of farming, others next to nothing, who have made money in other callings, and deliberately take farms because they prefer a country life, and without much anxiety as to commercial results. In many cases these men have burned their fingers, but their competition has tended to keep up rents.

Thus Mr Speir mentions of Nithsdale that out of 172 new tenants no less than fifty-three were bankers, merchants, or others entirely unconnected with agriculture.

To some extent, too, competition is increased for farms from the narrow margin of profit in nearly all industries, and the uncertainty of profitable openings abroad.

Again, the number of exhausted and useless farms, steadily on the increase, has directed competition towards farms in good and workable condition, from which there is still some chance of profit. " A well-farmed place is lettable still, and it is even more lettable because of the large number that are not well farmed."

Mr Riddell: "The good farmer is placed at a disadvantage, because at the end of his nineteen years' lease, if a farm is in very high condition, it makes a good many others covet it, and the landlord very often too."

Much of this competition is dishonest. Men are ready to offer a high rent for a farm which has been well worked for years, with the deliberate intention of exhausting the fertility, and thus compelling a reduction of rent when the farm is "run out." Such "land suckers" outbid the old tenant or the honest new tenant, and ultimately help to bring down the landlord too.

In Scotland, "at present, under the new leases with breaks at five years, there are a number of men who offer for farms in good condition, on the chance of leaving at the end of five years, and taking all they can out of them. These men compete with good farmers, and offer rents which the latter cannot pay."[1]

A Wigtownshire farmer says in despair about technical education and scientific farming: "If you are able through improved methods to raise prices, ultimately that will all go into the pockets of the landlords through competition."

Mr Ballingall (Fife): "Good land I have known gone down almost to wreck from the system of taking the highest rent. I believe in time that no more will be got for land than can be got out of it. By rack-renting you take away a man's hope. The first thing that suffers is the land." This is confirmed by Mr Riddell, who says that "farms let 'at the point of the sword' have, in the end, had a vastly greater fall in rents."

Again: "I have known plenty of cases where farms have been let at from £10 to £15 over the head of the old tenant, where there was no sufficient reason. There are plenty of good landlords. It is the middling class of landlords I am speaking about. The landlord is in a very different position to screw rent out of a farm when it is in high condition." In his own case, Mr Riddell, who had enormously enriched his farm, was not allowed to renew it on valuation, but was told he must compete with the rest, or "bundle and go."

The enormous number of changes of tenancy in the south-west of Scotland is certainly due largely to rack-renting eating up all possible profits. The balance sheets attached to Mr Speir's report show, he says, "that notwithstanding the capital invested, the remunera-

[1] Davidson, 51,026; Riddell, 54,668.

tion of the average farmer of moderate means is no greater than that of a first-class artisan." "Next to low prices, the most potent cause was generally considered to be the unwarrantable competition which exists among farmers themselves."

"The competition is so great that the difficulty of landowners and factors is not to take unreasonable rents."

Competition has also been deliberately stimulated. Thus Mr Ballingall says: "In former times it was not unusual for unfair means to be used when an estate was to let to induce one offer and then another, to get the highest possible."

Mr Rew states that at present in North Devon a practice is complained of, of "offering the farms by tender, and then selecting a tenant, and endeavouring to induce him to give the highest bid."

It is of course natural to say that the tenants are to blame for their own folly.

"The farmers were themselves to blame for raising the market price of the rent to a fictitious value." And again, "It is the tenant's fault that rents are high and not the landlord's, because tenants will bid against each other." [1]

In this opinion it is impossible to concur. It can never be to the real interest of the owner any more than it can be consistent with justice, for a landlord to charge a rent for agricultural land which he knows cannot be made by the produce of the land. He ought to be perfectly aware that the offer of an excessive rent must be either dishonest, reckless, or ignorant, and that the temptation of a temporary gain in times when the possible margin of profit is narrowed to a minimum, will be dearly bought by injury to his estate, as well as loss to the offerers. The tenant farmer is not to blame, if finding others are trying to get the same farm, and knowing that his only or best chance in these times is to secure a good farm, if possible, out of which he can get some immediate return, he is compelled to overshoot the mark and bid a sum which handicaps his own chances heavily,

[1] Wilson Fox, Garstang, p. 17; Rew, North Devon, p. 17.

and perhaps strangles half-a-dozen other struggling men. The landlord is to blame for ignoring the sound principles which in the end are his own best protection as well as the tenant's.

Mr Gillespie, who has advised and occasionally acted for landlords, says: "I had one instance where 30 per cent. more was offered for a farm. I never looked at the offer, because I thought it was far too much." The theoretical justification to the landlord who takes the highest bidder, is that "he gets it valued by the public, and he presumes these practical men know their business."

It is unfortunately established that in Scotland, Devonshire, and other districts, the system of encouraging competition to the utmost by letting farms on the tender system is widely prevalent, and in some parts almost universal.

On the other hand, the best landlords and the best agents repudiate this policy emphatically, and it is certain from the evidence that on some, if not a majority, of the best managed estates it is the definitely announced policy to let farms on valuation, and to select tenants mainly on the grounds of capacity, capital, and to some extent of hereditary and local claims.

Mr Punchard says: "The larger landowners have been in the habit of having their farms valued periodically, and let upon that valuation. On the other hand, the small or middle-class owner has been in the habit of letting his farms by tender. Of course, where farms have been let by tender, the rents have gone up very much more than where they have been let upon a valuation."

"One landlord may say, 'I do not want the farms put up to their value; I am content to take 10 or 15 per cent. less than the top market price.' Whereas another man, who may from necessity be obliged to get the last penny he can, will naturally say: 'You must let the farm by tender, and get as much money as you can.'"

Mr Gilbert Murray says that, although there is much competition for farms in Derbyshire, especially on good estates, farms are not put up to auction, nor let to the highest bidder; the rent is determined by expert valuation based on the current values of the produce.

On the Holker estates in North Lancashire, rents have remained unchanged since the valuation made in 1826. "The large farms are still paying rent on the old valuation. In a few cases the rents have been reduced."[1]

Sir Massey Lopes, even in Devonshire, has not let his farms by tender; his rents are moderate, and his tenantry go on from father to son.

The Duke of Richmond, who goes personally into every detail of his estates, takes the best evidence available, and then fixes the rent himself at what is, in his opinion, absolutely fair. "I should offer it to the old tenant at the rent which I considered, after consulting with my factor and commissioner, was the rent which ought to be paid, and if anybody else offered to give me a larger rent I should not take it . . . I should think that he did not know so much about it as we did." He is strongly against letting by tender. "I think it would be fatal to set them bidding against each other."[2] The tenantry have thrived and remained from generation to generation.

The evidence of Mr Muirhead, agent to Lord Aberdeen, is important on these points. On the Haddo Estate, which seems to have been always moderately rented, a revaluation by arbitration was offered to the tenants in 1886, and carried out on about one-third of the estate. The new rent was fixed for five years at a reduction of 23 per cent., and in 1890, things being better in that district, half of this reduction was withdrawn. At the end of a lease the farm is offered to the sitting tenant at a valuation which is based on the quality and fertility of the soil, the character of the buildings, position as regards railways, etc. It is only when farms are definitely given up that offers are received from outsiders, and the highest bidder is not taken, but the best qualified farmer. Small increases of

[1] Wilson Fox, Garstang, App. B. 6, p. 53.
[2] 22,686; 22 709; 22,603; 22,705.

rent in the last two years have occurred, but the changes of tenancy are extremely few, the old tenants remaining on.

The principle that a real valuation should be the basis of rent occurs again and again in the evidence.

Thus Sir Michael Hicks Beach had his estates revalued in 1855, on the basis of the prices of the chief commodities produced on his farms at that time. His farms, with one or two exceptions of changes of tenancy, remained at that valuation all through the times of inflated prices, and were then very heavily reduced, immediately after the losses of 1879. And now Sir Michael says: "My rents are infinitely below the point at which they were fixed by the valuation of 1855, and have been reduced in much greater proportion than the percentage of fall of prices. In making reductions, landlords have to consider a great many other questions besides the question of prices."[1]

Mr Gilbert Murray, in his interesting evidence, proposes as a solution which, in his opinion, would settle the land question for fifty years, a general revaluation of all holdings based on products and prices.[2] The gross returns of a farm are obtained by taking the average of each kind of produce, having regard to the rotation of crops observed, cereals with their straw, beef and mutton, wool and milk, the quantities being then put into their money equivalents, in the current market prices. From the gross returns so determined you are to deduct the whole cost of production, including labour, horse labour, seeds, insurance, depreciation on implements and machinery, and 5 per cent. interest on an average of £8 per acre capital as tenant's remuneration. The balance left is to go to pay rent, tithe, rates, and taxes.[3] It will be at once noted that Mr Murray's estimate for tenant's outgoings is obviously lower than in most of the farm accounts given in the evidence and reports. Mr Murray's proposal is that this valuation being settled, rents are to fall or rise by a sliding scale based on prices.

The principle of valuation suggested is clearly sound,

[1] 6127-33.   [2] 5141, etc.   [3] Vol. I., App. A., XVIII.

though it should not exclude variations from considerations of accessibility to markets and many other matters. But the principle of a sliding scale has not been accepted by the tenants with whom Mr Murray is specially connected, and does not seem to have succeeded in the cases where it has been tried, and, in its older form of corn rents, has practically been discarded. In some instances this has probably resulted from too high a valuation being adopted as the standard from which to start. But it may be doubted whether, even with the lowest and fairest valuation to start from, the automatic reduction of rents in proportion to prices could be got to work justly and smoothly in these tumble-down times.

In conclusion, competition cannot be regarded as a fair instrument for determining the value of agricultural land. The abuse of competition must inevitably transfer to the owner, one by one, every advantage which the farmer obtains in earning profits, either by his own skill and enterprise and outlay, or by improvements in agricultural methods and science, or by relief from local or other burdens, and must constantly tend to cut down the capital of the farmer to the narrowest margin at which he can be induced to go on living and working on his farm, and must, as it destroys hope and effort, tend to weaken and deteriorate agriculture. There is no reason why the wise and generous policy adopted by some landlords, and shown to be to their interest as well to their tenants by the history of their estates, of fixing a fair rent for agricultural land based on the quantity and current prices of produce, should not be made general. Parliament could render no greater service to agriculture than by facilitating this satisfactory result.

CHAPTER IX.

THE RELATION OF RENTS TO LANDLORD'S IMPROVEMENTS, THE CAPITAL VALUE OF LAND, AND TO MORTGAGES AND INCUMBRANCES.

THE relation of the outlay by landlords in permanent improvements and repairs has a material bearing on rents.

The evidence brought before us, though conflicting on some points, shows generally that the expenditure by many landlords, and especially the owners of large estates, has been heavy and continuous for many years.

By many witnesses it is stated that this expenditure has increased rather than diminished since agriculture began to decline, except on small estates, or where the owner's income is wholly drawn from his agricultural land.

In the good times, not only in Wales, but in many parts of England, and frequently in Scotland, a proportion of the permanent improvements—not large or constant, but occasional and irregular—was carried out by the tenants themselves.

"Frequently on the larger farms, in the good times, when money was plentiful, tenants put up a shed or other building, without even asking their landlord to do it, and as for the smaller repairs, the landlords were never troubled about them."[1]

But since depression set in, tenants have generally ceased from any such outlay, and the whole expenditure on improvements, and also most of that on repairs, previously undertaken in their agreements by tenants, has come upon the landlord.

Further, on changes of tenancy, new tenants have

[1] Wilson Fox, Lincoln, p. 14.

asked for much more in buildings, drainage, and other improvements and equipments for stock, dairying, and other modifications of farm working. And the evidence is uniform that with the fall in agricultural prices there has been a rise in the cost of building operations.

It may be doubted, for reasons stated later, whether there has been an increase in the outlay on improvements since the more acute period of the depression. In some cases exceptional efforts have been made to restore estates to a sound condition, but in general we believe the impression of some witnesses that there has been greater outlay as depression deepened, is due to the fact that there have been since 1882 and 1883 successive breaks down of tenants in many districts, and that the new tenants who took farms on the changes of tenancy have very naturally insisted on having better equipment of their holdings in order to have some chance of doing better than their predecessors.

Mr Wilson Fox is probably interpreting the facts correctly, for the country generally as well as for Lincolnshire, when he attributes the outlay on improved buildings to "the fact that both sitting and incoming tenants have asked for more, both in enlarged and extra buildings and in repairs, to which requests the landlords have had to accede, sometimes to retain, sometimes to acquire tenants."

Reasons have already been given from the evidence for thinking that most of this expenditure has been for new tenants.

The proportion of gross rents returned to the land in the shape of buildings, drainage, and other permanent improvements and repairs on many large estates varies somewhat, but this variation is in some cases probably due to the fact that estates that have been uniformly well managed and kept up, require less annual outlay, except where some considerable change is made in the methods of farming.

The amount expended in permanent improvements and repairs on some large estates is as follows:—

Lord Derby, in South-West Lancashire, on 43,217

acres, has expended £200,000 in twelve years, or £16,500, or 7s 8d an acre, each year.[1]

Lord Sefton, on 18,000 acres, £286,000 in twenty-two years, or about £13,000, or 14s an acre, each year.

On Mr Talbot Clifton's agricultural property of 16,000 acres, £5000 a year, or 6s 3d an acre, for half a century past.

Mr Turnor, on 21,000 acres in Lincolnshire, where the net rental has sunk from £21,327 in 1877-8 to £8754 in 1893-4, has spent about £5000 a year, sinking in the last few years to about £3000.

On the Earl of Ancaster's Lincolnshire estate of 53,993 acres, £689,197 [2] has been spent between 1872 and 1893, or at the rate of £31,327, or 11s 7d an acre, each year. The total gross rent received on this estate for the twenty-two years was £1,565,213. The remaining landlord's outgoings for tithe, land tax, owners' rates, management and miscellaneous outgoings (the last item as much as £174,512) were £350,354. The net income, after all deductions, was on the average £23,900, or about 9s an acre, and in 1893 was only £14,394, or about 5s 6d an acre. In 1876, the year of highest receipts of rents, the percentage for improvements and repairs was 36·92, in 1893, 37·37, showing undiminished proportionate outlay.[3]

On Lord Yarborough's estate of 54,139 acres, £98,391 was spent between 1879 and 1893, or about £6550, or 2s 9d an acre, each year.

On a large estate in Northants, the average annual rent from 1858 to 1878 was £45,536, and the average outlay on improvements and repairs was £8334, or 18 per cent. of the annual gross rent. But for the years 1891, 1892, 1893, the average payments are £10,432 on an average gross rent of £31,320, or 33 per cent. There has thus been an increase of over 23 per cent. in the expenditure in the last few years, and the amount of gross rent which is assigned to these objects has nearly doubled.

---

[1] Wilson Fox, Garstang, p. 8.

[2] Including £20,781 for drainage and embankment rates, which are of the nature of a rent charge for permanent improvements.

[3] Wilson Fox, Lincoln, p. 53.

The net agricultural rental has fallen from £27,194 in 1885 to £11,900 in 1893.¹

On another large estate which has always been low rented and excellently managed, between 1881 and 1893, out of a gross rent received of £220,787, the sum of £59,440 was expended, or an average of nearly 27 per cent. of the gross rent. On this estate a comparatively heavy outlay was incurred between 1880 and 1886 on drainage to restore the condition of the land after the wet seasons. The result of this prudent management has been that the net rental between 1887 and 1891 was 15 per cent. higher than in 1881, and even in 1892 and 1893 is still considerably more than half the gross rental.

On a Bedfordshire estate of 9476 acres, the outlay has been in the past fifteen years £41,445 8s 6d, or an average of 5s 10d per acre each year. This is about equivalent to 26 per cent. of the gross rent of 1879, and about 38 per cent. of that of 1893.²

The agricultural rents on Lord Chichester's estate at Stanmer have fallen from £9285 in 1877 to £5319 in 1893, but the improvements and repairs have been kept at £2500 to £2600, and in 1893 were £2678, or nearly 50 per cent.³

In the North of England the expenditure has been most widely extended since farming became more difficult. Thus of Northumberland, Mr George Grey, who is both an owner and agent, says: "Actually more has been expended on buildings than formerly, in the hope that increased facilities for feeding stock, etc., would assist the tenant in farming his land. As a rule, farm buildings and cottages are very good, and are far in advance of twenty years ago.⁴

Mr Hughes says: Farm buildings have been vastly improved in Northumberland within the last fifteen years. On the Waterford estate, 6000 acres, about 14 per cent. of the gross rental goes to improvements

---
¹ Pringle, Beds, Hunts, Northants, p. 29.
² Ibid., App. B. II., p. 100.   ³ Ingram, 3514, 3534, etc.
⁴ Wilson Fox, Glendale, p. 8.

and repairs, on Lord Tankerville's (20,000 acres) about 17 or 18 per cent.

Mr Pringle says of South Durham and the North Riding, that the landlords have spent large sums on permanent improvements. The comparative escape from the worst consequences of this long and severe depression is largely due to the way in which landlords have provided the best equipment for stock farming on economic and profitable lines, with covered yards.

Mr Spencer says of Oxfordshire, Gloucestershire, etc., that the average outlay ranges from 10 to 36 per cent. of the gross rental in those counties, is greater on large properties, and is generally maintained in spite of heavy reductions, and in some cases considerably increased since the depression. Much of the tenant's liabilities under covenants to repair has also been transferred to the landlord, who practically takes the whole cost.

The proportion of gross rent thus employed is in some cases prodigious. Thus Mr Hall,[1] on his Cambridgeshire estate of 5600 acres, expended in 1892—"a medium year"—on improvements and maintenance, £2753 out of £5105 gross rent, or over 54 per cent. On his estate in Bucks—2583 acres—the expenditure is £1191 8s 9d out of £2940, or over 40 per cent.

The "Particulars of Expenditures and Outgoings on certain Estates" show that—

On the Tollemache estate in Cheshire, improvements, repairs, drainage, etc., have taken about £5000 a year out of about £33,000, or 15 per cent.

On the Holkham estate of Lord Leicester, between 1872 and 1892, in 21 years £153,234 was spent out of £1,109,314 gross rent received, or 13·72 per cent. The outlay has considerably fallen since 1884.

On the Thorney and Wansford estates, out of £750,738 gross rent for 21 years (1872-92), £385,192 has gone to permanent improvements, drainage rates, etc., over 50 per cent.

On estates of about 27,000 acres in Beds and Bucks, out of £890,444 gross rent received, £233,239

[1] Vol. VI., App. III. and IV., pp. 462, 463.

were expended in the same period, or about 29 per cent.

On the Fitzhardinge estate, Gloucestershire, out of £723,293 gross rent, £249,927 went to improvements and repairs, or 34 per cent. These items have in 1892 fallen to 26 per cent.

For the same period—

On 24,500 acres in Devon, Cornwall, and Dorset, the gross rents are £736,026. Improvements and repairs, £155,067, or 21 per cent.

On Bolton Abbey estate, between 1880 and 1892 (13 years), out of £134,760 gross rent, improvements and repairs took £28,942, or 21 per cent.

On the Chatsworth estate, for thirteen years, out of £159,309 gross rent, £56,084, or 35 per cent.

On Lord Tollemache's Suffolk estate, repairs and improvements took 16·97 per cent. of the rents in 1872, in 1882, 35·81 per cent., but in 1892 had fallen to 8·27 per cent.

Of Scotch estates, improvements and repairs took—on Lord Wemyss's property, 9·92 per cent. of rents in 1872, 26·09 per cent. in 1882, and 14·19 per cent. in 1892; on Lord Breadalbane's estates, 23·27 per cent. in 1892; on the Poltalloch estate, 25·71 per cent. in 1872, 26·7 per cent. in 1882, and 39·68 per cent. in 1892; on Drummond Castle and Stobhall estates, 28·45 per cent. in 1872, 57·03 per cent. in 1882, and 32·28 per cent. in 1892.

On Lord Strathmore's estates 27 per cent. of the rental goes to improvements and repairs.

On the Underley estate, in Westmorland, of 22,000 acres, from a rental of £24,000, sinking in 1892 to £20,000, £102,000 has been spent on repairs and permanent improvements in the last twenty-eight years, or rather less than £6000 a year, or from 24 to 28 per cent.

Sir Massey Lopes, on his Devonshire estate of 9000 acres, in forty years expended £150,000 on improvements and repairs, two-thirds of it going to permanent improvements. His experience is that this outlay of about 6s an acre a year has left him where he was as regards rental. But he has retained his tenantry in a fairly prosperous condition, without the wreckage of generation after generation of farmers to be seen elsewhere.

Mr Lipscomb says that the constant and increasing outlay on the small farms of the Savile estates has averted changes of tenancy.

In Cornwall, where stock farming is increasing, landlords have increased their expenditure in providing the necessary buildings.

Mr Squarey thinks, as regards the south of England, that the amount of outlay on permanent improvements has been greatly diminished. The Lands Improvement Company is doing much less business.

Perhaps the most profitable permanent improvements which landlords could make in many parts of the country would be the subdivision of very large farms, and the equipment with buildings of smaller farms. But with existing resources and with existing prospects, this is nearly impracticable.

Sir Nigel Kingscote, one of the Commission, states that the expenditure on improvements and repairs on the agricultural estates of the Crown have been £257,016 5s 11d from 1879 to 1893. The rental was £112,900 in 1879, and £72,195 in 1893. The average outlay was over £17,000 a year, but has fallen to an average of £7800 in the years 1889-93. The heaviest expenditure was on drainage after the wet years.[1]

On the agricultural estates of the Ecclesiastical Commissioners, between 1880 and 1892 inclusive, £812,438 has been expended on improvements and repairs on an average rental of £295,000, about 21 per cent. per annum.

On the three estates of Guy's Hospital, in all 22,605 acres, about £6000 a year was formerly expended, but now, owing to reductions, only half that amount.

The Duchy of Lancaster draws about £19,800 from about 17,000 acres of agricultural land. On this there has been expended in improvements since 1880 about £63,500, or about £4000 a year.

The official information supplied by the Board of

[1] Vol. I, Appendix A. 1, etc.

Agriculture as to expenditures under the various Drainage and Improvement Acts since 1847, which have enabled owners to make the cost of improvements a charge upon the land, show that in forty-seven years the sum of £16,521,277 was so spent and charged, £8,978,731 being for drainage, £4,702,361 for farm buildings, £1,067,336 for cottages, £432,988 for fencing and embanking, and £566,357 for mansion houses, the last item beginning in 1872, after the passing of the Limited Owners Residences Act, 1871. Four millions was advanced by the Exchequer under the first Drainage Acts (nearly all repaid)—the remainder by the Land Improvement Companies and by landowners themselves, under the Improvement of Land Act, 1864, and the Limited Owners Residences Act. It is not possible to ascertain what has been expended and charged under the Settled Land Act, 1882, but the estimates submitted to the Board of Agriculture, where the Board approves the surveyor, have amounted, in 1893 and 1894, to about £200,000 each year.[1]

Since 1873, the heaviest outlay appears to have been for drainage in the six years succeeding 1879, and for farm buildings. There was also a heavy but steadily decreasing outlay on buildings between 1876 and 1888. But the expenditure since 1888 does not confirm the statements of several witnesses that outlay has been increasing with the depression, but rather tends to show that the opinion of Mr Squarey, Sir Michael Hicks Beach, and others, that in the last few years outlay has been very much less, owing to straitened means.[2]

Mr Elliott thinks this and the smaller prospect of profit from improvements are the main causes of the smaller amount in last six or seven years, though it is also suggested that under the Settled Land Act, some portion of this expenditure escapes public attention.

It would appear probable from the evidence that the largest application of gross rents to improvements have taken place on the best managed and on the whole most

[1] Vol. III, Appendices XXVII to XXXI.
[2] Appendix XXIX.

prosperous of the large estates, and especially where the owner has considerable other resources. But there is very striking evidence of extraordinary efforts on the part both of owners of large estates in exceptionally bad districts, and also of owners of small properties with no other resources to keep up their farms, who have clearly made enormous personal sacrifices to meet the necessities of their tenants, and to keep their estates in working order.

Thus, on a large estate in Essex (13,000 acres), where the net rental was still £7682 in 1881-2, the outlay on buildings and repairs had risen from £2020 in the former year, to £3184 in 1887-8, and to £4690 in 1892-3. When all the outgoings are deducted in the last year, the sum left as net income to the owner is only £652 13s 9d, or about 1s an acre.

Again, in the South Midlands, Mr Pringle found, "on going over the accounts of small properties, that efforts had been made to maintain buildings and drain land to the last possible penny." "Small landlords will submit to anything rather than lose a tenant or farm their own land." These small and helpless landlords are specially selected as victims by the unscrupulous farm wreckers, who "get all they can by reckless cropping in a year or so, and then bolt."

There is another side to this matter. The buildings and cottages on many Essex farms are reported to be wretched, and sheds and yards for stock keeping of the most undesirable description.

Mr Pringle remarks: "It is a pity that in the good times, when Essex farms were paying high rents, so little was done towards the equipment of estates with substantial farm buildings. It is evident that what cannot easily be done now, could, and I think should have been accomplished then."

Mr Rew says of North Devon: "The condition of the farmhouses, buildings, and cottages is, on larger estates, as a rule, good, though there are exceptions even there. On the smaller estates the condition is generally indifferent, and in some cases very bad. On the best managed estates repairs are well kept up, but improvements are not carried out to the same extent as formerly. Up to recently, interest on improvements effected by the landlord has been commonly charged to the tenants, but latterly it has been found impossible to do this, and consequently less outlay has been undertaken in this direction."

Similarly of Dorset, Mr Rew reports that while buildings are generally good on the larger estates, some are bad in respect of convenience, adequacy, or condition. "The times have checked expenditure on new buildings, as it is very seldom that any interest can be obtained for the money spent on them. On the smaller estates, buildings are frequently inadequate and in indifferent order." Some of the cottages, even on larger estates, are disgraceful.

The discreditable insanitary condition of many of the farm buildings in Lancashire, where rents run high, and the way in which stock and dairy farming is hampered by these defects, has already been alluded to.[1]

In Cambridgeshire, where there are few large estates, complaints are frequent that "most of the farm buildings and cottages are very bad. The drainage of farmyards is bad." "The buildings in East Cambridgeshire are very bad." At Ely it is said, "ordinary repairs have been kept up, but no substantial ones." At Parson's Drove, "buildings and sheds have been neglected by the landlords. The water in the streams is not fit to drink," &c.[2]

In Suffolk, though the farmers do not appear to complain, buildings, with a few exceptions on some large estates, are described as inferior and ill-adapted to help farming. "The dairy accommodation is wretched and discouraging to farmers," and "often near sources of contamination."

"In the Lothians, some owners are taking farms into their own hands, and setting them down to grass, and leaving the buildings alone rather than put new buildings

---

[1] Page 49. [2] Wilson Fox, Cambs., p. 14.

up. Buildings are getting so out of order as to hamper the business of farming."

There is also much evidence here and there that drainage is still in a most imperfect state, that in some districts the old drains laid many years ago are useless, and have not been replaced.

And the amount spent on drainage, and charged on estates under the Improvements Acts, in the six years following the disaster of 1879, is £710,125 for the whole of Great Britain.[1] This was a most critical period, and the area of land affected by the last season was enormous. On Lord Spencer's estate in Northamptonshire of 14,808 acres, nearly £17,000 has been spent in drainage since 1879, with the greatest benefit to the pasture land.[2] But if this is the proportion on one estate, it is hardly likely that the sum of £710,125 would cover any adequate proportion of the large area of land put out of condition by the wet seasons.

It is certainly an extraordinary circumstance, in this connection, that the outlay charged on estates under the Improvements Acts after the passing of the Limited Owners Residences Acts should have been so great in respect of mansion houses. It appears from the tables supplied by the Board of Agriculture that the expenditure for mansion houses during the period of depression between 1879 and 1894 inclusive was no less than £430,737, whereas during this period only £377,920 was borrowed and charged under the Acts for the erection of labourers' cottages. The expenditure for farm buildings was £1,831,718, and for drainage £1,047,274 during the same period. In one year, 1890, the amount for mansion houses is £77,844, whereas on labourers' cottages only £8311 was expended, and even on farm buildings the amount was only £67,080, or £10,764 less than on mansion houses. In the five years ending in 1894, the outlay on mansion houses was £169,592, on labourers' cottages only £67,864, and on drainage £12,227, and farm buildings £328,464. These figures do not of course cover more than the outlays arranged for under the Acts,

[1] Vol. III, App. XXIX. [2] Pringle, Beds, etc., p. 12.

but if they can be taken as fairly representing the proportion of loans applied by owners to the maintenance or development of their estates, it would appear that, since the depression set in, the outlay on the essential provisions for the well-being and effective working of estates—the outlay which would keep good labour on the land, and help farmers if possible to make a profit out of it, has been, in the cases where owners borrowed under the Acts, relatively subordinated to the comfort and dignity of the landowners' families, and that, as rents have been further reduced in the last five years, this relation of the several outlays has been still more sharply defined. Mr Elliott's explanation that some of this expenditure on mansion houses was made by new purchasers of estates out of money derived from other sources, does not seem to touch the point of the relative proportions of the outlays charged for the several purposes.[1]

Special significance also attaches to the very general demand of tenant farmers in many districts for amendments to the Agricultural Holdings Act, to confer on them the right to either obtain from the landlord, or to execute for themselves (with the right to compensation) the classes of improvements which they hold to be essential to the profitable working of the soil. It is impossible to suppose that this contention would be so frequently and forcibly advanced were it not that there must be a very large, and as yet unsatisfied, demand for the better equipment of farms.

The outlay by landlords on improvements has been generally regarded as a justification for rents which otherwise would be obviously thought to be high, if not excessive, in the face of falling prices.

Many owners seem to think that they are getting no rent at all for their land, unless they have first secured what they consider a fair interest on their own outlay in improvements. The whole of this outlay is regarded as capital invested in buildings, drainage, fencing, and other improvements, and it is clearly matter of conviction with

[1] Vol. III, App. XXIX.

many witnesses, who have come before us, that they are entitled to expect a full interest on the whole of this outlay, exactly in the same sense as from any ordinary commercial investment.

This view has naturally arisen from the fact that, with the exception of some large estates, interest has almost invariably been paid by tenants on such outlay, till margins having become too narrow, it became no longer possible to charge interest, and in the case of new tenancies, improvements have been insisted on as a condition of taking a farm at all.

Thus the enormous outlay for a long number of years on the estates of Lord Leicester in Norfolk and the Earl of Ancaster in Lincolnshire are compared with existing rents.

On the Holkham estate, the expenditure of two generations, by two successive Earls of Leicester, ranging from 1777 to 1892, amounts to the very large sum of £1,112,090. The rental in 1894, which was likely to sink still lower, was £28,700. If, as is assumed, the expenditure of two generations for a century back ought to be a sort of first charge on the land, the rents paid would only give an interest of 2½ per cent.

On Lord Ancaster's estate, since 1872 the sum of £1,039,551 in all was spent, and of this £689,197 was for improvements, repairs, etc.

The gross rent received (not the rent-roll), in 1893 was £53,196. This represents 5 per cent. on the total outgoings of the twenty-two years, if the whole of them are to be treated as interest-bearing investments, or 7½ per cent. on the outlay on improvements and repairs taken apart from the other outgoings. If the expenditure of 1893 on improvements and repairs, £15,015, is deducted from the gross rent, the remaining income for that year, £38,181, represents 3⅔ per cent. on the whole outlay for the twenty-two years, and 5½ per cent. on the improvements and repairs outlay.

But it is plain that in such calculations many essential considerations are unconsciously ignored. In the first place, in these accounts some items are not investments at all. Thus, in the case of Lord Ancaster's estate, the outlay of a million sterling since 1872 includes tithe, land-tax, local rates paid by owner, management, and miscellaneous outgoings, none of which can be an interest-bearing investment; and in the case of the Holkham estate, a large proportion of the enormous expenditure of two generations is quite out of date as an element upon which the rent of to-day could reasonably be calculated in the light of so much dividend upon an investment.

Mr Albert Pell, in his interesting article on "The Making of the Land in England," and in his evidence before the Commission, argues that agricultural land has really been made available by the expenditure of the landowners, and that this expenditure has been so enormous that it is probable that present rents only represent about 1 per cent. upon the total outlay. If owners had gone on from year to year investing the same amounts in consols or other securities, they would have had a large return. Sir Massey Lopes, in his evidence, advances the same contention.

But such reasoning is obviously fallacious. The landlords could only *ex hypothesi* have had these sums to expend on improvements, or to invest elsewhere from year to year, if their rents continued to be paid; or, if these sums were invested elsewhere, in a very few years the rents would have gone down to nothing, with the result that the landlord would be poorer, not richer, from this change of his arrangements. In fact, Mr Pell admits that the money was invested in making the land " lettable "—without it, it would, therefore, have not been lettable, but would speedily have reverted to waste.

The fallacy is threefold. In the first place, most of such expenditure is not truly of the nature of an investment. It is to some extent merely the essential preliminary to any rent being earned at all. And, in the second place, a very large portion has long since lapsed. Mr Pell himself holds that " no landlord would in fixing his rent take into consideration such expenditure unless made within a reasonable period," and could not go back to these outlays of half a century or more ago. And, thirdly, it seems to be quite forgotten that many of the items which swell these vast accounts are temporary and evanescent. Much that goes down as "repairs" consists of recurrent and transient payments. It is of the nature of the mere replacing of the wear and tear of the machine, or instrument which is let on hire, and which is unworkable and useless without this constant attention. If a jobmaster spends money year by year in keeping a carriage he lets out on hire in good order, he naturally does better business and is able to let his carriage on better terms than another man who neglects repairs, but it would be absurd for him to add up year by year his outlays on repairs as a species of cumulative investment, increasing for ever and ever, and expected to yield an interest on the wholly fictitious total of investments thus created. It would very soon exceed the selling value of the carriage. Much of the reasoning as to rents not producing a fair interest on landlord's outlay is equally unsubstantial and fallacious.

When the claims of tenants for their improvements are considered, the time limit of exhaustion is rigidly and jealously guarded. The proposals of all the Scotch tenant farmer witnesses, and of many of the English tenant farmer witnesses, that compensation should be given for long continued good farming, resulting in what they term "cumulative fertility," have been repudiated by witnesses representing the views of landowners and agents. But, at the same time, statements are made which imply the claim by landlords and their representatives to treat the landlord's outlay as a matter on which time has practically no effect whatever.

By the Lincolnshire custom a tenant is only allowed fifteen years for drainage, after which time it is assumed that no value worth pecuniary recognition is thought to remain. On what principle can it be justly held that, on an exactly similar outlay, a landlord should have a right to interest extending over generations?

Landlords' Improvements really paid for by Tenants.

In any case it must be recognised that, until the more recent and acute stages of the depression, agricultural tenants have themselves been clearing away for generations past, the capital and interest of the outlays made by their landlords. This is established in the evidence and in the reports. In some cases the repayment has been made in instalments repayable by specific agreement, in others by some proportionate increase of rent. In most cases it must be presumed that the whole outlay was thus repaid; in others, a part of the outlay. In his own case, mentioned by Mr Carrington Smith, a clause was added to his agreement providing that the money borrowed by his landlord for improvements on the farm was to be paid off by the tenant at the rate of 7 per cent. "I continued to pay principal and interest on the drainage until its repayment was finished; then, of course, the extra charge upon me ceased."

On an estate in South Dorset, the tenant is compelled to agree to pay 5 per cent. on all landlord's outlay and drainage, and also "to convey all materials for such improvements free of cost from a distance not more than ten miles."

But where no specific agreement has been entered upon, but there has only been an increase of rent on a general understanding that the increase was to pay for outlay by the landlord on improvements, it is probable that this increased rental has, in many cases, become crystallised as the accepted rent of the holding, and the addition made in respect of the improvement on which the outlay took place has not ceased at the end of the reasonable time within which the addition to rent would have cleared off both principal and interest.

Thus Mr Davidson says: "In the old days" (before the depression) "I think the interest on drainage was regarded as so much rent when you came to renew your lease."

Mr Stuart says of a Banffshire tenant: "The tenant

paid up the capital and interest in the course of a nineteen years' lease at the rate of 6¼ per cent., and then he was charged a larger rent on these improvements in his next lease."

Mr Speir states, as regards the south-western counties of Scotland, that the improvements have practically been executed by the tenants. The landlords have built most of the houses, but the tenants have done the cartage for great distances in hilly districts, meaning a heavy outlay for which no adequate return has been made.[1] And in many cases the principal and interest for the buildings has been paid by the tenant alone.

In the case of a Northants tenancy brought before us, a mill was erected by the landlord, and fitted with special machinery in 1893, the annual value of which was taken to be £100, and an addition of £50 a year was made to the rent, or rather the reduction of the rent from £732 to £400 was placed at £450, to cover part of the outlay.[2] And in many instances it has been urged that reductions of rent to tenants have been made in a certain sense by some increase in the outlay of the landlord in permanent improvements. If this argument is economically sound, it proves that these permanent improvements are being paid for by the tenant and not by the landlord.

If the evidence is conclusive, as appears to be the case, that this paying off by the tenant has been, till the last few years, the general practice except on a very few large estates, it is plain that the tenants have really borne in most instances the expense of permanent improvements, in addition to the outlay they have made from their own capital in developing and maintaining the fertility and condition of the soil, and frequently also in more prosperous times in carrying out permanent improvements themselves. The landlord's share in the transaction has been the advance of capital, and for the argument it matters nothing whether it has been borrowed from the Exchequer, or from a company, or from elsewhere, or expended out of rents received, or

[1] T. Carrington Smith, 8127.　　[2] Baker, 47,167.

other resources. It is capital advanced, and when repayment at a reasonable rate has been made, either in instalments by specific agreement, or in a rent increased, or maintained to cover the necessary amount, the transaction should be treated as wound up and done with, and it is wholly inadmissible to go on adding cumulatively, one upon the other, all these repaid outlays, and treat the immense sum, thus fictitiously piled up, as a permanent investment, to secure a fair commercial interest on which rents ought to be kept at some fictitious level, even when it is obvious that the greatest part of this accumulation of outlays has long since been paid off and cancelled.

The injustice to which these fallacious contentions naturally lead is obvious. It is still more striking when we consider the amount of evidence that where tenants have directly contributed their own capital to the permanent improvement of the landlords' property they have no security whatever, and are unable to obtain for their outlay any repayment from the landlord, either by instalments of interest and sinking fund, or by allowances out of rent, unless they have been able to make beforehand an agreement to cover their expenditure.[1]

Thus Mr Stuart says that, on the Duke of Fife's property, the tenants have executed permanent improvements very generally. He has built his own steading, steam mill, and done fencing, dyking, etc., and has got nearly as much value in the farm as the landlord has. Mr Stuart estimates the annual value of his permanent improvements at £80 a year, and states that, unless he pays less than half his present rent, he is losing the whole of this annual value of his improvements.

Mr Hutchinson, who erected buildings on his farm before the Act and without an agreement, and if he left would be handing over about £2000 to his landlord in the buildings, is clearly now paying and not receiving interest on his own expenditure.

[1] Rowlandson, 17,574; Pringle, Beds, Hunts, Northants, pp. 59, etc., J. Stratton, 6623, etc.

From such cases it is indeed clear, that so long as the power of fixing rents at discretion remains in the hands of the landlord, without restriction or qualification, from the moment a tenant spends a sum on an improvement, the improvement thus made belongs in practice to the landlord, and (if no agreement has been entered into to protect the tenant) it absolutely depends on the sense of fairness of the landlord whether he abstains or not from unjustly depriving the tenant of the value from the outset, or at any determination of the tenancy.

The only chance of forcing anything in the form of a repayment by the landlord of the value added to his property by the tenant's outlay is where the tenant is in a position to threaten the destruction of the improvement, as in the case of permanent pasture laid down by the tenant himself. By this consideration Mr Carrington Smith was enabled to get an agreement that he should receive £5 an acre for pasture he had laid down and improved for over twelve years, at the close of his tenancy, he engaging on his side not to plough it up.

These facts show that wholly different standards and different reasoning are applied to the interests landlords and tenants respectively have in any expenditure by which either party contributes to the value of the holding.

Again, in assuming that rent ought to cover not only a reasonable equivalent for the productive power of the land, but also include a full interest on accumulated outlays, it is forgotten that rent has also a necessary relation to the present capital value of the land.

This may be illustrated by a case from Mr Pringle's Essex report.[1]

An estate cost, in purchase money and improvements, £200,000, but would now only fetch £50,000 in the market. Before 1879 the gross rental was between £6000 and £7000; now (in 1893) it is below £4000. The owner says, "I get no rent at all from my land; I merely get about 4 per cent. on the cost of buildings, drains, and fences."

[1] Pringle, Essex, p. 18.

But, on his own showing, if the estate with the buildings and improvements would now sell for only £50,000, the present gross rental would represent about 8 per cent. on the present capital value of the whole land and improvements. Even deducting £1200, or 33 per cent. for repairs, etc., he is still netting 5½ per cent. on the current value of his land and improvements.

In this analysis, it has been wished to give the fullest attention to the important evidence of very large outlays having been made by many owners, without any charge of interest during the period of depression. It will be universally recognised that a broad and generous and considerate policy, and a wise foresight, has been shown by many wealthy landowners, in the free application to the useful and necessary work of restoring or maintaining agricultural land, of large sums from other investments and accumulations. It is certain that, even now, this immense outlay, made without imposing onerous conditions on the tenants of these estates, is bringing some small return to the owners in preventing the further diminution of rents, which, without this outlay, would speedily ensue. Most people also will agree with Mr Rew, that it cannot be expected that landowners should go on permanently expending income from other sources on their agricultural estates without the inducement of something like a commercial return, as many have now practically been doing for several years.

But it has seemed only right to expose the fallacies lurking under some of the reasoning as to landlord's improvements, and as to capital values of land and buildings, the economic depreciation of which ought to be frankly recognised, because it is obvious that these fallacies have operated, and are likely to operate, as incentives to unjust over-renting of tenants. And it is certain in practice to be as injurious to the chances of agriculture that the owners of land should treat what they consider a fair interest on their outlay as a sort of perpetual first charge like tithe, as it would be ruinous to railway interests if dividends should be taken first to suit the ideas of shareholders, and working expenses be left to take their chance afterwards.

The moral, as well as economic, injustice of some of the high rents, which are apparently being maintained, deserves special consideration.

It has been frequently said, with or without precision, that many rents in Ireland were only paid by the remittances sent to the tenants by children or other relatives in America. But it certainly can be said with exactness that the whole, or at any rate some portion, of the rent of many of the small farms in Lancashire, in Wales, parts of Scotland, and in other districts, is not made by the land itself, but is really being paid by the gratuitous labour of the farmer's grown-up children.

Mr Wilson Fox says: "At the present time in some districts it is the farmers' sons and daughters who have suffered rather than the land, for they have been and are giving their best energies towards its cultivation, receiving no reward in the present, and with but little prospect for it in the future." . . . "Some large farmers have told me that after feeding and clothing themselves and their families, and paying no wages to their sons and daughters, they have made nothing for the last year or two, while several have told me they have had to draw on capital." When the ordinary wages of grown young men and women in Lancashire towns are considered, it seems extraordinary that this heavy sacrifice should have been made to keep up the farms, and still more astounding that, even when this sacrifice was unavailing to prevent loss of all profits, the reductions of rent in Lancashire have not been vastly greater than the relatively small reduction recorded in evidence. The farmers asked Mr Fox: "Prices have dropped 30 to 40 per cent., and rents only 5 or 10 per cent.: how are we to get along?" They might reasonably have urged that they are paying a second rent by giving the labour of their children for nothing. And this injustice seems to prevail in parts of Scotland also, and where the Scotch settlers in Essex and other counties are struggling with difficulties.

And it is not confined to these instances. Mr Wilson

Fox remarks that rents are more reduced on large than on small farms, and this has led to the conclusion that small farms have suffered least, but this is really due to the heavy labour bill on the big farms; while one of his farmer witnesses is of opinion, "the 50 to 100 acre men have felt the depression least, because they and all their family work, and are not paid, their labour going to the landlord as rent."

Much of the inability of landlords to reduce rents to a level at which profits again become possible, or to provide the improvements and repairs on which profitable working must to some extent depend, is clearly due to the heavy charges on land, either in the form of mortgages, or under settlements for the benefit of members of the owner's family.

As there are no available records of mortgages and other charges, it is impossible to estimate with any exactness the amount of the existing encumbrances on agricultural land. But that they are exceedingly large is undoubted, and in some districts and on some estates absolutely crushing.

Sir Arthur Arnold, from his own experience and from the opinions of experienced solicitors in England, thinks that land is as heavily mortgaged in England as in Ireland, and that the total amount would be about £400,000,000. In his opinion, the existence of heavily encumbered estates, and their perpetuation through the system of settlement in a more or less paralysed condition, is eminently prejudicial to agriculture. Registration of title, and the accompanying record of all mortgages, would both facilitate borrowing money for improvements on easier terms, and "would very shortly lead to the extinction of insolvent landowners, and the easy transfer of land to persons well able to supply the capital for its cultivation."

The excessive pressure of encumbrances on many estates has been due to over-confidence of owners and solicitors in the future increase of values of land. In the times of high prices, rents were easily raised, without resistance by tenants, and the nominal capital value thereby enhanced. "Taking it for granted that rents would not fall, and that values would gradually rise, large sums were borrowed on the security of the high rentals. Mansions were enlarged or castles built, dowagers, wives, sons, and daughters were left annuitants, and all these payments formed deep and lasting drains upon the income of the landlord."[1] The margin which, if preserved, might in most cases have been ample to meet emergencies, was thus given away, and the net income, after paying mortgage interests and charges, became insufficient to admit of adequate reduction of rents, or of the full provision of essential improvements and works upon estates.

In this situation, it was not unnatural that most owners were tempted to regulate "the amount of a remission or reduction of rent more by the ability of the owner to give than by the right of the tenant to receive," and to absolutely forget that the balance of net income has nothing to do with the economic value of the land for letting purposes.

Again, both owner and mortgagee are interested in preventing permanent reductions in rent. The margin on which the selling value of the interests of either party rests would be diminished, and there is, therefore, the strongest inducement to keep up rents so far as possible.

In some cases where depression has cut deepest into values, as in Suffolk and Essex, the mortgagees would lose by foreclosing and selling under present circumstances, and there has been a disinclination to precipitate matters, and this may in some sense be helping to tide over, and even to reduce slightly the interest.

The extent to which the action even of liberally intentioned owners is paralysed by the fact that his mortgage interest and other charges remain a fixed quantity, while his gross receipts have been steadily lessening, is recognised as a serious hindrance to relief.

Mr Biddell says: "I do not think that he has been able to support the farmer out of his own pocket; he has had children to keep, and jointures to pay, and

[1] Pringle, Beds, Hunts, Northants, p. 58.

possibly he thought more of them than he did of the farmer."

Mr Kay gives the case of a farm let at 14s, which would be worth 25s if properly drained. But drainage is impossible; the estate is mortgaged to its full value, and is really bankrupt. "If I could borrow, or insist upon the landlord or the mortgagee borrowing, the £800 necessary to drain the land, on the low terms the Government could get the money, the land would be better worth the increased rent to me than it is worth what I now pay."

The effect of the growing proportion of mortgage interest to receipts in times of depreciating values is vividly described by Mr Everett, and "the grave imprudence of landowners in giving mortgages over a long period has taught them a severe lesson."

The accounts of an Essex estate of 643 acres strikingly illustrate the position of small owners.[1] Valued in 1881, on a rental of £1153, tenants paying tithe, at £20,700, the owner borrowed £9000, and has to meet the interest, £360. But his net rents now, less tithes, taxes, repairs, and management, are only £381 6s 6d. The balance received is only £21 6s 6d, and his four largest tenants had given notice.

In Lincolnshire "there are estates where little, if anything, goes into the owners' pockets. A reduction of 40 or 50 per cent. in gross rental means an alarming encroachment on private income, when all outgoings and also fixed charges and interest on mortgages have been paid. In some cases there are owners of land drawing nothing at all from their properties, and the mortgagees are taking what interest they can get, not daring to foreclose."[2]

The economic hopelessness of the position in many cases is illustrated by the inability of mortgagees to realise anything like the amount of the mortgage itself. Thus a farm bought for £22,000 in 1874, and mortgaged for £11,000, is valued at only £6796, not much more than half the mortgage. For a small farm, bought

[1] Pringle, Essex, App. B. 4, p. 54. [2] Wilson Fox, Lincoln, p. 47.

originally for £7803 and mortgaged for £5000, the highest bid at a sale was £3600.[1]

For a farm near Cambridge costing in 1874 £7700, mortgaged for £6000, the mortgagee would take £2000 now. Another farm bought for £10,000 in 1874, mortgaged for £8000, now offered for £3500.

Similar illustrations from Suffolk show even more astounding depreciation.

A farm bought in 1893 for £13,000, and saddled with three mortgages, was sold by the first mortgagees for £1800, a loss of 80 per cent., while the other mortgagees lost everything.

Another foreclosure sale shows a loss of 85 per cent. of the amount of the mortgage.

In such districts and on such estates there is complete paralysis, and no hope of reconstruction except by the land passing to new and stronger hands.

Mr Speir states how a North Ayrshire factor got over the difficulty in its less aggravated form. Heavy mortgages left no margin for indispensable new buildings, but the tenants were induced to build them by a deduction from the agreed rent sufficient to pay $7\frac{1}{2}$ per cent. on the outlay. " In this way the landlord succeeded in erecting new buildings without seriously trenching on his limited income, while the tenant received fair interest, and got his capital back by the end of the lease."

Suggestions are also made that annuities charged on estates should rise and fall with the letting value of the estates, and that there should be much greater freedom than that given under the Settled Land Act, 1882, to sell part of a property and use the proceeds in improving the rest of the estate.

Another suggestion of great practical importance bearing on this subject is that the life owner should be entitled to the absolute ownership of all improvements he makes on the estate. This is not only just in itself, but must be a strong inducement to many owners to

---

[1] Wilson Fox, Lincoln, App. B. 4, p. 154.

find money for improvements, who otherwise would have no margin with which to execute them.

This amendment of the law has also been recommended by a unanimous resolution of the Central Chamber of Agriculture. Its advantages are incidentally shown by the better position of tenants on Crown and corporate estates, where outlays may more readily be charged to capital instead of paid out of income.

It is urged that on heavily encumbered estates the tenants have no security, as to retaining the farms, or as to fair treatment. Till the passing of the Tenants Compensation Act in 1890, the claim of a tenant for improvements, or for tillages and crops, as against the landlord, lapsed if the mortgagee took possession, and thus stepped into the landlord's shoes. The Tenants Compensation Act transferred to the foreclosing mortgagee the landlord's liabilities to his tenants in these respects.

But on encumbered estates there is a double danger. The narrow margin tempts, or even compels, owner and agent to be unjust; and if the farm passes to the mortgagee, still less consideration is to be expected. In the latter case the sitting tenants have no chance. If they have improved their farms and kept them in high condition, the fullest competition value is exacted from them, or they are turned out to make a higher rent to be got from others. The usual history of heavily encumbered estates, whose values have been fictitiously written up by the lawyers as a basis for heavy charging of this created value, is rack-renting till the sitting tenant breaks or leaves, and then reletting at enormous reductions, when the land has inevitably gone down.

It must be recognised that even on estates whose encumbrances seemed moderate a few years back, the margin has probably in many cases become insufficient to meet in full and fair proportion the reasonable claims of tenants to a fair working rent and adequate equipment, and that on the most heavily burdened estates the position has, as we have shown, become quite hopeless. This state of affairs, where it exists, is rather an argument for prompt interference by the State to facilitate either the transfer of such estates to others who are more able to do justice to them, or to enable the owner to extricate himself from insolvency by loans on low terms for clearing off mortgages, than it is an answer to the claims of tenants to hold their land securely at a reasonable rent, which does not confiscate their improvements, or imperil their financial position. The tenant should be entitled to enjoy his land at a rent determined by the valuation of the holding as a food-producing concern, and not merely measured by the embarrassments and liabilities of his landlord, and has also a fair claim, as a tenant of an agricultural holding, to receive a reasonable minimum of essential equipment from the landlord, or, if he supplies it himself, to receive a fair compensation for doing so. When the owner is so involved that he can no longer either let his farms at their fair value, or give or pay for what is necessary, he is practically bankrupt, and his retention of his position is merely an obstacle to agricultural success. The sooner the situation is ended the better.

The breaking up of estates held by insolvent life-tenants under settlement would clearly be of the greatest benefit, not only to the tenants of the estates, who, in most such cases, would pass under new landlords with capital sufficient to work the estates well, and to make adequate reductions of rent, but also to the community at large. Where mortgages are heavy, it is obvious that the worst evils of the "absentee" system are operating perniciously to cripple agricultural enterprise by diverting tenants' capital from cultivation to the making up of interest out of proportion to existing values, and by withholding improvements which are absolutely essential to success.

It is the interest of all that such a state of things should be ended.

I agree with the recommendation made by the majority in the chapter on the sale of mortgaged land, but wish to add to that recommendation some further suggestions.

The restrictions on absolute ownership clearly intensify the mischief of insolvent and encumbered landlords. The abolition of entail and settlement as regards land, and the compulsory registration of title, with a clear and accessible record of every act and transaction as to the land, would remove many difficulties, would enable existing owners to sell their land to greater advantage, would increase their motive as well as power for selling, would stimulate the better distribution of land, and, in Sir Arthur Arnold's words, would tend to "bring the effective energy of a very large number of minds to deal with the land to increase its production."

This whole group of reforms would simplify the situation and enable estates now bound down by complicated interests, and in many cases paralysed by the prolonged and cumulative embarrassments of the nominal owner, to be extricated from their hopeless position, and promptly made available for the work of agriculture, and the benefit of the community.

I am also strongly of opinion that in any legislation affecting encumbered and bankrupt estates and facilitating their sale, it would be eminently desirable, now that a strong local authority in the shape of county councils exists, that provision should be made, giving to county councils a right of pre-emption on the sale of such estates, for any public purpose, and especially with the view of letting or reselling the agricultural land to those who will make the best use of it.

CHAPTER X.

The General Relations of Landlord and Tenant.

The general relations of landlord and tenant, as disclosed in this inquiry, form one of its pleasantest features. Even on the part of some of the sharpest critics among the farmer witnesses there has been a striking display of the good-will and consideration which seem to have been shown by the best type of farmer to his landlord all over the country.

And there has been evidence throughout the inquiry that the difficulties under which landlords labour, especially where their income is wholly agricultural, are frankly recognised, and a most generous interpretation put by tenants on the action taken by landlords both in making reductions of rent, and in endeavouring with a narrowed margin of income to keep up their properties.

The general feeling is probably expressed fairly enough in some passages of Mr Wilson Fox's report on Lancashire.

"Generally speaking, there has been a policy of give and take between landlord and tenants." "Landlords and tenants have both been hard hit, but we have met each other as far as we could."

The same tone of kindly sympathy with the landlords and readiness to accept even insufficient reductions was expressed by many witnesses.

But the accounts of some Lincolnshire farms which we have analysed demonstrate that this acquiescence and good-will on the part of the tenant, who has been bearing more than his fair share of the loss, is rather a matter of sentiment and of sympathy than of conviction that matters have really been equitably adjusted.

And, indeed, Mr Fox goes on to quote the opinion of Mr Calthorp, of Spalding, "whose experience and judgment," he says, "are so widely recognised." Mr Calthorp thinks :—" Notwithstanding the great reduction in rent, it will have to be still lower if the land is to be cultivated. In most cases here they would not have made a profit of late if no rent had been paid. Hence they have been living on capital. It is merely a question of time. My balance has never been on the right side in ten years farming my own land." [1]

And, in the face of the important evidence collected by Mr Fox as to the position of the Lincolnshire tenant farmers, it is quite out of the question to believe that they accept their rents as satisfactory.

"Many farmers have told me that they would give up to-morrow if they could see their way to get a reasonable amount of their capital back, but that they dare not leave at present prices and go out with their valuation worth half what it was when they entered, in addition to the loss of other capital."

"The present position of the large majority of farmers is very critical, there being in most cases no margin of capital left to meet a bad year or any abnormal losses. Here and there a large farmer has a private income independent of farming, or a celebrated flock of sheep or herd of cattle for which fancy prices can be obtained, etc., but the greater number of farmers, whose sole capital is invested in their land, are in the position I have described."

Besides the striking series of accounts, Mr Fox gives personal statements of responsible witnesses, such as the following :—

People who have kept their land up to the mark have done it out of capital. During the last ten years I have, on an average, paid £200 a year out of capital."

Mr Rew says of Norfolk : " Hundreds of men cannot break because they have not enough to break on. Their

[1] Lincoln, pp. 50, 51.

creditors let them go on in the hope of better times coming, and the landlords are afraid to stop them."[1]

In Suffolk, "more would quit if they dared, but are dipped too deep to move."

"Most farmers who have not had private means, or who have not had friends to help them, have gone. I am convinced that most of the labourers' wages have been paid out of capital."[2]

"The majority of the farmers have been drawing on capital for the last ten years. An average farmer cannot live on his farm at present prices and pay rent."

"I have farmed at a loss for the last thirteen years. It is not a question of rent at all. We could not make it pay anyhow."

"No land in the county of Suffolk to-day is worth any rental save the very best, situated near a town or railway."

Having regard to the large amount of similar evidence from the districts most affected by depression, it cannot be seriously maintained that tenant farmers in such districts are satisfied with their present rents.

The expressions of acquiescence which have been quoted are, it is obvious, mainly due to the desire of most of the farmers for a rise in prices which would enable the old conditions to be renewed, under which the margin was large enough to prevent any serious friction between the interests of owner and occupier, unless, indeed, the owner appropriated an unfair share of the returns in good times by greatly enhanced rents.

Further, an opinion crops up here and there in the reports, that the loss from low prices is so great that rent does not really matter. If farms were held rent free, many farmers say they would not be making anything. But this is obviously an argument advanced not against the reduction of rents, but for an artificial raising of prices. It is impossible to suppose that any tenant seriously wishes to go on paying rent out of capital till he becomes bankrupt, and the arguments occasionally

[1] Norfolk, p. 35.
[2] H. Biddell, quoted by Wilson Fox, Suffolk, p. 57.

advanced from this basis in the interests of landlords are transparently absurd.

Another consideration must not be forgotten. There has been, without doubt, a certain reluctance on the part of some to give evidence publicly, or to state openly what they were willing to state privately to Assistant Commissioners.

Thus Mr Speir, in referring to excellent meetings held in the south-western counties of Scotland, remarks, "While the public meetings in great part reflected the opinions expressed in private, they neither did so fully nor forcibly, because many subjects could be discussed in private which it would have been injudicious to mention in public, and many gentlemen who spoke on the subjects under inquiry without reserve while in private, did not for various reasons wish to appear in public debate."[1]

Mr Pringle also states, "I think the farmers speak more freely in private than in public;" and with regard to the worst instances of the unfair treatment of sitting tenants, statements were made to him confidentially which would not have been given at a public meeting.

In view of the evidence as to the payment of rents out of capital in the depressed districts, the actual figures of existing rents are significant.

Thus, in Suffolk, in the Blything Union, the average of rent over the 92,316 acres is 14s 8d. In the Plomesgate Union only 13·4 per cent. of the land is let at or under 10s an acre. In the Sudbury Union 24 per cent. is assessed as worth 10s an acre, tithe free. On seven large well-known estates, the existing rents are 13s 6d, 12s, 15s 11½d, 16s 6d, 13s, 14s 3d, 12s 7d. On other estates, farms up to 100 acres are not quoted below 17s 6d, and farms from 100 to 400 acres range from 8s 2d to 21s.

In Lincolnshire, on twelve important estates, rents for farms from 100 to 400 acres are quoted by Mr Fox, 10s to 28s, 22s 8d, about 15s, 25s to 26s, 18s 9d, 16s 9d, 18s 3d, 21s 5d, 25s 6d, 23s 6d, and 25s for fen farms

[1] Ayrshire, etc., p. 3.

where the landlord pays a drainage rate of 8s. Farms up to 100 acres are generally from 10 to 30 per cent. higher.

In Beds, Hunts, and Northants, Mr Pringle quotes existing rents as follows: Fine feeding land, 30s to 55s; inferior pasture, 5s to 20s; best fen land, 25s to 35s; best barley and turnip land, 20s to 30s; first-class clay loams, 22s to 27s; best class stiff clay, still well-farmed, 10s to 20s: second-class lands of all kinds from 9s or 10s to 16s and 20s, and only the very worst clays at 2s 6d to 10s. Similar figures could be quoted for other districts. But these suffice to show that, even with a very liberal allowance for additional remissions in exceptional seasons like 1893 and 1894, it is wholly impossible that the majority of farmers are at present on anything like equal terms with landowners as regards a fair distribution of the economic loss. Having regard to the evidence as to payment of rents out of capital, and to the extraordinary figures disclosed in the farming accounts, it is substantially established that on many estates, even where considerable reductions have been made, the owners are still receiving an income which their land is not producing, while the tenants are really subscribing out of their capital to keep the estate and its owner going.

A general review of this class of evidence should convince any impartial mind that, next to low prices, excessive rents have been the chief and most effective cause of agricultural decay, and are still the most effective check on agricultural recovery. Although the true economic meaning of rent is fully recognised by the ablest and most far-seeing landowners, and put in practice to some extent on their estates, in general the competition value has been taken, or, still worse, values which have long since become economically impossible have gone on being exacted, partly as a matter of habit, partly because tenants were not in a position to give notice, and either get a fair reduction or escape. The degree to which the mischief has proceeded has largely been in proportion to the nature of the soil. Where the soil could be worked cheaply, matters have gone less badly and held together better. But wherever the soil has presented serious difficulties, the course of events has presented the same features. There have been sweeping changes of tenancies. The few instances where the old tenants have remained are where they have been men of means of their own, and not dependent merely on their farming capital. But, in general, the old tenants on the bad soils have been drained of their capital, and have disappeared. In some cases the landlords have relet at once, at heavy reductions, long withheld from the old tenants; in other cases, they have had to painfully ascertain by their own experience in farming the land themselves, the amount of the losses they had been imposing on their old tenants for years past, and have at last let the farms to new tenants at heavy reductions, generally even then insufficient to give any real security to the new comers.

It cannot be seriously doubted that, under the existing system, many thousands of conscientious, intelligent farmers have been used up and swept away, because the full force of the economic pressure has been thrown upon their resources, which were admittedly only sufficient for the actual working of the soil. It is equally clear, from our inquiry, that at the present moment, in every district of the country there are still many men who have done well by the land, who are being gradually deprived of their capital and brought to ruin. Mr Pringle gives a description of this class of men which we believe will hold good of many counties in Great Britain.

"There are any number of farms still well managed, and producing as much as can be secured by liberal farming, where for years there has been a steady loss on each year's transactions. This has been possible simply because private capital and the savings of the good times are being burned up in this unquenched fire. 'A relation of mine,' says one of these men, 'has lost £20,000 on 1000 acres during the last fourteen years. The only upper class farmers who have survived are those who, like myself, are independent of their farms.'"[1]

I wish to press, with all the force the accumulated facts of this inquiry supply, the contention that the history of the past depression, and the present position of the working farmers upon the land, calls for urgent and immediate action of Parliament.

I am also profoundly convinced that, if the present opportunity is not seized to give by legislation fuller protection to the capital invested by tenants in cultivating and improving the land, and to establish sound business relations between landlord and tenant, and a workable machinery for guarding and vindicating those relations, a large proportion of the present occupiers will probably be brought to ruin before the rents are readjusted to prevent this result. Further, if prices improve, and confidence revives, it is plain that the full benefit of this improvement will rapidly be transferred to the landowners, and that, on the probable recurrence of bad seasons and low prices, the tenant farmers of that time will again be exposed to the same exhaustion of their profits and their capital. The features of these depressions, and the necessarily disproportionate losses imposed on the occupiers, at the time things go wrong, are now so clearly established, that it would be not only unjust to existing tenant farmers to postpone legislation any longer, but in the highest degree inimical to the future interests of agriculture.

[1] Beds, etc., p. 55.

CHAPTER XI.

THE AGRICULTURAL HOLDINGS ACT (1883).

THE only serious attempt to check some of the evils resulting from the existing system of tenure, and to give a certain amount of security to the position of tenant farmers in investing their money in the soil, has been the Act of 1883.

The Act of 1875 may be dismissed from consideration. At best it was a mere record of some of the existing customs, and it was at once made null and void by the contracting out clause, of which landlords promptly availed themselves.

The working of the Act of 1883 has been very generally condemned by witnesses of all classes, the substance of whose evidence is summarised in the following paragraphs.

The principle of the Act was that an outgoing tenant should be entitled to recover from the landlord, as compensation for any improvements legally made by him on his holding, the full value that the improvements would represent as a benefit or aid to an incoming tenant in entering on the holding.

With regard to the more permanent improvements, such as buildings, roads, bridges, and important alterations in the character of the holding, the consent of the owners is required, but this limitation does not alter the principle of the Act, which is to secure to the tenant a property right in the full value of his improvements.

This principle is obviously sound and just to all parties. In the first place, it treats compensation as a debt to be paid to the outgoing tenant by the landlord, and not by the incoming tenant; in the second place, it secures to the outgoing tenant the full market value of the improvement; and, in the third place, it sets no time limit whatever on the duration of an improvement, but gives the outgoing tenant an absolute right to get the full remaining unexhausted value of any improvement, however long the period since it was carried out, if any remaining value can be shown to exist. It in effect created by statute a property for the tenant in the whole added value his outlay or labour, so far as such outlay was in accordance with the Act, may have contributed to the holding.

The chief defects of the Act were that it provided no machinery to work out this principle effectively and equitably, and that it limited the application of the principle of the Act—the securing of the ownership by the tenant of his own improvements—to one class of tenants only, those who are leaving their farms.

The result of the first of these defects has been that in the working of the Act, the existing class of valuers have nearly everywhere in practice set aside its principle, and instead of estimating compensation for the whole of the improvements executed on a farm at whatever date, if any remaining value of such improvements can be shown, they have substituted for the principle of the Act time scales of exhaustion for fertilisers and feeding stuffs and other improvements, and have rigorously limited compensation to the expenditure of the tenant in the last two or three, or in the case of some manures, four to six or seven years. Further, they have in general paid no attention whatever to the manner in which such improvements have been carried out, and have simply applied a rule-of-thumb calculation to the actual bills for cake and manure, without considering the quality of the farming.

Of many evil consequences of this perversion of the principle of the Act, that most frequently and most cogently insisted upon by witnesses is, that the working of the Act has put the bad farmer on a safer footing than the good farmer. It has been established by the evidence that by the working of the Act in practice bad farming is encouraged, as the worst type of farmer may exhaust the fertility of his farm for years, and still obtain compensation by expenditure in the last years of his tenancy; and good farming is discouraged, because the best farmer enriches his land to the utmost in the first years of his occupation, and requires less outlay afterwards to maintain the fertility, but only receives a small proportion back of the outlay of the last year or two, while the previous outlay is in practice ignored. The bad farmer gets more for half spoiling his farm than the good farmer has a chance of getting for a long continued and ample expenditure in generous treatment of the soil, which, wisely done, increases for many years after the productive powers of the farm.

Mr Scott says: "The mere fact of a man spending some money at the end of his time does not of necessity do the land any good. The man who has farmed well all through under the Act gets no more than the man who has farmed badly and puts manure on at the end. The Agricultural Holdings Act is an Act for rogues."[1]

In the second place, the intention of the Act has been to a great extent defeated, at any rate in England, and the debt of the landlord to the outgoing tenant has been transferred to the incoming tenant. The Act contemplated a settlement between the two former parties, and this seems to have been carried out in Scotland, but the practice, in England, under the customs of most counties, of the incoming tenant paying for tillages, and in some cases crops, has been either kept up as regards improvements, or extended to them after the passing of the Act. This may inflict injustice on both outgoing and incoming tenants. A Wiltshire farmer says: "The outgoing tenant should have to do with the landlord and should not be handed over to the incoming tenant. This is a very convenient way of getting out of landlords' responsibilities." Cases are given where landlords have sold farms and handed their tenants over to the new

[1] Wilson Fox, Glendale, p. 21.

owners, who promptly repudiated the debts which should have been paid by the old owners.[1]

On the other hand, if the new rent represents the full market value of the farm, and thus includes the remaining value of the improvements, as is probable, it is clear that the incoming tenant is paying twice over for the improvements. Such a diminution of his capital must be prejudicial to agriculture, as well as inherently unjust.

Thus the intention of the Act to secure to the tenant a full property in the value of his improvements has been defeated, both for outgoing and incoming tenants, by the blunder of leaving an important reform in the hands of valuers of the old type, who were habituated to the working of the old system which the Act was meant to supersede. The proper course would obviously have been to create a new machinery adapted to carry out, instead of leaving the new principle to be perverted and evaded.

The much more serious defect of the Act of 1883 was that it limited the principle of property in improvements to tenants who were quitting their holdings, and made no provision for giving a similar security to tenants remaining in their holdings.

Sir James Caird protested in 1883, when the Bill was brought out, against this limitation, the effect of which was that Parliament was legislating not for the best but for the less deserving tenants.[2] The evidence brought before us certainly shows that the forecast of Sir James Caird, of the results of excluding the cases that ought to have been provided for, has been verified.

Sir James Caird urged against the Bill of 1883 that it did not protect just the men you really want to protect, and did not do what it was intended to do, and continued: "unless the interests of the sitting tenants, who are the real backbone of British agriculture, are equally recognised and dealt with, the Bill will fail to give that security which would promote good farming and justify legislative interference with contracts."

[1] Rew, Salisbury Plain, pp. 21, 22.
[2] Letter to the "Times," April 4, 1883.

The theory of the framers of the Act of 1883 was that it was sufficient protection in practice to give a tenant the right to full compensation on quitting, and that the possession of that right and power of exercising it would enable him to enter into a bargain with the owner on an equal footing, when the rent and other conditions of tenancy had to be settled between the two parties on the renewal of a contract of tenancy.

The evidence of practical farmers given before us, and the general complaints on this point in the sub-commissioners' reports, show that this result was not obtained, that the sitting tenant has not in general been able to make as good terms for himself as a new tenant, and that the full force of competition has been concentrated on the best farms where presumably there has been the heaviest outlay in tenant's improvements, and that, in consequence, the sitting tenant, instead of being able to retain for himself the value of his improvements, has had to acquiesce in its constant appropriation by the landlord.[1]

Before examining in detail the evidence as to the results of these two leading defects of the Act, and the evidence as to specific complaints as to many other defects in the Act, and its working, it will be convenient to state to what extent, and in what way the Act has been operative.

One effect of the Act has been the introduction of clauses in agreements securing beforehand some compensation for improvements not previously protected. By section 5 of the Act, agreements of this nature are treated as a substituted form of compensation, and are admissible if " fair and reasonable."

Very grave exception is taken by some Scotch and English witnesses to this system. The landlord is the stronger party in bargaining, and will impose his own terms. It is also urged that such an agreement involves the rigid application of time scales of exhaustion, and so tends to prevent the tenant from getting a fair compensation for long continued good farming.

" There should be no contracting out ; neither landlord

[1] See pp. 102-9.

nor tenant can foresee improvements that could be made in the course of nineteen years, and the result of agreements would be to limit the improvements; the tenant would not put his money into improvements that he was not to be compensated for."

Mr Lander's objection is rather that a time scale should be put in express terms into the Act, on the same method as in the Act of 1875, instead of leaving the scale to be settled under pressure of private bargaining. Mr Kay takes the same view, but it is not generally held.

Other witnesses strongly approve of the principle of arranging compensation beforehand by agreement, on the ground that they thus avoid the uncertainties of arbitration under the Act.

In any case, it would seem expedient to remove the uncertainty that exists as to the provisions of Clause 5, and to state definitely, in any amended Act, that the question of whether compensation under an agreement is "fair and reasonable" shall be determined in the same way as any other differences between landlord and tenant under the Act, and that an agreement fixing a time scale of exhaustion of specified improvements shall not bar general compensation for the high condition resulting from long continued good farming.

In its direct application, the evidence shows that in many, if not in most districts, the Act is practically inoperative.

"In Norfolk, not one per cent. of the tenancies changing hands come under the operation of the Act." This is the more remarkable as there is no local custom as regards tenant-right, "that is the reason why we want it most, and we get it least."[1] "In Lincolnshire, there are very few estates under the Act. The custom of the country is considered quite as good as the Act."[2]

In Suffolk "we treat the Act with contempt, none of us ever once think about it. The custom of the country gives us all we could get from the Act without the bother."

The Lincolnshire custom is preferred from the ease

[1] C. S. Read, 16,142.   [2] Lincoln, p. 25.

and certainty of the procedure, and the comparative liberality of the scales of compensation adopted, the general type of which is fully given by Mr Wilson Fox.

Mr Epton, on the other hand, thinks the Act is being more used in Lincolnshire. The Act is not utilised in Sir Massey Lopes' district of Devonshire; it is treated as a dead letter in the Andover district. From South Wilts a valuer of experience says the Act is "unworkable, but did considerable good by forcing bad landlords to give tenant-right." "The Act is everywhere described as a complete failure. The general opinion is that it falls far short of its intentions and pretensions." The Milborne St Andrew's Farmers' Club in Dorset states "the Act is quite a dead letter, tenants recognising it only as a means of being fleeced." In Berkshire "farmers generally seem afraid of it." In North Devon there seems more disposition to use the Act.

Mr H. H. Scott takes a more favourable view of its working. "The depression would have been accentuated had it not been for the Act; and is of opinion that an outgoing tenant keeps his farm in better condition owing to the Act." And, in Huntingdonshire, Mr Looker, an agent, says the Act is repeatedly called into operation.

Mr Middleton considers the Act has been to some extent a failure, more in the carrying out of it than the Act itself.

Mr Carrington Smith considers the Act is practically inoperative.

In Lancashire the Act has been but "little put in force, and in recent years has ceased to be acted upon."

From Scotland we have various comments.

"The Act has been a benefit, and the recognition of a good principle, but farmers are beginning to be afraid of it."

"It is too expensive and cumbrous in its working."

"The Act is a dead letter in Forfar; too much formality and expense."

The Act is disliked by landlords, and the position of the tenant under lease who wishes a reduction of rent, Mr Speir states, is made use of frequently by landlords to contract themselves out of the Act, the tenant agreeing to forego his claim under the Act on receiving an abatement in his rent.

Mr Hope says: "When the present Act was passed, it was regarded as a great boon to British agriculturists. The principle of the Act is admitted to be sound, but it is universally felt that the Act has conspicuously failed to secure the main ends for which it was intended."

Mr Stuart:—"The Agricultural Holdings Act should be improved out of existence. Its principle and intention seem fairly good, but it utterly fails to secure tenants' improvements."

And the main portion of the able evidence given by Scotch witnesses at the sittings in Edinburgh was directed to urgently demanded amendments of the Act. It is obviously in much wider operation in Scotland than in England, and a much closer attention has been given to the subject.

Mr Hope represents the general opinion that "the thorough amendment of the Agricultural Holdings Act, as the only certain means of giving tenant farmers the fullest encouragement to invest their capital in developing to the utmost the resources of their holdings, is by far and away the most important measure that can be passed by Parliament in the interests of agriculture."

The procedure of the Act is very generally condemned as costly, cumbrous, and uncertain. "The expenses of working the Act are far too great."[1] Mr Riddell's important compensation case cost him £200, though he was not charged a penny by his own witnesses, the award being £1063.

Thus witnesses say: "We want some easier and cheaper way of obtaining compensation for improvements."

"Tenants are afraid of litigation; what is wanted is a simpler form of settlement."

"Lawyers are called in, and a great many witnesses

[1] Davidson, 51,157; Wilson Fox, Garstang, pp. 19, 21; Gilchrist, 53,038. Olver, 37,570-1.

examined, who might be dispensed with," the remedy would be a " single arbitrator appointed at once."

"The expenses are excessive, especially where you come in contact with the antiquated forms of agreement."

"Both landlords and tenants prefer not to conclude tenancies under the Act, because of the fearful amount of legal uncertainty."

"It has been found both dilatory and expensive, and has spread dismay amongst the farmers as regards the Act."

"The expenses include cost and entertainment of witnesses and of referees; a valuer away from home two or three days requires from twenty to twenty-five guineas."

"I never saw a man make anything out of a claim under the Act; he might win the day, but he was in reality a loser."

"The expense is extreme—there is no end to the witnesses."

The Act does no good except to the arbitrators; "if you get them sitting, you cannot get them up again. If you make a claim, the landlord will make a counterclaim, and then they go to arbitration, and so waste all the money."

"The procedure is costly and risky."

Mr Speir says that the procedure must be made much simpler, and you must have an official valuator.

"The real difficulty is that the landlord's counterclaims are generally excessive, and lead to a lot of expense."

Mr Kay states that in a "friendly arbitration" "he was awarded, as tenant, £125, while the landlord's counterclaim was cut down to £30, but each side had to pay £30, besides all the private witnesses' expenses, and this for only two days' work."

Mr Davidson refers to a case in Scotland where an award of £200 cost £150 in the expenses incident to the arbitration. He adds: "as a general rule the arbiter's fees are a comparatively small proportion of the whole expenses in those cases where there has been complaint as to the great amount of expense."

The dread of extravagant counterclaims has, it is proved, deterred tenants from claiming under the Act.

The landlord has not only two months to think out his general claims for deterioration, but has a fortnight to consider his counterclaim after he has seen the tenant's claim in its details.

"It follows," says Mr Stratton, "that the person who sees his opponent's cards before playing his own is sure of winning the game."

"The counterclaim is always regulated by the amount of the tenant's claim."

"The tenant has almost always been swamped by a counterclaim, which always exceeds the tenant's claim."

Mr C. S. Read says that a claim under the Act is treated "like a declaration of war." "Instead of its being accepted as a matter of course, land agents hunt up every possible dilapidation and default on the part of the tenant. I have seen one claim on a small farm of no less than ninety-six different dilapidations brought against the tenant."

"I am quite convinced that the way in which counterclaims from landlords have been admitted has so frightened the tenants that they, you might say, bounce the tenants out of their claims altogether. No sooner does a tenant make a claim, than the counterclaim of the landlord is put in considerably above the amount claimed."

Counterclaims "have no limit according to the interpretation put upon the Act by the valuers of Norfolk." While the tenants' claims are backed with vouchers and receipts, the counterclaims are largely speculative.

The tenant's claim is therefore necessarily limited, while the counterclaim is unlimited. And we have had to note that while there has been little evidence to the effect that tenants' claims are often exaggerated, the evidence is almost unanimous that the counterclaims are generally enormously in excess of what an impartial arbitrator is likely to allow.

Mr Davidson refers to a case where the counterclaim of a landlord amounted to £1200. "I ventured to suggest £25 as a proper sum, and I think £30 was the award."

In another Scotch case, the claim of the tenant was £60, and the landlord lodged a counterclaim for £120. Mr Dickie, as arbitrator, "looked upon that £120 claim as an attempt pretty much to block the tenant's claim," and only awarded the landlord £2 2s. Some of the items were far-fetched, and some quite fictitious.

A valuer, with one of the largest practices in Hampshire, states that he never knew but one instance in that county in which, a claim having been made under the Act, it was not met by a counterclaim considerably greater.

Mr Adams says that not one farmer in twenty dare make a claim because he knows a counterclaim will be lodged, whether fair or not. While there is much evidence to the effect that when the reference is completed, the counterclaims are usually cut down to a moderate limit, there can be no doubt that the dread of these altogether disproportionate demands on the part of the landlord has had a most serious effect in deterring tenants from making use of the Act.

Similar results are attributed to the restrictive covenants, generally coupled with penal rents for their breach, which are still found in most agreements to let agricultural land.

Some of these documents, especially in Scotland, are stated by Mr Speir and other witnesses to be expressly designed "to break the Agricultural Holdings Act, and make its working null and void." There are special manuals instructing factors how to frame clauses for leases which set aside various provisions of the Act. These covenants are illegal, but tenants are compelled by the keen competition to sign anything to get a farm.

A number of such covenants are quoted. One of these ousts compensation for manures by a stipulation for the application of 70 cubic yards of farmyard manure per acre (whereas 30 would be a large amount) and limiting compensation to any excess over that impossible quantity. "Such clauses strangle agriculture."[1]

Another covenant excludes the time limit to four years for "waste" in estimating counterclaims.

Mr Speir says that during his inquiry he "had a great pile of leases sent in, most of which contained objectionable clauses" of this nature, with the obvious intention of nullifying the Act, by enabling the landlord to raise counterclaims.

Covenants are quoted setting aside (1) the right to apply artificial manures at all without consent; (2) the right to remove fixtures; (3) the right of the incoming tenant to compensation at the end of his lease; (4) the right of the tenant to execute or compel his landlord to execute drainage; (5) "no counterclaim in respect of deterioration or breach of covenant shall be barred in respect of such breach of covenant, or deterioration occurred more than four years before the determination of the tenancy." And these are not merely in old leases, but have been recently and are still being signed under pressure.

Mr Guild states that penal rents or clauses work very unfairly, and often defeat just claims. Leases should be put on the same footing as other contracts, viz., actual damage. "The penal clauses are always enforced where we have a claim to meet under the Agricultural Holdings Act, not otherwise."

The frequency of covenants and agreements which oust the operation of the Act creates obviously a strong feeling in some witnesses even against agreements for substituted compensation, the only form of agreement in lieu of the Act contemplated by the Act. The landlord uses competition and pressure on the tenant to contract himself out of the Act.

Again, in the hard times, landlords have in "many cases" made reductions during a lease only on the

[1] Speir, Ayrshire, p. 32, App. XI; 46,845; 46,922-3.

express condition that tenants should forego compensation for improvements at the end of the lease.[1]

Such a condition would possibly be held to be illegal, but in any case, it is transparently unjust that, in an ordinary lease which is not drawn up as an "improving lease," a tenant should thus be compelled to pay himself for the reduction made indispensable by the fall in prices.

Technical breaches of such covenants, whether legal or illegal, are used as a pretext to increase counter-claims, or to hold over the tenant the dread of large and indefinite liabilities. Mr Davidson has given two or three decisions to the effect that a rent receipt, handed to the tenant subsequent to any such alleged breach of covenant, should be held to bar claims for damages. But it is doubtful whether such a decision would be supported in the English courts.

It is complained in Essex that landlords and agents make no objection to breaches until the moment for a claim for improvements arrives, when they base their counterclaim upon what they tacitly acquiesced in. It is urged that in such cases the right to include such items should be held to have been abandoned. The penalties attached in covenants to cross cropping (ranging from £10 to £50 an acre for ploughing up pasture, and from £5 to £20 an acre for repeating a corn crop oftener than once in four years, from £5 to £10 for lopping trees, etc.), would entirely annihilate any claim for improvements, and farmers are frightened out of claiming, even when the landlord has suffered no damage.

English valuers differ on this point. Two leading Suffolk valuers hold, the one, that a landlord who has knowingly let things go, can claim nothing, the other, that the claim is good unless the breach of covenant has been formally condoned.

In Lincolnshire, some valuers take Mr Davidson's view, and hold that under a yearly tenancy dilapidations should not be allowed for more than one year. The

[1] Ballingall, 54,183-6 ; Speir, Ayrshire, p. 10; 46,914.

Lincolnshire Chamber of Agriculture stated that "after a receipt for rent, there should be no further claim." But this was contested by leading land agents.

At Devizes, Mr Spencer found opinion was that restrictive clauses were generally inoperative till a tenancy was being determined, when they were put in force.

A Kentish hop grower, quoted by Dr Fream, says of these restrictive and penalising agreements, "the tenant signs the agreement and trusts to Providence the landlord will not enforce it."

"Many of the farmers whom I visited," says Mr Pringle, "were absolutely ignorant of the conditions of the agreement which they had signed on entry. More than one had not gone the length of reading the document."

The evidence is uniform that, in practice, the full amount of penal rents for breach of covenant cannot be recovered, but are almost invariably cut down to the amount of actual damage proved.

The use of the power to apportion costs adversely to the party whose claims are least reasonable probably has had some effect in lessening the evil of excessive counter-claims.

Further, it has been decided in the case of Holmes and Formby, that the claim of the landlord under the Act can only be taken into account by way of reduction of the claim of the tenant, and even if, as in that case, the sum awarded to the landlord under the reference exceeded the sum awarded to the tenant, the umpire has no power to award this overplus to the landlord, and the county court has no power to enforce such an award.[2]

While these considerations operate to restrict the resulting mischief to some extent, it is plain that there is a far too widespread survival of covenants, in leases and agreements, which are wholly inconsistent with modern requirements and with modern law. This survival is, to a large extent, obviously part of a policy of retaining a maximum of power over tenants, so that if any dispute arises the dread of the results of a breach

[1] Wilson Fox, Lincoln, p. 27.   [2] Rew, Norfolk, p. 51.

of one of these covenants may bring the tenant to submission, whether as regards rent, or game preserving, or any condition of tenancy. An essential part of this policy has been to put obstacles in the way of the Agricultural Holdings Act, and to limit the possible compensation obtainable under it.

Such a policy clearly is prejudicial to the full development of agriculture, and any amending Act, to be of value, must remove, or lessen as far as possible, these opportunities for putting unfair pressure on tenants.

It is universally recognised by tenant farmer witnesses as well as by others, that adequate protection must be given to the landlord's as well as the tenant's interests, and that what should be arrived at is to place the two parties on a fair and equal footing.

The remedies suggested are several:

(1.) That notices of claim, for improvement by the tenant, and for deterioration by the landlord, should be put in on the same day, so that neither side should see the claim of the other.

(2.) That the heads under which the landlord can claim for deterioration should be specifically scheduled in the same way as the tenant's claims for improvements.

(3.) That the present limitation of "waste" in the Act to the last four years of the tenancy should be further restricted to the last two years.

(4.) That, at the beginning of every future contract of tenancy, a record should be made of the condition of the farm, the state of the buildings, fences, roads, and the cultivation of the several parts of the holding.

There is a strong consensus of opinion as to the first suggestion, which has long been advocated by the Central Chamber of Agriculture, and is now recommended by its committee. The suggestion is that notices should be given simultaneously by both sides.

It is hoped that the removal of the opportunity of capping the tenant's claim by a long list of dilapidations deliberately concocted in order to exceed the tenant's claim for improvements, and so to deter him from proceeding further, will have the result of compelling landlords and agents to put in practical demands on their merits. This hope is almost universally expressed by the tenants examined.

The date at which the simultaneous notices should be sent in, suggested by the Central Chamber of Agriculture and by a majority of witnesses, is twenty-eight days before the determination of the tenancy. Many witnesses, however, would prefer other dates. Thus Mr H. H. Scott prefers a date at or about the time of quitting, or within a month after quitting. Several witnesses assent to a date after quitting. One Scotch witness suggests, in reference to the Scotch Act, that the date of notice should be not as now four months, but six months before quitting, while other Scotch witnesses suggest that claims on either side should be submitted within three months after the determination of the tenancy. In his report on Roxburgh and other counties, Mr Hope says: "If both claims are put into neutral hands on the same day, it is thought that there would be less tendency to rake up vexatious counterclaims." But the compromise of one month before quitting has most support, one obvious reason being that the tenant still has time before quitting to make good a number of dilapidations as to buildings, fences, ditches, drains, etc., for which the landlord may have claimed.

As to the frequent difficulty of different portions of the holding being given up at different periods, it is suggested that the date for notices should either be twenty-eight days before the last portion of the holding is given up, or that separate notices should be given twenty-eight days before each portion is given up.

The Committee of the Central Chamber also recommend that "the landlord shall have power, within fourteen days after the determination of the tenancy, to amend his claim in respect of dilapidations to buildings occurring after the notice of claim has been delivered.[1]"

[1] Vol. III, App. VIII.

While approving of the general recommendation as to simultaneous notice, we may perhaps think that such a proviso would tend to nullify its object, and would lead to disputes and litigation by a revival of the counter-claim mischief in a more restricted form. It is probable that fair, prompt, and amicable settlements will be best arrived at by basing the landlord's claim on an inspection of the farm and buildings prior to the date of notice; and that the re-opening of claims on either side after that date is unnecessary and prejudicial.[1]

Further it would be shorter, simpler, and less likely to lead to litigation if the items of the claims and counterclaims were sent in in the first instance instead of after a preliminary notice.

It is also suggested by the Central Chamber that landlord and tenant would be placed on an equal footing, and counterclaims would be more likely to be strictly limited to the facts, if there was a schedule of dilapidations for landlords, in the same way that there is now a schedule for improvements for tenants.[2] Mr Druce, who thinks the schedules unnecessary, holds that, if there are to be schedules, there should be one for the landlord's claim as well as for the tenant's.[3]

Mr Read is strongly in favour of this proposal, but apparently his chief reason is that the landlord has, in his common law right, a second string to his bow. This common law right cannot be got rid of, and I am disposed to think the suggestion of the landlord's schedule is of little practical value, and that conceivably it might even lead to an ingenious expansion of landlords' claims instead of limiting them. The mere setting forth in an Act of such a schedule as that recommended by the Committee of the Central Chamber might be held to justify claims for specific deteriorations, which were largely due to unfavourable seasons like the wet season of 1879, or the drought of 1893, and for which tenants could not fairly be made accountable. Further, so long as rents are not brought into a reasonable proportion to the value of the produce obtained from the holding

[1] Rew, Wilts, p. 20.   [2] Vol. II. App. VII.   [3] 20,035.

and to farming expenses, I am strongly of opinion that money is now being paid in rents which, under other circumstances, would have been applied in keeping up the farm, and that, in practice, this is recognised on a large number of estates at the present time, on which it is in evidence that repairs, for which tenants are liable by their agreements, are now being carried out by the landlords.

Again, what the tenant claims for are specific acts of improvement, while much of the matters raised in the suggested schedule for landlord's claims are matters which may or may not have resulted, not from acts committed by the tenant, but from omissions on the part of the tenant.

What seems most conclusive of all against this proposal is that the schedules in the case of the tenant are only rendered necessary because improvements must be classified. If tenants were perfectly free to make any improvement of their own motion and get compensation, there would of course be no schedules. But this reason does not hold of the landlord's position.

The third suggestion, that the present limitation (in section 6 of the Act) of the landlord's claim for waste to the last four years of the tenancy should be further restricted to the last two years, is generally supported in the evidence.

While not endorsing all the considerations already adverted to on this point, or adopting the suggestion that a receipt for rent should be held to wipe off possible claims for waste, we may well hold that good farming will be promoted if landlords give timely notice to tenants as to any act or omission which is likely to deteriorate the holding, that the failure to so give notice ought to be held in general to bar the landlord's claim on the matter in question, that in any case two years is a fair period to fix, and that any damage caused before ought to have been dealt with by the owner at the time.

Several witnesses who are in favour of doing away with time scales for tenant's improvements, and wish to secure for the tenants a right, unlimited in time, to the unexhausted value of their improvements, have stated that in their view it is necessary to apply the same principle to landlords, and on the one hand to give compensation for increased fertility, and on the other for decreased fertility, without any time limit whatever. These witnesses cannot have considered the essential difference in the position of the two parties. The tenant is debarred from obtaining any form of compensation for his acts of improvement at any time during the course of the tenancy. Under the present law he can recover nothing, unless he actually quits the holding. Even if the proposals as to the compensation of the sitting tenant, recommended later in this chapter, were adopted, compensation could only be obtained at the determination of the tenancy, in the event of the terms of the tenancy being modified. The position of the landlord is wholly different. He can at any time, under the powers of the common law, take action against the tenant for deliberate acts of "waste," or for damage caused by the breach of any covenant. He has only himself or his agent to blame if he has not also, under the specific covenants of the lease or agreement, protected himself from "permissive waste" on the part of the tenant. It is more to the interest of all concerned, that matters of this kind should be dealt with as they arise, and that large and indefinite liabilities for an unlimited time should not be kept hanging over the heads of tenants.

Few suggestions made to us have been so strongly supported as the proposal that the exact condition of a farm, at the beginning of a tenancy, the state of the buildings, roads, fences, drains, and other equipment, and the cropping, and quality of cultivation of the several fields, should be recorded in a scheduled form, which can be referred to as evidence at any future period, as to whether the holding has been improved or deteriorated.

Such a scheduled record or inventory is held to be the best practical starting point, and that, even if the original surveyor or valuer dies, or is unable to report at the determination of the tenancy, it would approximately meet the real difficulty.

Mr Read suggests that the valuers at the entry should state whether the land was foul or clean, in a high state of cultivation or impoverished. Such a record would protect the landlord as well as the tenant. Mr Rowlandson thinks the cost of such a survey and record would only amount to about ten guineas for a 400 acre farm, and that it would be money well spent.

To facilitate the adoption of this system, the Committee of the Central Chamber recommend that every award should include a record of the condition, and when there is no award, it might be made an essential part of every agreement. Mr Parton suggests that the record should be retained by some Government official, and would extend the principle to the recording of any first-class improvements effected by the tenant with the landlord's consent.

Some of the witnesses are clearly of opinion that such a record could be made to act as a real measure of the improvement or deterioration afterwards. Thus, Mr Lander, Mr Reynolds, and others say, that on quitting, the tenant should either receive from the landlord, or pay to the landlord, the money value of improved, or deteriorated condition.

Mr Olver thinks this system would create a sense of security and confidence, and promote good farming.

Mr Pringle says that in the South Midlands, "the scheduling system" is universally accepted both by landlords and tenants, and that it is also wished that "at any time during the currency of a lease or tenancy it should be in the power of either party to have an intermediate report drawn up by the district arbitrator." He adds :—" By this system two very necessary and important points would be gained. (1.) If a landlord proposed to raise the rent on a holding increased in letting value by the improvements and exertions of the tenant, the tenant could, by having the holding rescheduled, prove to the landlord that before an increase of rent could be obtained, it would be necessary for him to pay as compensation the capital sum upon which the increase of rent would be the interest. .... (2.) It would enable the landlord to put a stop to spoliation and deterioration. A second report may be obtained as soon as improper farming is observed, and the landlord will thus get rid of a bad tenant, and get his compensation for deterioration, as decided by the first and last schedules, before the tenant has lost everything."

In Scotland, Mr Hope reports a general desire for the protection both of landlord and tenant, to preserve evidence as to the condition of the farm at entry. The farm should be inspected by the official valuator and his report deposited for reference. In this way compensation for "cumulative fertility" and for thorough cleansing of a farm could be equitably determined.

Mr Davidson thinks the particulars of the claim of the outgoing tenant would be better than any record.

Mr Guild, however, considers the principle essential as a measure of the rights of the parties, and recommends that the record should be kept by the Board of Agriculture.

Mr Riddell thinks a schedule of condition absolutely necessary to rightly establish the tenant's claim for increased fertility and condition.

Mr Speir and other witnesses, on the other hand, point out that another valuer twenty years afterwards can hardly be expected to interpret the schedule exactly in the same sense as the man who drew it.

Mr Hutcheson (Perthshire) thinks that, in practice, the system would lead to complications and difficulties in settlement.

Mr Forster (Northumberland) takes a similar view.

Mr Punchard thinks the proposal unworkable. You could not in general have the same man again.

While it is difficult to assent to the view that such records could be exactly appraised in money equivalents, so that the later of two records would enable an arbitrator to determine with any nicety how much should be paid by the one party to the other at the winding up of the tenancy, this system certainly should be encouraged in the manner recommended by the Central Chamber, as perhaps the best check on injustice, or fraud, or error. And the power to obtain an interim report by the arbitrator as to the condition of the farm, as enabling the landlord to bring a bad farmer to book and promptly stop depletive farming, is of special importance and should in such a system be provided for.

Freedom of Cultivation and Sale of Produce.

Much evidence has been laid before us as to the expediency of doing away with covenants restricting tenants as to cultivation and sale of produce. Every shade of opinion seems to have been fully represented.

On one point there is unanimity—that, whether tenants are to be guided and restrained by covenants, or left to use their discretion, no relaxation is advisable or possible, if the fertility of the soil is not to be fully maintained by adequate manuring and adequate working of the land.

There is much striking evidence that in the depressed districts landowners are largely at the mercy of farm wreckers, who deliberately run out the land by miscropping and selling off everything. In many cases, where there is no dishonesty, farmers are driven to sell hay, straw, and roots when, owing to loss of capital, they are no longer able to consume their crops at home. Unless such sale is accompanied by restorative treatment of the land, it must be the beginning of the end.

But it seems probable that the worst cases of depletive farming are occurring on estates where restrictive covenants are to be found in every agreement, and the question naturally arises whether these covenants really are the best and most effective means of promoting good cultivation.

The covenants are stated to be retained " as safeguards to be used in extreme cases when a bad tenant deliberately sets about damaging his farm." The evidence is conclusive that restrictions have been almost everywhere relaxed. "As long as a man pays his rent, and keeps his farm in fair condition, he can now do as he likes." "Landlords and agents shut their eyes."

And this is not merely yielding to the pressure of the times. It is probably also matter of policy. Some of the more recent agreements in Lincolnshire do not require more than "good and husbandlike" farming according to the custom of the country, and "not to take any two crops of the same kind in succession." The Duke of Richmond gives freedom to yearly tenants as well as to leaseholders, except during the last four years of the tenancy. The same rule prevailed in the leases on Leicester's estate, and apparently on the estates of the Duke of Bedford.

On the Crown lands, "when a tenant is farming well, it is considered desirable to allow him to do very much as he likes, provided he will leave his farm in a proper state of cultivation at the end of the period."

Mr Stratton thinks that the restrictive covenants are now obsolete, and practically abandoned, and are only effective or necessary as regards the last two years of tenancy.

Again, the opinion was freely expressed that the best farmers, if given a free hand, would largely carry out the order of crops which covenants impose on them.

It is urged that it is economically wasteful to insist on the consumption of straw, and in some cases hay, when the market value is three, four, or more times greater than its manurial value. The same restoration of fertility may be more cheaply made, and a profit obtained in addition.

It is also argued that it is suicidal to tie tenants down in these times to methods of farming, like the four-course system, which can no longer be made to pay.

And, without doubt, in many of the instances of success in the bad times, absolute freedom in the management of the farm, as well as practical sagacity, has been a main cause.

Mr Prout's success at Sawbridgeworth, while violating the two most cherished restrictions, viz., that wheat shall not be grown continuously, and that straw shall not be sold off—is in itself a *reductio ad absurdum* of the old ideas, and a complete demonstration that the true method is not to arbitrarily fetter the discretion of tenant farmers, but rather to give the utmost encouragement to intelligent enterprise, so long as the one essential point, the maintenance of fertility, is observed.

Mr. Druce, Secretary of the Farmers' Club and Assistant-Commissioner in the former Commission, says it is only fair in these days that the tenant farmer should have as free a hand as possible in farming his land and in the sale of produce. With a covenant to keep the farm, and leave it in good heart and condition, the landlord is safeguarded, and has a legal claim that can be enforced against the tenant at any time. "I do not think it right to treat the tenant as a man who means to ruin the land and to make all he can out of it and hurt his landlord." The holding should be left in the rotation usual in the district.

Mr Punchard says: "Any man who can be trusted can have freedom of cropping and sale at any time; it would be a very dangerous thing to put it into the hands of many farmers."

Mr Bowen Jones would have complete freedom in all future tenancies, the landlord restricting sales in the last year of the tenancy, and protecting himself year by year as to clean and thorough cultivation of the farm.

Mr Carrington Smith, and other witnesses, hold that all restrictions, except from breaking up of old pasture, should be got rid of: "No one is so good a judge of how land is to be cultivated as the man in occupation of the land."

Mr Owen Williams (Denbighshire) says: "When a tenant farmer is a practical man, he ought to know best how to cultivate his land, and he is certain to cultivate it to the best of his ability for his own benefit, as well as for the benefit of the landlord."

Mr Kidner puts the converse: "Restrictions will never turn a bad farmer into a good one."

Mr Rew reports general demands in North Devon of

"greater" freedom. Agreements teem with minute conditions, many of them impracticable. Adequate manurial return for hay and straw sold off, and restrictions as to cropping and sale in the last year of tenancy, coupled with the power to give notice to quit, are sufficient protection to the landlord.

Mr H. Biddell, speaking of the practice at present in Suffolk, thinks that tenants have a free hand, except that they must not sell hay or straw, or have more than half the land in corn the last year, this restriction being essential in the interests of the incoming tenant.

The Welsh witnesses generally make the same demands as most of the English farmers, but it was stated that on the whole there is more freedom of cropping in Wales than elsewhere.

Messrs Dean, very large farmers in South Lincolnshire, believe in absolute freedom, except that the tenant should leave on the holding the manure made from the produce of the farm during the year previous to quitting.

"A man who has not broken his course of farming in the last ten years could not have done. We have broken ours, and largely gone in for growing seeds. The general character of my land has been improved by this, and I have grown more corn afterwards. On two farms of equal quality, one has had everything sold off for twenty years, and the other has had nothing sold off. With artificial manure at one-fifth the cost of farmyard manure, I have been able to grow as much corn but not quite so much straw as on the farm where all had been consumed. It is a national loss if farmers are restricted. The landlord must protect himself by annual supervision."

The demand in Scotland for freedom to sell off is universal, but there should be a restriction on cropping at the close of a lease.

Mr Rutherford says when the manurial value of straw is from 10s to 15s, and its selling price is up to 75s a ton, "it would be no hardship to the landowner, and of immense advantage to the farmers, if they were allowed, whenever they thought fit, to sell straw or hay, provided they replaced the fertility in manure." This should be matter of agreement.

Mr Davidson takes a similar view, and wishes freedom of sale, coupled with the obligation to bring back the manurial equivalent to be made a statutory right, but holds that freedom to crop would be injurious.

This is also the recommendation of the Scottish Chamber of Agriculture.[1]

Mr Flockhart thinks freedom of cropping would encourage the men who come in for five-year terms to "run out the farm."

Mr Riddell is against freedom of cropping, and would make selling off subject to landlord's consent.

Other Scotch witnesses would sweep away all "rotation" clauses, and merely stipulate for good husbandry.

"In the neighbourhood of Edinburgh, there are practically no restrictions on cropping or sale, and the land is in the very highest state of cultivation. It is sufficient for the farm to be left in a certain rotation at the end of the lease. If a man technically miscrops, but makes an adequate return to cover the results of any change of cultivation, he should be held free from liability."

Mr M'Connell points out that high manuring, *e.g.*, with bone meal, will so increase crops that the stipulation to consume the produce becomes unreasonable and wasteful.

In the report of the Committee of the Central Chamber of Agriculture, freedom to sell off produce was recommended in this way, viz., that except in the last year of the tenancy, the landlord's consent is not necessary, if the tenant gives security that the manurial equivalent will be returned.

At a subsequent meeting of the Central Chamber a resolution was passed in favour also of freedom of cropping and sale of produce with similar return of what is necessary to maintain fertility.[2]

It appears to be not unusual to stipulate in agreements

[1] Vol. IV, App. VII.
[2] Proceedings of the Central Chamber, Feb. 1895.

and leases for a certain money value of manurial return to the land, either at so much an acre, or sometimes a specified proportion of the value of the hay, straw, etc. sold off.

Mr Rew draws special attention to the agreements in force on Sir Thomas Acland's estate, which provide that "hay and straw may be removed if a quantity of manure equal in value to one-half of the money for which the hay or straw is sold be within the same year bought back and expended on the premises, but after notice to determine the tenancy, such removal shall not take place without the consent in writing of the landlord or his steward."

This agreement would seem to be to the advantage of the landlord as well as the tenant, and there can be no doubt from the evidence that a concession of freedom of cropping or sale has its money value, and not only is thought certain to raise rents to a high figure, but actually has had that result in practice.

The general effect of the evidence points to one obvious conclusion. The real remedy against the farm wrecker or the hand-to-mouth tenant is a rigidly enforced regulation or agreement as to adequate manuring. This is a simple, direct, and easily applied check, while the elaborate contrivances by which lawyers have tied the hands of enterprising and practical men who know their business, and, if let alone, and encouraged to seize opportunities for new methods of cultivation, would benefit their landlords and the country as well as themselves, have done much harm in this way, and have effected little or nothing in stopping the mischiefs which they were intended to prevent.

Common sense much more than bare necessity has dictated the very general relaxation in practice of restrictive covenants, and it is now high time that legislation should sanction what has practically been agreed to between the best landlords and the best tenants. The sense of confidence thus created will lead to bolder and more enterprising improvement of agricultural methods.

I therefore recommend in any legislation amending the Act that a clause should be introduced on the lines of that first brought before the House of Commons in 1887 by myself in a Bill to amend the Agricultural Holdings Act, and since then annually in Bills. The clause, which is clause 53 in the Agricultural Holdings Bill, 1897,[1] provides that no penalty or damages shall be enforceable, and the tenant shall not be turned out for change of cultivation or sale of produce, if an adequate return of manure is made, or security given that it will be made at the proper season.

If these recommendations are adopted, and coupled with the recommendation of the Central Chamber of Agriculture that the four-year limit to claims for waste by the landlord shall be reduced to two years from the determination of the tenancy, the operation of section 6 of the Agricultural Holdings Act will be materially restricted.

It apparently escaped the observation of the framers of that Act that the effect of subsection (*b*) of section 6 is to read every tenancy agreement as if the tenant had agreed not to sell hay, straw, roots, etc., for, whether the tenant has so agreed or not, the landlord can claim to reduce the tenant's compensation on this ground. The section in fact extends the power of the landlord beyond the cases where the tenant has agreed not to sell off, to cases where the tenant has not so agreed, or even where he has by custom or agreement the right—sometimes not very clearly defined—to sell off.

This oversight has really given the landlord more than he asked for, and has caused some injustice in practice, Mr C. S. Read having been a notable sufferer from this unintentional extension of landlord's powers. It is necessary, therefore, to introduce into the section the words "contrary to the written terms of the tenancy," an amendment also suggested in the Bills referred to.

There is a further extension of landlord's powers under this section, which, in my opinion, should be more strictly defined. Outside the Act, a landlord has power at common

[1] See Appendix II to this Report.

law, to recover damages from a tenant for a waste committed, *i.e.*, waste which results from acts of the tenant, but not for "permissive waste" such as allowing a building to fall of itself from neglect, etc. But this section gives the landlord a new power, by enabling him to set off against a yearly tenant's claim for compensation a claim for waste which he could not maintain independently of the Act. I am of opinion that the claim of the landlord as regards any alleged waste, whether committed or permitted, should not be admissible under section 6, unless he shall have given notice to the tenant within six months of the commission of the waste to make it good, or in regard to permissive waste, unless he shall have given notice to the tenant (within one month after a notice to quit has been given by either party), to desist from any specified form of waste.

In Scotland, the spirit of recent decisions of the courts is that, if a receipt for rent has been given without comment, or if the landlord fails to proceed for waste within a reasonable time, he should be held to have lost his right by acquiescence.

It has already been noted that the practice of referees and umpires, and of the county ands uperior courts, has disallowed any recovery of penal rents beyond the amount of actual damage proved. I think that this sensible and just practice should now be made statutory, and recommend in any new Act the insertion of a clause to the effect of clause 7 in the Agricultural Holdings Bill, 1897, which makes provision to carry this out, Appendix II to this Report.

Compensation for Improvements.

The extension of the principle of the Act by increasing the number of improvements for which compensation is payable, and by removing the obstacles to the full application of this principle in all cases, has been advocated universally by tenant farmer witnesses.

There is a general and a growing demand on the part

of farmers, and of the more enterprising farmers, to have a statutory right to carry out all improvements which are suitable to the holding and necessary to give any chance of success. It is contended by some that the mere letting of land for a specific agricultural purpose is, in intent, a giving of consent by the landlord for the working of the land for that purpose by the most effective and remunerative methods, and that it is illogical and unjust that when the tenant wishes to carry out improvements of this character, and which are essential to this object, the landlord should have by law the right to withhold his consent, and thus compel the tenant either to desist from working his land in the most remunerative way, or to face the risk of having his whole outlay on such improvements confiscated by the landlord, on any determination of the tenancy.

These views are held most strongly where tenants have to make the heaviest outlay in order to carry out their business with any chance of success.

Dr Fream reports of the fruit and hop districts of Kent, that there is a general demand that the whole of the improvements to which, by this Act, the consent of the landlord is required, should be transferred from Part I to Part III of the First Schedule of the Act; in other words, that tenants should be perfectly free to execute any permanent or first-class improvements, with a right to subsequent compensation, whether the landlord consented or not.

The cost of growing hops runs to £60 an acre, and of the newer methods of permanently wiring for hops to from £20 to £50 an acre. Hop growers would require the security of a long lease, or the right to compensation before undertaking such an outlay.

Similar arguments are put forward by the market gardeners of the Vale of Evesham. The preparatory clearing of the land and the planting of fruit trees and bushes is very costly (running from £20 to £80 an acre), and has invariably been done by the tenant, and at his own risk. Up to the passing of the Market Gardeners' Compensation Act, 1895, these men were absolutely at the mercy of their landlords, though to a certain extent protected by a custom which allowed something like free sale of improvements, as between outgoing and incoming tenants. There was, legally, no property right to these large investments, and they were at any time liable to have their rent raised on their improvements, which was in fact frequently done. The market gardeners argued that whether the object of letting was specified in the agreement or not, it was quite understood that the land was let for this purpose, and that the act of letting ought to carry with it the landlord's consent to all improvements suitable for their business.

The Market Gardeners' Compensation Act, 1895, gave the sanction of Parliament to this contention. The Act provides, as regards holdings in future specifically let as market gardens, that the planting of fruit trees, bushes, strawberry plants and asparagus, and other vegetable crops, and the erection and enlargement of buildings for the purposes of the trade or business of a market gardener, shall be placed in Part III of the Schedule, and the tenant will be entitled to compensation without having obtained the consent of the landlord. Further, this provision is applied retrospectively to all existing holdings now in use as market gardens, on which such improvements were executed before the Act, unless the landlord has, prior to the execution of any such improvement, dissented in writing. The consent of the landlord is also dispensed with, in section 56 of the Agricultural Holdings Act, and the outgoing tenant can thus transfer his property right in his improvements to the incoming tenant without the intervention of the landlord.

The importance of the principles thus recognised for the first time by the legislature cannot be exaggerated. In my opinion, the only ground for distinguishing such cases from any other kind of agriculture is, that the money outlay exceeds the average outlay in ordinary farming. But this is clearly not a distinction in kind but in degree. There can be no reason in the relations of the parties, and the nature of the rights and claims involved, why the same principle, *mutatis mutandis*, should not be applied to all kinds of farming.

The desire for similar rights in ordinary farming is expressed most strongly by the energetic and successful type of farmer.

From Scotland the demand, as might be expected, is practically unanimous.

Mr Hope, in both his important reports on the great arable and grazing districts in Scotland, puts this point at the head of the suggested amendments of the Act.

"The schedules should be abolished, and all improvements executed by the tenant, and tending to give an enhanced letting value to the farm, should be paid for by the landlord at the termination of the tenancy."

In regard to buildings and some other permanent improvements, the landlord should, Mr Hope says, be protected by a reference to the official valuator, who should decide whether a proposed improvement was suitable and would add value to the holding. But as regards laying down to permanent pasture, or drainage, the tenant should have absolute freedom, with compensation for remaining value at the end of the tenancy.

Mr Speir points out that, in the south-west of Scotland the value of the landlord's property has been enormously enhanced by permanent improvements made by the tenants without statutory protection, and subsequently confiscated by the landlords. He quotes an instance of a farm where the rent has been increased since an early date in the century, from £30 to £220 entirely by tenant's improvements, for which there was no legal protection. "The removal of stones, levelling, road making, etc. have, as a rule, been done by the tenant, and if interest on all these outlays were allowed, a very small sum indeed would remain for rent."

Mr Guild, land agent, thinks that as regards buildings, roads, fences, and water supply, the drainage procedure should hold good, but as regards all other improvements no consent and no schedules should be required.

Mr Riddell thinks there should be compensation,

without consent, for improvements certified to be really necessary for working the farm to advantage.

Mr Speir approves of notice, and that the landlord, where possible, should himself carry out improvements. " He does it in such a way that the estate should benefit as a whole; whereas the tenants would only do it, if they did it themselves, to benefit their own time."

Mr Fyshe would abolish all schedules and put all improvements on the same footing, and pay for added value in every case, except that as regards buildings, if the landlord withheld consent, a decision should be taken as to whether they are necessary for the farm. " If not found necessary, they should not be paid for."

Mr Elliot would merge Part I in Part II, or else get rid of them altogether.

A committee of factors and tenant farmers agreed (with two dissentients) that, if the landlord's consent was withheld, the improvement might be carried out and paid for, if, previous to its execution, a reference determined that the improvement was necessary to the efficient working of the holding.

The Scottish Chamber of Agriculture, to cover the cases where landlords will not carry out or consent to improvements, recommend that the tenant should call in a qualified arbitrator, and that compensation should be given for such improvements as are certified to be necessary for the proper working of the farm, having regard to the purpose for which it was let.

In the North of England as in Scotland the procedure of the drainage clause is approved.

Mr Scott adopted this procedure in the Northumberland scheme of compensation, the owner to have the right on receiving notice to get a prohibition, if the improvement was found on a reference to be unsuitable.

But, among English and Welsh witnesses, the simple and more direct method of giving the tenant freedom to make what improvements seem to him desirable and likely to give him a chance of profit, and the right to compensation for their remaining value, has vigorous exponents.

Thus Mr Nunneley, who appears to have succeeded, where others have failed, and to have shown enterprise and resource in adapting his methods to the times, would allow a tenant to make any improvement he pleases, with the knowledge that if it was found to have added to the value of the holding, he should be paid for it, and if not, he would lose his money. He would put no limit on the tenant's outlay, but would give the landlord the right to claim for deterioration.

The drainage procedure under Part II he considers complicated and unworkable. Entire freedom is best.

"It is so important that the land should be as well cultivated as possible, that although I should be very sorry for a landlord who could not afford to pay for improvements, I consider the good of the country must override the good of individual landlords, and if a man is not in a position to pay for improvements, the sooner the land belongs to someone who can do so, be he landlord or tenant, the better for the landlord, the tenant, and the whole country. In practice, all tenants would give notice of intended improvements, as they would prefer the landlords to do them. Again, the valuer would, in considering whether an act was an 'improvement' or not, take into consideration the purpose for which the farm was let."

Mr Bowen Jones thinks that permanent improvements might well be carried out by the tenant at his own risk; whether the improvements were worth anything would be decided by the arbitration at the termination of the tenancy.

Mr Carrington Smith wishes that the tenant's claim for unexhausted improvements should be unrestricted by schedules, and that he should have a right, of which he could not be deprived, to recover the full value of any agricultural improvements made by him, without the consent of his landlord. The arbitrator would decide whether it was really an improvement or a waste of money.

Mr Bear thinks it is a restraint of agriculture to prevent the improvement of land, and if the landlord and tenant system is kept up, it should not be allowed to be a bar to improvement. If the landlord objects, he does not think a reference as to the suitability of the proposed improvement necessary, but would prefer to leave the improvement perfectly free and open, the tenant to take the risk of a loss. If he erects an unsuitable building, the valuer will not allow him for it.

Among Welsh witnesses, Mr Owen Price thinks that permanent pasture, improving watercourses, making fences, reclaiming waste land, should be transferred to Part III of the Schedule.

The proposals of the Central Chamber of Agriculture on this matter take a middle course. The report of their Committee recommends that the following improvements should be transferred from Part I to Part II of the Schedule and put on the same footing as drainage as to procedure, viz :—Laying down of permanent pasture, making of gardens, orchards, and osier beds, not exceeding one acre, improving of roads, of wells, watercourses, water supply, and application of water power, and the reclaiming of enclosed waste land. The landlord's consent is to remain necessary for the rest of Part I.

It was stated, however, by Mr Lipscomb that the proposal to transfer the whole of Part I. to Part II. was originally adopted by the Committee, and only struck out at the final stage of their report.

The arguments urged to the contrary are that such a right would unfairly restrict the rights of an owner over his own property, and that tenants could, in many cases, by using such a procedure, involve themselves and their landlords in embarrassments and loss.

Mr Wilson Fox thinks the demand is not made in Lincolnshire or Suffolk. The tenants in the latter county are too impoverished, and even if they could carry out permanent improvements, in many cases they could not recover compensation from owners practically insolvent.

Mr Stratton thinks it might be a hardship to lay down in grass without some consideration for the wishes and abilities of the landlord.

I attach more importance to the argument, frequently advanced, that an improvement which increases the letting value, or prevents it from falling, clearly increases, not diminishes, the general assets of the owner. The provision of the money may, in many cases, cause difficulty and limitation of the power to improve, in some cases may operate as a complete prohibition at the present time. But I believe that the granting of State loans on cheaper terms, and the influx into agriculture of some of the vast accumulations of capital now bringing next to no returns, which we expect to see follow a satisfactory amendment of the law as to tenants' improvements, will be found to remove the anticipated difficulties, perhaps slowly, but surely.

In respect of improvements like laying down permanent or temporary pasture, which has been found in practice to be the best expedient for making farming pay in these times, we think that the arguments advanced by many witnesses establish an unanswerable case for giving the tenant a free hand, and a right to full compensation.

It is proved that this class of improvement must be carried out with skill, judgment, and considerable outlay, if it is to be successful at all. If it is badly done, it may only lead to further expense in cleaning the land, and recommencing the operation. It is, therefore, to the interests of all concerned that there should be the strongest inducement to the tenant to do it well, if he does it all.

In the present state of the law there is the strongest inducement to the tenant to adopt temporary and inferior methods. He has no security. In most cases where application is made, consent has apparently been refused, and the tenant has been compelled to lay down at his own risk. And if he has gone to the expense of laying down well, he has no other means of extorting compensation than the threat to destroy the improvement he has made. By this threat, some tenants have been able to obtain agreements guaranteeing them a small compensation.

Mr Stratton dwells strongly on this defect of the Act. "There is no encouragement for high farming. Rather than lay land down, I should prefer to have it in my own hands, and break it up, and have a couple of crops before leaving." "It is very damaging for the farm if the owner wishes to let it again." "I know many farmers who are about to leave who do that. They feel: 'If I leave this down in grass, there will be plenty of competition for this farm: if I plough it up, I can take it again on my own terms;' the Act should be amended to enable the outgoing tenant to leave that grass land, and so prevent this evil, and put a premium on the best farming."

Mr Olver says that "farmers who have laid down to grass sooner than take the trouble to bargain as to compensation with the threat to break up, say to themselves: 'I will plough it, and then I am safe.' They take two crops of corn, and leave the land impoverished."

This crucial instance of how the limitations of the Act lead inevitably to bad farming, deterioration of the land, and wholly unnecessary economic waste, is only an exceptionally striking illustration of what applies generally to the defects of the Act and of its working. Many witnesses who have come before us have urged that the more the principle of compensation is extended to all acts which increase the value of the land, and the more complete and adequate the compensation for remaining values, the more probable it is that the improving and enterprising tenant will continue his good farming up to the end of his tenancy. On the other hand, the more restricted the improvements, and the scale of payments for them, the more certain it is that many tenants will be compelled to find their compensation by robbing the soil.

Strong evidence was given from Scotland as to this result of insecurity.

Mr Rutherford, who deals in manures, states that tenants now often ask for "something that will reduce the fertility of the soil, because if we leave it full of condition we will be rented on our improvements."

He adds:—"On four farms I manage we pay in rent and manures £3244. This year the amount spent in feeding stuffs was £3030, and the same last year. Unless we are to receive ample compensation under the Act we shall be at a decided disadvantage in getting these farms into a quite exceptional state of fertility, and expose ourselves to be outbid by 'land suckers,' who offer an increase in order to enter and suck the fertility out."

"In another ten years there will be no need for an Agricultural Holdings Act under the present system; the bulk of the best men are getting so frightened as to say, 'if we are to have no security we must make preparations.' There have been cases of insufficient compensation which have 'shaken the faith of the best farmers in keeping their farms in very high cultivation.'"

The same feeling is expressed by Mr Dutfield from Monmouthshire: "Tenants find they would do better often by the old bad principle of letting the farm down a little in the way of cropping, and going out and making no claim."

And this view of things seems to be acquiesced in by some land agents, in our opinion most unwisely.

Thus the agent of a large Lancashire estate says: "A tenant takes a farm and farms it highly to benefit himself; of course, after some years, the farm is improved. The tenant has only done his duty, and what is best for the farm, and having really repaid himself he wants to be repaid a certain sum by the landlord as well. But tenants generally settle the 'betterment' question for themselves by farming the place out, and they sometimes overdo it, and make a loss for themselves in the last year.[1]"

Not only is deliberate bad farming thus encouraged, but, by the time scales of the ordinary valuers, the bad farmer is able to concoct a claim, and get considerable compensation for outlay in the last few years, when he has been systematically depleting his farm, and deserves to be penalised, not compensated.

[1] Wilson Fox, Garstang, p. 40.

Mr Nunneley puts this well: "In my own district I can point to farm after farm which has been run down and practically ruined by the outgoing tenants, who have yet been enabled to claim compensation in considerable sums for improvements. On the other hand, I can point to many a good farmer who has farmed well, and has lost a considerable sum of money, who has left a very large amount for his successor and his landlord."

This double robbery, of the land first, and then of the landlord, is further explained by Mr Rutherford: "The man who is up in his business as a 'land sucker' may be using a great amount of cake, and at the same time be using sulphate of ammonia or nitrate of soda. He is practically exhausting at the same time as he is putting fertility in. To give compensation to that man would be ridiculous compared with the man who had been boning his place, and causing increased fertility."

Under the present Act, which the landlord can only use if it is first set in motion by the tenant making a claim, it is possible to rob the soil with practical impunity, if the bad farmer is content with that, and does not proceed to try to rob his landlord also.

It is matter of demonstration that it would be to the interest of the owner of land to have his land improved in all ways which make it a more productive and more valuable instrument of agriculture, to have the highest and most thorough cultivation carried on continuously, throughout and up to the end of a tenancy, and that the restrictions and limitations, and faulty administration of the Act which make so many tenancies consist partly of a long process of restoring condition, and partly of a diligent extraction of fertility to be put in the tenant's pockets, to make good the compensation which is denied him, bring with them the natural and inevitable results of economic blundering of the worst kind, and constitute year by year an immense waste of national wealth. I am therefore of opinion that such an amendment of the law as will secure at once freedom to carry out all suitable improvements, and full compensation for such improvements to the tenant executing them, cannot but be of the greatest benefit to the owner and to the community at large.

It would only be just also that such an amendment of the Act should be accompanied by provisions giving the landlord power himself to set the Act in motion, and to effectually check dishonest and depletive farming.

Continuous Good Farming.

The nineteen years' lease in Scotland, and long leases generally in other districts, have naturally led farmers to enter on a carefully planned out treatment of the soil to secure the maximum productivity. The question of compensation for cumulative fertility or continuous good farming is bound up with this system. The direct result of a long lease is to encourage the immediate fertilising of the soil to the highest point in the shortest time, in order that the tenant may draw the maximum of benefit from his generous treatment of the soil during the currency of the lease. But although this motive of self-interest operates to a certain extent, it is thwarted by the motives suggested by the administration of the Act.

"The use of the time scales has been unfortunate. If two farmers were to start together on a nineteen years' lease, and one of them was to make his farm his bank for the whole time, and the other farmer had done nothing for the farm, under the system of scales they would get very much the same amount awarded to them."[1]

"It pays a man better to leave his land foul and impoverished than it does to leave it clean and fertile."[2]

The history of Mr Riddell's experiment on the Corsehope farm and the working of the Act in that case are highly instructive.[3]

Mr Riddell on entry, seeing that the method of cultivation by breaking up and cropping the hill pastures would exhaust the farm, laid the whole down in grass, and fed very heavily with cake for the first few years on the new grass. There was also a heavy outlay in bone manures and on liming during the earlier portion of the

[1] Riddell, 54,537, &c. [2] C. S. Read, 16,572. [3] Riddell, 54,544-54,748.

lease. There was in all about £20,000 expended during the lease. None of the land after being once laid down was broken up again, and thus the whole added fertility was left in the soil. The result was an immense increase in the carrying capacity of the farm. Between three or four times more stock could be kept than when Mr Riddell entered. In Mr Riddell's opinion the longer he farmed the land the more power he had to improve it. "I found I could improve far more at the end of nineteen years than I could at the beginning, and for five, six, or seven years at first, proving beyond a doubt that the idea that it would be exhausted in three, four, or five years was ridiculous."

The result of this treatment on the market value of the farm was striking. While nearly all the farms of similar position and quality in the neighbourhood went down from 40 to 50 per cent. in rents, Corsehope farm was relet at approximately the same rent.[1] Mr Riddell estimates that the owner is reaping a benefit of £300 a year.

Mr Riddell made the very moderate claim of £2700. The time scales were applied so as to limit the compensation to the last six years, amounting to £763. But the proof of the increased fertility was so unanswerable, and the facts as to the enormous outlay in the earlier years of the lease so obvious, that the oversman decided to award Mr Riddell an additional sum of £300 "for the extensive use of feeding stuffs during the lease." In other words, he presented his landlord with £300 a year for an indefinite period, and was compensated with about one's year purchase of the improvement.

The contention of the majority of Scotch witnesses is that the tenant should receive a full and adequate compensation for the whole added value of a holding caused by the long-continued high farming.

Mr Elliot says he "treated land the same way as Corsehope, and it is growing grass to-day, though it is

[1] And this farm has been relet for a second term without further reduction.

twenty-five to twenty-eight years since it was done. Plenty of it was not worth a shilling an acre formerly. It is magnificent pasture to-day."

Mr Rutherford holds that the full recognition of compensation for "cumulative fertility" would be the best remedy. The inability of farmers to get allowance for their earlier outlays, however beneficial, has been the great cause of "land sucking" and deterioration, has been thus indirectly one of the main causes of the agricultural depression.

Mr Ballingall says, "The administration of the Act offers a premium to inferior farming, and acts as a deterrent against high continuous farming. It is grossly unfair, because there is plainly a fertility in some land that will stand for half or more of a long lease, and the tenant gets no more than another man who has only given enough manure to keep the land from poverty."

Mr Davidson points out that this is not the fault of the Act, but the habit of valuers to include everything under "cast-iron" scales rather than consider the whole circumstances of each case.

"I see nothing in the Act to prevent an arbiter, in considering that a farm has been well farmed through a sequence of years, from applying an appropriate scale." "It is obvious if a farm is in a high condition, and receives in the last years of the lease the same fertilisers in the shape of feeding stuffs, there must be a larger residue; the crops presumably would draw on the old reserves, and what had since been applied, whereas, if the farm is in low condition, and you only apply sufficient to grow crops in the last years of the lease, less compensation should be given than in the former case."

Mr Davidson states that he has himself awarded a general compensation for high condition produced by these anterior outlays, and there has not been, though there might have been, appeals. There should be specific outlays proved, and the carrying and productive power of the farm, and the cleanly state in which it is left, would also be considered.

In the north of England, where leases have more prevailed and the conditions of agriculture are more similar to Scotland, the same demand is made with much the same arguments.

Thus Mr Scott, while thinking the Act has encouraged farmers to try to keep up the condition of their land, and that landlords would now have had their land in much worse condition but for the Act, thinks also that "a bad tenant may get too much from the Act, and a good tenant is not likely to get enough. For instance, a good tenant may make the principal part of his expenditure in the first years of his tenancy, and get the farm into such good condition that it requires less during the last three or four years; therefore he will get less compensation. A bad tenant might put on very little the first few years of his tenancy, and might throw on a great deal of manure and a great deal of food the last three or four years of his tenancy, and possibly get more compensation."

"The Act does not give compensation for condition; it would be a great advantage if condition were valued."

Mr Forster is in favour of compensation for general improved fertility, and thinks it can be tested by productive power of the farm. He holds that compensation for general improvements is promised in "about the first sentence of the Act, and that is what I want carried out."

Mr Wilkinson says: "The increased fertility of the soil, due to continuous good farming, should be the property of the tenant. The operation of the law by which an outgoing tenant receives compensation based on the quantities of fertilisers and feeding stuffs used during the last three or four years, is not a sufficient recognition of his interests. Indeed, the law operates in a way detrimental to continuous good farming, because such a farmer is liable to a demand for an increase of rent, owing to the increased fertility, and consequently increased letting value, without getting compensation for it."

Mr Rowlandson thinks "for the benefit of the community there should be an allowance for continuous good farming. At present we often have claims for the deterioration of the land, and if the tenant has improved the state of the farm in its cultivation he should be paid for it." The schedule of condition at entry would make it perfectly feasible.

Under the present system of valuations "a tenant is allowed one-third of his expenditure in cakes during his last year, and one-sixth on the previous year, but a tenant having been two years on a farm receives precisely the same payment as if his expenditure in cakes and manures had been going on for thirty, or forty, or fifty years. In the latter case the tenant is entitled to considerably more than the tenant who has only been using cakes for two years. Any practical man can see at once, especially on grass land where cake has been largely used, the value of the land has been increased. The valuers have limited the principle of the Act, and it would be better that compensation for continuous good farming were placed in the schedule, with the intimation that it ought to be paid for."

Mr Rowlandson himself made an award of excess value in consideration of large consumption of cake, and very considerable improvement, and it was not appealed against.

Mr Punchard says: "We have a practice among the local valuers of varying the rate of compensation. If we find a man has been continuously farming high, we allow him a higher rate of compensation than when it has been partial or casual."

Mr C. S. Read strongly supports compensation for continuous good farming, and wishes to put into it cleanliness and thorough working of the land.

Sir John Lawes would approve of compensation for the fertility accumulated in grass well laid down and liberally fed.

Mr Middleton says that an incoming tenant would rather pay compensation to the man who had been farming high for twenty years, than to a man who had been farming for only three years. He would get better value.

Mr Sheldon points out that some improvements last even for fifty years. "I could show you the effect of boning the land fifty years ago, and you can see the improved quality of the grass to-day. It depends upon the character of the land."

It may be gathered from the evidence that there is no general disposition to challenge the justice of the tenant's claim to have long continued expenditure in enriching his farm fairly considered and allowed for, except the contention discussed earlier in this Report, that the tenant will have practically reaped the full benefi of these outlays during the course of his tenancy.[1] This view seems to us unsupported by evidence, whereas the permanence of the fertility induced by such treatment of farms seems to us established. There can be no doubt also that it was the intention of the Act to allow just this type of compensation.

The real question is how far such compensation can be practically arrived at.

Mr Bear and others, who prefer the method of free sale of improvements to compensation by valuation, are of opinion that "any attempt to value improvements that have been carried out on a farm for years past is almost impossible."

Mr Riddell's view that an expert agriculturist can really estimate rise of condition and general improvement, aided by a scheduled record of the state of the farm at entry, and by the evidence which would be produced both of the actual outlays and also of the increase of crops or of stock carrying power, seems a sufficient answer. I am therefore of opinion that it should be made perfectly clear in an amended Act that the tenant is entitled to be compensated for improved condition irrespective of time limits, and I also hold that the evidence under this head makes it still more necessary to alter the administration of the Act.

[1] Pages 109, 110.

Laying down of Pasture.

It is strongly urged by a number of witnesses that the laying down of permanent pasture should be an improvement for which the consent of the landlord is not required. The Committee of the Central Chamber of Agriculture recommend that this improvement should be transferred from Part I to Part II of the Schedule. Others would class this and other permanent improvements under the head of improvements which can be carried out if approved by an arbitrator.

The Scottish farmers, who have had the fullest experience of the beneficial results of laying down, seem particularly unanimous that the tenant should have a perfectly free hand, but in some cases recommending that notice should be given. Mr Hope reports that the landlord's consent has, in many instances, been refused to the detriment of all concerned, and from England there is much evidence to a similar effect, and also that landlords decline to enter into agreements to compensate tenants who have laid down pasture.

The great help that pasture, whether permanent or temporary, gives to the farmer, and the certainty that laying down must result in the accumulation of fertility, makes it practically certain that a landlord cannot suffer from the conversion of arable into pasture land. In the future wording of an amended Act it must be assumed, with regard to all improvements, that compensation will not exceed the actual money value of the improvements handed over by the outgoing tenant.

It further appears from the evidence that the conversion of arable into grass land, and the laying down of land in temporary pasture, has been adopted by thousands of farmers as a means of saving themselves from ruin when the prices of corn fell below the minimum cost of production. This change has not only kept these farmers going, but has already greatly benefited the landowners who have been enabled to receive rents which could not possibly have been paid them, even out of tenants' capital, if this change of cultivation had not been carried out.

I therefore recommend that laying down of permanent pasture should be transferred to Part III, or, in other words, permitted without restriction as to consent or notice, and further approve of the new item of Part III, recommended by Mr C. S. Read and by the Central Chamber, that compensation should be given for temporary pasture, if two years down or longer, and the land in clean condition.

Other Improvements.

The desire to have compensation for home-grown corn consumed on the holding is practically universal among tenant farmers, and has become keener in proportion as low prices and bad seasons have compelled farmers to use a larger proportion of corn for feeding purposes. In some counties the grievance is greater than others. Thus in Cornwall, "nearly all the corn grown is consumed on the farm; this Act is unfair, as it only compensates for bought corn." It will be perfectly easy to arrive at the proper amount by estimating the crop, and having a record of the amount sold off.

"In a very large proportion of the farms south of Edinburgh, towards the Lammermoors, almost the whole of the grain crops is consumed on the land, and without any compensation."

Mr Treadwell, who uses his own corn largely, to the value of, in 1891, £981; in 1892, £772; in 1893, £963 in 1894, £667, is strongly in favour of compensation for its use.

The great majority of witnesses of practical experience favour the proposal, and think fraud could be prevented.

"I am quite convinced that it can be carried out in fairness to both parties, but you must put the whole responsibility upon the tenant, of proving that he has first grown the corn and then used it."

Mr C. S. Read thinks there is no more difficulty in checking fraud as to home consumption of corn grown on the farm than as to taking it off one farm and putting it on to another, as is done now. The onus of proof must be on the claiming tenant, he must keep books to show what became of his produce, and substantiate his claim by this evidence, and the evidence of his men and his tradesmen.

The book containing the entries of home-grown produce used should be signed each day, and falsification made a criminal offence.

Mr Guild thinks the principle of compensation should be extended also to hay and other produce.

On the other hand, Mr Forster strongly opposes the proposal as leading to fraud, and Mr Middleton and the Cleveland Chamber think it unworkable. Mr Looker, a Hunts land agent, takes the same view. So does Mr Peile, a Scottish agent. I can see no insurmountable difficulty in granting this form of compensation with the checks suggested by Mr Read and others. And it is obviously illogical that two farmers should be able, by continually selling corn to each other, to obtain compensation, while the use of the same corn by the producer on his own farm brings no compensation.

A still more vexed question is whether there should be compensation for feeding stuffs and corn consumed by horses. It would seem, on the whole, fair that they should be granted on the conditions laid down by the Central Chamber that such compensation should be restricted to horses "exclusively engaged or kept on the holding."

The Central Chamber and most of the witnesses wish to strike out the proviso in section 1 of the Act, as to the "inherent capabilities of the soil." The argument is that whatever these capabilities may be, they are paid for already by the tenant in the rent, and that it cannot be just that they should be taken into account in reduction of the tenant's claim for the value of his improvements. Others think it wholly inoperative, and had therefore better go.

Mr Bowen Jones, on the other hand, thinks that "if there are any inherent capabilities they should belong to the landlord," and Sir John Lawes thinks that "fertility," being the natural property of the soil, should belong to the landlord, while "condition" is what really is caused by and should belong to the tenant. He does not, therefore, object to the proviso.

On the double ground that the inherent capabilities are already paid for in rent, and that the proviso offers an indefinite opportunity for whittling down a tenant's claim without adequate and producible evidence, the Central Chamber are probably right in wishing that the words should be struck out.

Several witnesses strongly favour the older principle that compensation should be based on outlay, and hold that the principle of the Act that the "value of an improvement to an incoming tenant" is too vague and unsatisfactory a standard to work upon.

Thus Mr Kay thinks that the words of the Act lead to misunderstanding and to the ignoring of improvements, and that compensation should be awarded on some schedule stipulating a return to the outgoing tenant of some fixed proportion of his outlay.

Mr Dobson thinks it would be desirable to keep the schedules in a new Act. The valuer might specify for which class of improvement the compensation was awarded, and then, if necessary, a further sum for general improvements beyond the items mentioned.

But the great mass of authoritative evidence is altogether the other way. Thus Mr Scott:—"If it were enacted that a certain portion of what the outgoing tenant had spent would be repaid to him, that would be still worse than the present Act, which does not sufficiently take into consideration the improved condition and fertility of the soil."

The able group of men in Northumberland, with whom Mr Scott has been identified, have tried to get just valuation of quality, as well as quantity by classification. Their object was to grade compensation according to the skill and thoroughness with which any improvement was carried out, and the cleanliness and good cultivation accompanying it. By combining time scales of exhaustion with a division into three classes, of excellent, creditable and bad management, they sought to secure for the best and most skilful farmer a proportionate reward.

But the experience even of this scheme has not been satisfactory.

Mr Scott, who was one of the committee who drew it up, now says:—" I have come to the conclusion that it is quite impossible to fix a scale for compensation. I thought it possible at one time, and helped to frame the Newcastle rules, but I now believe that claims must go to arbitration." "Taking lime, for example, on one part of my farm it will last twenty years, and on another part ten years." Other local experts agree that no hard and fast line is possible.

Mr Riddell's contention, that the arbitrator should determine what is due to the tenant by a careful examination of the quality and condition and productive power of the farm, comparing this result with the evidence of its previous condition, and using the figures as to outlay merely as evidence of what has been done, and not as a mechanical measure of the result seems sound, and should be the guiding principle of valuations.

To sum up the evidence as to compensation for improvements and the extension of the principle, while there is much to be said for getting rid of classification by schedules altogether, and allowing a perfectly free hand to the tenant to carry out any improvement on the understanding that he does so at his own risk, and will receive nothing for it, unless it is held on a reference at the determination of the tenancy to have added to the value of the holding, great weight must attach to the evidence of a general wish, on the part both of the tenant and the landlord, that the more important improvements should be carried out by the landlord, and this result will be better obtained, and the relations of landlord and tenant more readily adjusted, if the whole of the more permanent improvements, now set forth in the first part of the schedule, should be put together with drainage in a separate schedule. The procedure of the Act as to drainage is too cumbrous, and has been shown in evidence to have been for that reason inoperative. I therefore recommend that as to all improvements in the new schedule, the tenant should be perfectly free to carry them out, but that he should give notice to his landlord of his intention to do so. This would enable the tenant to carry out the improvements himself, without the delay and complication of the drainage procedure, if he chose to do so, while it would lead in general to a prompt and satisfactory agreement as to the improvements being carried out by the landlord, and would enable the landlord to take prompt steps to protect himself, in case the tenant proposed to erect unsuitable buildings, or make undesirable changes of cultivation.

Clause 2 of the Agricultural Holdings Bill, 1897, and the Schedule to that Bill have been drawn to give effect to this recommendation.

Retrospective Compensation for suitable Improvements.

Furthermore, the important principle sanctioned by Parliament in the Market Gardeners' Compensation Act, 1895, that a tenant who had, previous to the passing of that Act, carried out on a holding in use as a market garden, improvements for which that Act gave compensation, should be compensated, might be extended with excellent effects to ordinary farms. Mr Rowlandson and several other witnesses have stated to us that they have carried out important and costly improvements on their farms, relying wholly on the honour and good faith of their landlords, and without, of course, any legal security whatever.

In the event of a reference under the Act, I think it highly desirable that the arbitrator should have power to determine whether any such improvement was suitable to the purposes for which the farm was let, and therefore an improvement which might be assumed to have been contemplated in the letting of the farm, and that, in the event of the arbitrator deciding that the improvement was suitable, he should allow compensation for it retrospectively, according to the precedent of the Market Gardeners' Compensation Act.

And, in the event of such an amendment of the Agricultural Holdings Act being sanctioned, it should be provided that necessary and essential changes in the cultivation of the farm, like the laying down of permanent pasture, or the erection of suitable buildings and appliances for dairy work, where likely to succeed, should be declared, in such an amending Bill, to be suitable and proper improvements which should receive compensation, and that compensation should be awarded for them, unless it is proved that the landlord had dissented in writing from any such improvement.

Clause 3 of the Agricultural Holdings Bill, 1897, gives effect to this recommendation.

Compensation for the Sitting Tenant.

Assent has already been given to the view of Sir James Caird, that the most serious defect of the Agricultural Holdings Act, 1883, was that it restricted compensation to the tenant who was leaving his holding, and gave no direct protection to the property rights in his own improvements of the tenant who was remaining in his holding, and entering on a new contract of tenancy.[1]

In the analysis of the relation of rents to agricultural depression, it has already been pointed out that the force of competition, increasingly directed towards farms in high condition, operates to prevent the improving farmer from obtaining such a reduction of rent as will leave the material return from his outlay in his own pocket, and that the more continuously and effectively a tenant has maintained and improved the condition of his farm, the more certainly is the whole value of his improvements transferred to his landlord by rack renting.[2]

I now proceed to consider suggestions for the pre-

[1] Page 157. [2] Page 107.

vention of this injustice by amendments of the provisions of the Act.

The suggestion made by Sir James Caird, and defeated in Parliament, in committee on the bill in 1883, was, that the words "on quitting his holding" should be omitted, and compensation for improvements be recoverable on the termination of a tenancy, whether the tenant left, or entered into a fresh contract.

The compensation might be in a lump sum, or might, by agreement or award, take the form of a reduction of rent for a number of years corresponding to the probable period of exhaustion of the improvements, or of a charge on the holding for a similar number of years. In case either of these alternatives to a cash payment of the whole sum due were adopted, and the tenancy was terminated before the specified period had run out, the actuarial value of the remaining reductions of rent or instalments might be paid over to the tenant. This scheme of Sir James Caird was worked out in Clause 10 of the Agricultural Holdings Bill, 1894, in the form approved by Sir James Caird himself in 1887. This clause is omitted from the Agricultural Holdings Bill, 1897, partly for simplification, partly because its procedure would naturally be arrived at by agreements between the parties.

Several of the Scottish witnesses put the case for this method of compensation very clearly.

Mr Black says, if the tenant on renewal is not getting cash payment—"I do not know a case where he ever has got payment if he was continuing in the holding— I think he is entitled to a reduction in the fixing of his rent under the new lease."

" But as a rule the practice has been that the proprietor, either through his factor, or a valuator, has put a rent upon the farm—the sitting tenant has the option only of taking it at this rent or leaving it. The landlord values the farm as it stands, improvements and all, and charges rent for the full value. It would be a sound principle for the landlord, when it was ascertained what the amount of compensation due to the tenant for improvements, if he left, would be, to allow a proportionate percentage of reduction off the rent."

Mr Elliot thinks the sitting tenant should be compensated either by fixing a proportionate rent, or by paying in money. If this is not done at the determination of the tenancy, he will certainly on renewal pay rent on his improvements. " Farms are valued [for a new lease] at what they are considered worth at the moment, without taking into consideration the tenant's claim. " When the new rent is fixed, the remaining value of the tenant's improvement should be determined."

There should be a reduction from the rent proportionate to the value of the improvements.

Mr Elliot does not think that in practice the landlord would ask a still higher rent to cover this, but he might do so.

Mr Dun doubts if you could give the sitting tenant money compensation, but wishes to "arrange matters so that he could take his farm again as easily as if he had run down its condition; it would be a great advantage to him and to the country."

Mr Fyshe thinks the adjustment would be easy by the help of the record of condition. The rent would be determined by the arbitrator according to the condition of the farm, and some interest on the improved value caused by the tenant should go to the tenant.

Mr Ballingall thinks it should be arranged amicably between landlord and tenant that if he has been an improving tenant, and has added to the value, the landlord should make the rent cheaper on that account.

"The official valuator would go over the land, and value it in its present high state, and then consider the outlays. He might say the land is £50 better for these, and therefore he takes that off his valuation, and says, "That is the valuation I think you should pay." "It would be the interest of the compensation the landlord would have had to pay if the tenant left."

Mr Rutherford thinks the tenant should be entitled to have the value he has added, allowed to him. The record of condition, the vouchers for cakes, manure, etc., and the relative fall of rent as compared with similar farms, would enable the official valuator, on viewing the farm, to accurately measure what is due to the tenant. Supposing the farm had fallen in these times 28 per cent. while others had fallen 40 to 45 per cent. the difference capitalised really belongs to the tenant.

He would, on renewal, be quite willing to "let the award lie over, but that in the event of the tenant leaving the holding, the money should be handed over to him." "It would be left as a sort of guarantee to the tenant." It would be repaid gradually to the tenant in the form of a deduction from the valued rent.

Among English witnesses, Mr Carrington Smith wishes full compensation for all improvements at the determination of a tenancy, whether the tenant quits or not. The payment by the landlord to the tenant would prevent an increase to the rent, inasmuch as it would put it into the tenant's power to make his bargain before his rent was increased.

The obligation of the landlord to pay the capital value of the improvements before the rent was raised would prevent the renting on the improvements, and fixity of tenure would not be needed to secure the tenant.

Mr Gilbert Murray, from the land agent point of view, is willing to compensate the sitting tenant either in a lump sum or by a proportionate reduction of the future rent.

Mr Dobson, a Cumberland farmer, says that this would be the greatest advantage an amending Bill could confer. If the words "on quitting his holding" were struck out, it would be impossible to have a farm revalued without compensating the tenant for his improvements.

If it is argued that the tenant, after receiving compensation for his improvements, is stopping and enjoying the use of them, the answer is that the landlord is compensated by a higher rent than he otherwise would have received.

Mr Sheldon, on the same point, that the landlord,

having paid for the unexhausted improvements, the tenant would go on and get the benefit of them, explains that, in return for paying for the improvements, the landlord would get a higher rent not only from natural causes, but from the tenant's improvements themselves.

Mr Long thinks the absence of protection for the interests of tenants remaining on the farms in a new tenancy "is the greatest blot on the Act, and the greatest misfortune for agriculture."

Mr Lander states that one of the main reasons for compensating the sitting tenant is, that farmers who farm highly are less able to get reasonable reductions of rent, and that the remaining value of the improvements should be fully considered before the new terms are settled, and a sufficient reduction of rent allowed to cover the improvements.

Mr Nunneley explains clearly that what is wanted is that the tenant, when remaining in a new tenancy, should have allowed to him the full remaining value, just as if he were leaving; the rent should not be raised without a settlement. Where the tenant gives notice, with a view to a reduction of the rent, and the landlord says "your land is worth the money in the condition it is," the tenant can say "it is owing to my outlay," and should be entitled to get a fair valuation. "He would then be in the position of a new comer, and would pay in rent what the farm was fairly worth." The landlord would of course have to pay the compensation if he was letting to some one else, so that the arrangement is absolutely fair for both sides.

The above evidence sufficiently indicates the gravity of the mischief to be provided against, and the methods of such provision.

Further, no serious objection was made in evidence to this proposal.

Mr Rankin, speaking as a landowner, says of the principle that a tenant, if he wishes to remain, should have a valuation of what he did for the farm, that he sees "nothing to disapprove of in it; I think it is fair and just."

But several witnesses have pointed out difficulties which seem to them to make the remedy impracticable.

Thus, Mr Bowen Jones thinks it might be done where a rise in the rent was proposed, but that it would be very difficult to apply to the other case, much more frequent, when the improving tenant cannot get an adequate reduction of rent.

Mr Gillespie recognises the injustice, and that it might be desirable to devise some means of allowing a certain percentage from the rent, but thinks it is impracticable.

But the point most pressed is that the payments which it has become customary for the incoming tenant to make, not only for tillages and sometimes crops, but for manures and cakes, would have to be made by the sitting tenant after the tenancy was renewed, and thus he would be compelled to repay to the landlord what had been awarded to him as outgoing tenant by the arbitrator, and thus at the end he would be where he began, and the whole proceeding would be nugatory, except that if the parties did not agree, there would be the needless cost of a reference.[1]

This is clearly an ingenious fallacy, based upon a practice which several witnesses rightly think inconsistent with the principle of the Act and with justice.

Mr Nunneley says: "I have always held that these improvements ought to be paid for by the landlord, and not by the incoming tenant. It makes too large an inroad on the incoming tenant's capital, besides which he does pay twice over. A farmer takes a farm at a high rent because of the good condition it is in, and he has to pay a sum to the outgoing tenant for the manures and cakes which have brought it to that condition. I have always contended that the landlord ought to pay for the manures and cakes which have brought the land into that condition."

The ground for proposing compensation to the sitting tenant is that the rackrent will be charged by the land-

[1] See Nunneley, 56, 174-56, 209.

lord, including the full remaining value of the tenant's improvements.

If the full market value is charged, the incoming tenant ought in no case to make any such payment at all, and when the incoming tenant is the old tenant renewing his tenancy, it will be only a repetition of the wrong sought to be remedied for him to make such a payment, and he will rightly retain his compensation as a set-off to the rackrent.

If, on the other hand, the rent is reduced so as to leave a fair margin for the remaining value of the improvements, no question arises, as the sitting tenant will have received his compensation in the rent.

Furthermore, it is obvious that the question would never arise where only the minimum of compensation could be claimed for fertilisers and acts of husbandry. The proposal would only come into play in cases where the tenant has a very heavy investment of his capital in his holding, either in the way of more permanent improvements, or in high continuous farming bringing about the maximum of fertility, where in fact the tenant would be in a position to make a very considerable claim, if he was quitting his holding.

In such cases, at present, the landlord is able to exact a rackrent, because his tenant fears that his loss by realising in bad times would eat away any possible compensation, and therefore is willing to make any sacrifice to remain and make what he can out of his investment.

It is, of course, plain that unless there is some power, judicial or otherwise, to fix a fair rent, a landlord who is determined to act unjustly might, even with this proposal made statutory, effect his purpose by raising the rent so as to more than cover the compensation. But, in practice, the remedy suggested by Sir James Caird would in general lead to an amicable settlement, by placing the tenant in a more advantageous position to bargain, and removing the perilous insecurity in which he now stands to a great extent.

The natural and just procedure would be to

fix between the parties by valuation or agreement the rent of the farm in its existing condition, and then assign to the sitting tenant the value of his improvements by allowing a percentage upon the money value of the compensation he would have got, if he had left the farm, as a deduction from the rent. There is no reason why, in general, such an arrangement could not be come to, and this probably is substantially the practice now on the best managed estates.

This change would have as a result that the landlord, instead of being tempted to squeeze the tenant because of his reluctance to abandon his improvements, will consider that, whether he drives the tenant away or keeps him at an unfair rent, he will have to pay the full value of the improvements, whereas he may save his money by giving the tenant a reasonable deduction off the rackrent and let him remain. The reform substitutes a motive of common sense for a thoroughly base, though often unconscious, motive.

Compensation for Disturbance.

Another proposal frequently made in evidence, with the view of putting the tenant on a more equal footing in bargaining as to rent and conditions of tenure, and of giving him greater security as regards both the retention of the holding, and of his interest in his improvements, is that, under certain circumstances, compensation should be paid for disturbance.

The proposal was, it appears, originally adopted by the Committee of the Central Chamber, and only struck out at the last moment from their report, and has twice received the approval of the Chambers.

Mr Latham, who has had notice to quit, owing to the bankruptcy of his landlord, thinks that in such a case, or on the death of an owner, or in the case of capricious eviction, the tenant should receive compensation for a disturbance such as it is almost impossible for him to foresee. Such a change of ownership through death, or bankruptcy, may drive out a tenant who has built up an important business connection.

Other grounds stated by tenant farmer witnesses are the eviction of tenants for action taken in regard to the enforcement of the Ground Game Act, and resistance to illegal agreements in violation of that Act; or again for political or religious motives, of which several instances have been brought before us.

Mr Barlow thinks there should be compensation where a tenant is forced to quit, capriciously or otherwise, and whether the disturbance is because of killing rabbits, or because of excessive rent, or any other cause.

Mr Kidner thinks that the loss of business and family connections, and the heavy money loss of removal, create a strong motive compelling a tenant to consent to pay excessive rents; thinks there should be compensation "when a man cannot stay on his holding, either from not being able to get his rent properly adjusted, or because the landlord wants to remove him from any cause whatever, except in the case of bad farming. The compensation for his improvements on quitting would not nearly meet his loss in general."

Mr Long advocates compensation for disturbance equal to trade loss, where an owner reserves a farm for his own use, and turns out a farmer who has established a business connection.

Mr Bear, who prefers "free sale" as the measure of tenant's improvements, and the best method of securing the tenant's interests, says that if "free sale" is not granted, you should have compensation for disturbance when a landlord gave notice to quit, because a tenant was carrying out improvements which were shown to be for the benefit of the holding.

Mr Wilkinson, while not advocating fixity of tenure, thinks a tenant has insufficient security, and is often compelled to accept unjust, and unreasonable, and vexatious conditions, and unjust rents, rather than leave the farm, and suffer great loss and expense. "I think the tenant should be protected from arbitrary notice to quit by being allowed compensation for disturbance.

We want to be able to deal with our landlords on equal terms, and not for them to be able to say, 'sign that agreement or quit your farm.' We are tired of that sort of thing in Northumberland, and not going to tolerate it any longer." Where a man is refused a reasonable reduction of rent, and forced to quit his farm, "he is entitled to fair compensation if he has to put his stock on the market in bad times."

Mr Olver says "it is considerable cost for a tenant to move from one farm to another. Suppose a man may be on a farm for many years; he lays out his money and improves it, something turns up between him and his landlord, and he is turned out, and there are no means of getting back his capital again, I think he ought to be paid under those circumstances."

Mr Reynolds, answering the objection that compensation for disturbance is one-sided, and that you cannot compel the tenant to stop at a rent fixed by a court or arbitrator, says "the landlord would have nothing to complain of, because the farm would let directly, assuming that, if we have a court to fix a fair rent, it will fix a fair rent."

Mr Lander thinks it indispensable to the security of the tenant to provide compensation for disturbance. To effect this reform, together with compensation to the sitting tenant at the determination of a tenancy, and limitation of penal rents to damage proved, are, in Mr Lander's opinion, remedies in substitution for a Land Court, which will place the tenant on a more independent and equal footing for the adjusting of rent and other matters.

Mr Pringle, in his report on the South Midlands, refers very strongly to the general sense of insecurity of tenure, there being large numbers of cases in which the old tenants had been forced out of their holdings by the refusal of sufficient reductions of rent. "Compensation for improvements can never be regarded as equivalent to peaceful continuance and enjoyment on fair and reasonable terms."

In view of the frequent recurrence during the evidence

to proofs of a strong feeling on the insecurity of tenure, considerable weight must attach to these suggestions.

So far as it has been possible to gauge the feelings of tenant-farmers during our inquiry, there is at the present time a general reluctance to being bound down to pay a stipulated rent for a long period. Leases and fixity of tenure are not in favour, at any rate in England. But the sense that the more a tenant does to improve his farm the less power he has to arrange fair terms for continuing his tenancy is, in my opinion, wholly inconsistent with the well-being of agriculture. And it is, without doubt, the one idea most tenaciously held, and most frequently dwelt upon, by the majority of the tenant farmers who came before us.

The landlord should have the fullest power to obtain, at the proper times, the rent agreed upon, and to insist that the tenant shall not persistently injure his land by acts of waste. But beyond these powers, which are necessary to protect the landlord's interests, it is not unreasonable that a pecuniary check should be put on any arbitrary action, which compels the tenant to leave his holding, a pecuniary check reasonably measured by the loss thus caused to the tenant. And such arbitrary action could hardly be confined to capricious or unjust eviction. Injustice as cruel may be inflicted by the refusal of a fair reduction of rent, which compels a tenant to quit his holding, and to lose the savings and investments of half a lifetime. I submit that in such cases where a landlord refuses to reduce the rent reasonably, or to submit the matter to arbitration, the tenant should be entitled to some compensation for his loss by removal. It would contribute to steady and improving occupancy and benefit all concerned if the tenant's position were made more secure by giving him a legal right to be compensated for his losses in being compelled to leave his farm, owing to the action of his landlord, except for non-payment of rent and for bad farming.

Law of Distress.

Many practical witnesses have expressed their opinion that the total abolition of the law of distress would be of great benefit to agriculture.

"I would abolish the law of distress in the first instance, so that the landlord and the tenant should be on an equal platform in making the original bargain as to rents."

"It not only increases unfair and unsound competition for farms, but directly leads to bad farming."

"The abolition of the law would tend to reduce rents, perhaps 10 per cent., and would bring in men with real capital."[1]

Mr Sheldon thinks that the great advantages in credit and in other ways, would more than counterbalance any change in the way of paying rents more promptly, and of late years arrears are not generally allowed.

"The landlord, as preferential creditor, is taking in the form of rent the interest on his capital, whereas another creditor may lose, through that action of the landlord, not only his interest but his principal. I have known cases where the landlord has actually seized and taken implements and machines, sold to a tenant by a neighbouring agricultural machine maker, who has lost the whole."

The lessening of competition would, in Mr Kidner's opinion, promote better farming.

Mr Kay condemns the present law, as stimulating competition by unsubstantial men, and leading to other creditors not being paid, while the landlord secures payment in full. He does not think the abolition of distress would cause rents to be paid in advance. It would operate to cause the agent or landlord to make more careful inquiries in selecting tenants.

Mr Bear and the leading northern farmers, Messrs Rowlandson, Scott, Wilkinson, Forster, and also Messrs Lander, Olver, Brown, and Wyatt from the south and western counties, all desire the abolition of this power. So does Mr Owen Williams in Wales, with qualifications.

Mr Dutfield and others do not think abolition would

[1] Carrington Smith, 9782-93, etc.

lead to payment of rent in advance, and that abolition should apply to future tenancies.

On the other hand, witnesses from the south and east, like Mr Read, oppose abolition, on the ground that it would press hardly on struggling farmers.

Mr Edwards thinks that it would damage the chances of young beginners in farming.

Mr Biddell believes abolition would limit the numbers of those who rise from very small occupations to large ones.

Mr Johnstone thinks the law of distress does the farmers no harm.

Mr Fisher objects to abolition, as it would lead to prepayment of rents. Its retention is beneficial to farmers. The landlord is the most lenient creditor.

Mr W. J. Clark quoted by Wilson Fox says:— "Abolition might lower rents, but would lead to many farmers being sold up."

Another Cambridgeshire farmer says: "If the law of distress were abolished, we should get the land 10s an acre cheaper here. I should not mind paying rent in advance."

The land agents and owners generally oppose further restriction of the right of distress as unjust to the landlord and prejudicial to tenants, especially those starting in farming. The abolition would only benefit the other creditors.

Mr Druce does not think abolition would be beneficial, but thinks the procedure unsatisfactory. He and other witnesses strongly urge that the law should be amended, so that in all cases the intention of Parliament, that distress should be strictly limited to twelve months, should be carried out. Under certain agreements at present, it is possible for distress to be levied for eighteen months to two years.

Mr Middleton probably expresses an opinion widely held that many prefer things as they are, as the landlord is the easiest creditor to deal with, and the tendency of the law of distress is rather to protect the small farmer.

The balance of evidence seems to show that it must ultimately be to the benefit of farmers of all classes to have this right of the landlord abolished, that the right tends to maintain rents at a fictitious level, and to limit the freedom and enterprise of farmers.

The desirability and the necessity of having one, simple and complete, procedure for the recovery of compensations and payments under the custom of the country, as well as under the provisions of the Act, has been brought before us by several witnesses.

Mr Read complains that "a tenant, if he has any advantage in his lease or agreement, or by custom, is not allowed to bring that forward to augment his claims, whereas the landlord can claim the lease or the agreement, or the custom of the country, or the Act against the tenant." Mr Read should have added that the landlord has also very large powers under the common law, whereas the common law presumes everything against the tenant, because all improvements by the common law fall to the land, and go to the owner, unless law or agreement steps in.

Mr Lipscomb emphatically supports this suggestion.

Mr Druce says: "As a matter of convenience, and in fairness, it is only right in my opinion that the Act should be amended so that the whole payments on the determination of a tenancy, including all matters and things which are commonly payable under the custom of the country, may be included in one award, and enforceable as one sum."

In the case of Farquharson v. Morgan, although it was stipulated in the agreement that tillages and some other matters usually payable under the custom should be paid for under the Act, it was held that the county court judge had exceeded his powers in confirming the award of the umpire on appeal, and in issuing an order under the 24th section of the Act, to recover the whole amount of the award, including, as it did, items not specified in the Act, as payable under and recoverable by the procedure of the Act. The tenant thus suffered heavy loss because he relied on his agreement, the stipulation of which could not be carried out by the machinery of the Act.

Such a case is a vivid illustration of the absurdity of the methods by which the rights of landlord and tenant are attempted to be adjusted. It is obvious that the consolidation of valuations and of procedure for recovery is imperatively necessary. These considerations show also that the proceedings under a new Act ought to be simple and rapid and decisive enough to make it easy to include all the matters that have to be decided between outgoing tenant and landlord and incoming tenant, settled by one man and in one award. Simplicity of settlement is one of the strong reasons why so many farmers in some counties prefer to go out under the custom than under the Act.

In a new Act, therefore, a clause should be included to the effect that where a tenant is entitled, under custom or otherwise, to claim compensation in respect of tillages, crops, seeds, straw, hay or manure left on the holding, or for cartage, or in respect of a proportion of rent, rates or tithe, or for any other matter or thing connected with the holding, he may claim under the Act as if any such thing were included in its schedules. This provision is embodied in clause 50 of the Agricultural Holdings Act, 1897.

Valuers and Arbitration.

It has already been pointed out that one of the essential defects which had perverted the operation of the Act was the lack of machinery to carry it out.[1] The Act was left to the discretion of the existing valuers.

The evidence shows a practically unanimous opinion that the present type of valuer and modes of valuation are unsatisfactory, and have done more than anything to defeat the intentions of Parliament.

Mr Pringle states this point forcibly :—

"Wherever I went there was a perfect outcry against the manner in which, and the parties by which, the Act

[1] Page 155.

had been administered. 'Any fool can be a valuer;' when a farmer failed at his business he could take to valuation, for so long as he gave the amount, and stated the articles he had valued, it mattered not how his conclusion had been arrived at." Again, " The landlord is a fixture, the tenant removable, so that the valuers lean to the landlord; the odds were all in favour of the side which had most power and could give most jobs."

The referee and umpire system has failed, and will never satisfy either landlord or tenant in deciding compensation for improvements or a fair rent.

"The valuers in Norfolk 'boycott' the Act."

"If the present valuers exercise their powers as they now do, no Act will be of use in Norfolk." The tendency of valuers is shown by the suggestion from Norfolk that "all agents should be struck off the lists of valuers."

The leading farmers who gave evidence strongly condemn the present state of things.

Mr Rowlandson:—" I hope that you will do away with a certain class of men that I should like to see eliminated."

Mr James Stratton:—"It would be a great help to have an official arbitrator; the valuers do not seem to know what to do, and their action has not conduced to the encouragement to leave farms in the high state of cultivation so much desired."

Mr Middleton:—"It would be an advantage if the proper men were selected; it would cheapen the working of the Act, and it would be more equitably worked." There are men carrying on arbitrations who do not grasp the provisions of the Act.

Mr Lipscomb:—"I am perfectly confident that the complaints made against the Act are largely due to the faulty administration by valuers. I scarcely ever meet a valuer who is acquainted with the provisions of the Act."

"I constantly find that valuers do not comply with the Act, and appoint an umpire before they proceed to business. These delays are most injurious; they are costly, and nobody gains but the valuers." He suggests that "the umpire should be called in at once, and so get rid of two out of the three paid persons, except at the formal meeting."

Mr Forster's evidence on this point is suggestive. His experience is that the umpires appointed by the Board of Agriculture are always land agents, whose living depends upon the landlords. The landlord always insists on referring it to the Board of Agriculture.

"We take any unobjectionable man instead." "What we want is an impartial person to act in all cases through the county."

Mr Hope, in his two reports, seems to express the general opinion of the ablest farmers in Scotland that "many of the arbiters who at present administer the statute fail to do so in the spirit of the Act, and there is the greatest dissimilarity and irregularity in the awards made by them."

Mr Druce thinks that "many of the existing arbitrators are unsatisfactory; I do not think they are quite as good men as they ought to be, therefore troubles arise from land agents being so often umpires and valuers; they cannot help themselves from being on the side of the landlords. The farmers think that it is not a fair tribunal."

"I want the person who determines the question of compensation to be as strong and as well qualified a man as possible, and to get rid of the class of valuers who have had no education, and very often no practice."

The almost universal demands are that (1) cases under the Act should be decided by men of a higher status, of more knowledge, more responsibility, and of more independence; and (2) that procedure should be cheapened and simplified by having cases decided by a single arbitrator.

Some witnesses are still of opinion that the present system of having two referees and an umpire is satisfactory and should be maintained. Many farmers believe it necessary to have their own valuer to represent them.

But the great majority of witnesses are clearly in

favour of settling compensation cases by a single arbitrator, officially selected and appointed.

Mr Hope points out the cost and complication of the present system. "There are usually engaged in ascertaining the rights of the two parties, two arbiters, an oversman, a solicitor as clerk, and two solicitors acting for the landlord and tenant respectively, and a considerable number of skilled witnesses." He adds: "One natural result of such a process is to cause a strong feeling of hostility, and make each side view the other's claim as an attempted fraud."

The wish is to substitute for those arrangements an official valuator or arbitrator who would decide authoritatively, impartially, and in accordance with the intentions of the Act.

Other Scotch evidence is to the same effect.

The Amending Agricultural Holdings Act for Scotland in 1889 by which either party can require the sheriff to appoint a single arbiter, has led to more frequent decisions by single arbiters, but not as yet in a majority of cases.

Mr Ferguson says: "It would be far better for everybody concerned if representative practical men in districts or counties should be appointed under Government to arbitrate between the landlord and the outgoing tenant." "A sole arbiter would be far the best." "There should be an official referee with power in difficult cases to call in one responsible person, and to get advice from a neighbouring referee." "My opinion is that a sole referee should take whatever legal or other advice he considers necessary, and decide accordingly."

"The Government arbitrator would be supposed to be a man who would approach it from both sides of the question."

Mr Davidson "would rather have an official valuator than a casual appointment by a sheriff, but would leave the parties free to select beforehand their own man instead of the official arbitrator. It might be well to limit the selection by the sheriff to an official list sanctioned by the Board of Agriculture.

Mr Black thinks it would be cheaper and more

satisfactory to have every question settled by an official referee.

The independence of such an official is insisted on by Mr Ballingall, who says "the parties should not be allowed to nominate him, because that would bring in the wedge of friendship or partisanship."

"The sheriff is not an agricultural expert, and might not pick out the best man. We want officials who are officials and nothing else, who are not dependent on either proprietors or tenants for their business. We should have a permanent official for a defined district."

Mr Stuart is also strongly for appointment by the Crown, instead of selection by the sheriff. Mr Peile, a land agent, approves of a judicial valuator in place of the present system.

Two views crop up in the Scotch and English evidence. Some witnesses adhering to the idea of having some form of option, would prefer an official list from whom the arbitrator for any particular case must be selected; others, attaching most importance to absolute independence and judicial impartiality, wish for an official arbitrator with a definite circuit.

Mr Speir says: "You might have for all Scotland a list for each of the three or four districts, or you might have a single person for each of the districts. The former plan has a good deal to recommend it, but against it is this, that if you have a great many people doing the work you are sure to have many that are not suited for it, and you will have conflicting decisions, you will never have any continuity or uniformity of opinions on courses to be followed. Whereas, if you appointed a single man in a certain district, approaching in some respects to a sheriff in a county, you will then have uniform decisions and working. They might be applied to by either landlord or tenant as to any dispute which arose, or was likely to arise. A new tenant going into a farm might wish a record of condition, or on the dissent of the landlord to any proposed improvement, might apply for a decision from these gentlemen. They might become a court of conciliation which would decide any difference between an old tenant and the landlord about rent, but they could only do so if they were entirely independent of either landlord or tenant. With a large list, there is a difficulty as to the independence. If the arbitrator has to draw upon either side for his work, he must be biassed. You must have him, like a sheriff, absolutely above partiality."

Again, such an official would lessen not increase friction.

"Many tenants lose a good landlord and landlords lose a good tenant for the want of a mediator. That is happening every day. I know of cases where had both parties only known where they could have got an unbiassed opinion they would have gone and asked it and abided by it. Several landlords and factors during my inquiry have said, 'If you could only get a person in whom we had confidence, we would be only too glad in case of little differences to apply to him and be guided by his advice.' But his payment should not be from the State; let a stamp duty be paid on all the work which he does, as in the registration of deeds. All his work would be charged to the parties who employ him, and it would then go into some general fund, which would pay the cost of keeping up either the one, or the dozen, or twenty who might be employed."

Mr Guild: "I think it would work very much better and be more satisfactory to have one for a district, and he should give his whole time to it." "Four or five arbiters would do very well for the whole of Scotland, and if you had them sitting as a court of appeal, with the addition of a sheriff or legal adviser, it would be the means of getting a sound and safe judgment."

Mr Fyshe would have State-appointed and State-paid valuators for counties or groups of counties. Three of the four or five necessary for all Scotland would form a court of appeal. The Act would be administered from Edinburgh by a local branch of the Board of Agriculture. No appeals beyond this court of valuators should be allowed.

There is also a strong feeling that the practical knowledge of such arbitrators and the uniformity of their decisions will tend to diminish the number of cases in which the parties take action.

While Mr Hope wishes the appointment of the official arbitrator to be made by the sheriff of the county, the majority of witnesses are clearly in favour of appointment by the State through the Agricultural Department.

From the north of England similar suggestions are general.

The principle of a single arbitrator to do the whole valuation, to be an official, and not selected by the parties, is strongly supported by Cumberland land agents.[1]

Mr Kay, who represents one of the farmers' organisations in Lancashire, takes a similar view, and thinks the costs would be greatly lessened by making the county court judge the official umpire. There should be an official list of valuers from which the parties might select referees appointed by the county council, and not more than half of these land agents.

The Cumberland farmers "would prefer some fixed tribunal with a legal president and practical assessors, working under a fixed scale of fees."

Mr Punchard approves of the single referee principle, but would not make it compulsory. Arbitration now since the Act of 1889 is usually by one person, and that procedure should be extended to the Agricultural Holdings Act.

Mr Forster thinks "the Act fails from want of confidence in the umpire."

"The best plan would be for a person to be appointed to act in all cases through the county, an impartial person, appointed by the county council. Farmers would know when they were investing their money in improvements, what they had to expect." It would diminish litigation; "it is the uncertainty that causes the mischief."

Mr Bowen Jones wishes arbitrators appointed by the county council, or the Board of Agriculture.

[1] Wilson Fox, Cumberland, p. 18.

The proposal of an official arbitrator has for a number of years been advocated in the northern counties.

Mr Coleman, reporting on Lancashire to the Richmond Commission in 1882,[1] says: "It will be absolutely necessary that the umpires, to whom matters that cannot be settled between outgoer and incomer in the ordinary method of arbitration must be referred, should be men of capacity, judgment, and impartiality. It would be very desirable that Government referees should be appointed for different districts, to whom matters in dispute should be referred, who would hear evidence and decide without appeal. Some scheme of this kind will, as far as I can judge, satisfy the farmers of Lancashire."

Again, Mr Albert Greg, president of the Lancaster Agricultural Society, suggested an impartial court in certain centres to decide questions of improvements and dilapidations.

Mr Scott would remedy the cost of procedure by having official valuators or commissioners, or referees appointed for each district, and a court of appeal, so many of these referees meeting together quarterly; the law courts to have nothing to do with it.

It would be better that these inspectors or referees or arbitrators should have nothing to divert their minds from their work. They should be, as it were, inspectors, and in that case, we should have them as a first court, and then, if there was an appeal, it would go to three or four of them, and would be decided by the majority. That would cheapen the whole process. "Legal gentlemen are very fond of evidence, but we would hope that the official referee would not be equally fond of it."

Mr Pringle has stated with much clearness the wishes of representative farmers in the South Midlands on this question.[2]

What is wished is "the appointment of county or district arbitrators, assisted when necessary by boards of assessors." "Upon the following points all are agreed:

[1] Wilson Fox, Garstang, p. 21.
[2] Pringle, Beds. Hunts. Northants, pp. 61, 67.

The arbitrator must be so placed that any possibility of showing favour or manipulating awards will be prevented. His awards must state fully the reasons which have guided him in his decisions. He must be a servant of the State, employed, paid by, and accountable to Government. He must be familiar with the value of land and the customs of farming in the district."

The court, or board of assessors, should be composed of representatives of landlords and tenants, to advise and assist the arbitrators in doubtful cases. The general feeling was that the arbitrator should be appointed by the Board of Agriculture, and the assessors by the county councils.

Another method is suggested by Mr Lander, from Shropshire, and Mr Kidner from Somerset, both of whom wish an official arbitrator to be appointed by the district council for each district. The parties might act as their own valuers, and have this official as the umpire. Mr Kidner seems to think the arbitrator could be elected in some way by the parties interested. He would be paid by both sides on a fixed scale. Mr Middleton also wants to have some choice in the selection of these men.

Mr Druce thinks the appointment of all umpires ought to be made by the Board of Agriculture; the umpire in these cases ought to be a man who has the *imprimatur* of his capacity stamped upon him by the Board of Agriculture. There should be a certain number of men nominated by county councils in every county, and approved by the Board of Agriculture, and every reference under the Act should be to one of these men. In that way you would get as strong a man as possible, and do away with a desire for an appeal. The stronger you make the arbitrator or umpire in the first instance the better.

He favours the plan of settlement by a single referee, and that the referee should be selected from the official list, not by the choice of the parties, but in rotation.

Mr Rowlandson, Mr Lipscomb, and others support generally the recommendation of the Central Chamber of Agriculture, that all umpires should be selected from an official list, nominated by county councils and sanctioned by the Board of Agriculture, or, in other words, the proposal first made in the Agricultural Holdings Bill of 1889. Mr Lipscomb thinks it will still be necessary for most farmers to employ some one as a valuer to draw up the details of a claim. "I should only be too glad if this initial man were entirely set aside, and that the umpire should he called in at once." "The sooner you go to the umpire the better so as to get rid of the constant meetings, which is one of the causes of the trouble.

Mr Olver would have an official valuer or surveyor appointed by the county council, who should make records of condition and decide compensation cases.

Mr Looker and others prefer a list, and freedom of selection, "as every one would not have confidence in one man."

Mr Carrington Smith would leave the landlord and tenant, as now, to appoint their referees in the first instance, and then call in an official umpire instead of letting the referees appoint the umpire.

The opinions thus expressed by many practical and representative men are conclusive that the present system of references is obsolete, and a serious hindrance to the main purpose of any Act to determine the mutual rights of landlord and tenant. It is clear that the most satisfactory machinery will be the impartial judgment of a single arbitrator whose qualifications secure him the confidence of all parties concerned.

As to the manner of appointment of this official opinions differ widely, and much may be said for several of the conflicting suggestions. I am disposed to think that the higher the authority given to such an arbitrator, and the more judicial his functions, the weightier become the arguments for leaving the appointment to the Government instead of imposing on a local body a somewhat invidious task, into which personal and local considerations may enter, as well as the question of the perfect fitness of candidates for the office. Local and practical knowledge of the several features of the agriculture of the district would seem an indispensable qualification, and the Board of Agriculture ought to obtain satisfactory evidence as to this qualification from the county or counties concerned before making any appointment.

There is the even more important difference of opinion as to whether there should be a number of such official arbitrators appointed for a county or counties from which list umpires or single arbitrators are to be selected by the parties or the county court, or by some other authority, or a single official arbitrator appointed with jurisdiction over a specified tract of country like a county court judge.

The opinion of practical men would seem to have been steadily moving in the latter direction. The former scheme would seem a halfway house between two antagonistic systems, and to retain some of the mischief of the old system, without the full benefits reasonably expected from the "single and authoritative arbitrator" proposal. Much weight should attach to the contention that an arbitrator of the type contemplated by Mr Scott, and by most of the Scottish witnesses, would give decisions on broader and at the same time more consistent grounds, and would act as a better exponent of the intention of Parliament, and that procedure of this kind raised above the mere partisan efforts of competing referees would greatly lessen litigation, and settle disputed points on simple and definitely ascertained principles, with the minimum of friction, of outlay, and of cost. So long as the door remains open for either party to try, in selecting from a list, whether officially sanctioned or not, to get the man with a bias towards the interests of his side, the obvious evils of the present system cannot be quite eliminated.

There is no reason why, if sufficient care is taken in the appointment of such arbitrators for definite districts, men of high character and absolute impartiality, as well as of practical agricultural experience, should not be secured for posts of this kind, in whom both landlords and tenants would feel complete confidence. The suggestion of Mr Speir, as to their payment from a general fund into which all fees should be paid, irrespective of the localities, deserves full consideration.

CHAPTER XII.

Arbitration as to Rent.

IN the preceding chapter we have considered how far under the existing law, the interests and the freedom of the working agriculturist are protected, and the necessity for further protection in order to secure fair play for agricultural effort. It is obvious, on full consideration of the evidence as to insecurity, and of the various suggestions for strengthening the law, that the really essential difficulty, which all these suggestions are meant directly or indirectly to overcome, is the weak position of the tenant in bargaining as to future rent.

The theory of the promoters of the Act of 1883 was that "in any negotiations between a landlord and an existing tenant for the renewal of a tenancy, in any claim which the tenant makes in times of depression and low prices for a reduction of rent, or whenever in better times the landlord demands a rise in rent," the position of the tenant in bargaining will be strengthened by his statutory right to recover from the landlord, on quitting his holding, the full remaining value of his improvements.

The evidence taken before this Commission shows conclusively that this theory has not been confirmed by experience, and that, so far from being stronger in bargaining, the improving tenant who has a large amount of capital invested in his holding is powerless to obtain fair conditions, and that his position is the more hopeless just in proportion to the interests he has at stake. It has been found that, at any given moment in a period of low prices and general depression, a tenant farmer of this class is bound to estimate that his immediate loss in quitting his farm, selling off stock, and in removing to another farm, would much more than balance any possible compensation he could obtain under the Act.

The three main suggestions made to remedy these evils, viz., compensation for increased fertility, due to long continued good farming, compensation for loss by removal when a tenant is disturbed in his holding, and compensation to the sitting tenant at the determination of a tenancy, when the terms of renewal are being considered, have been fully discussed and approved in the preceding chapter.

These three amendments of the law, with the equally important amendment as to its administration by a single official arbitrator, would very materially alter the position of the tenant as regards bargaining for a fair rent. At the same time it has been admitted that it would be, though less probable, still perfectly possible to defeat these objects by unjustly enhanced rents.

I therefore proceed to consider the evidence given as to the necessity and desirability of determining rents judicially, or by some form of arbitration.

The mass of evidence which has been analysed in the earlier chapters and the very serious considerations it has been necessary to weigh and examine, as to the economic impossibility as well as the injustice of rents shown to be paid at the present time, have convinced me that the onus of proof must rest on those who oppose any reasonable scheme for reducing rents to an equitable and workable level. And reasons have been stated in Chapter X for some doubt as to the alleged acquiescence of farmers in the present state of things. And, in the evidence of many witnesses, there has been declared a strong desire for arbitration as to rents, at the same time that they express distaste and disapproval of what they call a "land court."

Further, it is obvious that the demands and suggestions should be examined as regards the substantial facts and grounds alleged, and without regard to the merely verbal distinctions made with imperfect appreciation by some witnesses; and also it is not quite reasonable to expect that practical witnesses, who come before us to formulate such demands, should be prepared to submit precisely drawn proposals. The demands themselves and the general grounds on which they are advanced, seem sufficient to call for close scrutiny, with the view to meet the real necessities from which they spring.

There can be no doubt that the strong feeling in favour of judicial rents which accompanied the early years of this depression from 1879 to 1882, and was then expressed in the proposals introduced in Parliament by the late Mr James Howard, on behalf of the Farmers' Alliance, was for some years, more or less, slackened by the hope of getting something out of the Agricultural Holdings Act, and has again developed on somewhat bolder and more decisive lines owing to the general disappointment at the results of the Act, and under the urgent stimulus of the more acute stage of depression which has prevailed since 1892.

That there is a strong and widespread demand at present is shown in evidence.

Mr Pringle says that although farmers in Essex were somewhat indifferent as to the Agricultural Holdings Act, "I had continuous evidence of their desire for better security in the form of continued occupation at fair rents, no charge being put upon their improvements." "The principle of the Irish Land Act was generally approved of, and the system therein devised of ascertaining a fair rent was recognised as practical and equitable. Courts of arbitration should be established, to which parties who failed to agree upon future rents could repair." At meetings at Ongar and Braintree resolutions were passed asking for the immediate extension to England of the Irish Acts, and "that in view of the failure of the Agricultural Holdings Act, and the present insecurity to the sitting tenant, and the desire to attract fresh capital to the land, arbitration courts should be established by the legislature as soon as possible."[1]

[1] Pringle, Essex, p. 35.

In Lancashire, where the movement in this direction has grown into an important organisation, extending also to Cheshire and Cumberland, there has been a widespread demand for fair rents to be fixed by arbitration, in some reasonable relation to the prices of produce. For this purpose a land court is suggested, and fixity of tenure, and free sale are associated with the proposal.

In Lancashire, and also in Cumberland, where the Farmers' Association favours a land court to determine rents, it appears that the details of any scheme have not been unanimously agreed on, and there is divergence of opinion. Fair rent and fixity of tenure, it was held by some, would naturally follow from absolute security for improvements. "They had no other object in view in asking for an arbitration court for rent than to prevent men from bidding a higher price than the land was worth." The president of this association thought "they would be satisfied with some form of voluntary arbitration, to which landlords and tenants could appeal to settle a question of rent."

But the essential point to notice is that there is a universal sense of grievance as to rents, for which some solution should be found. Mr Bird, a Westmoreland farmer, probably expresses the view in saying that, "though he was against a land court, the feeling was growing in favour of arbitration, owing to rents not having been adjusted to the present price of produce."

In Dorset, Mr Rew reports a resolution: "That some court of appeal be formed, to which a tenant might apply, without prejudice to his occupation, for a re-assessment of his rent, or for the adjustment of any other grievance." A land court was also suggested, because improving tenants could not get the same reduction of rent as bad farmers.

The evidence collected by Mr Rew in North Devon throws much light on the real drift of opinion. The general letting of farms by tender, and the keen competition thus provoked, leads to frequent "protests against the present rents as excessive."

Resolutions in favour of arbitration in all cases of

dispute, and that land valuers should be appointed to arbitrate, were adopted at South Molton and Barnstaple.

Here, as in Lancashire, all the issues have not been thought out. Mr Rew says: "Many who voted for the resolution did so with a vague idea that when a landlord refused to grant a reduction of rent an appeal might be made by consent of both parties to an official valuer, who would decide the matter in a friendly way." Others obviously wanted compulsory arbitration with enforceable decisions as to rent.

Mr Pringle, whose striking statements as to the insecurity of the improving tenant have been quoted earlier in this report,[1] states that the tenant farmers of the South Midlands submitted to him that "unless something is done to fortify the position of the good tenant, and protect him when disputes about rent arise, we need not expect capital to be invested in farming. They desire not the shadow but the substance of security."

He adds: "I have no reason to believe that landlords as a body would oppose the introduction of any reasonable system for the better security of the sitting tenant."

"Already the propriety of arbitration has been admitted by some landlords; in some agreements of recent preparation *all matters in dispute* are referred to arbitration."

The general view of the farmers is, that the best way of overcoming the difficulties of settling disputes about rent or other matters would be by "an arbitrator in the service of the State, and with local knowledge." "Beyond the question of fair rent, and what might be called 'disturbance of the sitting tenant' there did not appear to be any other matters seriously requiring settlement."

As in other districts, the farmers had not closely thought out the procedure.

Arbitration would, apparently in their view, mean that where farms had to be revalued for future rent, this should be done by an impartial official, instead of by a man selected by the landlord.

Mr Pringle thinks the desire is for compulsory pro-

[1] Pringle Beds, etc., pp. 60, 61.

cedure, not for a merely voluntary Board of Conciliation: "There is nothing at present to prevent landlord and tenant calling in a third party to value the rent, but that would be conciliation which would hardly be worth anything."

An advisory board of practical men is also suggested, to help the official arbitrator, where necessary, as assessors.

While desiring some form of compulsory arbitration as to rents, objection was taken to a land court; the objection being partly to the name, partly because they disliked public examination as to their rent in court. "I think it is the name of the thing, and perhaps the functions of this arbitrator may be just the land court over again."

In his report on the North Riding and Durham, Mr Pringle states that "farmers insist that rents must be greatly reduced. It is the general opinion that to bring about a fair and reasonable reduction some system of arbitration should be set in motion. Anything like compulsory interference between landlord and tenant is objected to, and land courts, although recommended by a few, are not, generally speaking, desired. Tenants prefer to arrange rents, if possible, without the intervention of a third party, but failing a satisfactory agreement, they feel that arbitration should be at hand. To this proposal some landlords make no objection. The owner of a very large estate said: "Provided that an entirely impartial arbitrator could be found, arbitration would not be objectionable to me." "On another large estate, arbitration has already been called upon to settle disputes as to rent."

He adds: "It is to protect the tenant, who by good and liberal treatment has made his farm a place to be desired, from being rented on his own good management that arbitration is suggested."

An excellent farmer who pays 36s an acre, and has been refused a reduction, because the landlord could get the same rent from a new tenant, says the high state of cultivation would enable a new man to make a profit at that rent by running out the farm for five years, when it would be worth perhaps 20s. " Personally, I do not care to get all the good out of the land and then give it up. I should prefer to farm as I have done for years, but at a fair rent. As a general rule, I think a landlord and tenant should make their own bargain, but a land court, or the appointment of Government arbitrators would be a very great boon to the farmer to appeal to in special cases such as I have related."

In Scotland, Mr Speir gives as the general opinion that agriculture needs a re-adjustment of rents to prices: " if the rent is wrong, no amount of legislation in other directions will make the farm right." The desire for a land court and judicial rents is very much on the increase."

Mr Gilchrist and Mr M'Connell would refer the fixing of a fair rent to the arbitrator, to be based on produce and prices.

In Aberdeenshire there is a strong demand for judicial rents.

Mr Black, Secretary of the Morayshire Farmers' Club, told us that a demand for reductions of rent based on a careful valuation resting on the fiars prices of all produce over a term of years had proved itself sound, and was now carried out on a number of farms.

On Lord Aberdeen's estate a re-valuation was given to tenants who desired it by voluntary arbitration, resulting in a reduction of 23 per cent. on a rental of about £11,000.

Farms are re-let on that estate on a valuation based on the quality and fertility of the soil, the state and suitability of the buildings, situation as regards railways, and the demand for land in the neighbourhood.

The wish for arbitration as to rent is put strongly by several English farmer witnesses.

Mr Kidner thinks that the insecurity of the sitting tenant can only be remedied by the determination of the rent by an independent authority, for some fixed term, probably five years, and revised when " grown out of proportion to the times." A rent would be fair " at which a man with good management would be able to live on the farm, and obtain a fair return for his outlay."

Mr Kidner's main ground is that the tenant's capital is inseparable from the soil, and to encourage its investment it is necessary to restrict the power of the owner from selling the use of the land at the highest obtainable price.

Mr Wilkinson asks for a court of some kind to deal with compensation cases, the reasonableness of conditions of tenure, and "of rent, in exceptional cases," where reasonable reductions are refused.[1] This is essential to enable tenants who have heavy investments of their capital in enriched fertility of the soil, and in valuable stock, to escape being squeezed into unfair terms.

Mr Wilkinson further contends that English should have as good security as Irish farmers, and that if a distinction is sought to be based on the fact that Irish tenants have put up buildings, it is untenable, because the value of the Irish investments in these improvements is not comparable with the thousands of pounds put into the farm by an English tenant in the shape of cakes and manure and other heavy outlays.

But Mr Wilkinson is not in favour of the full application of the Irish Act, with fixity of tenure and dual ownership. His object is to protect the invested capital of the tenant, and to prevent its confiscation in rent.

"I hold that the landlord should not have my improvements or live on my capital any longer. What belongs to the landlord let him sell at the best price, but he has no right to sell what belongs to the tenant."

An appeal as to rent should not be made oftener than from five to seven years. Mr Wilkinson would apparently leave it open to either party to give notice to quit during such an interval with compensation for disturbance, if the circumstances called for it.

And he especially insists on the right of appeal as to rent, where a tenant has been refused a reasonable reduction, the tenant having also in this case the right

[1] 31,394-7.

to compensation for disturbance if no agreement is arrived at, and he has to quit.

Mr Riley, who does not himself desire Irish legislation for England, but states that tenants are making nothing and paying rents largely out of capital, and that the keen competition for improved farms in high condition, prevents adequate reduction of their rents, quotes several farmers who wish to apply to this state of things an adequate remedy.

Thus, a farmer whose holding has been in the family 300 years and is splendidly farmed, can get no sufficient reduction, though his landlord is offering his Irish land at fourteen years purchase to the Irish tenants.

Another first-class large farmer says: " The only relief is an Irish land law for England. The best landlords need have no fear of it; it would only catch the bad ones who want more than the land is worth. Why should not the industrious, law-respecting English farmers have the same laws for land as the Irish?"

Mr Reynolds thinks rents must be brought into a fair proportion to the fall in prices, and that the old tenants will not be able to obtain such "reductions without some authority at the back of them, in the nature of a land court." The term for a judicial rent should be five years; but, like Mr Wilkinson, he would give the right to the landlord to get rid of his tenant, with full compensation for unjust disturbance.

Both parties would retain their freedom, and could not be injured. If the tenant gave it up, not liking the rent fixed, the landlord would be able to let the farm at once, supposing the rent reasonable. The court must be presumed to fix a fair rent.

Mr Nunneley says as to arbitration for rents : " If it could be fairly provided, I think it would be a good thing." The difficulty he sees is that though the law might compel the landlord, it could not compel the tenant to stop if dissatisfied. He thinks that among tenant farmers there would be rather a preponderance of opinion in favour of some kind of arbitration. He, himself, is not in favour of fixity of tenure.

Mr W. Smith, then M P. for North Lonsdale, introduced in 1893 a Bill applying, with some modifications, the provisions of the Irish Land Act and the Crofters Act, to English conditions. A land court is to be constituted of the county court judge, with assessors representative of landowners and of tenant farmers. A fair rent for five years, with power of renewal, fixity of tenure subject to payment of rent and good farming, and free sale of tenant's improvements, with power to the landlord to object to an unsuitable tenant, or to resume, paying the agreed sum, and fixing of reasonable conditions of tenure, are the essential points of the Bill. The court can also give the tenant permission to carry out permanent improvements, or assign an increased rent to the landlord, as interest on his outlay on improvements. The Bill is compulsory, and would practically exclude every other form of tenancy. The Bill is also meant to exclude competition values. An outgoing farmer, in selling his good will, would not be able to pocket the whole difference between the fair rent and the top competition price, because the amount passing between the parties would be determined by the court.

The Bill is really the outcome of the Lancashire and Cheshire movement, and reflects the impressions Lancashire farmers formed of their own fate from what they saw in Essex. The Bill has been approved by many agricultural meetings, and its principles were supported by about one-third of the delegates at the great conference in St James's Hall in 1892.

Mr Smith rests his case for these proposals on the steady eating up of tenant's capital by excessive rents, and the absolute insecurity of the improving tenant, both as to his property in his improvements and his retention of his holding. Mr Smith gave instances of the capricious eviction of tenants, in one case for political motives, in another because the tenant had taken part in the organisation of the movement for a better tenure system.

"What I think the court is needed for is that the farmers should know that there was in case of need an impartial authority to which they might appeal to redress their wrongs."

Security would rapidly develop agriculture, and if it had been granted before, "the depression would not have been so acute."

"I am quite certain that there is not one acre in a hundred in this country which is farmed up to the degree that it might be farmed."

Mr Smith does not wish the tenant to transfer an ever-increasing burden in the form of a tenant right as in Ulster; if necessary, he would shorten the judicial period to prevent this.

As to free sale, Mr Smith admitted that it might fail as a measure in times of rapid fall of prices, and therefore he left the Agricultural Holdings Act for the tenant to fall back upon in that emergency.

He was strongly of opinion that the provisions of his Bill were essential, and that full compensation for improvements, coupled with compensation for disturbance, would not really cover the present insecurity of the tenant, but he felt that there was a reluctance on the part of many tenants to accept fixity of tenure, and himself wished a shorter term than five years for a judicial rent to run.

Mr Worthington, a thorough supporter of these views, thinks that fixity of tenure would not deter a landlord from making improvements, and that the three F's are the only cure for the insecurity of the improving farmer, to whom no reduction is allowed. Farming will improve if the tenant's property is made absolutely his own by the power of free sale. Where improvements had to be valued, they should be valued by the land court, and a record of condition at entry would be kept at the court from which to calculate improved condition. If there were a land court, landlords would come to terms with their tenants, and there would be few or no appeals.

The landlord, under this Bill, would be able to get rid of a bad tenant at any time by application to the court. Otherwise these proposals give, by the power of renewal and bequest, a perpetual tenancy.

In the Scotch evidence, we had to note a protest by several witnesses against fixity of tenure on the ground that it led to a monopoly.

Many land reformers will feel doubt as to the wisdom of a practically perpetual tenure being given to individual tenants and their legatees. While there is a strong desire to give full protection to the rights and interests of those who till the soil, it may reasonably be held to be inconsistent with the general interest of the nation to create what are virtually fresh monopolies.

Mr Cooke, representing the Federation of Farmers' clubs in Cheshire, warmly approved of Mr Smith's Bill being carried out to encourage high farming by absolute security, stop capricious evictions for political or sectarian reasons, or because of game preserving, and to set aside unfair and restrictive covenants and penal rents, which still abound and are used illegally to coerce tenants out of their statutory rights. The landlord will be bound, but the tenant may quit, and his improvements would in that case be valued to him by the court.

Dr Fream mentions a strong wish for a land court in parts of Kent and Hampshire.

Mr Bomford approves of conciliation courts to settle disputes as to rent, and "thinks the very fact of there being a court of that sort would make the landlord and tenants practically agree to some compromise, and so settle their own affairs."

Mr Spencer quotes an Oxfordshire farmer who was refused a reasonable reduction, and said: "What we want is a land court to deal with the rent. If I could get my rent reduced, I would say nothing about the depression. *Many farmers would like a land court, but are afraid to say so.*"

With regard to the objection that arbitration would be unequal, as it would bind the landlord while leaving the tenant free to leave if dissatisfied, attention should be directed to the excellent results of Lord Tollemache's leases in Cheshire. This lease is for nineteen years and binding on the landlord, while allowing the tenant, if times go wrong with him, to leave at a year's notice.

The result on that estate has been contentment and splendid cultivation, and a readiness to pay somewhat higher rents than elsewhere.

Mr Cooke states that what is wanted in the proposals of the Bill is to secure pretty much the legalising of a lease like Lord Tollemache's.

Mr Bear, who in 1881, 1882, and 1883 took a leading part in promoting the proposals of the Farmers' Alliance, is of opinion that compensation by valuation always has been, and must be, a failure, and that free sale is the only satisfactory measure of the value of improvements. Fixity of tenure, and fair rents are only desirable to facilitate bargaining. The Farmers' Alliance proposed a term of seven years, during which the rent could not be altered. The landlord would have the right of pre-emption at the market price. This price would *ex hypothesi* be the highest offer of an outsider. And the offer [of the outsider must clearly be based on some kind of valuation. The first Bill of the Alliance, giving free sale alone as the procedure, was discarded in favour of a second Bill giving the alternative of procedure by valuation.

Mr Bear states that the free sale proposals were not generally acceptable to the majority of farmers.

Professor Long supports the "three F's" proposals in their entirety, holding that the invested capital of the tenant cannot be properly secured without fixity of tenure at a fair rent. Compensation under the Act is, he contends, a mere farce. "If the most is to be got from the land, and a satisfied and prosperous tenantry to be kept upon it, you must give them a very distinct interest in the soil, and induce them in every way to put their money and labour into it. Fixity of tenure exists to-day in the case of many good landlords, and I would not wish for more than they give; but it is the majority who are bad, or rather who do not do their duty to their tenants, whom I should like a law passed to control."

He thinks that fixity of tenure, by encouraging larger investment, will make it necessary to give freedom of sale. If land courts were adopted, agreements as to rents would probably be registered in the court, so that no revision could take place, after the contract began, till a reasonable period. Existing leases would have to be set aside, if the five years' system were adopted.

Professor Sheldon, like Mr Bear, is an advocate of free sale; fixity of tenure and fair rents are hardly, in his opinion, required if tenants had security to obtain the full value of their improvements when they left, and this they can best have by free sale. He would limit free sale to improvements only.

He admits that there are difficulties in this proposal, both as regards reserving to landlords their right of pre-emption and choice of a new tenant, and as regards the detachment of the increase of value of land due to improvements and to other causes.

Free sale of improvements is obviously open to several objections. In the first place, it will not work in bad times, and throws you back on a system of valuation. Without valuation, an outgoing tenant, when things are at their worst, would get nothing, and would be ruined. In the second place, you have to guarantee the purchaser that he shall have the same rent as the seller, or at any rate that he shall know beforehand at what rent he shall enjoy the holding. But if the transfer is made during the course of a five years' term, unless there is at the same time a reference to the court to fix a judicial rent for another five years, the new tenant cannot be sure at what rent he will sit, and, under Mr Smith's Bill and similar Bills, he must necessarily wait till the end of the term to know exactly how the court will decide. In the meantime some sudden change of prices, or the condition of agriculture, may materially alter the decision anticipated by the purchaser at the time he enters into his bargain. The whole transaction is therefore speculative, and does not rest, as an improved system of valuation would rest, on an exact appraisement at the moment of the remaining value of the improvements of the outgoing tenant.

As to fixity of tenure, much evidence was given that farmers generally have too little confidence to care to be tied down, for even as short a period as five years, to pay a stipulated rent without power of escape. It will have been noted that the supporters of Mr Smith's Bill and similar proposals are anxious to reserve to the tenant the right of withdrawal, while binding the landlord. And the general indisposition to take leases has been marked all over the country. Even on the generously managed estates of the Duke of Richmond, with all the advantages of practical freedom of cultivation, and the division of the rates, leases are declined and yearly tenancies asked for. Leases have been abandoned on the Holkham and other estates. And after producing admirable results in high continuous farming in Northumberland, they are lapsing now.

In Scotland, the same tendency has been shown in the demand for five-year breaks at option of tenant in the nineteen years' leases. Though there has been some reaction in some counties in favour of the longer unbroken tenancy, Mr Speir himself would "prefer to be clear of a lease altogether, and to have full compensation for any added value," and other witnesses are of the same opinion.

While noting these difficulties in the working, and as to the acceptability to farmers of proposals to introduce the "three F's," it must be admitted that these difficulties may reasonably be viewed as partial, and in some sense temporary. The evidence as to agriculturists who put large amounts of money into agriculture, like the fruit-growers in Worcestershire and elsewhere, and the hop-growers in Kent, establishes incontestably the fact that the more money is thus put in, the less possible it is to contest the fairness of the demand of men, who have so much invested, to the right to some mode of free sale, and of fixity of tenure, and to some machinery for preventing the frustration of their demand by unfairly enhanced rents. These are plain undeniable economic facts, which will, in my opinion, have to be dealt with ultimately, even though our present problems seem to be of a more restricted character, and the proposals of Mr Smith and others do not command general assent.

In reviewing the evidence given before the Commission and collected by the Assistant Commissioners, it is obvious that the preponderance of opinion expressed is against the proposal of a land court, so called.

Mr Middleton says:—"The feeling against any tribunal for fixing rents has been most emphatic. I am opposed to any outsider fixing the prices of any article."

Mr James Stratton and Mr Johnson (Ixworth) take much the same view.

Mr Kay thinks it unfair to compel a landlord to take a certain rent, when he himself can go to market and take the market price, or keep his cows. "The landlord ought to be able to do the same with his land. I fail to see that I ought to deprive the landlord of the liberty which I, as a tenant farmer, demand for myself."

The true method, in his opinion, is to make the landlord pay fully for any misuse of his freedom which injures others.

Mr Rowlandson, Mr C. S. Read, Mr Dewar, Mr Bell, Mr Edwards, Mr Parton, and others all prefer that bargains should be made between the parties, without any interference by an outside authority to settle the terms.

Mr Scott explained that in his scheme for official arbitrators, "their powers were not to extend in any way or form to the question of the regulation of rent between owner and occupier."

"That," he says, "is the general opinion of intelligent farmers all over the country."

A number of the English witnesses are opposed to the fixing of rents by judicial authority, including several who advocate very advanced proposals regarding compensation and security of tenure. Most of these witnesses express their objections in the form of dissent from the idea of a legal tribunal, before whom the relations of landlord and tenant are supposed to come in the form of a trial in court, while others base their objections on the desire to preserve freedom to make their own bargains.

Mr Wilson Fox has collected a variety of opinions in Lincolnshire in these directions.[1]

Thus: "Several farmers stated that they would sooner give up farming than go before any tribunal to settle questions between them and their landlords."

"Land courts are not wanted to deal with rent, but they might deal with the interest we pay on mortgages."

"We are dead against a land court. If we cannot look after our own interests, we do not want any one else to do it for us."

"There is not a single party in this room who would like any one in the room to assist him and his landlord in fixing a fair rent, though we are all friends. Much less should we like an outsider called in. We can, and we prefer to, fight our own battles."

A Lancashire farmer who is a strong Protectionist, says: "If we are to have a land court, we are all fools in a lump if we cannot make a bargain."[2]

More closely-reasoned objections are offered by several witnesses, who think that if the system of fixity of tenure and judicial rents were established, there would not be the same disposition, and probably a refusal, to give temporary abatements of rent in some exceptionally bad season. Others also attach much importance to the contention that, when the owner becomes a mere rent-charger, he will no longer care to invest his capital in permanent improvements and repairs.

Further considerations, to which weight must be attached, are made as to the difficulty of working any such system.

Thus, Mr Fyshe, a Scotch witness of much ability, says: "When you find one farm let at £200 of a rise, and another going to be let at 40s an acre, and an offer comes in for 50s an acre, in one week, it is difficult to find a remedy, unless this [land] court is directed to take

[1] Wilson Fox, Lincoln, pp. 20, 21.
[2] Wilson Fox, Garstang, Appendix P.

possession of the liberty of the subject, and allow valuators to say, 'Well, Mr Landlord, there is the value of your land. You can take what tenant you like.'"

At the same time, it must be remembered that Mr Fyshe considers "high rents" the first cause of agricultural depression, and this intense competition is as unwise as it is ruinous. And he, and many other witnesses, who appear to doubt the practicability of fixing fair rents, and compelling both parties to agree upon terms which will alone make the working of a farm an economic success, make the very strongest recommendations as regards the securing of tenants from being rented on their own improvements.

With regard to the contention often advanced that judicial rents would, in England, be unjust to the landlords, and would not have the same justification as in Ireland, because in Ireland permanent improvements have been carried out by the tenants, while in England they have been carried out by the landlords, this contention, for reasons fully stated in chapter IX, should be treated as fallacious, and should be discarded in the settlement of this question.

As Mr Wilkinson has pointed out, the English farmer has often a larger money stake invested in his holding than the Irish farmer; and it is matter of demonstration that, for all intents and purposes, the so-called landlord's improvements in England have been substantially paid for by the tenant, and therefore the supposed distinction does not, as a matter of fact, exist.

On careful consideration of all the evidence as to the dissent of practical farmers from any procedure for determining fair rents, I am convinced that part of this alleged repugnance is due to very natural disinclination on the part of tenants to others knowing the state of their affairs, and to the equally natural fear that the intervention of an official between them and the landlord or agent may suspend friendly relations. It is also obvious, from the mass of evidence we have considered as to the present unfortunate position of most farmers, that they must be disinclined to face the risk of supporting any proposals which they know are cordially disliked by those in whose power the present state of the law places their whole investments in the soil, and their business future to so large an extent.

Large numbers of farmers, also, who may not be so much embarrassed, or influenced by these motives, probably rely more on their own judgment in making a bargain than they would on an official decision; the same motive is seen operating in the failure of the legislation to promote selling of cattle by live weight.

Much more importance should be attached to the dread of most tenants of being bound to pay a rent which may be fair when fixed, but may become impossible to pay owing to sudden falls in prices of special products, or to disastrous seasons, and to the undoubted probability that landlords would not, after a fair rent was fixed, be inclined to give remissions also.

No doubt many grave difficulties will have to be encountered and overcome in introducing any changes, however ultimately beneficial, in the present system of tenure in England.

But, assigning all the weight which is due to the reluctance of many tenants, and to other drawbacks and difficulties, I feel bound to state that the objections made to interference with rents do not appear to me to have anything like the force or weight which should undoubtedly attach to two central and indisputable facts which our inquiry has established.

The first is the universal demand of the best type of farmer, the man who throws his money and his whole ability and energy into the improvement of the land, for absolute security. This demand is put with clearness by Mr Pringle in one of his reports.

"The desire of the farmers is for better security in the form of continued occupation at fair rents, no charge being put upon their own improvements."[1]

The necessity for meeting this demand has been proved to demonstration in this inquiry.

The second is that the rents which have been charged during the period of depression have been, and still are,

[1] Pringle, Essex, p. 35.

economically impossible over a large part of the country, and have been, and can only be paid, in many cases, by the steady depletion of tenants' capital, and the consequent progressive deterioration of the soil.

Reductions of rent have generally been insufficient, and the evidence has been nearly uniform that competition has tended to make rack-renting, relatively to prices and returns, more oppressive, to penalise the enterprising and improving farmer more heavily, and to render his position more hopeless and intolerable. The economic waste resulting from this state of things is a matter of national concern.

While, therefore, having noted several serious objections to proposals like those of Mr Smith's Bill, I feel convinced that it is my duty to recommend some simple and adequate means for facilitating the reduction of rents generally to a fair economic level.

Assuming that official arbitrators, with the powers and qualifications suggested in the previous chapter, have been appointed, it is natural to suppose that the determination of the letting value of a farm, when in dispute between landlord and tenant, would be not infrequently referred to the arbitrator by consent of both parties. As he will have to decide in the case of a sitting tenant, the proportionate reduction of rent which is necessary to exclude the tenant's improvements from the new rent, and in the case of a tenant who is obliged to leave owing to the refusal of a reasonable reduction of rent, the amount of loss sustained by the tenant, it is plain that this official in the discharge of these duties, must not only form but frequently express an opinion as to the relation of the total rent to the real productive value of the farm as an agricultural instrument.

If, as is generally anticipated by those who advocate their appointment, these officials acquire the confidence of both parties, I think it eminently probable that in the re-valuation of farms or estates, their experienced judgment will be thought helpful in voluntary arrangements. The fact that they will draw up the record of condition of farms at the beginning of tenancies, and that the decision of any ultimate questions which may arise will rest in their hands, must inevitably make it advisable in the interests of both parties, to refer to them voluntarily any arrangements as to rents, in which there is a difference of opinion as to the real value of a holding.

The remarkable evidence given by Mr Pennant puts the whole matter in its natural, and practical, and workable light:—

"You want people who will give confidence to both landlord and tenant. I think [official arbitrators] appointed by the Board of Agriculture, who would be really good men, would be very valuable, because where there was a difference between landlord and tenant, the parties would voluntarily refer the matter to these men instead of having any litigation."

"The great point is their knowledge and their independence, so that persons will have confidence in their decision."

"They would become experts, and I think people would be only too glad to refer the matter to them."

"The sitting tenant would get what he wanted without any unpleasantness with his landlord."

"Any matter that [the parties] chose would be referred to a competent individual. I will take the case of myself. I had spent a considerable amount of capital on a farm, and improved it very much; I thought in consequence of that that the rent ought to be so much; in fact, we agreed that it should be, but when the improvements were done the tenant thought the rent was too much; we agreed to refer that to a person in whom we both had thorough confidence, and he decided for us, and I acted upon his decision. I and the tenant were fortunate enough to find such an individual. I want to create individuals of that character—it can best be done by the Board of Agriculture—and then I am sure that landlords and tenants like myself and my tenant would make use of them in the future with very great advantage."

"I think they would employ these arbitrators whenever there was a difficulty, and *you would have practically no litigation.*"

In any matter arising out of the Agricultural Holdings Act, "when it comes to litigation, these arbitrators and these alone must be employed."[1]

When so simple and rational an expedient for attaining, and from time to time amicably readjusting on equitable lines, the rights and claims of the two parties to an agricultural tenancy is contrasted with the injustice—none the less bad because it is generally unconscious—which in so many cases has been shown, in our evidence, to impose on tenants the heaviest share of economic loss, and to transfer, by a process none the less iniquitous because it is strictly legal, the investments of the tenant to the pockets of the landlord, I venture to think that most impartial men would, on full consideration, heartily welcome machinery which would put friendly and effective arbitration, such as Mr Pennant suggests, within the reach of all.

Under present conditions, when estates are re-valued, there is a general practice of calling in expert aid from without. Sometimes, as on the Haddo estate, the re-valuation is actually carried out by valuers on either side, with an oversman, exactly like a reference under the Act.

In other cases men of wide agricultural experience and recognised impartiality, like Mr Rowlandson, are employed—probably with the satisfaction and confidence of both sides—to re-value estates.

Mr Rowlandson, asked whether tenants in his district have been able to get a reduction where it is fair and right to have it, replies: "It has been very often left to valuation, and I have valued thousands and thousands of acres for reductions of rent. Sometimes I have acted for both; sometimes for the tenant and sometimes for the landlord."

[1] Pennant, Vol. IV., 57,421-57,476.

If the official arbitrator were employed for a similar purpose, we cannot see that any grievance could arise, and the decisions would be of still higher authority than those of unofficial valuers.

And there is clearly a willingness on the part of some landlords to get this matter of rent settled on fair and workable lines which satisfy both sides.

Mr Wilson Fox mentions the case of a landowner who, with a view to meeting his tenants as far as he could over the rent question, asked each of them to name what they considered a fair rent. "Though some of the rents named entailed large reductions, they were all accepted by the owner," who has since granted them abatements also where necessary.[1]

Mr W. J. Harris, whose estate is in Devonshire, and who recommends the artificial raising of prices by import duties, thinks that the rise in rents, which would naturally follow, ought to be prevented in the interests of the community, and could be prevented by a court of appeal to fix rents. "The appeal would go before surveyors who would examine the farm, and see whether the advance in rent was justified or not." "I have no objection to an outside court, if fairly constituted." "I do not think it would have a bad effect upon the relations between landlord and tenant."[2]

In this connection much importance attaches to the valuable suggestions of Mr Gilbert Murray, which seem to go to the root of this matter, and which may be quoted here:—

"I should make a valuation of every holding in the kingdom, and fix the rent according to the value of the produce to-day. The first thing I should ascertain would be the productive power of the soil, by going over every field and taking them separately, and estimate the average produce; I should not altogether fix it according to the state of the cultivation at the present time. I should try to arrive at a medium; the farm being in the high state of cultivation, and worth more and would produce more at the present time than

---

[1] Lincoln, p. 21.   [2] Harris, 4845-53.

an average of produce, I should not take it at that. I would take it at an average, or normal rate."

"If made general and compulsory, this proposal would settle the land question for the next fifty years."

The valuation might be made by valuers to represent either side.

Mr Murray combines this suggestion of a general re-valuation on sound economic lines with a proposal for rents on a sliding scale.

While reasons have been stated in Chapter VIII for holding that a sliding scale would not be an acceptable solution, clearly this suggestion, the general re-valuation recommended by Mr Murray, is well worth consideration. Such a re-valuation might be carried out most cheaply either by the proposed official arbitrators alone, or with the aid of a certain number of assistants temporarily appointed to work under them, or again, re-valuations agreed upon between the parties might be registered in the offices of the official arbitrators, and unless challenged by either party before the arbitrator within any given time, be held to have the effect of decisions made by the arbitrator.

With regard to arbitration for the settlement of individual cases, I recommend that either party shall have the right to apply to the official arbitrator to have a fair economic, as opposed to a competition, rent fixed, and that the rent thus fixed may, by agreement between the parties, be fixed for any period they agree upon exceeding three years, but that if there is no such agreement for a longer period, the rent fixed by arbitration shall be unchanged for three years. Clause 20 of the Agricultural Holdings Bill, 1897, contains this provision.

In view of the existing disinclination to being bound by a fixed rent for a long period, it might be suggested as a fair solution of that difficulty if, on the one hand, the tenant were allowed to give notice to quit, if he thought fit, before the expiry of the three years, but in that case to lose any claim for compensation for disturbance, and if, on the other hand, the landlord were allowed to determine the tenancy also by notice, giving the tenant in that case whatever compensation for disturbance the arbitrator thought just, in addition to the remaining value of his improvements.

If a sound system of valuation, based on the quantities and prices of produce, and the real economic value of the farm, were insisted on, and the adventitious enhancements created by reckless competition and by the selfish and impolitic reliance on competition in many cases, were rigidly excluded, there can be little doubt that the essential mischief of the present condition of affairs would be arrested within a reasonable period, and a stimulus given to vigorous and intelligent development of agriculture such as it has never had before.

This is far more than a mere question of justice to the persons concerned. It is a question of national, and of supreme national interest. Whether you take the view that, so far as we can reasonably look ahead, foreign competition and the development of new areas will keep down prices, and make the struggle from time to time a desperate one for the home producer, or whether you take the view that population is certain to overtake production so rapidly that increased demand will make it profitable again before many years to cultivate all classes of land with the energy and outlay exhibited twenty-five years ago, the one imperative condition for minimising loss, or for attaining the highest degree of prosperity, is to get and keep that true equilibrium in farming economics, which maintains and develops the resources of the working agriculturist directly employed in his work, and prevents the wasting of those resources, and their diversion to other objects. Such a policy alone can secure the highest cultivation of the soil, the maximum production of food, and the widest distribution of employment. Any reasonable or acceptable machinery for such a purpose should be welcomed by the landowner as well as by the tenant farmer.

CHAPTER XIII.

LEGISLATIVE PROPOSALS.

IT will be convenient to sum up concisely the proposals that have been laid before Parliament, to meet the many points that have been fully discussed in the two preceding chapters.

Omitting earlier proposals, and confining this summary to Bills brought in since the beginning of the great depression, it is interesting to note that the first practical suggestion of value came from that veteran agriculturist, Sir Thomas Acland, in an admirably simple Bill in 1881.

Sir Thomas Acland's Bill affirmed, for the first time, that the measure of compensation must be the value to the incoming tenant—the principle of the Farmers' Alliance and of the Act of 1883. He proposed that compensation should be assessed by and recovered in the county court, except when the parties agreed to arbitration. Such a Bill would have obviously created cheaper and more effective machinery than the complicated Act of 1883.

The Farmers' Alliance Bill of 1882, to which Mr Bear alluded in his evidence, proposed to create a county committee representing owners and occupiers, from which assessors should be chosen for the county court. The Bill gave a choice between free sale of improvements by the outgoing tenant and a reference to the county court with these assessors.

In a subsequent Bill, introduced by Mr Howard in 1883, provision was made for the fixing of fair rents by the court, constituted as in the Bill of 1882, and the term for which they were to run was fixed at seven years.

Mr J. W. Barclay, late Member for Forfarshire, and Dr Robert Farquharson, M.P. for West Aberdeenshire, introduced for Scotland, for several successive years, a more carefully considered Bill, applying the principle of the "three F's" to Scotland.

The same proposals have been, with modifications, brought forward in the Bills successively introduced for Wales by Mr J. Bryn Roberts, M.P., Mr T. E. Ellis, M.P., and Mr Vaughan Davies, M.P.

The Bill on these lines, introduced by Mr William Smith, then M.P. for North Lonsdale, has already been fully discussed, and is printed in Appendix A, xxvi, vol. I. of the Minutes of the Commission.

Bills to amend the Agricultural Holdings Act, 1883, have been introduced by myself and other members annually, from 1887 onwards.

The first of these Bills had for its main object to enact the proposal of Sir James Caird to protect the interests of the sitting tenant, the proposal of the Scottish Chamber of Agriculture to put all first-class improvements on the footing of drainage, and enable tenants to obtain, or make them, on giving notice, freedom of cultivation and sale of produce, and, among other minor proposals, gave a right to revision of rents where prices had fallen since the contract was entered into.

In subsequent Bills, proposals were added to protect the rights of tenants of mortgaged holdings (a proposal afterwards enacted in the Tenants' Compensation Act, 1890), to give compensation for continuous good farming, and to substitute a system of officially appointed valuers or arbitrators for the present valuers, and to have cases of agricultural compensation settled by a single arbitrator.

In the Bill of 1891 an attempt was first made to consolidate the whole of the existing Acts relating to agricultural holdings, and in the Bills of 1892, 1893, and 1894 this process was further carried out, with numerous minor changes, suggested partly by resolutions passed by the Chambers of Agriculture and other agricultural organisations, partly as the result of the inquiry initiated in 1891 and 1892 by the proprietors of the "Mark Lane Express."

The Bill of 1894, the most complete of this series, was, as regards the schedules, largely based on the decisions of the Committee of the Central Chamber of Agriculture appointed in that year to report on the necessary amendments to the Agricultural Holdings Act. Improvements were divided into (1) those for which either consent of the landlord, or the favourable decision of a referee under the Act was necessary,[1] (2) those in respect of which notice only is required, which head included besides "drainage" the various improvements transferred to Part II by the Committee, among them the "laying down of permanent pasture."

This Bill also added clauses giving compensation for disturbance, in pursuance of a decision of the Central Chamber Committee,[2] and abolishing the law of distress for rent in agricultural holdings.

In 1895, the Agricultural Holdings Bill was modified further by a clause providing for a scheduled record of condition at entry and quitting of farms, and by restricting the schedule to a small group of permanent improvements, as to which consent or reference would be required, and leaving drainage by itself in Part II. This change was made to meet the views of a number of important witnesses before this Commission, including Mr Druce and Mr Carrington Smith.

Mr George Lambert, in 1895, having secured a day in the ballot, introduced a Bill to amend the existing Act, which was based on and included, with slight modifications, most of the amending clauses of my Agricultural Holdings Bill, 1894, and the schedules to that Bill. Special provisions were inserted by Mr Lambert to give tenants compensation for damage by game, and compensation for disturbance not only for capricious and unjust eviction, but also in the case of a "landlord refusing without good and sufficient cause to grant a renewal of

[1] This proposal was originally adopted by the Committee, and only struck out of their report by a narrow vote on the final revision.
[2] This proposal was also struck out at the final revision of the report.

a tenancy, or requiring a higher rent or more onerous conditions as terms of such renewal."

The second reading of this Bill was carried on May 15th, 1895, by 218 to 189, but owing to the dissolution, the Committee stage of the Bill was not reached.

At the meeting of the Central and Associated Chambers on May 28th, a resolution in support of the Bill was carried without dissent, after an amendment restricting approval rigidly to those points which were covered by the report of the Committee of the Central Chamber had been rejected on a division.

In 1896, Mr Robert Price introduced a Bill combining most of the proposals of the Agricultural Holdings Bill, 1894, with the scheme, which has since been very fully laid before Parliament in the Welsh Land Commission Report, to appoint agricultural registrars or assessors to the county courts, and making the county court, through this additional "agricultural county court judge" the instrument for arbitrating on all questions of dispute between landlord and tenant, including rent. The term fixed as the period for a judicial rent to run was three years.

The Agricultural Holdings Bill, 1897, which contains in the form of legislative proposals the recommendations made in this Report, is printed in Appendix II to this Report.

It will be seen that Mr Price's suggestion, in a modified and simpler form, is adopted in clauses 25, 20, etc. of the Bill, while the principles of the Market Gardeners' Compensation Act, 1895, are applied to all holdings. The procedure is further simplified by omitting the "notices" of claims altogether, and complete freedom to make improvements is given, subject to giving notice in the case of some permanent improvements.

CHAPTER XIV.

RAILWAY RATES.

WHILE several witnesses have expressed the opinion that railway rates have not been a cause of depression, are not seriously complained of, and are not in fact excessive, and other witnesses have expressed their opinion that it is impracticable, or might lead to worse mischief to completely alter the principles on which traffic is managed, the bulk of the evidence given and collected by the Assistant Commissioners is to the effect that agriculture has been seriously prejudiced by excessive or preferential railway rates.

The Central and Associated Chambers of Agriculture have placed this question second in their "Statement" of matters which demand the prompt attention of Parliament, and immediately after the question of local taxation, which was made the subject of our Second Report.

The Shropshire Joint Committee of the County Council and Chamber of Agriculture puts "the lowering of railway rates and charges" third in their list of remedies, and report practically unanimous complaints of excessive rates and undue preferences both at home and as regards foreign produce.[1]

Mr Pringle states the general feeling to be that the railways ought to take their fair share of the depression, and that railway shareholders are receiving 3 to 5 per cent., while farmers are getting nothing on their capital.

Mr Bell, a Scotch witness, urges that, while the effort

[1] Vol. III, App. A1.

now is to bring producer and consumer together, the policy of the railways has been to throw everything into the hands of the middlemen by the heavier charges on small traffic.

It has been strongly represented that recent legislation instead of decreasing has increased the pressure of railway rates on agriculture.

Mr H. H. Scott says: "The railway companies have accentuated the depression by raising rates." "The companies seem to ignore the principle that such high rates of carriage strangle trade."

Mr William Smith, late M.P., points out that mischief has resulted from home rates having remained at the same level, while foreign freights have been steadily falling. Thus Californian freights have fallen from 80s to as low as 17s 6d or 20s per ton, but railway rates from Lincolnshire remain practically the same. The result is that it is impossible for millers to use Lincolnshire wheats to mix with foreign wheats.

Excessive short-distance rates are very generally complained of, and recent legislation has made them even worse than before. The absence of competition is the usual pretext.

In the south-west of Scotland, Mr Speir states that the inequalities are so great that farmers are often compelled to cart to more distant stations to avoid the higher rates. He adds: "Consignments, as a rule, to and from farms are small, and seldom over very long distances, but the rates under 2 tons are excessive and handicap farmers very much."

Very serious complaints have reached us from districts where fruit and vegetables are the staple products.[1]

Mr Olver said that the heavy rates on early potatoes, and other vegetables and flowers, seriously restrict the growth of these crops.

Mr Woodward, speaking of the vale of Evesham, stated that "the railway rates are a great drawback. Our heaviest item is the carriage of the produce to the

[1] A. Spencer, Oxfordshire, &c., pp. 13, 38.

consumer." The companies have declined, he states, to take fruit at reduced rates in lots of 2 to 3 cwts.

Mr Rew illustrates the excessive rates imposed on non-competitive traffic.[1]

"Apples and old potatoes are charged 8s 9d in 2-ton lots from Salisbury to London, while from Dinton and Tisbury, only a short distance farther, the rates are 18s 9d for apples and 17s 4d for potatoes per ton, and in 2-ton lots 10s 6d per ton."

In the case of another rate quoted by Mr Rew, of 17s 4d per ton for new potatoes, in any quantity between April 1st and June 30th, it is clear that the railway company is insisting on having a share in the higher profits of a "season" traffic, in addition to a fair return for the cost of the service.

Mr Wilson Fox gives several railway accounts of vegetable growers in Lincolnshire. The accounts show that generally about two-thirds of the value are taken up by railway charges and salesman's commission, and that the share absorbed by the railway was 15s 5d out of 31s 6d, 16s out of 40s 6d, 48s 1d out of 92s.

The charges for potatoes from Spalding to Leeds in 1893 are quoted at £5 17s 8d for a lot of 4 tons 6 cwts., £4 1s 11d for 3 tons 3 cwts., and £3 18s 6d for 3 tons 2 cwts. At the then prices of potatoes this was an enormous share in the gross value to be taken by the railways.

The small men in the fen districts of Suffolk, Norfolk vegetable growers, Gloucestershire fruit growers, complain that railway rates "swamp their profits" if not cause actual loss.

In the case of a perishable article such as milk, there are general complaints of the high ratio of the railway charges to the value of the produce carried.

Mr Stratton says: "It is monstrous that the railway company should take an eighth of the gross value of my milk for carrying it sixty miles." If conveyance by passenger train is alleged as a reason, Mr Stratton

---

[1] Rew, Salisbury Plain, p. 38.

replies that without "passenger service" the milk traffic would not extend beyond thirty miles from London.

In Ayrshire, dairy farmers are paying as much as one-third of their rent for carriage of milk alone.[1] Mr Cooke, a Cheshire farmer, complains that the rate on milk is 13 per cent. and on skim milk 33 per cent. of its value.

In Leicestershire, the railways have substantially gone back to the 1892 rates, but would have raised them 50 per cent. but for the agitation.

Mr Adams, a Berkshire farmer, says the produce of one cow out of seven has to go to pay the Great Western Railway. And "farmers have to agree not to hold the company responsible for milk spilled, or not delivered," and have now to pay on "empties" which formerly came back free.[2]

Mr Reynolds says the milk trade is crippled by these conditions.

Mr Carrington Smith shows that rates have been indirectly increased by $6\frac{1}{4}$ per cent., by charging on the imperial instead of the barn gallon.

Mr Spencer: "The milk rate from Wootton Bassett to Paddington has been increased by 1d to $1\frac{1}{8}$d per gallon. On the amount sent from that station alone this would mean an increased cost per annum of £319 7s 8d falling on the senders."

On such figures as these, it may well be considered whether such an increase in the gross revenue of a company, from one out of many rural stations, does not greatly exceed any increase in cost of services which can be alleged as a reason, and whether this is not an instance of an attempt to recoup the company, out of a traffic specially at the mercy of railways, for reductions enforced on other classes of traffic.

Many complaints are made that railway rates are in some cases "practically prohibitive," and destructive of traffic.

In Norfolk, farmers say they are debarred from selling hay and roots by heavy rates to good markets. An

---

[1] Speir, Ayrshire, p. 36.
[2] Rew, Norfolk, p. 71.

offer for hay had to be refused because the lowest rate to Wickham Market was £1 per ton.

Mr Dewar, a successful Scotch settler in Norfolk, points out that it would be a great advantage to be able to sell off straw and bring back town manure at low rates. If the rate for town manure in his district was reduced from its present amount (7s 6d) to 3s 6d, a large quantity would be taken.

Farmers in Lincolnshire were compelled to send cattle by road at 1s a head into Leicestershire because the rate was 3s to 4s.

From Forfarshire to Worcestershire a bull cost £6 15s (while it would only cost £4 4s to bring one all the way from Canada), and a loose box for sporting dogs only cost £5.

In Lancashire, the rates on manure brought from towns were so high as to prevent its free use. The railway charges quoted were double or three times the price of the manure.

The prohibitive character of some rates was intensified where there was no competing route. Districts which most need cheap access to markets were placed at a great disadvantage as compared with coast towns.

Mr Pringle reports a general feeling in the South Midlands that the railways were using their powers unduly to extort from farmers rates excessive in themselves, and wholly disproportioned between long and short distances.

The rates on corn from Cardiff to Birmingham, 110 miles, are 8s 4d a ton, while from Cambridge, the same distance, the rate is 12s 6d ; and from Isham, sixty miles, the rate is 8s 4d, the same as from Cardiff.

The rates on beasts and sheep, which were raised twenty-two years ago, were raised in 1892 very largely by the new truck rate. Thus, before 1872, the rate per beast from Welton to London was 3s 9d, was raised then to 4s 9d and in 1892 to 7s 1½d. "Now we have to run by truck rate, and if we have an odd three after filling our waggon we have to pay extra. Load the waggons ever so tightly, it costs us 1s over the old rate per bullock."

In the poultry fattening districts of Sussex, Mr Rew found some complaint of the heavy rates on fowls brought from Ireland for fattening. The increases made in 1893 had been lowered three months after, but no return had been made of the overcharges. Mr Rew adds: "Probably this was the case in many instances, and the railway companies, therefore, made a considerable profit by the action which was on their behalf admitted to have been a 'mistake,' and was condemned by the Select Committee."

The same complaint comes from the dairy industry in Derbyshire, where cash or monthly prepayment had been insisted on, so that the overcharges in 1893 were practically irrecoverable.

The strongest feeling has been expressed by many witnesses that the competition of foreign produce has been unfairly intensified by the policy of the companies in giving preferential rates to imported articles, to such an extent as to substantially operate as a form of protection to foreign products. Further, the increases made in 1893 were applied only to home traffic, thus aggravating the evil.

The natural market for corn from the South Midlands is in Birmingham and the "Black country." But the rates on corn from the distant seaports are equal or lower. If the rates were in fair proportion it would mean an addition of 3s a ton, or 9d a quarter, to the value of the corn.

The rates on cheese from Leicester, about half-way, are slightly in excess of the rates on American cheese from Liverpool to London.

Mr Berry, as a representative both of the Central Chamber of Agriculture and of the Mansion House Association, gave, to illustrate many hundreds of similar instances, figures showing the differences in railway charges on foreign and home produce for the same distances.

Thus, the through rate from Calais to London for butter is £1; the water rate, including dock charges, being 15s, leaving 5s for local rate from Dover to

London. The English farmer pays 12s 3d from Dover, while the Canterbury farmer pays 11s 9d for quantities over 3 cwts.

Onions from Calais to London cost 14s 5d, owner's risk, and the cross-channel rate is 13s 4d, owner's risk, showing that the seventy-two miles from Dover to London is covered at the rate of 1s 1d, whereas the rate for English onions is 12s 3d, company's risk.

Potatoes from Calais to London cost 13s 9d, water rate 8s 4d, leaving 5s 5d for the local rate from Dover, whereas the English rate is 10s 6d from Dover and 10s from Canterbury.

Apples from Calais to London cost 15s, with a water rate 13s 4d, leaving 1s 8d for the railway charge on this side, while the English rate is 12s 3d from Dover and 11s 9d from Canterbury.

This is a preference of 10s a ton in favour of foreign apples, and, taking 5 tons to the acre, is a bounty of 50s an acre against the English fruit grower.

The difference of about 5s a ton in the case of potatoes is a bounty of 40s an acre against the home producer.

Mr Berry admits that the English farmer would not be greatly benefited by the raising of the through rates on foreign produce in such cases, as it would come more cheaply direct to London by water; but he urges that the companies are clearly carrying foreign produce at some profit, and could therefore reduce the charge on home produce. He agrees that foreign consignments are packed and delivered so as to be more readily handled and compactly loaded. "But," he adds, "I believe that is being made an unfair use of against us. I do not think there is anything like the difference which has been suggested."

The demand formulated by Mr Berry is that "our one ton ought to be carried at the same rate that the railway company carries two or three tons of foreign goods, that is if we can give them a fair average load. Under no circumstances whatever should foreign produce be carried at a less rate per ton per mile than English produce."

A fair allowance should be made for ease and convenience of handling and loading, but 5 to 15 per cent. would be reasonable, whereas, even in the case of hay, hops and fresh meat, as to which the traders were successful in the Southampton rates case, the companies under the present law were able to justify differences in their charges of 300 to 400 per cent. on the ground of services rendered.

Mr Berry is strongly of opinion, and expresses the opinion of the Central Chamber of Agriculture, that, having regard to the results of the Southampton case and the facts as to undue preference, that "no redress whatever can be given to agriculturists until the law is so altered as to put English produce on something like all-fours with foreign, and that it was not the intention of Parliament that all these differences should be allowed."

Several witnesses draw attention to the helplessness of traders. "We have great difficulty in finding whether railway charges are the legal rates or otherwise, or how they compare with others." "It is quite impossible for a single farmer, or even bodies of farmers to take any case before the Railway Commissioners, we consider there should be some cheap tribunal to which any farmer or trader who had a grievance should be able to go at a very moderate expense." There are great difficulties in proving undue preferences.

Mr Berry thinks it difficult to get redress. Every case has to be fought, which means money, and that is what agriculturists have not got. The conciliation clause is useful, but in the congested state of business at the Board of Trade means protracted delay, and after all is done, the Board can only advise the companies, and has no control.

And although it will be seen from the review of decided cases under the Acts that the Courts have been enabled to give a status to associations of traders to obtain in some sense general redress as regards unreasonable rates and preferences, it does not follow that individual agriculturists can share in these benefits without having themselves also to set the law in motion, with all the risk of loss and disappointment.

It would, therefore, be a reasonable suggestion that the decision of individual cases of a simple character should be devolved on county courts.

Since the commencement of our inquiry, it has been satisfactory to note that action has been taken, both on behalf of the agricultural interest to facilitate the collection and despatch of produce so as to assimilate the services rendered for home and foreign produce, and for small and large consignments, and by the railway companies in voluntarily reducing rates and offering greater facilities, especially for small consignments.

Particulars of the new traffic arrangements in 1896, were furnished to the Commission by the Great Eastern, Great Northern, Great Western, London and North Western, London and South Western, London, Chatham, and Dover, South Eastern, North Eastern, and London, Brighton, and South Coast Railway Companies.

The Great Eastern, "as an experiment," were carrying all kinds of farm and market garden produce from nearly all their stations to London at 1d per 5 lbs., in boxes of specified shape, carriage prepaid. Special reductions have also been made as to rates for corn, feeding stuffs, and manures, natural and artificial, for distances over forty and sixty-five miles.

The Great Northern made similar arrangements for small packages from rural stations on their lines to London and other large towns. The rate ranges from 6d for 20 lbs to 1s 2d for 60 lbs prepaid. The Company furnish a list of farmers, market gardeners, and others desirous of forwarding produce direct to consumers.

The rates for stable, farm yard, and other manure, in 6-ton lots from London, were also reduced experimentally from 12 to 30 per cent. The rates on fresh meat and dead poultry were also reduced.

The Great Western Company from August 1896, arranged a reduced scale of rates for fresh meat, dead poultry, butter, eggs, fruit, and vegetables, in consignments of 10 cwts, 1 ton, 2 ton, and 3 ton lots. Mixed consignments will be charged at the reduced rates, if the minimum quantity is made up by a combination of the various articles. The Company also announced lower rates for manures and feeding stuffs, grain, cider, potatoes, and roots.

The South Western Company also adopted a reduced tariff for fruit and vegetables, packed in consignments of 1 cwt. and upwards, reduced rates for meat, including cartage in London, and for grain, green crops, vegetables, roots, oil-cake, and packed manure, in loads of not less than 6 tons (which can be made up of any of these articles), between non-competitive stations. There is also a reduced scale for live stock for short-distance traffic between "local and non-competitive" stations.

The London, Chatham and Dover Railway Company issued reduced rates from all their stations to London markets for fruit and vegetables, and also for feeding stuffs and roots and packed manures in 6-ton lots. The reductions are about 18 per cent.

The South Eastern Railway Company, in November 1895, reduced the rates from London to all non-competitive stations 25 per cent. on manure in bulk in 6-ton lots, outside a radius of twenty miles. In July 1896, fruit and vegetables for London, cattle feeding stuffs, and packed manures in 6-ton lots were reduced 15 per cent. The cartage on hops in London was reduced 25 per cent.

The North Eastern Company in February 1896, adopted an experimental scale of reduced rates between local non-competitive stations (1) for manure in bulk, a minimum truck load of 5 tons; (2) for grain, potatoes, roots, feeding stuffs, packed manures, minimum of 5 tons; (3) for part truck, small truck and medium truck loads of live stock.

The London, Brighton, and South Coast Railway furnish tables showing reductions in rates for manure in bulk, since prior to December 1881, of from 21 to 29 per cent.; for grain, oil-cake, and potatoes, since 1880 of 34 per cent. on the average; for roots, since 1893 from 16 to 23 per cent.

It is to be hoped that the policy thus adopted will be extended to all parts of the railway system, and may be further expanded in its details, especially as regards small consignments, and that it may result in a considerable increase in traffic and receipts to the companies.

At the same time, it may be observed that the adoption of this policy is a clear admission of most of the contentions agriculturists have put forward for years past, and demonstrates how large a share of the gross profits of agriculturists has been appropriated by the companies for years past.

As the scope of our own inquiry on this subject was restricted, owing to the recent inquiry by a Select Committee and the Act of 1894, the results of which are not yet fully before the country, it seems desirable to briefly indicate what has been done and what still may remain to be done.

The Select Committee of 1893 had to inquire "into the manner in which the railway companies have exercised the powers conferred upon them by the Railway Rates and Charges Order Confirmation Acts (1891 and 1892), and to consider whether it is desirable to adopt any other than the existing means of settling differences arising between the companies and the public, with respect to the rates and conditions of charge for the conveyance of goods."

The report of the Committee makes it clear that it was not intended by Parliament that the systematic classification of charges provided for by the Act of 1888 should be so manipulated that the companies could recoup themselves for the reductions made in maximum rates in some cases by raising the rates in other cases, even where rates so raised were still below the new maximum rates. The Board of Trade, in fixing the new maximum rates, did so on a definite understanding that the new maxima, where higher than the previous rates, were so fixed only to cover any possible increase in the future in the cost of services. This understanding was explicitly confirmed by the representatives of the companies. But, in the new schedules of rates issued in

1893, the companies set aside this understanding, and generally imposed the full maximum rates, making enormous increases in many instances. This course was emphatically condemned by the Select Committee, who also, in dealing with the modified claim of the companies to an increase limited to 5 per cent. over the rates current in 1892, reported that " It was not the intention of Parliament, that the companies should raise their non-competitive actual rates, even by 5 per cent. all round, for the purpose of recouping themselves for the reductions of other rates, which Parliament has pronounced to be unjust and unreasonable."

Evidence given before the Committee showed that, even with the revision limiting the increases in most cases to 5 per cent., the result on the Great Western line was that the Company were raising the rates on some traders by £94,000 a year, in order to recoup itself for reductions to other traders to the amount of £80,000 a year, and thus making a net gain of £14,000 a year on the previous total amount of receipts.

The general effect, therefore, of the Act of 1888, and the subsequent proceedings of the Board of Trade and Parliament in pursuance of that Act, had been, while giving to traders certain advantages in the simplification and systematising of rates, to enable the companies to increase their rates, and to give those increased rates a legal validity which they had not under previous legislation. In the opinion of the Committee, the effect of section 24, sub-section 20, of the Act of 1888, to wit: " That the rates and charges mentioned in a provisional order to be framed in accordance with the Act and confirmed by Parliament shall, from and after this Act comes into operation, be the rates and charges which the railway companies shall be entitled to charge and make," whether it was fully contemplated by the Board of Trade and Parliament, during the passing of this Act, or not, was to clear up any doubts as to the meaning of the Act of 1845, and to make it certain that no rate thenceforward could be questioned at law if within the maximum allowed by the Provisional Orders of 1891 and 1892, except those which are open to objection on the ground of undue preference.

With this exception of undue preference, Parliament left no remedy for unreasonable rates within the maximum, except the conciliation section, (31), of the Act of 1888, under which the Board of Trade has no power to enforce any conclusion it may come to on the point in dispute.

The situation was in fact this. Parliament in 1888 had created machinery for the benefit of traders who were suffering from excessive charges. But the fixing of maximum rates, with wide allowance for the future expenditure of railways in carrying out their services, and without any statutory check on the misuse of these maxima to the detriment of traders, had enabled the companies to carry out not merely a policy of complete recoupment for reductions, but also to secure an increase in their gross receipts.

In view of the fact that some companies "may continue to enforce on certain traders grave additional charges" to carry out this policy of recoupment, the Committee recommended legislation "to protect traders from unreasonable raisings of rates, even within the maximum charges, and from such unreasonable conditions of transport as cannot now be made the subject of arbitration."

The Act passed in 1894, in pursuance of these recommendations, throws on the railway company the onus of proof that any increase in a rate or charge made subsequently to 1892, whether directly or indirectly, is reasonable even where such increase leaves the increased rate within the authorised maximum. Complaints are made in the first instance to the Board of Trade under the conciliation section, and if not there adjusted, can be carried before the Railway Commission, who have jurisdiction.

In my opinion the Act of 1894 is defective in principle and in its procedure, and cannot be considered as anything more than a temporary expedient. Objections were taken, during its passing through the House of Commons, (1) that by limiting complaints and jurisdiction to the increases made in rates, it was made difficult, if not impossible, to go into the constituent elements of the whole rate so as to determine, in the only complete and satisfactory way, whether the increase was reasonable or not, and (2) that the Act was legalising rates existing in 1892, whether reasonable or not, and so to some extent defeating the purpose and intentions of Parliament in the legislation of 1888, and subsequent years.

These objections seem well founded, and the first of them has received some illustration in the arguments on which the recent judgments in the Northampton case, by the Railway Commissioners and the Court of Appeal, and in other decided cases, upon which comments are made further on, seem to have been based.

The precise value of the existing law, as a remedy against undue preferences and unreasonable rates, is best measured by some recent judgments of the Railway Commission.

The cases of undue preference depend on the interpretation of section 27 of the Act of 1888. That section throws the onus of proof on the company to justify differences of charges to different traders or districts for similar merchandise and for similar services, specifically empowers the court, or the commissioners, to take into consideration whether the differential charge is necessary for the purpose of securing in the interests of the public, the traffic in respect of which it is made, and whether the inequality cannot be removed without unduly reducing the rates charged to the complainant, and especially provides that, in the case of foreign versus home produce, no difference of treatment shall be sanctioned " in respect of the same or similar services."

In the case of the Liverpool Corn Trade Association *v.* the London and North Western Railway Company, decided in 1890 in favour of the complainants, undue preference was alleged in respect of a charge of 8s 4d a ton for 2-ton lots on corn from Cardiff to Birmingham, the distance being taken as 127 miles, whereas 12s 9d per ton was charged from Liverpool to Birmingham, taken as ninety-eight miles, on 2-ton lots, and 11s 3d on

s

4-ton lots. The preference enabled Cardiff to undersell Liverpool at Birmingham by 3d to 4d a sack. The company argued that the Liverpool rate was reasonable, and that the low Cardiff rates could not be raised, as they were necessary to secure the traffic in the interests of the public, because of the low competing rates from the Severn ports.

Mr Justice Wills delivered an elaborate judgment, as this was the first interpretation of the section. He held that the justifications, because of competition and because of the impossibility of re-adjustment without undue reduction to the complainant, are matters which only may be taken into account, and in addition to all the other considerations. On the one hand the commercial interests of the company were not to be disregarded unless the public also were interested in securing the traffic, nor on the other hand was the mere question of securing the traffic, even in the interests of the public, to be conclusive in favour of the company.

The inequalities complained of were in themselves illegal, and it was immaterial even to prove existing injury to trade. They could not be justified on the ground that the traffic could not be secured, unless the rates from Cardiff were thus low, because no interest of the public was established in securing an alternative route, as such a route already existed.

But the subsequent case of the Liverpool Corn Traders' Association *v.* the Great Western Railway Company was decided in August 1892 in precisely the opposite sense. This judgment seems to have been governed by the decision of the Court of Appeal in the case of Phipps *v.* the London and North Western Railway Company, in March 1892, when Lord Herschell held that the fact that a trader had access to a competing route for the carriage of his goods, may be taken into consideration by the Railway Commissioners or the Court, in deciding whether lower rates charged to such trader are an undue preference under the Acts of 1854 and 1888. Lord Herschell held that the Act of 1888 did not alter the considerations under the Act of 1854, but made it clear that both the interests of the Company and of the public might be considered, and that it was in general to the interests of the public to encourage traffic from greater distances by rates low enough to make competition possible. The intention of Parliament was that the court should weigh all the consequences of either raising the low rate, or of unduly lowering the high rates.

Accordingly, in the Liverpool corn trade case against the Great Western Company, the decision, on much the same issues as in the case two years before against the North Western, was in favour of the Company on the ground that it was impossible for the Company to secure the grain traffic from the Severn ports, in face of the competition of the Midland Railway and of carriers by water, unless the low rates were maintained, while the inequality could not be removed without unduly reducing the rates from Birkenhead, which were rates applicable to the whole port of Liverpool, and that it was necessary to maintain the irregularity of rates, if the Midland markets were to have the benefits of both sources of supply. One of the Commissioners, Sir F. Peel, however, delivered a judgment substantially on the lines of the North Western case of 1890.

An appeal was dismissed on the ground that no question of law was raised, and that on questions of fact, there was no appeal from the Railway Commission.

The judgment of the Railway Commissioners in the case of the Mansion House Association v. the London and South Western Railway Company in April, 1895, gives the first interpretation of the "proviso" added in the House of Lords to section 27, to exclude undue preference for foreign produce. The complaint was that while imported bacon and hams, butter, cheese and lard, hops, and wool paid 6s a ton from Southampton Docks to London, seventy-six miles, and hay 5s a ton, the rates from Southampton Town were 17s 6d, 17s 11d, 20s 10d, and 17s 11d respectively, and for hay 9s 8d a ton for the same distance; and the rates from Botley (also 76 miles) were about 1s 2d to 1s 9d higher still. The traders' contention was that the proviso forbade a differentiation of rates in favour of imported goods, and explicitly shut out the considerations that might be advanced to justify lower preferential rates in respect of home traffic.

The Company relied, in their first replies, on the plea that the low rate from Southampton Docks to London was (1) an apportioned amount of a through rate, and (2) that it was necessary to enable them to compete with the water route to London. But on coming into court they had to abandon these pleas as untenable, in view of the wording of the Act and of the proviso, and to rely solely on the plea that the services rendered in respect of the foreign produce cannot be treated "as the same or similar services" as those in respect of home produce, when they can be rendered at a lower cost, and with larger returns, owing to the conditions of the traffic, uniformity of packing, ease of handling, etc.

The Commissioners held that, as regards the local charges in England, foreign and home produce should stand on the same footing, and that justification of a lower charge because of less cost of service ought to be admitted as between foreign and home produce in the same way as it would be between one kind of home traffic and another, and that this justification could not be excluded by the proviso simply on the ground that the goods in question were imported.

What the proviso really is intended to exclude is any advantage to foreign goods because of the distance of their place of origin, or any consideration of what may be necessary to secure traffic because of sea competition outside the United Kingdom. " If the railway company have proved facts which would justify the admitted differences had the goods in both cases been home goods, the company are not debarred from relying on those facts as an answer because the goods which received the benefit of the differences are of foreign origin."

Sir Frederick Peel thinks that the proviso requires differences "to be judged solely with reference to services rendered by the railway company," and that " differences in rate or treatment shall be such only as the degree in which the services may not be similar may make reasonable."

The foreign consignments are of greater average weight, and load more compactly, so that on the average the return is stated at 4.4d per truck per mile to 3d for home goods. Again, the foreign steam-pressed hay loads 4 tons to the truck to 2½ tons of English hay, while foreign hops load 3 tons to 2½ tons of English.

The limits of justification being thus narrowed to differences of cost of service, the Commissioners ordered a readjustment of rates as regards hay, hops, and fresh meat, but rejected the traders' complaint as to the other articles on the ground that the traffic in them was insignificant.

This judgment would seem to fully justify the contention of agriculturists that the excessive differences in rates on foreign produce are substantially due to the action of the companies in competing for imports by a policy of putting very low charges upon them, and recouping themselves by unreasonably high rates on home produce. It is clear that the considerations of less cost of services relied on can fairly account for only a small proportion of the enormous differences ranging, in this Southampton case, from 57 per cent. on fresh meat, and 63 per cent. on hay, to 220 per cent. on bacon, butter, and wool, and 276 per cent. on hops. Further, it appears that the differences in cost of service, such as they are, are probably exaggerated. The Salisbury meat traffic runs through Eastleigh, seventy-one miles to London, without stopping in a fast train exactly like the meat train from Southampton docks. And hops and other foreign produce are, it is shown, frequently run up in half loaded trucks, so that the consideration o close packing is non-operative.

It might also be urged that the ground stated for refusing to order a readjustment in the rates for bacon, etc., is unsatisfactory, inasmuch as it might permanently check any attempt to develop new traffic, such as curing factories, or creameries.

By the decisions of the Railway Commissioners and the Court of Appeal in the case of the Mansion House Association *v.* the Great Western Company, where the Association made general complaints of unreasonable increases in the rates on certain classes of goods, it was settled that such complaints could be made under the Act of 1894, by an authorised association, without proof of loss to any individual trader, or without any trader paying money into court.

Lord Esher held that as the Company had raised their rates in respect of a whole class of articles, instead of looking into the question as to each of those articles "in an ordinary, fair, business manner" before they raised the rates, in which case they would have had ready to hand reasons why they raised the rate on each particular article. Unless, therefore, they could justify the whole by some common reason, they could not call on the complainants to name the articles individually complained of. The onus of proof, therefore, remains on the company, as in the case of an individual complaining trader, and an increase of rate on a particular article.

The present state of the law as to the extent of the right given to traders under section 33 of the Act of 1888, to have the component parts of a rate, when it is within the maximum, split up and separately stated, has been decided on April 14th, 1896, in the case of the New Union Mill Company *v.* the Great Western Railway Company. The judgment of Mr Justice Collins and the Commissioners was that the Act is complied with if the company choose to state, on their own responsibility, that the whole charge is for conveyance only. The court cannot compel a company to state charges for terminals if the company choose to say, "We make no charge for terminals." The Act of 1894 makes no difference. "It may or may not be that section 4 of the Act of 1894 does entitle a person under those circumstances to a rebate, notwithstanding the railway company assert that no charge is made in respect of the particular matter in respect of which he asks for a rebate. I do not decide that point."

It appears obvious that the law so interpreted undesirably limits the facilities for establishing cases of undue preference or unreasonable increases.

The desirability of effective machinery for properly establishing the real charges made in railway accounts, is shown by a comparison of the analysis of rates for grain in 4-ton lots from Liverpool and Birkenhead to Birmingham with the figures given in evidence, in the case of 1892, by the Great Western Company for the purpose of rebutting the allegation of undue preference.

The analysis of 1896 is "collection by cart from dock warehouse in Birkenhead, 8d; delivery by cart in Birmingham, 1s; conveyance ninety-eight miles, 9s 7d (= 1·17d per ton per mile), total, 11s 3d."

The analysis used in evidence in 1892 runs thus: "Collection by cart from Liverpool warehouse, 1s 4d; lighterage across the Mersey, 2s; unloading from lighter, 4d; storage at Birkenhead, including loading into and unloading from warehouse, 1s; do., do., at Birmingham, 1s; cartage in Birmingham, 2s; conveyance ninety-eight miles (= ·44d per ton per mile) 3s 7d; total, 11s 3d."

In the case of Rickett, Smith & Co., the Derbyshire Silkstone Coal Company, and the Grassmow Company against the Midland Railway Company for indirectly raising their rates on coals by about $3\frac{1}{2}$ per cent., by altering the allowance for wastage, it was practically determined that increases of rates within the maxima have now to be justified by proof of increased cost of services rendered, and a majority of the Commission decided that this increased cost had not been made out by the company.

In the case of the Mansion House Association *v.* the London and North Western Railway Company, where complaint was made of increases (mainly between London and Northampton) in class and special rates, and in rates on small parcels, and on the live stock rates to Northampton from Hereford and Welsh stations, and from Bletchley, the defence of the Company was wholly in the cartage charges. But while the Company showed an increase in the cost of cartage of 12 to 15 per cent. within the last ten years, the increases, if treated as increases only in respect of the cartage item, are shown to be not 12 to 15 per cent. increase on the old cartage charges, but from 28 to 36 per cent. "It follows, then, either that the increase in the cartage charge has been excessive, or, as is more probable, that the increase has never in effect been made as suggested, but has fallen to a large extent upon the railway portion of the aggregate rate." Judgment was therefore given, and an order made to discontinue the increases.

It is to be noted in this and other cases that the limits imposed by the several Acts of Parliament obviously preclude that complete disclosure of the railway accounts, and distinct proof of the several items of costs of service and of details of charges, by which alone a completely satisfactory decision could be arrived at. The real amounts charged for cartage, and the real cost of cartage previous to 1893, were clearly matters of more or less probable conjecture, and not of demonstration.

In connection with this and other cases, attention should be drawn to the general unwillingness of railway companies to treat the decisions of the courts in these cases as a standard, by which to regulate other similar charges. The policy seems to be, as far as possible, to compel individual agriculturists and traders to go to the expense of proceedings, rather than to re-cast charges, which have been indirectly shown by these test cases to be indefensible in part or whole.

In conclusion, it cannot be denied that the present state of the law and of its administration as to railway rates, so far as the interests of agriculturists are concerned, is confused, incomplete, and unsatisfactory.

It might be conceivable to leave the railway companies and the traders free to arrive at adjustments by commercial and economic friction. But this has not been done. The State has undertaken to supervise and to some extent regulate the charges made by the railways, in view of the qualified monopoly that has been secured to them. The object of such regulation is that, while the vast capital invested in railways should be fairly protected, the industries of the country should be enabled to have their products and their raw materials carried at reasonable rates which do not confiscate their possible profits, nor give unfair advantages to one set of interests as against another, nor operate to restrict the development of trade. Now that it has been recognised as a proper function for State control, it is certainly not desirable that the legal and administrative machinery for this object should be inadequate, as the review of the cases referred to, and the considerations by which the judgments were governed, compels us to believe.

Further legislation is therefore needed to enable traders to bring to the test, and the courts to determine the reasonableness of all rates, and of any part of a rate, whether made or increased before 1893 or not, and within the maxima fixed by the Provisional Order Acts of 1891 and 1892, and more especially to enable both traders and the courts to test with precision the real cost of all services and accommodation provided by railways, and the relation of the charges and rates imposed in respect of such services to the cost so determined. Power should also be taken to decide all minor points arising between traders and the railway companies by the county court procedure, or some cheap and simple delegation of the duties of the Railway Commission.

I am also of opinion, in view of the observations of several of the judges who have had to give decisions in respect of section 27 of the Act of 1888, that legislation is necessary to indicate more clearly what weight is to be attached to considerations of competing routes as a justification for differences of rates as between one place, and one set of traders and another.

CHAPTER XV.

SMALL HOLDINGS.

As the chapter in the Majority Report dealing with this subject seems somewhat incomplete, and to present too strongly the less favourable view of small holdings, some further extracts from the evidence and reports is here appended, with some further conclusions and recommendations.

It is to be regretted that the Commission did not take directly the evidence of representatives of occupying owners or tenants of small holdings. But a large amount of evidence of this nature was collected by several of the Assistant Commissioners, and especially by Mr Wilson Fox, Mr Pringle, and Mr Rew.

An obvious and initial difficulty in arriving at just conclusions on this topic is due to the still prevalent lack of sympathy with, and insight as to, the aims and methods of small farming. Among the large farmers and land agents, there is still a reluctance to recognise the economic function which land reformers naturally attribute to small holdings. Small holdings and job labour naturally go together. And the majority of the large farmers do not seem yet to realise what the systematic development of allotment and small holdings can do for agriculture, in maintaining on the spot a permanent supply of efficient and skilled labour.

In my opinion, labour cannot be much longer organised on the old lines—at any rate to the extent common in the "seventies" and the "eighties." Labour must necessarily become more independent, and the natural relations between the big farmer hiring labour and the labourer must tend to become more elastic. Labour can no longer be bound down to 12s a week, harvest wages, eighteenpenny cottages, and rood allotments. If the best labour is to be retained for agricultural work there must be reasonable opportunities for men to raise themselves little by little, by getting land to cultivate, or by working up a small stock of cattle, or by poultry, eggs, or milk.

And the transition to the new state of things will not lessen, but increase, the supply of labour for carrying on the work of the larger farms economically and effectively. The interests of the two classes are not antagonistic, but bound together, and the movement of the time, checked like everything else in agriculture for the moment by the acuter stages of depression, must inevitably in the long run, when times get better, not only tend to raise the condition of the rural population, but to bring to agriculture a more thorough organisation, a more eagerly competing enterprise, and a higher degree of prosperity than has ever hitherto been known.

To deal with some of the typical cases brought before us.

In the Isle of Axholme, small holders have had exceptional advantages and exceptional drawbacks. The land is rich and workable, but from that very reason there has been too keen competition, too eager desire to acquire land at any price, and with capital borrowed on almost any terms.[1] The small owners have suffered most, not because their labour and industry have been fruitless, but because they have discounted the future too freely, and imposed on themselves, in the interest on mortgages, a rent which, at current prices, even that rich soil could not pay. Interest does not generally admit of remissions like rent. Where mortgagees have abstained from exacting the full interest, it has remained as an arrear of debt to be cleared off in better times.

---

[1] In the "seventies" good land ranged up to £120, and inferior to £60 an acre. Confidence in rising values was so great that a man who could pay a deposit of 10 per cent. only could borrow the balance without difficulty.

The eldest son, on inheriting, has too often put heavy charges on his little estate for the benefit of the rest of the family, just as big owners have overburdened their big estates. Bequests and sales have led to minute subdivisions into strips and plots of land often wide apart. This means loss of time, doubling the cost of labour,[1] and also makes thorough working and manuring more difficult. Many of these men have been ruined, and their land gone to the lawyers.

On the other hand, many, even of the heavily mortgaged small owners, have in past years cleared off their mortgages, or have in later years been able to transfer, in some cases, to a new mortgagee on easier terms.

Mr Pringle describes them as hardworking, thorough in management, frugal and thrifty in their home life. Their "work is neatly and seasonably performed, their root-crops and corn stubble remarkably clean." The heavy cropping requires liberal returns of manure, which in bad times has not been always available; but, taking the Isle of Axholme as a whole, the standard of agriculture is extremely high. The houses, too, are commodious and comfortable. In the good times, money had been spent freely on buildings and domestic comforts.

Of the smaller holdings, 80 per cent. are freeholds, and 90 per cent. are under arable cultivation. Wheat has, of course, decreased its area materially, while oats have increased over 40 per cent., and there has been a rapid and persistent development of special crops, such as celery, carrots, beetroot, and other vegetables, which take up most of the land formerly left in fallow.

One drawback is the comparative scarcity of job labour for small holders, to whom the addition of wages from time to time would be a great help.

The suffering in North Lincolnshire is not confined to the small freeholders. Mr Pringle gives cases which showed that tenant farmers of large farms are as badly off as the small owners, and on an estate of 3500 acres the rent has fallen from £6860 in 1882 to £3365 in 1892,

---

[1] Amounting, in some cases, to £3 14s an acre.

while the arrears of 1882 were £2068, and in 1892 were £6700. Many of the larger tenants, with insufficient capital, seem to have collapsed, and their farms have been taken by new men at great reductions who are doing better by improved methods, and by converting their rich soil to market gardening. When celery can be grown at a considerable profit, and the early potatoes, grown between the celery rows, fetch 90s to 96s a ton, it is only lack of capital, or freedom, or excessive rents which can prevent a reasonable amount of prosperity.

The balance sheets of a farm of 73 acres, for eleven years from 1882 to 1892, occupied by a tenant, show a net loss over the whole period of £470.

Mr Bear, in his book on "Small Holdings," says, "The houses reminded me of those I had seen in Jersey rather than of the cottages of farm labourers, and I was most struck with the well-fed and happy appearance of the people." This account is confirmed by Mr Pringle.

On the whole, results are much what might be expected. At present values the old mortgages could not be realised, and the interest upon them is an enormous burden. Land is kept by great sacrifices, both on the part of parents and children who work without wages. The economic pressure has fallen heavily upon these people. But their lives have been happy, self-reliant and independent. Adaptation is rapidly meeting difficulties for those who can hold on, and where there is any capital to work the land well the position is improving, and if prices are but slightly better, the small holders who pull through will reap the fullest fruits from all their sacrifices.

It must be remembered, too, that although the pressure of hard times has been tremendous, these men have even in such times an advantage from ownership not shared by the yearly tenant. While the latter have been swept away in wholesale ruin in many districts, the small owner has in most cases been able to cling on somehow, and so keeps his chance of recovery.

And it is plain from Mr Pringle's report and other

evidence, that the solid comfort and prosperity of former times has left considerable resources to draw upon.

In the New Forest, where the policy of consolidating farms wholly failed, and 100 acres is about the largest type of farm, the commoners and cottagers with small holdings ranging from 6 to 20 acres (the most workable size being 12½ acres), have done well by turning out cows, ponies, and pigs in the forest, under the rights secured to them by Acts of Parliament.

Mr Briscoe Eyre, who came specially to give evidence as to this district, said :—

"Everybody turns out something. Many labourers double their wages by stockkeeping, and some have been known to save all their wages for a series of years, making their living by their forest rights. A labouring man will get hold of one animal somehow, a cow, or a mare, and then that makes the foundation of his fortunes. . . . When once they have something like £5, either in stock or money, they then go steadily up in the social scale."

"They reckon that if a man turns out a lot of pigs of all sizes in a good mast season he can clear 10s per pig."

There is an immense deal of money made in the Forest by ponies, and efforts are being made to improve the breed.

Though ordinary farm land in neighbouring districts has fallen one-half, these small holdings have not gone down at all in value.

Land which would sell in larger holdings at £20 to £25 an acre, fetches in small holdings about £40 an acre.

Small holders, who are the sons of the labourers of the past generation, are actually investing their savings in these little holdings, if they can buy them, to pay 4 or 5 per cent. At recent sales in the Forest, land in small portions has sold up to £100 an acre.

Mr Eyre says the industry and thrift of the small holders, and "the way in which they seem to have money whenever they want it for their own purposes," is astonishing. Labourers who worked at 12s a week have now holdings of 12 to 50 acres, while a labourer's son who started with a heifer of his own, when only seventeen, now deals in cattle, sometimes to the amount of £500 a week. The average amount to each depositor's credit in the savings bank is £17 7s 11d as against £14 12s 2d for all England. A little carting adds to their profits.

Of a small holding about one-fourth would be arable, with potatoes, turnips, vegetables, and winter food for their cows. The rest is pasture and orchard. There is spade culture and high manuring. Dairy-fed pork, butter, poultry and eggs are sold to itinerant dealers.

The majority of the holdings are let, and at rents double the usual rent of the district, because of the grazing rights. But the tenants can well afford it.

Although the old race of small owners, called locally "statesmen," have been dwindling in Cumberland and Westmoreland, from the many temptations to sell their land, from changes in their family tastes, and other causes, the northern counties throw a most encouraging light on the policy of promoting small holdings.

Mr Coleman, reporting to the Richmond Commission, said that "the prosperity of the farmers in Cumberland and Westmoreland is attributable mainly to their extraordinary industry and careful habits, which are induced by the desire to improve their condition."

The agent to the Netherby Estate says: "The farmers who have been foremen and labourers keep climbing up. They are never satisfied to stand still." A man who has risen from a shepherd to a large farmer says: "I think a small farm should be a stepping-stone to a large one."

Lord Lonsdale's agent stated: "We have plenty of big farmers who began life as farm servants, and now have 300 or 400 acres. They make the best farmers, being steady hard working men who know their business."

Lord Leconfield's agent: "Wages have been good, clothing and the other necessaries of life cheap, so that a thrifty man could save, and in middle life take a farm

[1] Wilson Fox, Cumberland, p. 36.

and do well, increasing the area as time went on. There is one man not far from here paying £350 rent. He and his wife were both farm servants."

A foreman on Sir Richard Graham's estate at £14 the half-year, began to farm at £35 rent, went to a 150 acre farm, and then, with a large family of children to help him, took 500 acres. "At last a farm rented at £1000 a year fell in, and he was able to take and stock it all with his own money. He then took another 700 acres at £1000. By this time he was farming 2000 acres at a rent of £2100 a year. The family are still farming this acreage, and 1000 acres in addition.

Many similar instances are reported by Mr Wilson Fox.

In the Appendix to his Report, one man tells the story of his life, and how by steady industry he was able to buy 80 acres and build a house out of the profits of farming, and even to pay off the debts of relatives to the amount of £2000.[1]

Others have done well, but complain that rents are far too high, and that they have kept afloat by withholding any wages from their children.

"All round here the farmers' sons and daughters work for nothing. I do not know one case where a father pays his sons and daughters wages. They give their sons a shilling or two to buy tobacco."[2]

The last few years have been hard for small men with insufficient capital.

One man says: "Up to ten years ago we did well and saved a lot of money, but for five or six years I could not have done without the interest on the money saved."

The same thrifty and industrious spirit is shown in Northumberland, where many have risen from being labourers and shepherds to large farmers.

Those who have taken small farms recently have suffered most, but "those who rose to the position of small farmers between 1864 and 1873," says Mr Scott, and made some money before the depression began,

---

[1] Wilson Fox, Cumberland. Appendix B 1, p. 53.
[2] Ibid., p. 39

have done fairly well since, not only because they had saved money, but because they have not lost the economical habits of their youth."

Some striking instances of successful small farming are given in Mr Wilson Fox's Lancashire Report.

One man farming 63 acres has done well throughout the depression near good markets by high farming, and by judicious application of capital to altered methods. "It is better to have a small farm, and farm it very well, than a big one and farm it indifferently."

In the districts of special farming, such as the fruit districts of Worcestershire and Cambridgeshire and the cheese-making districts of Leicestershire, small holdings have a natural function which seems to be ordinarily discharged with success, even in bad times.

In counties like Suffolk, where there is little good pasture land or land suited for market gardening, small farms and freehold farmers are rare. Most of them have suffered severely and been squeezed out from want of capital, while their land and buildings are in bad condition. The necessity for an excessive number of hours at labour from want of capital to hire labour tells heavily on the older men. Men of exceptional energy and capacity, if the soil is good, and the rent low, can make small farms pay, if they work harder than a labourer. The few who do at all well, are combining some other trade with their small farms.

In the fens of Cambridgeshire and Lincolnshire, the easily worked and fertile soil is more favourable, and the results not unsatisfactory, save where the enormous weight of mortgages or excessive rents have swept away the chances of profit.

Thus, in the Chatteris neighbourhood of Cambridgeshire, numbers of small holders have been able to pay rents of over £2 an acre, besides heavy drainage and other rates, and have made a good thing out of holdings of 4 to 50 acres, growing potatoes and early carrots, besides other produce. The rents have been nearly double those of adjoining large farms, but till the last year or two the rents do not seem to have oppressed

T

them. On the whole they have done extremely well till the worst pinch came.

At Willingham, the industry of many small holders makes something out of asparagus, potatoes, and fruit. Elsewhere "men who work hard can still get along on 30 to 40 acres," though it is generally by adding other industries. And most of them have too little capital for essential improvements, such as claying their land.

In South Lincolnshire, the competition for small freehold farms in the good times, and the ease of mortgaging, saddled many men, as in the Isle of Axholme, with charges which have crippled many of them in these times of fallen values.

The majority who bought their holdings left 60 to 80 per cent., or even the whole sum on mortgage at $4\frac{1}{2}$ up to 6 per cent. In the east and south of the county, the highly productive marsh and fen land sold for £80 to £120 an acre up to 1879.[1] In the good times land paid well, even at those rates. But "those who bought about 1878, and started on their farms with no margin of capital, found themselves face to face with steadily falling prices, with a series of wet seasons, with a rate of interest to pay representing a rent much higher than those who were renting land next door to them," and with no prospect of a remission, unless it was thought by the mortgagees that they would lose by foreclosing.

After 1879, stock and capital gradually melted away. If the mortgagees foreclosed they would lose at least 20 per cent. of the money advanced.[2]

One of these small freeholders says: "I have brought up a family and nearly worked them to death. They said, 'Father, we are not going to stop here and be worked to death for nothing,' so they went off into shops and left me and the old woman to struggle along."

Another:—"I and my three boys, the eldest eighteen, work the land, and my wife and daughter when wanted. We have been working eighteen hours a day for several days, and average ten to twelve during the year. I have

[1] Wilson Fox, Lincoln, p. 60.
[2] Calthorpe quoted by Wilson Fox, p. 67.

been here twenty years, and have just been scraping along. Last year we lost money. We eat very little fresh meat."

Another :—" We work much harder than labourers, in fact, like slaves. The only advantage we get is we are our own masters. We live very carefully. I just keep going. I pay the interest on my mortgage, and I am not in debt."

Things are less gloomy where there are opportunities for earning wages by occasional work on large farms in the neighbourhood, or wheat carting, coal selling, or other small industries, can be combined with the cultivation of the small holding.

In specially fertile districts, such as the Wainfleet and Kirkton districts, and where early potatoes, or other high priced crops can be grown, small holders seem to be doing well, with energy and thrift, even at rents from £3 to £5 an acre. A labourer bought 13 acres at £70, and 10 acres at £110, and rents 22 acres at £3, and has in the past thirteen years paid off £100 of mortgage, and kept a family of seven children.

Another bought part of his 10 acres at £100, and part at £80. He says :—From 1879 to 1882 we lost money, and it has been a struggle ever since, as we got behindhand. We are paying our interest, and just getting our living. No doubt a small freeholder or tenant can make a living in this district, if he works hard. Many people here paying £4 an acre are doing well.

Another, who began as a farm lad at 9d a day, and worked as a labourer till 1874, bought 9 acres at £82 and rents 60 acres at 32s 6d. "Since 1882 I have paid interest and rent and kept going, but have saved nothing. I brought up six children."

Two others, who bought at £115 and £130, and who also rent additional land, have paid interest and rent, and get food and clothes. "Every one works hard in Friskney; the land was never so well farmed. The hardest time was between 1879 and 1881. We were nearly all broke then, and it has been taking all our time to get square. The small men are just about living."

Mr Wilson Fox gives one instance of energy and adaptiveness evolving remarkable success.[1] A man who bought 12 acres at £106 an acre, and growing early potatoes, bulbs, fruit, flowers, also keeping pigs, poultry, and bees, and taking up each new line that pays, actually made a profit of £86 and £111 in 1893 and 1894, and has "always made money," and, since he got his land into condition, has always saved money, and has cleared off nearly all his purchase money in these bad times.[2]

In spite of the enormous difficulties, the men who are fit for the work, with energy and capital enough, can do well, if the price is not too high.

The temptation to start with small savings on too large a scale has been the real cause of disaster.

A living is obtainable from as little as 10 acres of "early potato ground," but with mixed farming from 30 to 50 acres seems necessary.

The occupiers of small holdings of from 2 to 7 acres, who also work as labourers and do higgling, are doing well, and so are small shopkeepers who combine small farming with their business.

The life has undoubtedly been hard, the work heavy, and in the worst times, anxiety has been oppressive, but on the whole Mr Wilson Fox's summary of the evidence he obtained as to their position from small holders shows that the majority are holding on fairly well, with occasional losses and a very narrow margin, but certainly not worse off than the large farmers. The worst instance he quotes, we note, is one, not of an owner, but of a tenant of 30 acres.

In the more favoured districts, such as Wainfleet and Friskney, the state of things is much better.

The competition for small farms is great and increasing. "Foremen and labourers get good wages, and the necessaries of life are cheaper."

They save money more easily. They can also rent and stock a farm for less money. Many are thus

---

[1] Page 72. [2] This man values his land at £120 an acre now.

tempted to try their fortune notwithstanding the price of produce.

On sixteen estates in Lincolnshire there are 1447 holdings under 50 acres, 204 from 50 to 100, 243 from 100 to 200, and 321 between 200 and 500, and 96 over 500 acres.

There is no doubt some sacrifice of possible interests of children in the work of small farms, where the labour, practically unpaid, of the wife and children, is essential to success.

The whole question turns on the natural aptitude and tastes of the would-be small farmer and his family. It is a hard, but independent and wholesome life, and those who enter on it with vigour of mind and body, and capital enough at a reasonable figure, plainly do very well indeed.

A small owner of 60 acres says:—" Small holdings are a benefit to the community. People who employ no labour and keep pigs, hens, cows, and grow vegetables can live. Borrowing money has done the harm, both when buying land and stocking the farm."

But small holdings may be looked at from another point of view than the benefit of the small holder. " The increase in the number of such holdings would create a larger resident population of hardworking thrifty character, with local interests, and less likely to migrate if they could get a fair margin of profit."

The suggestion is made by many of the heavily mortgaged small freeholders that the State should advance money at a lower interest to set them free, and that this margin would pull them through.

It must be remembered that some of the land specially suited for small holdings is very heavily rated, both for ordinary purposes, and for the special drainage needed in the fen countries. Heavy railway rates have also been a great drawback to success in the more remote districts.

The whole question is economic. The advantage of the security which attaches to ownership is lost, if in bidding a price a purchaser is really saddling himself for all time with the top rent the land could fetch at the highest point of prices and prosperity. And the loss is still harder to meet if the buyer is paying, not with savings, but with borrowed money. The result is fixity of tenure at a rent increasingly unfair, and too often complicated embarrassments and loss owing to lack of ready money.

It is obvious that the ultimate result for those who are in a position to hold on depends upon prices righting themselves. There can be no doubt that if prices and times improve, those who pull through till then will certainly have as bright a future as any class of agriculturists, and will have this advantage over tenants, that they will be able to reap the full gain of the good times, which, in the case of tenant farmers, will be shared with or appropriated by the landlords.

Perhaps the greatest obstacle to small holdings is the lack of capital which prevents landowners from making and equipping small farms, and labourers from stocking them. Loans on cheap terms are needed to enable landlords to meet the outlay on buildings and other improvements.[1] In Cumberland and Westmoreland, farm servants are frequently enabled to start farming and climb up by the landlord stocking the land with sheep, at 4 or 5 per cent. additional rent on their value. For the small tenants, credit banks might be useful machinery as in Germany, or there might be some simple form of loaning State money through the Post Office.

In this connection the evidence given by Mr Wolff as to the success of co-operative credit banks for agriculturists in Germany and Italy is of great practical significance. The development of any such system as that of the Raiffeisen or Luzzatti banks in England must inevitably be slow. Their success clearly has depended, on the Continent, on the slow evolution in the leaders of this co-operative movement of a special type of knowledge of accounts and of human nature and affairs. These things are

[1] Mr R. Roberts shows that the additional rent obtainable from smaller holdings would more than pay interest on a Government Loan. Wilson Fox, Lincoln, App. B, 13.

not done in a day. Great credit attaches to Mr Wolff, to Mr Yerburgh, and others, who have endeavoured to spread exact information and to cautiously initiate experiments in this form of co-operation in this country. I am convinced, from the evidence of Mr Wolff and his excellent treatise on "People's Banks,"[1] that if any such system as that of Raiffeisen had been in effective operation in England, most of the disasters of the over-speculative small holders would have been prevented, or at any rate, mitigated. And it is obvious that the ultimate development of small holdings in this country will be quickened, and directed into economically sound channels, if this movement for spreading co-operative credit banks takes root, and becomes a source of strength and guidance in agricultural districts.

Mr Pringle found everywhere in the South Midlands that want of capital is an obstacle to success in new forms of farming, or in the subdivision of large farms. Here and there, there are hardworking men who begin at the foot of the ladder and steadily climb upwards. Two brothers in Hunts, once labourers at 9s a week, took small farms and worked up, through all the bad times. They can hardly read or write. They have recently taken two farms of 300 acres each, their land is fully stocked and they can command £5000 between them. They farm on old-fashioned lines, but do it with a very fine margin.[2]

Smaller farms would in general be more workable and profitable both to landlord and tenant, but loans for equipping with buildings at 3 to $3\frac{1}{2}$ per cent. are essential.[3]

Lord Wantage, who had done much to promote small holdings, both on his own estates and through the Small Farms and Labourers Land Company, said there was increasing demand for farms from 50 to 100 acres, from men who worked themselves with their families. And they are excellent tenants.[4]

"Small men of that sort are more punctual rent payers, and are less exacting as to buildings."

[1] "People's Banks." By Henry W. Wolff. Longmans.
[2] Pringle, Beds, etc., p. 45. [3] Lord de Ramsey. [4] Lord Wantage, 4411-6.

The Small Farms Company has shown that "the inclination of this type of man is to buy an acre or two on which to put their buildings and their house, and rent the rest." They are industrious, and have greatly improved the poor soil of the farm on the Berkshire Downs which Lord Wantage handed over to the Company.

It is found to be better, Lord Wantage says, not to have too many small holdings together, as outside employment is needed to supplement the earnings from the land.

His own small tenants prefer a yearly tenancy, on an honourable understanding that they will not be disturbed, if they go on paying rent. "Even if they fall into arrears, they will not usually be disturbed."

One difficulty in small holdings is that the village system naturally leads the men to try to get the choice bits of accommodation land. If population were better distributed, there would be less competition between the would-be small farmer and the big farmers for the choicer bits of land.

Lord Wantage gave an interesting account of his experiment in profit sharing on his farms in hand, which amounted to 2344 arable, 1833 meadow, and 250 acres of down land. Dividing a fourth of the profits, the bonus to the men has ranged from 60s down to 10s. This system has stimulated active interest in the work, and increased results, while the labourers learn to understand better the position of profit and loss from year to year.[1]

"I would adopt the system on any farm of any size which I was cultivating myself."

"The trouble is nothing compared in my estimation with the advantages which are to be got by it."[2]

Its effects are shown in the aggregate increase of population in the two parishes concerned, while the population of the whole union has been decreasing.

Lord Wantage also favours large allotments, finding many men work them well.

[1] Lord Wantage, 4490, 4512.   [2] Ibid. 4628, 4675.

The Small Farms Company have found their tenants prosper, and a vacant holding has applicants instantly after it.

Sir Massey Lopes has many small holdings on his estate in Devon. There are advantages in grazing rights on Dartmoor. Those who are helped by their families and do not hire labour have done fairly well. He encourages small pasture holdings in the villages for the local provision of milk and butter. The yeoman farmers are generally disappearing, and one great difficulty of the small tenants is the wish of their sons to get off to the towns.

Wherever there is a possible profit in working small farms, as in many of the grazing counties and in Wales, there has been a tendency to divide large farms, and this economic movement it would seem of benefit to the country to encourage as far as possible.

What, then, are the essential conditions for success? First, that the land should be either bought or hired at such a price that leaves some room for profitable working; second, that the land should be productive and exceptionally easily worked; third, that there should be a quick and easy access to a good market, and that railway rates should not eat up all possible margin of profit. It is also—at any rate in the present stage of development—desirable to have work available for small farmers on large farms in the neighbourhood, or opportunities for supplementing income by carting, etc.

The persistence of the feeling of jealous criticism of the small holder cannot but be regretted. That criticism is economically unsound, for where the conditions are suitable, it is better for all concerned that a considerable proportion of farms should be small, more produce is got, and more human well-being accomplished.

It does not follow because men were tempted to start with insufficient, or with borrowed capital, at a moment when prices and values were steadily moving upward, and thus the back wave has hit them with exceptional severity, where they were heavily mortgaged, that freehold farming is to be rejected. On the contrary, there is ample evidence both of the value to the community of this type of agriculturist, and of the strenuous industry and self-denying thrift which always accompany its development.

It is too often argued from the casual utterances of a few despairing men that they would have been better off and have had fewer hours of labour as labourers, that the effort to achieve independence is a mere folly. The almost degraded position of the agricultural labourer in England, a generation or even half a generation ago, and the instinctive desire of the most energetic type of labourers, to emancipate themselves by means of allotments and small holdings is the direct answer to this specious fallacy. Both in the interests of agriculture, and of the social elevation of the rural population, it is, in my opinion, the plain duty of the legislature to promote, by every practicable and sound method, the development of a system of small holdings, and to create facilities and machinery which will enable small holdings to be freely formed where the conditions of soil, markets, and population are favourable, and under conditions which will provide against the special dangers under which so many small freeholders have suffered hitherto.

Sir Arthur Arnold, then President of the Free Land League, made important suggestions to the Commission. In his opinion, small holders produce more, and the best agricultural results are to be obtained "where a man's total energies are given to the cultivation of his own land."

The Allotments and Small Holdings Acts are useful, but the results wholly insignificant and insufficient. "What we look forward to is a much wider extent of distribution of land by alteration of the Land Acts, and that a very much larger breadth should pass into the hands of possessing cultivators."[1]

He recommends the application to Great Britain of the system of land purchase, restricted to holdings under £50 a year rent. This would not at present operate largely, but under altered conditions of the law there

[1] Arnold, 33,955, etc.

would be a gradual and, in the end, a very signal alteration in the distribution of the soil.

The Glebe Land Act has not, he contends, operated to put land within the reach of the small holder, but to add glebes to large adjoining estates.

The glebe lands still amount to about 650,000 acres, widely distributed. These lands, together with other lands of a similar public character, amount to about 2,000,000 acres. Sir Arthur Arnold recommends that the whole of these lands should be placed at the disposal of county councils and other local authorities, or, if found more expedient, administered by a special commission. He would allow the lands to be sold, or let for small holdings, allotments, and similar purposes.

A Bill (Mortmain Law Amendment) was introduced in 1884 by Lord Randolph Churchill with somewhat analogous objects.

I wish to support these suggestions most strongly, and also to urge the necessity of amendments to the Allotments Act and the Local Government Act, 1894, removing the restriction of the land provisions of those Acts to the labouring population, and giving a free hand to parish, district, and county councils to acquire and let or sell land to occupying cultivators in whatever way seems most expedient for the wants of each locality. I am also of opinion that the suggestions made in Chapter IX as to the sale of encumbered estates, or estates in bankruptcy, with some right of pre-emption vested in county councils, would operate beneficially if county councils availed themselves of such an opportunity with public spirit, and thus placed additional facilities for acquiring small holdings on reasonable terms within the reach of the rural population.

Aid should also be given administratively and by the dissemination of information for the purpose of leading to the general adoption in the rural districts of the co-operative credit system or people's banks, which have been of such immense benefit to small holders in Germany and Italy.

CHAPTER XVI.

TUBERCULOSIS.

THERE was a consensus of opinion from all witnesses examined on the point, as to the success of the several Acts passed to check the various diseases which have caused heavy loss to stock farmers in the past.

Whatever differences of opinion have been expressed from certain districts of Scotland and the eastern counties as to the restriction on the importation of live cattle, and whatever complaints are made as to special hardships in the administration of the Swine Fever Act (Contagious Diseases Animals Act, 1893) the legislative policy of the last few years for the purpose of stamping out disease may be taken as having the substantially unanimous approval of all practical agriculturists.[1]

Important evidence was also laid before the Commission as to the grave losses to agriculturists from tuberculosis.

Mr Speir says that it is far more prevalent than supposed; that throughout Ayrshire and Wigtownshire the losses to farmers are enormous, and in themselves sweep away profits. A Wigtownshire farmer lost twenty-three cows out of fifty in a single year, while in many cases a "full stock" has died off in a year or two.

Mr Speir quotes the opinion of an expert, that there are few stocks free from the disease, and that almost 75 per cent. of the cows must be more or less affected.

The opinion of dealers and veterinary surgeons is,

[1] Murray, 5191, 5218, 5403; Lopes, 17,090; Duke of Richmond, 22,610; Lander, 33,487; Finney, 35,452; Brown, 35,826; Pears, 36,343; Elliott, 37,965; Bowen-Jones, 44,747; Stratton, 6459; Read, 16,297, 15,932, 12,207; Hope, 48,418; Hutcheson, 24,436, &c.; Bell, 26,291; Dewar, 31,771; Fyshe, 53,925; Ballingall, 54,194; Wilkinson, 31,365; Stratton. 6732-7; Johnson, 7882; Lipscomb, 20,683.

that the disease is vastly more prevalent than formerly. The losses are heavy in fat bullocks as well as cows. The Ayrshire Butchers' Society, formed for compensating purchasers of animals condemned after slaughter, estimates 12 to 14 per cent. of the animals which passed through their hands to be affected.

This society urged that tuberculosis should be scheduled as a contagious disease, like pleuro-pneumonia, while generally through these Scottish dairying counties there is, Mr Speir states, even greater unanimity in favour of compulsory slaughter of animals affected with tuberculosis than there was as to pleuro-pneumonia, and farmers would accept almost any compensation, however small, rather than go on as they are.

Mr Speir suggests that animals detected by the tuberculin test should at once be excluded from the dairies, should be branded, and that some compensation should be paid for the loss on sale of the carcase. The grave danger from tuberculous cows continuing to give milk is insisted on from all sides. The diseased animal may give saleable milk up to the very last stages of the disease.

Mr Hope found tuberculosis very prevalent, especially in the in-bred pedigree stock of the northern counties of Scotland, though there is a general reluctance to admit its extent. There is a universal demand among stock-owners in favour of compulsory slaughter with compensation.

While, in the case of cattle slaughtered for pleuro-pneumonia in Edinburgh, it had been found that 20 per cent. of the carcases showed tuberculosis also, Mr Hope is of opinion that the per-centage of tuberculous cattle is now still greater.

By those witnesses who speak for the districts most affected, and who have given the most attention to the subject, tuberculosis is insisted on as the most important question of agricultural administrative reform at the present time.

Mr Kay who, in the name of many Lancashire farmers, strongly advocates scheduling tuberculosis and compensating for slaughter as for pleuro-pneumonia, says that cattle and cows are being constantly condemned by the medical officers of the Lancashire boroughs, and that the loss to either farmer or butcher is now enormous, as inspection of slaughtered animals has shown that at least one in five is affected with the disease. In nearly all cases the disease cannot be detected by ordinary inspection when the animal is alive.

"It is," says Mr Kay, "one of the greatest causes of depression in Lancashire, more particularly in the dairy districts."

Mr Stratton thinks there are few herds now free from it, and that the matter calls for urgent attention.

Mr Wilson Fox states, in his Lancashire report, that unhealthy and ill-constructed cattle sheds and byres, with want of space and air, have contributed to the spread of tuberculosis. Instead of 600 cubic feet of air, in some cases a cow gets only 260 cubic feet, and there are no means of isolating diseased animals. One witness stated that, if the Dairy and Cow Sheds Act was put into force in the Chorley district, seven-tenths of the buildings would have to come down. The granting of compensation, on compulsory slaughter, would be equivalent to a reduction of 10 to 20 per cent. in the rent.

Besides the direct and total loss, there is an indirect loss in the price of animals sold off, when slightly affected. The extent of the disease has been greater owing to winter dairying, close and heated air, insufficient ventilation, and overcrowding.

Mr Patrick Wright, Professor of Agriculture at Glasgow, thinks the prevalence of the disease is largely due to ignorance of sanitary conditions. Many of the byres in the country are hotbeds of disease and infection.

Mr Speir is of opinion that infection is the chief cause, in-breeding also contributory, and close confinement being a third cause. The contamination is easy and rapid in crowded, close buildings.

In Wigtownshire, he estimates 75 per cent. of the cows to be affected, and, having applied the tuberculin test to many stocks in Ayrshire and Lanarkshire, has found farms with 75 and even 90 per cent. affected.

" In only one case have I found every animal free."

The loss by death to breeders is chiefly in yearlings. The rest of the loss falls to the stock farmers who buy for dairy or feeding.

For ten years past Danish agriculturists have been working on a policy of isolation, but the impossibility of diagnosing the disease at its initial stage has, till Koch's discovery of tuberculin, made isolation and disinfection almost useless.

Experiments made by Professor Bang and others demonstrated the enormous per-centage of latent tuberculosis, and showed that "mild methods were out of the question."[1]

A law was passed in 1893 appropriating about £2700 (since increased to £5000), for five years for providing free tuberculin tests for young cattle to owners who were in a position to separate healthy from re-acting animals. But the testing of whole herds was soon adopted; the advantage to the farmer of knowing promptly how he stood as regards his whole stock being obvious, enabling him to divide his herd and immediately start upon the gradual process of clearing away the disease. The veterinary surgeons being on the premises for free testing of the young stock, the testing of the grown stock by private arrangements is carried out at small additional cost.

The first year, 327 herds only were tested by 69 veterinary surgeons, while in October 1895 there had been reports of tests on 1972 herds by 210 veterinary surgeons. The first reluctance of the farmers has been changed to an eager demand throughout the country.

Reporting up to August of 1896, Professor Bang says the number of inoculated animals was then 53,000 out

---

[1] This and the succeeding paragraphs summarise the main points of Professor Bang's important Report on "The Application of Tuberculin in the Suppression of Bovine Tuberculosis."

Deutschen Zeitschrift für Thiermedicin und vergleichende Pathologie, XXII, Band. Translation made for the use of the Massachusetts Agricultural College, U.S.A.

of nearly 1,700,000 head of cattle, and that under the test 38·7 per cent. had re-acted. Of those tested, the large herds—those with 50 head or more—showed the worst results. About two-thirds of these herds show 59 per cent. of re-acting animals, and about one-fourth show over 75 per cent. In the small herds, there are many found wholly exempt from disease, while more than one-half have less than 25 per cent., and only a tenth show 75 per cent. or more. The existence of entirely healthy herds upsets the theory that the bacilli of tuberculosis are everywhere present, and gives more basis for the hope that the disease can be extirpated. Doubt is also thrown on the hypothesis that "in and in" breeding is a cause of spread of the disease, Mr Bang has found two herds most of which originated from the same cow, and had been increased by in-breeding, but were absolutely free from taint. The importation of breeding animals for the improvement of big herds has, in his opinion, caused infection, which has been spread from the larger to the smaller farms.

The test has been found to be faulty in Germany in 13·14 per cent. of instances, and in Denmark in 9·7 per cent. of instances. In some of these cases dissection has shown tuberculosis to exist, though there has been no re-action. In other cases where there has been re-action, and dissection shows apparently healthy tissues, it is quite possible that minute tuberculous deposits have escaped attention. "Knots from the size of a needle's head to that of a pea, in a hidden lymph gland surrounded by fatty tissue, may be overlooked even by those of most experience." Thus the proportion of cases in which the test is a fairly certain indication is probably greater even than 86 to 90 per cent. In the great majority of cases, the reaction merely indicates latent tuberculosis, and the test gives no guide as to the degree to which the disease has advanced, incipient tuberculosis giving sharper re-action than old standing cases. Again, there is serious difficulty from the different degrees of susceptibility of different animals and different stages of the disease. On a repetition of the test, even after twelve months, diseased animals may show no re-action, though it seems probable that the majority show a repeated re-action even after a short interval. "Intentional deception," says Mr Bang, "could therefore be practised to no great extent, and the cautious cattle buyer could hold his newly purchased animals apart from the healthy ones until an additional test has been made."

The use of tuberculin is also, in his opinion, practically without risk.

The test cannot be treated as legal proof, or as infallible, but it is "an excellent means for recognising tuberculosis."

As to remedies, Professor Bang condemns compulsory slaughter as proposed in France, and unsuccessfully attempted to be carried out in some of the United States. The number of animals showing disease is too great. The cost to the community, or the loss to the stock owner would be too heavy.

The Danish policy is to test the whole herd, to separate the healthy from the unhealthy, to kill only the evidently sick animals, to rear on sterilised milk the calves of the re-acting cows which are only slightly attacked, carefully withdrawing them from any chance of infection, and to test the healthy section of the herd once or twice yearly.

It seems to be established that, except where the parents are seriously affected with general tuberculosis, pervading the blood and principal organs, the calves are usually born healthy, and acquire the disease almost entirely by infection.

Co-operative dairies, otherwise of immense help to agriculturists involve the risk of disseminating germs of disease, unless the skim milk handed back to the farmers for the use of calves is sterilised by sufficient heating.

Mr Bang says :—"On farms where this method has been used collected evidence shows that all the calves were healthy, even where tuberculosis had widely spread among the grown animals."

U

The interesting experiments carried out by Professor Bang at Thurebylille, with not the most satisfactory means for separation, seem to go far to establish the soundness of this theory. "With the exception of two cases of inborn tuberculosis, and one doubtful case, thus far no calf of the re-acting cows since the beginning of the experiment has later shown itself to be tuberculous." A careful and vigilant persistence in the method seems likely "to gradually change a tuberculous herd into an entirely healthy one," all the suspicious animals being isolated and gradually got rid of, under circumstances which prevent them from spreading the disease further.

Sir T. D. Gibson-Carmichael, Bart., M.P., has carried out an experiment on nearly similar lines with his herd of Aberdeen-Angus cattle at Castlecraig since 1894. An interesting report has recently been prepared by Mr James Wilson, Fordyce Lecturer in Agriculture, Aberdeen University.[1]

In this experiment the calves have been treated on the hypothesis that "milk as it comes from the udder is germ free except when the milk gland is in a diseased condition." The calves of the re-acting cows were accordingly allowed to suckle till the autumn, but kept separate from the calves of the sound cows until they had been subjected to the test. Of twenty bull calves in 1895, seven were from tuberculous cows. Yet the whole of these passed the test in the autumn of 1895, and again in January 1896, two of them having been sold before this second test.

The experiment, so far as it has gone, seems to show that this policy must certainly restrict and arrest the spread of disease, that it is possible to breed safely from slightly diseased animals, and that the disease may steadily be eliminated.

If it is objected that the cost of the inoculations, and of the close observation and repeated examinations of temperature of the inoculated animals, on the precision and accuracy of which the whole value of the process

[1] "The Results of the use of Tuberculin in the Castlecraig Herd." Edinburgh, G. P. Johnston. 1896.

depends, is too heavy, it should be borne in mind that the alternative of compulsory slaughter of all affected animals would involve a vastly greater expenditure or loss. The apparently reasonable prospect of clearing a herd from disease within a few years should be viewed as a probable addition to the assets of agriculturists, the amount of which, if the policy is successful, must, in any case, greatly exceed the cost of the remedy. Taking even the most moderate estimate of the extent of tuberculosis, and assuming that of about 2,700,000 cows, 30 per cent., or 900,000, are affected; of other cattle under two years of age, out of 2,600,000, 10 per cent., or 260,000, are affected; and of 1,600,000 cattle over two years of age, 20 per cent., or 320,000, are affected, making a total of nearly 1,500,000 head of stock out of nearly 7,000,000, it is probable that the pecuniary benefit to agriculturists would not fall short of a million sterling per annum, and might conceivably greatly exceed that sum. If the higher estimates of the prevalence of this disease arrived at by Mr Speir be taken, the results would be much greater. In either case it is plain that the cost of such a remedial policy as is being adopted in Denmark, represents a very small percentage on the enormous addition to agricultural income which extirpation, or reduction to a minimum, of disease would mean. Any immediate sacrifice made by agriculturists would be an investment bringing heavy and increasing returns in a very few years.

In a memorandum laid before the Commission, Mr Speir puts the cost of the tuberculin at 6d to 7d for each animal, and the veterinary attendance at about 6d each animal, but this does not include the taking of the temperatures during the next twenty-four hours after injection. He suggests, as a fair division of liability, that the State and the county should each pay two-fifths, and the stockowner one-fifth of the cost. Taking the four south-western Scotch counties, the charge would amount to a 3d rate. There are veterinarians enough, and the total cost of the four counties would be about £3000 a year, while the extirpation of the disease would, he estimates, save a present loss of £66,000 a year. I cannot but think that both these estimates are slightly below what is probable.

The important letter recently addressed by M. de Leclercq, President of the Shorthorn Society of France, to Lord Brougham, President of the English Shorthorn Society, and urging that cattle should be sold subject to the tuberculin test, emphasises the danger and the possible losses to this country of temporising with this matter. Some of the highest priced animals imported from England, including the champion bull "Nonsuch," have proved, on being tested and afterwards slaughtered, to be seriously diseased. The French Government have interdicted importation of cattle which do not pass the tuberculin test at the frontier, and take special precautions to defeat frauds alleged to be attempted by the repeated inoculations just before importation. Belgium and Switzerland are taking steps in the same direction, and in Buenos Ayres, where most of our export cattle go, Bills have been introduced to make the test compulsory.

M. Tisserand, Director-General of Agriculture in France, thinks the disease has been and is increasing, and that an attempt should be made to extinguish it everywhere. Tuberculosis is a disease of slow evolution, and may exist for a very long time without external symptoms; the animal may live unsuspected, and arrive at the slaughter-house in apparent health, but will show by post-mortem examination numerous tubercles in the lungs, muscles, and other organs. While in contact with others, it is a constant source of infection.

The Government should, M. Tisserand insists, have power to order the test, and to order the isolation of reacting animals. In his opinion, the English shorthorn breeders will be obliged, sooner or later, to satisfy the foreign purchaser, or lose their export trade.

It must, therefore, be deeply regretted that the English Society has thrown cold water on the reasonable French demand.

It is sufficiently established, by the post-mortem test following the tuberculin test, in Denmark, in France, in the United States, as well as in this country, that the chances of error in the application of the test are very small, and that some of the cases when it has apparently failed are due to insufficiently exact and comprehensive searching of the tissues where the disease may be, in all probability, lurking. This being so, to promptly ascertain their own position would be a great gain to practical farmers.

In the vast majority of cases, farmers applying the test with care and knowledge, will at once be able to isolate the diseased cattle or cows, purify their dairies, and fatten and sell off the very slightly diseased animals, before the disease has ruined their selling value. This policy will reduce to a minimum the losses which many men, under such circumstances, are doubtless reluctant to face. And the successful results attained in Denmark, and in such experiments as those of Sir T. D. Gibson-Carmichael, give every reason for the encouraging hope, that, with skill and persistence, under favourable conditions, as regards the arrangements of buildings and of pastures for purposes of isolation, farmers will find in a few years that they will have worked the disease out of their stock, to their lasting advantage as well as to the advantage of the whole community.

On these and other grounds, I submit that pending the adoption of any definitive policy of dealing with tuberculosis which may result from the recommendations of the Special Commission which is now inquiring into this question, it is expedient that, without further delay, the Board of Agriculture should forthwith take steps—

(i.) To disseminate accurate information in a concise and readable form as to the methods and results of the attempts to deal with tuberculosis made by the Danish, French, and other Governments;

(ii.) To establish one or more stations where tuberculin of guaranteed and uniform quality can be obtained on reasonable terms by agriculturists who wish to test their herds; and

(iii.) To prepare in connection with these stations, lists of veterinary surgeons who may satisfy the Board of Agriculture that they are competent to apply the test with precision.

CHAPTER XVII

GENERAL SUMMARY OF CONCLUSIONS AND RECOMMENDATIONS.

A.—CONCLUSIONS.

THE conclusions arrived at in this Report may be thus summed up :—

(1). The decline of agriculture from the prosperity of twenty-five years ago, although led up to, and from time to time aggravated, by unfavourable seasons, has been mainly due to the fall in prices of agricultural produce.

(2). The fall in prices has been largely, if not exclusively, brought about by the rapid development of agricultural production in new districts abroad, by the quickening and cheapening of means of transport, and by inventions enabling producers in the Colonies and abroad to place foreign and colonial meat and dairy produce on the home markets in saleable condition.

(3). Besides the fall in prices, the chief cause of agricultural depression has been the excessive rent put upon agricultural land.

(4). Contributory causes have been excessive and preferential railway rates and charges, the organised and fraudulent sale of adulterated articles of food, and, in a minor degree, the local and Imperial burdens on land.

(5). It is impracticable, and would be prejudicial to the general commercial interests of this country, and it would be immediately prejudicial to stock and dairy farmers, and would ultimately, if not immediately, be prejudicial to all agriculturists, to attempt to raise prices artificially by protective duties, either directly imposed on agricultural imports, or by differential duties, or by any system of bounties.

(6.) Changes in the currency system, with a view to raising or maintaining prices, have not been shown to be necessary, or even certain to produce the results expected, but have been shown to be perilous to commercial stability, even if adopted by international agreement, which is at present improbable.

(7.) If agriculture is to be helped, Parliament must deal with the causes of depression which are within reach, and can be met equitably and with practical results.

(8.) The most effective help Parliament can render to tenant farmers is by the extension of agricultural arbitration to rent, and by giving real security to tenants' capital invested in the soil, and to their tenure of their holdings.

(9.) Any legislative help Parliament may render to agriculture by making the relations of landlord and tenant more equitable, and by giving greater security to the investment of tenants' capital, should be based on economic evidence, and be directed to putting the relations of landlord and tenant on a strictly business footing.

(10.) While the gross returns from farming have fallen enormously, what may be called the reproductive items of expenditure, the outlay on labour, and on fertilisers and feeding stuffs are practically stationary, and, therefore, ends can only be made to meet by a reduction in the non-reproductive items, the chief of which is rent.

(11.) The analysis of the accounts furnished by farmers, and from the great estates, makes it certain that, in the great majority of cases, rents have not yet been reduced to the point at which the economic loss from fall of prices would be fairly shared between landlord and tenant, and in consequence of this landlords are still drawing rents which, in many cases, are largely paid out of tenants' capital, and which, in most cases, absorb practically the whole profits which farmers might otherwise obtain, and deprive them even of the most modest return from their capital invested in farming.

(12.) These inferences, from the accounts supplied, are more than confirmed by the mass of evidence—substantially unchallenged—to the effect that excessive rents have brought, and are bringing, vast numbers of farmers to ruin, that rents have been insufficiently and too tardily reduced, and that the soil has been steadily deteriorated by the ruin and impoverishment of tenants, owing to the disproportionate share of the diminishing receipts which has had to be taken for rents.

(13.) The ruinous results of rack-renting in all parts of the country have demonstrated that competition cannot safely be taken as the measure of agricultural rent, which should rather be based on a valuation of the average money returns obtainable from the land, a principle recognised on some of the most wisely and generously managed estates.

(14.) The large sums of money expended in the purchase and improvement of estates are not a sufficient justification for high rents, for the reason that to charge anything like interest on the original capital value would be to transfer the whole economic loss to the tenant; and, as to landlords' improvements, the tenants have, in fact, paid for them, and are still paying for them in the reduced rents, while much of the outlay of landlords cannot be treated as in any sense an interest-bearing investment.

(15.) While the bad farmer, who reduces the value of his farm, is able to make easier terms for a renewal of his tenancy, the improving farmer who invests large sums in increasing the fertility of the soil, is unable to obtain in most cases a reduction of rent in fair proportion to the fall in prices, for the reason that his farm is coveted by other competitors—a competition all the keener in bad times, when farms in high condition are fewer, and therefore more eagerly sought for.

(16.) The results of this state of things have been grave insecurity of tenure, constant discouragement to high farming up to the end of a tenancy, and serious injustice to the very class of farmers who most deserve the protection of the law.

(17.) The attempt made in the Agricultural Holdings Act for England, and the similar Act for Scotland, to give greater security to tenant farmers in bargaining with their landlords, and fuller and more easily enforceable property rights in their improvements, and thus to check or remedy some of the evils resulting from the existing system of land tenure has largely failed.

(18.) The chief causes of the comparative failure of the Act have been (*a*) that no suitable machinery was provided to carry out the Act; it was left to the old type of valuer and the old methods of valuation, with the result that the main purpose of the Act, to give the tenant the full remaining value of his improvements, has been largely frustrated; (*b*) that compensation was restricted to quitting tenants and no provision made to protect the interests of sitting tenants, with the result that the best type of farmers have been constantly compelled to acquiesce in rents which transfer the tenant's interests in the soil to the landlord.

(19.) These perversions and limitations of the Act have operated to encourage bad and defective farming, and to discourage the thorough and generous and persistent cultivation and fertilising of the soil, and have placed the most deserving class of agriculturists—those who have steadily

GENERAL CONCLUSIONS

persevered in developing and maintaining the highest standard of good farming—under disabilities which ought to be removed.

(20.) The procedure of the Act is costly and unsatisfactory, the rights of tenants to compensation are frequently defeated by unreasonable counter-claims and by penal and restrictive covenants, and the administration of the Act is largely in the hands of valuers of inadequate knowledge, independence, and responsibility.

(21.) The Act is incomplete, and does not cover all the matters which should be covered, and leads to the defeat of justice by frequent appeals.

(22.) The Act gives no sufficient protection to the landlord against dishonest and depletive farming.

(23.) It is contrary to the interests of agriculture to restrict the cultivation of the land in the way which may be found to pay best under present circumstances, or the sale of produce so long as the soil is thoroughly worked and manured.

(24.) It must be to the benefit of all interested in the land that all reasonable and suitable improvements, which tend to increase the value of the land for the purposes for which it is let, should be encouraged by giving freedom of action to tenants and compensation for any remaining value of such improvements, and that the recent recognition of this principle in the Market Gardeners' Compensation Act should be extended to all kinds of farming.

(25.) The preferential right of the landlord to distrain for rent has been and is prejudicial to the interests of agriculture.

The following changes of the law and improvements in its administration may therefore be recommended.

B.—RECOMMENDATIONS.

I.—AGRICULTURAL HOLDINGS ACTS.

The present Agricultural Holdings Acts for England and Scotland should be amended so as to provide as follows :—

Scope of the Act.

(1.) Full compensation for the cumulative fertility resulting from continuous good farming, irrespective of any arbitrary time limit.

(2.) Freedom to carry out, and compensation for all improvements suitable for the purposes for which the holding is let, whether the landlord consent or not.

(3.) Tenant's improvements to be classified in two schedules, the first to comprise the more permanent and costly improvements in respect of which consent shall no longer be requisite, but a notice shall be required ; the second schedule to comprise all other improvements in respect of which neither consent nor notice shall be required.

(4.) The first schedule should include buildings, except those required for market gardening, silos, irrigation, roads and bridges, provision of water supply, permanent fences, embankments, the reclaiming of unenclosed waste land, and drainage.

(5.) The laying down of permanent and temporary pasture and grasses, the consumption of home-grown corn and other produce, the remainder of the improvements now classed in Part I of the First Schedule to the Act, the improvements now classed in Part III of the First Schedule to the Act, and all other improvements not specifically placed in the proposed first schedule, for which notice is required, should be classed in the second of the proposed schedules.

(6.) Compensation should be given retrospectively, as in the Market Gardeners' Compensation Act, 1895, for suitable improvements prior to the passing of a new Act, where the landlord did not dissent from such improvements at the time.

(7.) All tenants' claims and payments under the custom of the country or agreements should be brought within the procedure of the Act, so as to be included in one award with the specific compensation provided by the Act, and enforceable as one sum.

(8.) A tenant remaining in his holding at the determination of his tenancy, and entering on a new contract of tenancy should be enabled to protect himself from being rented on his improvements by the right to claim compensation for their unexhausted value without quitting, or to obtain a proportionate reduction from the new rent.

(9.) A tenant arbitrarily compelled by the act of his landlord to quit his holding, except for nonpayment of rent and for bad farming, should be entitled to such compensation as will cover his loss by removal.

(10.) Tenants should be free to cultivate the land and sell produce to the best advantage, so long as they maintain its fertility.

(11.) Tenants should be entitled to claim compensation for damage to their crops by game.

(12.) Claims for penal rents, or breaches of covenant, should be limited to actual damage proved, and claims for waste should be limited to two years, and not be enforceable unless the landlord shall have given reasonable notice to the tenant to make good, or to desist from the waste specified.

(13). The landlord should be given an equal right with the tenant to set the Act in operation.

Procedure of the Act.

(14.) The claims of the tenant for improvement, and of the landlord for deterioration, should be served on the other party simultaneously.

(15.) A record of the condition of a holding should, so far as possible, be inserted in every contract of tenancy, and in every award under the Act.

(16.) References under the Act should be determined by a single arbitrator, from whose decision there shall be no appeal except upon a point of law.

(17.) For each county, or portion of a county, or group of counties where expedient, the Board of Agriculture should appoint an agricultural arbitrator, whose qualifications should be practical experience of the agriculture of the district, judicial capacity and absolute independence and impartiality, such arbitrator to be paid partly out of a general fund created by fees, partly by the State, and to be removable, for cause shown, by the Board of Agriculture.

(18.) All matters in dispute, including rent, should be referred to the agricultural arbitrator.

(19.) The preferential right of the landlord to distrain for rent should be abolished as regards agricultural land.

II.—RAILWAY RATES.

The Railway and Canal Traffic Acts should be amended so as to enable traders to test the reasonableness of every rate or condition, and to test all evidence bearing on those questions, and to create a cheap and accessible machinery for deciding all cases, and to remove uncertainty from the decisions of Parliament and the courts as to undue preference.

III.—ADULTERATION OF FOOD PRODUCTS.

The recommendations of the Select Committee should be forthwith carried into law, and the existing and improved machinery at the disposal of the Local Government Board, Board of Agriculture, and Board of Customs should be set in motion more effectively than hitherto.

I further recommend the appointment of one or more special Commissioners for a period of five years to supervise and report upon the administration of the various Acts and regulations.

IV.—SMALL HOLDINGS.

The restrictions in the Allotments Acts and Local Government Act, 1894, should be removed. With a view to the better provision of land, glebes, Crown and ecclesiastical agricultural lands, and other land of a public character should be placed at the disposal of county councils. County councils should also have a right of pre-emption of land sold under bankruptcy, or under any new legislation for dealing with encumbered estates.

Co-operative credit banks for agricultural districts should be encouraged, and any legal difficulties removed.

V.—TUBERCULOSIS.

This cause of immense pecuniary loss, both to agriculturists and to meat dealers, and of continued peril to the public health, should be dealt with without further delay, and facilities for voluntary action by agriculturists should be forthwith provided by the Board of Agriculture.

VI.—DIVISION OF RATES BETWEEN OWNER AND OCCUPIER.

I wish again to repeat here the recommendation made by the Richmond Commission, and by myself and several other Commissioners in the Second Report of this Commission, that there should be an equitable division of all local rates between the owner and the occupier.

APPENDIX.

I.

REASONS FOR DISSENTING FROM THE REPORT OF THE MAJORITY.

[NOTE.—It has been suggested that the following statement of objections to the main report of the Commission, which appeared as the first chapter of my separate report, should be reproduced in the present volume. It is therefore placed as an Appendix for purposes of reference only, the general argument and conclusions being complete without it.]

I regret that I am unable to concur in the Report of the Majority of the Commission.

While assenting to the introductory chapter recording the course of our proceedings, and the scope and manner of our inquiry, I think it is much to be regretted that the general Report of the Commission dealing with the whole of the causes of agricultural depression, and the whole of the proposals that might be made either as remedies or mitigations, by legislative or administrative reforms, has not been completed and issued before now.

Most especially is it to be regretted that the one topic upon which most evidence was taken and upon which a great majority of witnesses were practically unanimous—the Amendment of the Laws relating to Agricultural Holdings—has not been reported on at an earlier stage of our proceedings, or at any rate at the same time as the Second Report dealing with "Burdens on Land."

Legislation on this question has for years been urgently needed, and I think it was perfectly possible for the Commission to have reported on this subject in time for such a report to have been the basis of legislation either in the Session of 1895 or the Session of 1896.

This protracted delay has unfortunately withheld from

tenant farmers for three Sessions longer that statutory protection for the money they invest in their holdings, which their ablest representatives have unanimously asked for, and which men of impartial and sound judgment and of adequate experience have professed a readiness to give them.

As to the Report itself, it arranges with skill and effect many of the most important points brought out in evidence, it contains much precise and useful information, and many suggestions and recommendations with which I heartily concur.

The statistical tables and summing up of evidence in the chapters on the "Fall in Prices" and "Foreign Competition" are carefully prepared and well digested, and will be found of great value.

I also wish to express my cordial assent to several of the chapters in Part III, especially the well-considered chapters on the "Sale of Mortgaged Land," and on "Agricultural Education."

But having said thus much, I am, to my regret, bound to state that I find the report defective in method, inadequate as a presentment of the facts laid before us, one-sided in its handling of essential issues, and misleading in several of its conclusions.

Agricultural depression, with its causes and their possible remedies, is from beginning to end an economic question. The subject can only be adequately handled from an economic standpoint, and by a logical and complete examination of the whole of the facts.

But, in the Majority Report, there is no consecutive and comprehensive analysis and attempt to classify, and approximately estimate, in their economic relations to each other, the whole of the causes contributing to the state of things that we wish to see bettered.

Thus, while the fall of prices and foreign competition are exhaustively dealt with, and the permanence or increase in certain items of the cost of production are recognised, the obvious inference that the margin left for rent must dwindle when prices have fallen, and the ratio of the cost of labour and other outgoings to the gross receipts from the land has risen, and that, therefore, high rents in bad times rapidly become a more and more intensely operative cause of acute depression, is left undrawn and unstated.

In the Majority Report there is nowhere any adequate appreciation of the disastrous effects upon agriculture of the policy of diverting the working capital of the tenant farmer from its proper application, the thorough cultivation of the soil, to the making up of rents, which have, by the fall of prices, lost their economic basis, and now assign to the landlord a wholly unfair proportion of the proceeds of the land.

The Report thus leaves out of sight, and practically excludes from consideration, some of the most serious economic elements of the situation.

While describing a disastrous condition of things in many parts of the country, it substantially fails to give the true or any complete explanation of how things got into so bad a state. Further, in consequence of this limited and one-sided inspection of the facts, the report also fails, and necessarily must fail, in making any suggestions or recommendations which would have adequate effect and reach the real sources of the evil. As it leaves out real explanations, so it leaves out real remedies.

The really essential problem to solve is to enable a tenant farmer of average capacity and average capital to earn out of the land the minimum profit which will encourage men in his position to cultivate it properly. This result, with falling and uncertain prices for agricultural produce, is, on some land and in some districts, not to be attained under any conditions which the State can provide by legislative or administrative help, or which landowner or tenant can bring about.

But the evidence taken by this Commission shows that it could be attained in many parts even of the worst districts, if the real causes of agricultural distress were honestly faced and dealt with.

Such portions of our evidence as Mr Hunter Pringle's graphic history and analysis of the ruin of parts of Essex, where many landlords spent too little in equipping their estates with improvements in the good times, and when bad times came, did not reduce rents till the bankruptcy and disappearance of one tenant after another, and consequent deterioration of the soil, compelled them to reduce rents; and, again, in Scotland, such evidence as Mr George Riddell's description of the too frequent treatment of the improving tenant, conclusively establish that the really essential feature of the agricultural depression, and the chief of those causes of disaster which can be reached and remedied, is the faulty system of the tenure of agricultural land. A report which does not face and attempt fairly to arrive at some solution of this question is of no practical value whatever.

And, in effect, this is admitted in the summing up of the recommendations of the majority (paragraph 600) where the recommendations are described merely as palliatives.

It is evident throughout the report of the majority that the situation has been considered almost exclusively from the standpoint of the landlord, and has not been threshed out solely from the economic point of view.

In this connexion, I feel bound to contrast the terms of the Second Report of the Commission where the pressure of burdens upon agricultural land is dealt with.

"Excessive burdens may undoubtedly throw land out of cultivation, and it appears from the evidence that they have already had this effect in certain parts of the country. In other cases, where the results have not yet been equally disastrous, the imposition of excessive burdens on land must tend to discourage the investment of capital, the application of enterprise, and the employment of labour on land, and thereby operate directly to the detriment of the whole agricultural community, and ultimately to the injury of the community at large."

But if the case needs to be stated so strongly for the relief of agriculture from, according to the recommendation of the Second Report, three-fourths of the rates imposed upon land, or a sum of only about 1s 10d an acre on the average, I submit that a very much stronger demand ought to be made in respect of a reasonable relief from the burden of the item of rent, which has been shown to amount on an average to over 20s per acre on many great estates in England and Scotland

Further, I cannot think the various contributory causes of depression are marshalled or handled in a satisfactory manner, and that the arrangement of the Report in that respect leaves much to be desired.

To deal in detail with those portions of the Report of the majority in which I am unable to concur :—

The Report seems to me to insufficiently recognise the facts established in our inquiry :—

    (1.) That the depression has been continuous since the Richmond Inquiry;

(2.) That, while in the earliest stage of the depression investigated by the Richmond Commission, bad seasons were the chief cause of mischief, a persistent, though at times fluctuating, fall in prices coincided with the arrival of better seasons and the improvement of the condition of the soil ;

(3.) That any real and general recovery of agriculture was thus made impossible, because any economic advantages from the better seasons from 1884 to 1890 were more than counterbalanced by the fall in prices;

(4.) That the three exceptionally bad seasons of 1892, 1893, and 1894 coincided with a still deeper fall of prices and culminated in the most acute and widespread stage of the depression, in the autumn of 1894 and summer of 1895.

The Depression in England.

Chapters I and II, stating the condition of agriculture in the arable and in the grazing districts of England, are fairly complete, but, in my opinion, fail to set forth as distinctly and vividly the real position of the majority of agriculturists in those districts as it has been laid before us in the carefully prepared reports of Mr Rew, Mr Wilson Fox, Mr Pringle, and others, and by many of the ablest agriculturists who spoke from local knowledge and practical experience.

Especially I note, in paragraph 40, the inadequate reference to the striking evidence in Mr Pringle's report on the condition of agriculture in Bedfordshire, Huntingdonshire, and Northamptonshire ; the disastrous effects of the bad seasons, not only on the heavy clay arable land, but on the finest pastures in the country, the steady spread of ruin among large classes of farmers, bringing agriculture into the position of a bankrupt industry, the wholesale changes of tenancy, and the share that excessive rents have had in intensifying the features of the depression.

As to Hampshire (paragraph 41) a single quotation is selected from Dr Fream's report, to the effect that tenants are in some cases " keeping on their farms at their own rentals," while the statements from the same report, that " north of

Andover, with rents down to nothing, many of the tenants continue losing money;" that, in another district, "the tenants had borne the brunt of the bad years, and now, when it was too late, the landlords were offering reductions which at an earlier stage might have saved the tenants from collapse;" and that farmers had reported to Dr Fream, "the disinclination and refusal of landlords in most cases to meet their tenants," and that "good farmers have not been sufficiently well treated and met by the landlord, and so long as any balance was thought to be at the bankers, *no reduction* was made" are withheld. Further, if rents were referred to, Mr James Stratton's important evidence, that, although rent had been reduced 50 per cent., it would have to go down 25 per cent. more, should have been quoted.

The effects of the depression in Berkshire, Notts, and the East Riding, and in Kent (paragraphs 42-47), seem insufficiently indicated.

The effects of the depression in the counties of Somerset, Devon, Cornwall, Shropshire, Herefordshire, and Worcestershire (paragraphs 54, 55), seem to be underrated in the report, partly because here, as throughout the report, there is a disposition to measure depression by the actual reduction in rents, or, in other words, to treat it solely as a landlords' question, whereas there is much evidence that rents are complained of as excessive in these counties, and therefore it is probable that in the practical result to the tenant farmer, the degree of loss, which, having regard to the conditions of the district and its type of agriculture might otherwise be slight, is made severe by the postponement of an adequate reduction of rent.

The references to Lancashire, Yorkshire, Durham, and Northumberland (paragraphs, 60, 61), seem to me inadequate and misleading. The reports of Mr Wilson Fox on the Garstang district of Lancashire, and the Glendale district of Northumberland, supported by much evidence from witnesses, show that depression has been acutely felt by tenant farmers in both these counties, and that there have been heavy losses by all classes of farmers, and that the position of many is precarious. As to Lancashire in particular, high rents and insecurity have clearly operated to make the fall of prices more difficult to meet. Mr Pringle's report on Durham and the North Riding brings the disastrous losses of large classes of farmers, and their inability to make a profit, even out of stock farming, in many cases, into the clearest light, and is supported by the evidence of several of the ablest practical farmers in England. While this state of things is partly recognised in the paragraph, it is not correct to state that the position resembles that of Cumberland or Westmoreland, where it is known that there has been the very smallest degree of depression.

Depression in Wales.

The paragraphs relating to Wales (62-64) do not give a satisfactory statement of the evidence laid before us. It may be true that owners in Wales "have not hitherto experienced the effects of the depression to any serious extent." If this is true, it is obviously because rents have not been materially reduced, and, as one land agent admitted, are in some cases paid out of capital, and in other cases out of the wages of the children of farmers. But, for this very reason, it is clear that the tenant farmers have suffered severely. They have had to meet the heavy fall in prices of many articles, and occasional disastrous losses in prices of other articles, and further to meet a continued increase in the cost of labour and production generally, without having, except in a very limited degree, the help by reduction of rent which has been given more freely in many parts of England.

In these paragraphs, as elsewhere in the report, the conclusions arrived at are vitiated by the omission to recognise that, if agriculture is to go on, and the worst features of the depression are to be remedied, when prices have gone down and the cost of production has gone up, the items of rent and other non-reproductive items must go down to the point which leaves a profit. It is therefore impossible to place confidence in them.

Depression in Scotland.

Similar comment is reasonable as to the estimate of the effects of depression in Scotland. The paragraphs fail to describe fully and accurately the real state of things. In this connection it should be noted that, owing to extreme pressure of time in the examination of witnesses in Edinburgh, the character, extent, and acuteness of the depression were generally assumed, and witnesses were questioned chiefly as to remedies and practical suggestions.

The facts of the situation in Scotland had already been laid before us by Scotch witnesses examined in London, and in the Sub-Commissioners' reports. It is clear from that evidence that tenant farmers have suffered severely in all parts of Scotland, and that, except under favourable circumstances of position, or soil, or crops, or markets, even those best off have been only able to make two ends meet, and to secure a bare living. If they had not made money in the previous good times they could not have held out now. As a great agent puts it: "The farmers are getting only their living for their labour, and probably some of them with £10,000 invested are getting very little interest, whereas in former days they got a good profit." But those who have been less fortunate are described as being too deep in the mire to get out, while in several typical districts of Scotland, the rich arable south-eastern counties, and also the south-western arable and dairy counties, there are shown to have been enormous changes of tenancy during the depression, involving in a striking proportion of cases the total ruin of the unfortunate tenants.

The report of the majority lays everywhere stress on the evidence of competition in the demand for farms. I am convinced by the unvarying tenour of evidence as to the causes and character of this competition, as is stated more fully elsewhere,[1] that it is largely due to other causes than supposed profits from agriculture, and that, in regard to farms whose tenants have kept them in high cultivation, such competition is, to some extent, fraudulent and with a view to the exhaustion of the fertility created by high farming.

It seems to me plain that while Scotch farmers have to a certain extent made a saving by lengthening rotations, and reducing the labour and horses employed in cultivation, the general increase in wages and the cost of production, and the maintenance of relatively very high rents have, as in Wales, intensified the depression inevitable from the heavy fall in prices. And it must be remembered that

[1] Chapter VII.

although Scotland has escaped one or two of the worst seasons which have crippled agriculture in England, notably 1879, Scotland has had also exceptionally bad seasons both for crops and stock, and the fall of prices, especially in wheat and potatoes, has been disastrous in some of the most highly rented districts.

The situation in Scotland would have been much worse if the security of long leases had not so widely developed the system of high farming. At the same time, the wholesale ruin and injustice caused by high rents when fixed for as long a period as nineteen years, strikingly illustrate the defects in the law as to agricultural tenures which have contributed so largely to intensify depression throughout Great Britain.

Effects of Depression on Owners.

Again, in discussing the effects of the depression on the owners of land, I think the report is fallacious in assuming that land was, on the average, sold at thirty years' purchase in 1875, and only at eighteen years' purchase in 1895. The calculations based on this assumption greatly exaggerate the undoubtedly heavy fall in the capital value of agricultural land.

On the other hand, I dissent from the statement that the average reduction of rents in the most depressed districts has been 50 per cent. While it is established in evidence that in many districts rents have, on individual farms, after repeated changes of tenancy, been reduced from 50 to 70 or 80 per cent., and in some cases to nominal amounts, it is obvious from the returns under Schedule A of the Income Tax, which show for the annual value of "lands" a fall from £55,618,428 in 1875 to £46,317,729 in 1894, or only £9,300,699, or 16 per cent., that rents, on the whole, have not come down to anything like the amount that would seem proportionate to the ascertained decrease in the value of the products of agriculture.

I am also compelled to dissent from the reasoning in this section of the report in paragraphs 83, 84, 85, which seems to rest on the assumption that all sums expended by the owner on land are interest bearing investments, and that rent should be considered as a return on landlord's outlay rather than as an assignment to the landlord of a reasonable share in the produce of the land after the cost of production has been met.

It is urged, in paragraphs 63, etc., that the estate accounts show that the great landlords have suffered severely, but in my opinion these accounts establish exactly the reverse. Those of the English estates show that the arrears of the agreed rents are inconsiderable—less than 9 per cent. —and that taking twenty years' purchase, which is a moderate but fair " all round estimate " for the estates in question, the rents actually paid represent nearly 5 per cent. on the capital value, and the net rent nearly 3 per cent. It is beside the mark to quote Mr Mill to show that real rent has disappeared in such a case, as it is obvious that in the agreed rental the annual value of the land, together with the use of the whole results of the landlords' outlay, is expressed. Further, as is shown elsewhere (Chapter IX), the calculations of the outgoings are misleading and exaggerated, and include some payments which do not belong to estate maintenance, and others which are part of the ordinary local outgoings of any resident.

Effects of Depression on Occupiers.

The section dealing with the depression in its effects upon occupiers is, in my opinion, a wholly inadequate presentment of the enormous mass of facts and figures supplied by farming witnesses of authority from all parts of the country, and by our Assistant Commissioners in their reports.

Use is made of the tables in the Memorandum by Mr Little on the farm accounts (Appendix III to Final Report).

I have considered these accounts in several aspects, and especially in their bearing upon the actual years during which depression was actually present, and I have considered the careful and instructive comments upon these accounts, giving many further facts explaining their bearing upon the position of farmers, which were inserted in the reports by our Sub-Commissioners after direct local inquiry from the farmers themselves.

I am convinced from this examination that, so far as the farm accounts can be taken as a fair illustration of the position of farmers (and the Report of the Majority admits that the accounts may be taken as representing "conditions more favourable than the average,") they show that the position at best is that, while some are making a little more than nothing, some also are making less than nothing.

The tables of the Memorandum purport to put the position in a better light.

But the comparatively favourable result thus set forth, showing an average profit of 25·66 per cent. of the gross rent over twenty years, is arrived at by including the four years before 1879, which in most parts of the country were years of extreme prosperity. Such a calculation is worthless and misleading as a measure of the "effects of the depression on the occupiers of land," and I am surprised that it should have been put forward at all.

This calculation is further vitiated by the fact that the number of accounts for the years 1879 to 1881 inclusive, when the most sweeping disasters occurred after the bad seasons, is very small. If the number of accounts had been as large as that for the period 1890-93, the amount of losses which would probably have been recorded would have swamped the accounts for the remainder of the period to 1894, and made the resulting average widely different from what Mr Little has obtained.

Taking the whole of the English tenant farmer accounts, which are sufficiently precise, and taking the averages for these accounts for all the periods they cover, it appears that the average annual rents over the 38,941 acres involved amount to £39,530, and the average net profit over the whole of the accounts has amounted to only £852. The ratio, therefore, of the average net profit over the whole area is only 2·15 per cent. of the average annual rent, whereas the figures obtained from Mr Little's tables show a ratio of 25·66 per cent.

But if the calculation is confined to the last five years, the tables of rents and profit and loss handed in by Mr Lambert show a still more striking contradiction to the figures arrived at by Mr Little's revision of the accounts.[1]

Mr Pringle, in his report on the South Midlands, gives the profit and loss account for eleven farms, over periods ranging from four up to thirteen years, and covering an

---

[1] Appendix IV to Final Report.

area of 4986 acres. The total profits were £13,913 18s 7d, the losses £10,106, the net profits being thus £3806 19s 8d, or a profit of 1s 10¾d per acre per annum, or $1\frac{1}{10}$ per cent. on £8 capital. Two of these accounts are of exceptionally favoured farms.

In another table he shows that the average rents of eight farms amount to no less than 7½ times the profits of tenants.

The figures from Lincolnshire are still more striking.

Mr Wilson Fox, in the appendix to his report on Lincolnshire, gives ten accounts of tenant farmers for periods ranging from one to eleven years, over an area of 7341 acres. The average rents for the whole are £8457, the average profits £543 18s 4d, and the average losses £385 15s 4½d, or a net average profit £158 2s 11½d, or about 1·86 per cent. of the average annual rent.[1]

I am convinced from these and similar figures, which can be produced from all parts of the evidence and reports, that the contention in paragraphs 110 and 111, that the position of farmers, as regards profits, is only from 40 to 50 per cent. below what is assumed for income tax purposes to be their ordinary and average range of profits, is fallacious and seriously misleading.

These statements, however they may be supported by rearrangement of figures, are inconsistent with the obvious inferences from all the more recent farm accounts, with the careful records of their own inquiries handed to us by our Sub-Commissioners, and with the tenour of the great mass of evidence from landowners and agents as well as from tenant farmers.

Cost of Production.

Further, I cannot think that the arrangement of the report is satisfactory as regards the "Cost of Production," paragraphs 157-167. The economic position of the farmer can only be arrived at by an analysis of the whole of the farm out-goings, including necessarily rents and other non-reproductive items. The chapter on the cost of production deals imperfectly, and in some respects inaccurately, with the two

---

[1] The items for produce consumed in farmhouses, which are erroneously entered in two accounts on the side of expenditure, are here transferred to receipts.

essential outgoings of labour and fertilising, and excludes the consideration of rent in its relation to the rest of the outgoings. The question of rent is relegated to Part III, "Miscellaneous Subjects bearing on the Agricultural Position," as if rent was not the really vital factor in the outgoings of a farm, turning the balance sheet of the farmer to profit or loss, exactly in the proportion that it is fair and reasonable, or excessive and unjust.

Mr James Hope puts the matter fairly in his report on Perthshire, etc.

"The real solution of the difficulty caused by low prices induced by foreign competition is to be found in a reasonable readjustment of rent. The basis upon which all rents ought to be calculated is the revenue expected to be drawn from the farm after making due allowance for working expenses, interest on capital invested, and a fair return for the skill and labour of the farmer. The balance remaining over, after meeting the cost of production, represents the sum which the tenant can afford to pay as rent."

Agricultural Holdings Acts.

The chapter of the Report of the Majority dealing with this subject may be taken to represent the barest minimum of the amendments of the law to which general assent is now everywhere given. While many of its positive proposals are obviously sound, I regret the refusal to entertain many proposals which have been assented to with practical unanimity by the principal agricultural associations of the country, and have been warmly supported by witnesses representing the landlord, as well as the tenant interest, in our inquiry.

Here, as in all the essential topics of the inquiry, I think it illogical and, in its results, unfair to limit the subject artificially by excluding the real considerations out of which legislation to protect the rights of the tenant in his improvements obviously originated.

The origin of the Agricultural Holdings Acts clearly was the insecurity of the tenant in investing money in improving his holding. The Acts were a strictly limited reversal of the legal presumption that everything done to, or put into the soil became the landlord's property, and their intention was to put an end to the confiscation of the tenant's improvements, the usual method of which has been by including the annual value added thereby in the rent of the holding.

While in the paragraphs as to compensation for the sitting tenant, and for unreasonable disturbance, the Report has been obliged to touch on the subject of rent, the discussion is deprived of reality and practical value by the exclusion from this chapter of the representations made to us by nearly every tenant farmer witness, and reported to us by our Assistant Commissioners, that the most serious objection taken to the existing Acts is that, while they give too much help to the bad and unscrupulous, they give little or no protection to the improving farmer, and that the legal protection to the best type of farmer becomes less just in proportion to the greatness of his investments in the soil. This is the key to the real demand for reform, and it is ignored by the report of the majority.

I also regret that the report does not assent to the reasonable proposals for freedom to make improvements, and as to cropping and sale of produce under reasonable conditions, which were shown to have had the support of the English and Scottish Chambers of Agriculture, and especially that no encouragement is given, in the recommendations, to that most essential improvement, in these times, the laying down of pasture.

I have also to note that the report wholly omits any recognition of the extensive concessions to tenants, as to the right of making improvements and obtaining compensation, retrospectively as well as in future, given by the Market Gardeners' Compensation Act, 1895. Market gardens, it should have been remembered, are included under the provisions of the Agricultural Holdings Act (England), 1883.

LAND TENURE.

I take exception to the chapter on Land Tenure, because it does not grapple with the real points at issue.

Changes of tenure are suggested in order to prevent certain forms of economic injustice to tenants, which our inquiry has proved to have a wide and disastrous operation in crippling agriculture, as well as in bringing men to ruin who have done, and are loyally doing their best by the land.

But instead of dealing with the established facts, out of which the demand for reforms of tenure springs, the report merely criticises the details of proposals and arguments such as those advanced by Mr William Smith, formerly M.P. for North Lonsdale, and quotes the opinions of well-known opponents of tenure reform in Wales and elsewhere, without going into the merits of the questions involved.

As I have pointed out elsewhere, the essential facts to deal with are :—(1) the practically universal demand that rents should be reduced to a level which would enable the tenant to make some profit, or at any rate equitably share his losses with his landlord ; and (2) the practically universal protest of the tenants who put money into their business against the absolute insecurity of their position.

In the face of substantially unanimous evidence from all parts on these points, it seems inconclusive, if not altogether irrelevant, to urge, as any answer to such a demand and protest, that there are frequent expressions of dislike to having rents fixed by a "Land Court."

There is, probably enough, a repugnance on the part of many farmers to disclose their affairs in public, and that is naturally their idea of what a "Land Court" would mean.

But it would be not only in contradiction to our evidence, but contrary to common sense, to argue that because many farmers have this dislike to publish the state of their affairs before an open tribunal, farmers generally are hostile to any and every form of practical machinery which would bring within their reach reasonable rents and complete security for their investments.

On the contrary, I submit that our inquiry has demonstrated the necessity, in the interests of agriculture, of meeting satisfactorily the mischiefs shown to be prevalent, and has farther shown a striking convergence of practical opinion, in the direction of a workable machinery.

The Majority Report omits to set forth the important suggestions made from many quarters,[1] and submitted also

[1] Middleton, Kidner, Pringle, J. Hope, Rowlandson, Sheldon, Forster, Hutcheson, Ferguson, Bell, Scott, Lander, Olver, Looker, Bowen-Jones, J. Speir, Davidson, Wilkinson, Stuart, Black, W. Elliot, Flockhart, Fyshe, Pennant, O. Williams, Dutfield, Price, Brown.

to the Richmond Commission,[1] as to the appointment of official arbitrators, and the bearing of these suggestions, directly and indirectly, on rent and conditions of tenancy, as well as on compensation for improvements.

Further, in the case of the reports and evidence of Mr Pringle and of Mr Speir, both of whom deal with this question, the paragraphs of this chapter are seriously misleading, and withhold matter which should be stated.

While Mr Speir's evidence on the strictly limited point of judicial revision of rents of land held *by lease* is correctly quoted, the following passages of Mr Speir's report should not have been withheld :—

"*Everybody is of opinion that nothing can rid agriculture of the millstone about its neck so much as a readjustment of rents in accordance with present prices.* . . . Everywhere evidence was submitted to me that, while many matters connected with the owning and occupying of land require amendment, many farmers say that, 'unless the hiring of land is regulated in some way, so as to prevent [reckless competition], legislation in other channels will be of little avail. *They say, if the rent is wrong, no amount of legislation in other directions will make the farm right.*"

"Few farms yield the profit they might do if farmed to the highest possible capacity consistent with economy. . . . Just now there is little security for money so invested, and, until the Agricultural Holdings Act is very materially amended, it will not be possible to divert much more money into farming."

"Almost every farmer who gave evidence before me on this matter mentioned this as a *sine quâ non* of success: 'the nearer occupancy and ownership approach each other the better would the land be farmed.'"

"The number is, comparatively speaking, small who are decidedly in favour of a land court *to the exclusion of every other means*, but a very large proportion say that, unless some better scheme is devised than the present Act, they will be forced, against their inclinations, to favour the establishment of a court to fix rents."[2]

---

[1] Speir, Ayrshire, &c., p. 11. *See also* Pars. 47 and 17 of Mr Speir's Report.
[2] Coleman ; Report on Lancashire, &c., Richmond Commission.

I submit that this is as strong a statement of the real case for tenure reform as can be imagined, and that this chapter, as it stands, gives a wholly misleading impression of the results of Mr Speir's inquiry.

Paragraph 422 is also misleading and incorrect.

Mr Pringle, who, in my opinion, has rendered excellent service as an Assistant Commissioner in all the districts he has visited, found in the South Midlands a district where arable farming had passed through much the same stages as in Essex, though for various reasons the last stage of exhaustion of some Essex districts had not been reached.

Both as to Essex, and as to Beds, Hunts, and Northants, Mr Pringle laid before us much evidence of the feeling of farmers on the questions of unfair rents and insecurity.

In this paragraph, the passages of the Essex report are ignored altogether.

As to the Essex farmers, Mr Pringle states:—

"I had continuous evidence of their desire for better security in the form of continued occupation at fair rents, no charge being put upon their own improvements.... Any compensation which might be obtained by an outgoing tenant under an Agricultural Holdings Act is but a poor substitute for continued enjoyment at a fair rent. The principle of the Irish Land Act was generally approved of.... It was suggested that courts of arbitration should be established, to which parties who failed to agree upon future rents could repair."

Resolutions in favour of these proposals were adopted at meetings of farmers at Ongar, Chelmsford, and Braintree, with the qualification, to secure unanimity, that arbitration should be optional and not compulsory.[1]

I feel bound to comment on the exclusion of this important evidence from the chapter on tenure.

Further, in his report on Durham and the North Riding, Mr Pringle again draws attention to the general demand on the part of farmers:—

'If nothing can be done to raise prices, rents must be greatly reduced. *It is the general opinion* that in order to bring about a fair and reasonable reduction some system of arbitration should be set in motion. Land courts, although recommended by a few, are

[1] Pringle, Essex, p. 36.

not, generally speaking, desired. Tenants prefer to arrange rents, if possible, without the intervention of a third party, *but failing a satisfactory agreement, they feel tha tarbitration should be at hand. To this proposal some landlords make no objection.* The owner of a very large estate said : 'Provided that an entirely impartial arbitrator could be found, arbitration would not be objectionable to me.' On another large estate, arbitration has already been called upon to settle disputes as to rent. . . . . Given a person whose mind is free from bias or partiality, it is thought that his presence would be of immense benefit, and his assistance freely sought and fully acquiesced in."[1]

And the vital reason for such arbitration is also clearly stated. Mr Pringle goes on :—

"It was frequently stated that the tenant, who by good and liberal treatment has made his farm a place to be desired, is in a most unfortunate position when seeking a reduction of rent. It is to protect such a man from being rented on his own good management that arbitration is suggested. Both in Durham and Yorkshire, I heard of numerous cases where landlords had sent away good tenants, owing to disagreement upon the question of a fair rent, and after a time had been forced to accept lower offers from strangers."

These passages from the Yorkshire Report are also withheld, although obviously of the highest value as matter upon which the judgment of the Commission should be given.

Mr Pringle found similar opinions general in the South Midlands. His evidence when examined as to his report is conclusive.[2] Thus he says :—

"The Bedford Agricultural Society, the Huntingdon Agricultural Society, and the Northampton Agricultural Society and Chamber of Agriculture, selected all my witnesses for me,"—(100 in all)—"including landlords as well as tenants."

"My note-books show that almost one out of every two tenant farmers that I saw spoke on this subject—

[1] Pringle, Durham and York, 29.
[2] Mr Pringle's Evidence Vol. IV, 47,607 to 48,246.

MR PRINGLE'S EVIDENCE

that the business relations between landlord and tenant might be put on a more satisfactory footing."

"They have the feeling that, providing the landlord were to die, the tenant has no security whatever, and that he may be turned out if the landlord likes, if any difference arises about rent."

"I heard of a great many cases illustrating this insecurity of tenure. I would not take evidence of that character from any person unless he was able to substantiate it. Estates would be picked out for me, and cases would be given of where a good tenant had to leave because he did not offer a sufficiently large rent, and the farm would be taken in hand for a year or two, and finally it would be let to some other person for a lower rent . . . the farms were pointed out to me that had gone through this."

"I have no hesitation in saying that 75 per cent. of the tenants who have mentioned that matter to me would adhere to some system of arbitration. My note-book is full of evidence of that."

"There is a very strong opinion that the time has come when there is some system wanted for amicably and quietly settling disputes between landlords and tenants upon all points."

"The principle of arbitration was in the minds of those men before I went near them at all, and they had also opinions upon what this arbitrator ought to deal with, and the qualifications that were necessary. These, as they came before me one by one, were all noted down in my books, and I tried to condense the thing and produce it to you in this form."

"The men who mentioned this question of the determination of the rent were chiefly those who kept books."

"They do not like the idea of a land court."

"The general feeling was that the work should be done through the board of assessors or their representative (official arbitrator) appointed by the Board of Agriculture."

"If official arbitration could not be carried out without the publicity that is inseparable from a court, and the friction caused by landlord and tenant appearing in person before a court, I am sure the great majority of those who mentioned the matter to me would prefer to go on as they are."

"There is nothing in this report except what I have heard."

"Many tenants, and they appear to be good tenants, feel that in these present times .... there is far more liability to differences and disputes than there used to be, and that there ought to be some way of protecting the sitting tenant from the differences of opinion."

Mr Pringle then goes on to quote from his note-books what had been said to him by a number of tenant farmers, substantially of the same tenour as his report and his evidence, premising that the whole of these communications were made confidentially and that the tenants might object to their names being given.

The whole of these extracts from his note-books were taken from interviews with farmers *in Bedfordshire.*

In my opinion, the idea of arbitration, not definitely worked out in a Parliamentary Bill, but in the rough, practical form which would commend itself to men who, in his words, want a peaceful and easy machinery for insuring "continuous enjoyment at a fair rent," not by litigation, but by a reference to a local agricultural expert, in whom all parties could place perfect confidence, could not be stated more simply and fairly than in Mr Pringle's report and evidence.

But this suggestion is not attempted to be discussed on its merits by the Majority Report. The only answer to it is a quotation from the evidence given before the Commission by two of Mr Pringle's witnesses, *not from Bedfordshire but from Northamptonshire.*

Important replies of both these witnesses are withheld which bear materially on the proposals and the reasons given for it.

In reply to the question "Is there any strong opinion in Northamptonshire in favour of having official arbitrators to whom you would refer all these questions—a sort of land court?"—(Mr Nunneley.) "I do not think there is any strong feeling in favour of it. *I think among tenant farmers there would be rather a preponderance in favour of it.*"

Mr Britten, who has been nearly forty years on the same farm and under the same landlord, stated that if he had not received a 30 per cent. reduction he would have been ruined, and even with it he has made a very poor interest on the capital he employs, that he knew of cases where reductions had only been 10 per cent., others where there had been no reductions, and cases where new tenants have had greater reductions than the old ones were offered. Those who had no reductions had fared very badly, are in a desperate position, and near starvation.

It is obvious, therefore, that Mr Britten admits the whole case on which the proposal of arbitration is based, and that his reply that " tenants have, as a rule, been enabled to take care of themselves" must be taken with much qualification.

I regret, further, to note that the passages to a similar effect in Mr Rew's valuable report on North Devon have also been excluded from this chapter in the same way as the passages from Mr Pringle and Mr Speir.

After stating with precision the complaints made by farmers as to insecurity, the position of the sitting tenant, and the results of competition, Mr Rew goes on :—

"I am bound to say that it was more common to protest against the present rents as excessive, and to say that landlords ought to reduce them."

Resolutions in favour of arbitration in all cases of dispute between landlord and tenant, including the question of rent, were adopted at meetings at South Molton and Barnstaple.[1]

Mr Rew explains that, in his opinion, those who advocated the fixing of rents by an official authority had not thought out all the conditions and consequences of their proposals, or in all cases made up their minds whether arbitration was to be voluntary or compulsory. *But they wanted it to meet the case of tenants who could not get a fair reduction.*

It is unsatisfactory that the report of the majority ignores the proofs thus afforded in our inquiry that this legitimate demand for reasonable valuation of land for rent is not being met, and ought to be met by some machinery.

And I submit, further, that the omission to discuss arbitration on its merits, or even to allude to such a scheme of revaluation as that suggested by Mr Gilbert Murray is a grave defect in the report and likely to arouse much doubt as to its adequacy and impartiality.

In this connection it is a matter of surprise that this

[1] Rew, North Devon, pp. 17 and 18.

chapter contains no reference whatever to the evidence given by Mr Pennant, a Welsh landowner.

Mr Pennant strongly approves of official arbitrators being appointed by the Board of Agriculture, men of character and local knowledge, who would command the confidence of landlord and tenant, and be independent of both.

With such arbitrators "the sitting tenant would get what he wanted, without having any unpleasantness with his landlord."

Asked if the sitting tenant who had made improvements "would not be entitled to have a reduction from his rent according to the value of the compensation due for that improvement," Mr Pennant replied :—

> "Any matter that they chose could be referred to a competent individual. I will take the case of myself. I had spent a considerable amount of capital on a farm and improved it very much; I thought in consequence that the rent ought to be so much, in fact, we agreed that it should be, but when the improvements were done, the tenant thought the rent was too much; we agreed to refer that to a person in whom we both had thorough confidence, and he decided for us, and I acted on his decision. I and the tenant were fortunately able to find such an individual. I want to create individuals of that character, and it can best be done by the Board of Agriculture, and then I am sure that landlords and tenants would make use of them in the future, and would be glad of them."
>
> "Of course a sitting tenant should not be rented upon the unexhausted value of his improvements; this was a case of increased rent in consequence of improvements done by myself, but the tenant had helped me in doing them, and we wanted a person to decide fairly between us, and we secured the person."
>
> "They would employ these arbitrators whenever there was a difficulty, and you would have practically no litigation."
>
> "All cases under the Act must be referred to them.[1]"

Other omissions and inadequate or misleading references or quotations may be pointed out in this chapter.

I have selected the above as a sufficient illustration of my

[1] 57,421—57,479.

initial comment on this chapter, viz., that it does not touch the real issues raised, and does not attempt either to challenge the existence of, or to suggest any practical solution for the serious difficulties, economic and legal, in the relations of landlord and tenant which the agricultural depression has brought more vividly to light, and to meet which suggestions as to reforms in tenure have been made.

Rents.

The whole reasoning of the chapter on rents is vitiated by the assumption that there is perfect freedom of contract in bargaining. It ignores the mass of evidence, in my opinion conclusive, as to the inability of the improving farmer to reduce his rent by bargaining, to the point which leaves him the results of his improvements and high cultivation, and it ignores also the conclusive evidence as to the force of competition, in keeping up the rents of such farms to a level which transfers the whole, or major part of the profits, to the landlord.

While it is perfectly true that the further shrinkage in agricultural prices and in land values could not accurately be predicted in the earlier years of the depression, it is plain from facts brought before the Richmond Commission in 1881-82, before the Commission on the Depression of Trade and Agriculture in 1885, and the present Commission, that the attention of landlords and agents has been vigorously and unceasingly called to the necessity of permanent and adequate reductions of rent, and that these reductions have in most cases been postponed till the last moment, and in a great number of cases have only been made after the ruin and removal of the old tenants.

I submit that the chapter in the Majority Report on rents fails to present the facts laid before us as to the extent to which high rents, and rents which absorb and confiscate tenants' improvements, have led to crushing reverses, to wholesale ruin, to the sweeping away of large numbers of old tenants, and to continual and widespread deterioration of the condition and the productive power of the land.

I think that the evidence cannot but produce on any impartial mind a profound conviction that, next to the fall in prices, the greatest and most destructive cause of agricultural depression has been the draining away of tenants' capital in paying rents, which it was impossible to pay fairly out of the produce of the land, and at the same time to pay adequately for labour, manuring, and the expenditure essential to the proper maintenance of agricultural condition.

I would once more draw attention to the paragraph in the Richmond Commission Report, which thus sums up the subject of rent :—

"While we strongly object to any legislative interference with arrangements on the question of rent between landlord and tenant, we are of opinion that it will be for the interest of both parties that rent should be so fixed by voluntary agreement as to enable farmers to meet the difficulties of their position."

In his Supplementary Report to the Richmond Commission, our colleague, Mr Clay, said :—

"A readjustment of rent is most urgently required by the large majority of farmers in the country, and it is for the interests not less of landlords than of tenants that a readjustment should take place at once to meet the altered circumstances with which farmers have now to contend. The report, in my opinion, should distinctly recommend full readjustment of rent for the adoption of the landlords. An abatement of rent for one or two years will not meet the difficulty, or allow tenants to recoup themselves and do justice to the land; what is required is a permanent reduction of rent to give tenants some hope of regaining their lost capital, and an impetus to increase the fertility of their farms by the continued high cultivation of the land. . . . Evidence has been given that rents have been unduly forced up by class laws, false and inflated competition, also by the letting of farms by tender, and screwing out of tenants more than what could be honestly paid from the produce of the soil."

I hold that the evidence taken in our own inquiry shows that neither in point of time nor in degree, have rents been reduced in anything like fair proportion to the heavy and progressive fall of prices, and that therefore it is clear that over-renting has been to an even greater extent an operative cause in the disasters of agriculture in the last few years than it was at the period of the Richmond Commission.

It seems to me scarcely reasonable to treat the question

of a "fair rent" as of extreme difficulty (par. 436), when well-known landlords like the Duke of Richmond and Sir Michael Hicks-Beach have indicated clearly that rents should not be fixed by competition but by valuation, and land agents of repute, like Mr Gilbert Murray, have approved the necessity of a careful re-valuation based on prices and productive power.

Doubt is attempted to be thrown on the contention of tenant-farmer witnesses, and on the inferences drawn from the farm accounts submitted to the Commission. It is a sufficient reply to point out that in an exceptionally bad year, 1892, after thirteen years of progressive depression, the accounts of twenty-nine of the most important estates in England and Wales show a rent actually paid averaging over 24s an acre, and a net rent, after deduction of outgoings of the most comprehensive character, including items extraneous to estate maintenance, of nearly 14s an acre. Without further evidence from other quarters, these estate accounts demonstrate that, although agricultural prices are down from 25 to 40 per cent., and the cost of production has increased rather than diminished, an altogether disproportionate share of the value of the produce is still being assigned to the owner, and a fair balance has not yet been struck between the parties.

I take exception also to the statement in par. 438. The only fair way of estimating the proportion of profits to rent is by taking the average. I have already given reasons and figures which go to prove that the calculations in the Majority Report are misleading; and that, so far as the farm accounts throw light on the matter, the average profits have nearer 2 than 26 per cent. of the rent. To reach the income-tax standard of seven-sixteenths, the average profits should have been, not £852, but £16,331.[1]

The reasoning of paragraphs 440 to 449 rests on the assumptions (1) that tenants in general can and do avail themselves of "the annually recurring opportunities" of getting rents revised; (2) that "the market price paid for land is the best if not the only available test of its value;" and, apparently, also (3) that landlords are justified in accepting the competitive rent, without considering for themselves whether it can or cannot be paid out of the actual earnings of the land.

[1] pp. 88-92.

The inference is drawn that "rents are now, generally speaking, adjusted to the conditions of the farming industry," and "the main burden of agricultural depression now rests upon the owners and not upon the occupiers of the soil."

It is, in my opinion, difficult to reconcile these conclusions, and the *à priori* reasoning on which they are based, with the admissions, that "readjustments" have not been universal, and, in paragraph 445, that farmers do pay too high rents from reluctance to lose their homes and to sacrifice their capital.

I submit further that these assumptions and conclusions are in conflict with most of the evidence given by tenant farmers, and, as regards making competition the measure of rent, are refuted by the evidence of some of the best representatives of the landed interest. This is fully shown in Chapters VIII and IX of this Report.

I regret also that in par. 445 there is no recognition of, or attempt to meet, the statements made by the great majority of tenant farmer witnesses that reductions of rent have usually been refused to old tenants, which on a change of tenancy have to be made for new tenants. It is really beside the point to affirm that tenants go on, of their own accords, paying too high rents in order to retain their homes and avoid the loss of removing and selling off.

In reference to other chapters of the Majority Report I have further to state that in some respects the chapter on small holdings, and especially its lack of practical suggestions seems to me unsatisfactory, and that question has, therefore, been dealt with in a special chapter.

The same remark applies to some extent to the subject of railway rates, to which I attach great and urgent importance.

FARM ACCOUNTS

APPENDIX II.

SUMMARY OF FARM ACCOUNTS.

NOTE.—Five of the 76 Tenant farmers' accounts here given, Nos. LII, LIII, LIV., LV., and LXXIX, only give acreage, and profit and loss. These accounts cover 4025 acres. The remaining 71 accounts, covering 38,941 acres, give details, and the totals and percentages of outgoings at foot of this table refer to those accounts and that acreage. The totals of profit and loss refer to the whole area of 42,966 acres.

References to Farm Accounts.	Acreage Total.	Arable.	No. of Years Averaged.	Average Outgoings per Annum.	Average Cost of Labour.	Percentage of Outgoings.	Average Cost of Fertilising Items.	Percentage of Outgoings.	Average Rent.	Percentage of Outgoings.	Average Rates and Taxes.	Percentage of Outgoings.	Tenant's Capital.	Average Profit.	Average Loss.	Percentage on Tenant's Capital +Profit -Loss.	Per Acre +Profit or -Loss.	Remarks.	Reference in Reports of Sub-Commissioners.
				£	£		£		£		£		£	£	£ s.		s. d.		
Beds I., &c., p. 62	256	—	6	1794	576	32·1	437	24·36	365	20·34	—	—	3750	—	119 15	-3·2	-9 4	Rates and taxes included in rent. Interest taken at 150l.	Pringle, App. C. I. (pars. 103-4).
Beds II., p. 63	200	200	4	1390	809	22·23	176	12·66	423	30·43	50	3·00	2500	83	—	+3·3	+6 4½	Insurance included in rent	Pringle, App. C. II. (pars. 103-4).
Beds III., p. 64	922	600	12	3471	909	26·18	416	11·98	1122	32·30	155	4·47	—	151	—	—	+3 3½	—	Pringle, App. C. III. (pars. 103-4).
Beds IV., p. 66	800	—	7	3379	866	25·62	880	26·04	560	11·67	60	2·04	—	—	140 0	—	-10 5	—	Pringle, App. C. IV. (pars. 103-4).
Beds V., p. 69 " VI., p. 71	275	—	6	1459	411	28·10	378	25·9	184	12·10	—	—	2050	—	201 0	-9·0	-21 1¾	Interest taken at 1022, 10s. Details given under X.	Pringle, App. C. V. (pars. 103-4).
Beds VII., p. 72	—	—	—	—	—	—	—	—	—	—	—	—	—	—	—	—	—	By Mortgagee.	Pringle, App. C. XV. 6 (par. 139).

Beds VIII, p. 7	467	400	1 (1893-94).	1193	306	33·19	160	18·49	360	30·18	40	3·45	—	—	—	—	−6 10	—	Pringle, App. C. XV. (pars. 15, 110).
Beds VIIIa., p. 73	670	335	1 (1893-94).	1532	597	38·97	190	12·40	568	36·75	43	2·80	—	—	—	—	−15 10	—	Pringle, App. C. XV. (pars. 15, 110).
Beds IX, p. 73	560	420	1 (1893-94).	2376	654	27·53	473	19·90	731	30·77	153	6·44	—	—	—	—	−21 9	—	Pringle, App. C. XV. (par. 139).
Beds X., p. 73	540	976	1 (1893-94).	2352	790	33·59	826	35·12	350	14·88	76	3·23	—	—	—	—	−11 11	—	Pringle, App. C. XV. (par. 139).
Cambs XI., p. 74	505	408	21	6834	912	13·34	1065	24·22	1117	16·34	119	1·74	5500	363	—	6·6	+12 10	—	Wilson Fox, p. 58.
Cambs. XII., p. 76	401	240	17	5076	498	7·83	516	10·16	851	16·78	95	1·87	4500	409	—	9·1	+20 4	p. 60.
Cambs XIII., p. 78	665	—	20	4765	1023	21·47	1127	23·65	1057	22·12	272	5·70	—	145	—	—	+4 4	Tithe included in rates and taxes.	p. 62.
Cambs XIV., p. 80	400	350	1	2944	635	21·57	902	30·6	859	12·19	—	—	—	—	405 0	—	−23 3	—	App.
Devon XV., p. 80	245	—	2	1852	304	16·41	722	38·58	387	20·89	67	3·62	—	53	—	—	−4 0	—	A. 1. D. Rew, App. C. II., p. 64 (par. 28).
Dorset XVI., p. 81	420	165	1	2047	581	21·9	647	24·4	735	27·7	—	—	—	—	3 0	—	−0 12½	No valuations given; loss probably greater than shown	Rew, App. B. 3 (par. 30).
Dorset XVII., p. 81	686	420	1	1211	490	39·	237	19·	318	23·	—	—	—	—	277 0	—	−8 2	Rent includes rates, &c.	App. B. 3 (par. 30).
Dorset XVIII., p. 82	202	160	1	1017	306	36·	197	19·5	1	28·	—	—	—	—	78 0	—	−7 1	„	App. B. 3 (par. 30).
Dorset XIX., p. 82	1122	335	1	2757	575	20·8	479	13·6	1158	42·8	—	—	—	—	264 0	—	−4 8	„	App. B. 3 (par. 30).
Dorset XX., p. 82	940	297	1	3059	678	22·	859	28·8	989	29·7	—	—	—	—	42 0	—	−1 0	„	App. B. 3 (par. 30).
Dorset XXI., p. 83	—	—	—	—	—	—	—	—	—	—	—	—	—	—	—	—	—	In owner's hands	App. B. 4.
Dorset XXII., p. 84	—	—	—	—	—	—	—	—	—	—	—	—	—	—	—	—	—	Imperfect	„
Dorset XXIII., p. 85	840	—	18	2493	878	35·20	510	20·45	565	22·46	78	3·13	—	279	—	—	+6 5	—	App. B. 5.
Essex XXIV., p. 87	950	620	12	10,688	1529	14·30	2755	25·79	952	8·91	127	1·19	12,881	466	—	+3·64	+9 7	—	Pringle, App. C. I. (pars. 109-10).

Summary of Farm Accounts—continued.

No. of Years Averaged	Average Outgoings per Annum.	Average Cost of Labour.	Percentage of Outgoings.	Average Cost of Fertilising Items.	Percentage of Outgoings.	Average Rent.	Percentage of Outgoings.	Average Rates and Taxes.	Percentage of Outgoings.	Tenant's Capital.	Average Profit.	Average Loss.	Percentage on Tenant's Capital. + Profit — Loss.	Per Acre. + Profit or — Loss.	Remarks.	Reference in Reports of Sub-Commissioners.
5	3067	523	17·	884	28·82	550	17·93	54	1·76	3450	435	—	+12·60	+13 8 £ s. d.	—	Pringle, App. C. II. (par. 102).
—	—	—	—	—	—	—	—	—	—	—	—	—	—	—	—	Pringle, App. C. II. (par. 102).
6	3676	895	24·35	1099	29·92	972	26·	—	—	4130	—	212 0	−5·	−6 1½	By owner	Pringle, App. C. IV.
5	1215	233	19·	398	32·9	170	14·	—	—	—	118	—	—	+19 9	Rates and taxes with rent	" V.
3	1689	267	16·27	566	34·5	305	18·5	—	—	1448	—	111 0	−8·	−11 2	Rates included in rent	" V.
1	1706	356	20·87	321	18·81	290	17·	—	—	2450	—	106 0	—	−7 8	Rates, &c. included	" VI.
—	—	—	—	—	—	—	—	—	—	—	—	—	—	—	—	" VII.
—	—	—	—	—	—	—	—	38	2·28	—	—	—	—	—	By owner	" VIII. (par. 106).
5	2099	573	27·30	453	21·56	347	16·5	—	—	3775	—	195 0	−5·17	−11 4	By owner under paid manager	Pringle, C. App. IX.
—	—	—	—	—	—	—	—	—	—	—	—	—	—	—	Five farms managed and worked by owner.	" X. (par. 107).
9	20,343	5151	25·82	5091	25·03	2782	13·68	780	—	20,000	782	—	+3·91	+4 1½	4 per cent. interest charged on capital, rates, &c., including tithe.	Pringle, App. C. XI. (par. 111).
3	1019	304	29·	89	8·7	92	9·	—	—	1700	—	180 0	−15·8	−21 10	—	Pringle, App. C. XII. (par. 113).

Essex XXXVII. and XXXVIII	—	—	—	—	—	—	—	—	—	—	—	—	—	—	—	—	—
Herts XXXIX., p. 118	350	270	2	2852	628	21·8	—	21·5	450	15·7	78	2·5	—	—	—	—	Spencer, App. E. II.
Herts XL., p. 118	—	—	—	—	—	—	—	—	—	—	—	—	—	—	—0 6	—	" App. E. III.
Hunts XLI., p. 119	462	300	13	1649	390	23·05	380	23·04	344	20·86	27	1·64	4000	194	—	+4·8	+8 10	Pringle, Beds., &c., App. C. VII. (pars. 103-4).
Hunts XLII., p. 123.	400	300	7	3387	512	13·34	450	14·33	462	12·05	76	1·95	3500	53	—	+1·5	+2 7	Pringle, Beds., App. &c., C. VIII. (pars. 103-4).
Kent XLIII., p. 12.	—	—	—	—	—	—	—	—	—	—	—	—	—	—	—	—	—	Fream, App. L.
Lincoln XLIV., p. 127	474	234	11	1836	452	24·6	400	21·7	478	20·	95	5·17	3055	200	—	+6·5	+8 3¼	Wilson Fox, App. A. 1. A. (pars.105,&c.).
Lincoln XLV., p. 128.	320	298	9	1333	434	32·59	229	17·17	235	17·63	116	8·85	2309	—	52 0	−2·2	+3 6	Wilson Fox, App. A. 1. B. (pars.105,&c.).
Lincoln XLVI., p. 129.	491	392	6	2333	499	21·38	532	22·8	692	29·6	—	—	3400	123	—	+3·61	+5 0	Wilson Fox, App. A. 1. C. (pars.105,&c.).
Lincoln XLVII., p. 130.	—	—	—	—	—	—	—	—	—	—	—	—	—	—	—	—	—	W. Fox, App. A. 1. D. Farmed by owner.
Lincoln XLVIII., p. 131.	1200	900	10	4450	1249	28·06	535	12·02	1579	35·48	249	5·59	7407	169	38 0	−0·51	—0 5	App. A. 1. E.
Lincoln XLIX., p. 132.	790	600	5	4903	736	16·03	1311	26·73	603	12·3	—	—	5822	—	—	+2·89	+4 3	" App. A. 1. F. Rates and taxes in rent.
Lincoln L, p. 133.	—	—	—	—	—	—	—	—	—	—	—	—	—	—	—	—	—	" App. A. 1. G. By owner
Lincoln LI, p. 134.	—	—	—	—	—	—	—	—	—	—	—	—	—	—	—	—	—	" App. A. 1. H. " "
Lincoln LII., p. 135.	592	407	6	—	—	—	—	—	—	—	—	—	—	—	242 0	−6·73	−8 0	" App. A. 1. I.

352 AGRICULTURAL DEPRESSION

Summary of Farm Accounts—continued.

References to Farm Accounts.	Acreage Total.	Acreage Arable.	No. of Years Averaged.	Average Outgoings per Annum. £	Average Cost of Labour. £	Percentage of Outgoings.	Average Cost of Fertilising Items. £	Percentage of Outgoings.	Average Rent. £	Percentage of Outgoings.	Average Rates and Taxes. £	Percentage of Outgoings.	Tenant's Capital. £	Average Profit. £	Average Loss. £ s.	Percentage on Tenant's Capital. +Profit—Loss.	Per Acre. +Profit or —Loss. d.	Remarks.	Reference in Reports of Sub-Commissioners.
Lincoln, LIII., p. 135.	1800	—	15	—	—	—	—	—	—	—	—	—	15,119	—	488 0	−3·2	−5 9¾	Produce for house is taken, but no account kept.	W. Fox, App. A.1.J.
Lincoln, LIV., p. 135.	538	448	11	—	—	—	—	—	—	—	—	—	4500	—	106 0	−2·4	−3 7½	"	App. A.1.K.
Lincoln, LV., p. 185.	1000	384	15	—	—	—	—	—	—	—	—	—	10,000	33	—	−0·33	+0 5	"	App. A.1.L.
Lincoln, LVI., p. 136.	969	639	2	6799	1417	20·8	680	10·	1314	18·0	347	5·75	6500	—	42 0	−0·64	−0 11¾	—	App. A.1.M.
Lincoln, LVII., p.136	1600	—	1	10,872	1523	14·	607	6·	1700	16·6	100	1·05	8500	—	232 0	−2·8	−2 10	—	App. A.1.N.
Lincoln, LVIII., p. 137	635	400	1	3136	680	21·6	846	26·	727	23·	—	—	4000	—	1 0	−0·3	—	—	"
Lincoln, LIX., p.137.	812	560	1	3853	885	22·8	407	11·5	1017	26·2	175	4·5	5000	—	302 0	−0·05	−7 3¾	—	App. A.1.O.
Lincoln, LX., p. 137.	150	100	2	633	226	35·7	171	27·	160	25·5	18	2·8	1000	—	25 0	−1·5	−4 0	—	App. A.1.P.
Lincoln, LXI., p. 138	73	—	12	299	95	31·7	12	4·5	56	28·	18	6·7	—	—	59 0	—	−16 2	—	App. A.1.Q.
Norfolk, LXII., p. 142	425	383	13	3303	644	10·47	856	25·91	467	14·13	—	—	—	265	—	—	+12 9¾	In addition to arrears of rent of £271.	Pringle, Axholme App. B.
Norfolk, LXIII., p. 142	750	600	9	3739	1005	28·43	753	20·14	880	23·53	64	1·71	—	25	—	—	+0 7½	Rates, taxes, and tithes included in rent.	Rew, Norfolk, App. E. 1 (par. 45)
Norfolk, LXIV., p. 145	—	—	—	—	—	—	—	—	—	—	—	—	—	—	—	—	—	Tithe included in rent.	Rew, Norfolk, App. E. 2
Norfolk, LXV., p. 146	490	300	1	3309	682	20·61	639	19·13	523	15·16	51	1·54	6000	—	189 0	−3·77	−7 7½	By owner. Tithe included in rent.	E. 3. / E. 4.

Location	(1)	(2)	(3)	(4)	(5)	(6)	(7)	(8)	(9)	(10)	(11)	(12)	(13)	(14)	(15)	(16)	(17)	Notes	Reference
Norfolk, LXVI, p. 147	208	—	—	1681	390	23·20	351	21·23	354	21·07	—	—	2500	—	24 0	—0·96	—2 4	Tithe, rates, &c., included in rent.	" E. 5.
Norfolk, LXVII, p. 147	—	—	—	—	—	—	—	—	—	—	—	—	—	—	—	—	—	By owner	" E. 6.
Norfolk, LXVIII, p. 148	—	—	—	—	—	—	—	—	—	—	—	—	—	—	—	—	—	"	" E. 7.
Norfolk, LXIX, p. 148	640	425	3	1743	622	35·69	147	8·43	556	31·69	—	—	—	185	—	—	+59	Tithe, rates, &c., in rent.	" E. 8.
Norfolk, LXX, p. 148	—	—	—	—	—	—	—	—	—	—	—	—	—	—	—	—	—	By owner	App. E. 9, 10, 11.
Norfolk, LXXI, p. 149	—	—	—	—	—	—	—	—	—	—	—	—	—	—	—	—	—	"	Rev, Norfolk, App. E. 9, 10, 11.
Norfolk, LXXII, p. 149	—	—	—	—	—	—	—	—	—	—	—	—	—	—	—	—	—	"	Rev, Norfolk, App. E. 9, 10, 11.
Northants, LXXIII, p. 150	431	47	5	3561	277	7·8	*	—	707	21·6	—	—	—	—	112 0	—	—5 2½	Grass farm	Pringle, App. C. IX., (pars. 103-4).
Northants, LXXIV, p. 151	324	226	7	2321	464	20·	947	14·9	389	16·7	—	—	4000	241	—	+6·	+14 10¾	Strong land	Pringle, App. C. X.
Northants, LXXV, p. 152	316	84	9	728	202	27·75	61	8·38	333	45·74	29 3·98	47 5·3	2414	99	—	+4·1	+6 3¼	Heavy land	" App. C. XI. (pars. 103-4).
Northants, LXXVI, p. 155	—	—	—	—	—	—	—	—	—	—	—	—	—	—	—	—	—	By owner	Pringle, App. C. XII.
Northants, LXXVII, p. 157	—	—	—	—	—	—	—	—	—	—	—	—	—	—	—	—	—	Co-operative farm	" App. C. XIII.
Northants, LXXVIII, p. 162	218	—	1	859	238	27·5	262	29·	204	23·7	—	—	—	—	249 0	—	—22 10	—	" App. C. XV.
Northants, LXXIX, p. 162	95	—	1	—	—	—	—	—	—	—	—	—	—	52	—	—	—10 11	Details imperfect	" App. C. XV.

* No figures separately given.

354 AGRICULTURAL DEPRESSION

Summary of Farm Accounts—continued.

References to Farm Accounts.	Acreage. Total.	Acreage. Arable.	No. of Years Averaged.	Average Outgoings per Annum. £	Average Cost of Labour. £	Percentage of Outgoings.	Average Cost of Fertilising Items. £	Percentage of Outgoings.	Average Rent. £	Percentage of Outgoings.	Average Rates and Taxes. £	Percentage of Outgoings.	Tenant's Capital. £	Average Profit. £	Average Loss. £ s.	Percentage on Tenant's Capital. + Profit, − Loss.	Per Acre. + Profit or − Loss. s. d.	Remarks.	Reference in Reports of Sub-Commissioners.
Northumberland, LXXX., p. 163.	494	96	10	2190	490	22·4	450	20·5	422	19·0	39	1·8	—	126	—	+4·03	+5 6	—	Wilson Fox, Glendale, App. A, 3.
Suffolk, LXXXI., p. 167	500	—	20	4756	809	17·	2092	42·5	641	13·5	212	4·7	6460	448	—	+6·	+15 2	In same family 60 years; continuously well farmed	Wilson Fox, Suffolk, App. A. 1. A.
Suffolk, LXXXII., p. 168	230	—	15	1464	375	25·	588	42·	180	12·1	77	5·	1933	63	—	+·36·	+5 5½	—	Wilson Fox, App. A. 1. B.
Suffolk, LXXXIII., p. 168.	560	460	11	3799	876	23·	1337	35·	486	12·7	76	2·	—	—	18 0	−·36·	−0 8	Housekeeping charged in accounts.	Wilson Fox, App. A. 1. C.
Suffolk, LXXXIV., p. 174.	260	150	18	1874	891	17·66	614	32·70	245	13·07	25	1·33	1800	168	—	+8·4	+12 11	Rent includes tithe	Wilson Fox, App. A. 1. D. See 49,783, 49,815.
Suffolk, LXXXV., p. 175	500	310	8	5824	982	17·5	1664	31·25	630	11·8	50	·94	5731	456	—	+7·9	+15 5	Profits due to dairy development. See 49,766. "If it were not for the 500l. for milk he would have made no profit."	Wilson Fox, App. A. 1. E. See 49,785, 49,815, 49,903.
Suffolk, LXXXVI., p. 176.	1750	—	1	7548	2002	27·3	3083	40.8	1554	20·5	—	—	—	192	—	+2·1	+2 2¾	By owners	Wilson Fox, App. A. 1. F.
Suffolk, LXXXVII., LXXXVIII., LXXXIX., pp. 176-180	—	—	—	—	—	—	—	—	—	—	—	—	—	—	—	—	—	—	Wilson Fox, App. A. 2, A., B., C.

	Total number of acres, 42,966.			Total outgoings, 217,424l., or 5l. 12s. per acre on 38,941 acres.	Total cost of labour, 47,099l., or 1l. 4s. 6d. per acre.	Percentage of labour to total outgoings, 21.9.	Total cost of fertilising and seeds, 47,548l., or 1l. 5s. per acre.	Percentage of fertilising to total outgoings, 22.5.	Total rents, 39,530l., or 1l. 0s. 7½d. per acre.	Percentage of rent to outgoings, 18.5.	Too imperfect to set out total.	Too incomplete to set out total.	Total average profits, 6555l. / Net profit, 110l. on 42,966 acres. (Total average losses, 6452l.)			Except where mentioned in this column, no interest on capital is charged, and no charge is made for management.	
Sussex XC., XCI., XCIII., p. 132	—	—	—	—	—	—	—	—	—	—	—	—	—	—	—	Accounts illustrating profits from poultry farming otherwise imperfect.	Rew, Heathfield, App. V., VI., VII.
Warwickshire, XCIII., p. 165.	215	65	1	667	260	39·5	137	21·5	165	24·7	31	4·5	—	150 0	—	—13 11	—	Turner, Stratford-on-Avon, App. B.
South Wilts, XCIV., p. 186.	760	—	1	3251	783	24·	1100	33·8	579	17·8	104	3·75	—	13 0	—	—0 4½	—	Rew, Salisbury Plain, App. CIV.
South Wilts, XCV., p. 186.	827	—	26	4164	774	18·58	1128	27·08	820	19·69	122	2·03	6000	54	+0·9	+1 3	300l. interest on capital, included. A typical Wilts sheep and corn farm, farmed by man of exceptional ability.	Rew, Salisbury Plain, App. CV.
Yorkshire, XCVI., p. 195.	837	767	15	4196	1000	24·	1029	24·02	925	22·0	107	2·4	10,044 73 8	90	—	+0 1·05	A splendidly-worked farm.	Pringle, Yorks and Durham, App. C II. (pars. 26, 53).
Yorkshire, XCVII., p. 203.	550	275	13	3407	549	16·11	481	14·12	647	19·00	57	2·55	5500	21	+1·8	+8 7	—	Pringle, Yorks and Durham, App. C III.
Yorkshire, XCVIII., p. 208 (all grass).	500	—	4	1083	145	14·03	194	18·78	375	36·40	19	1·84	—	—	—	+0 10	—	Pringle, Yorks and Durham, App. C IV. (par. 52).

APPENDIX III.

AGRICULTURAL HOLDINGS BILL.

Introduced by Mr CHANNING, Mr ROBERT PRICE, Mr LAMBERT, Mr LUTTRELL, and Mr STEVENSON.

MEMORANDUM.

THE object of this Bill is to consolidate the laws relating to agricultural holdings in England ; to equitably extend the principles of compensation for improvements adopted in the Agricultural Holdings Act, 1883, in the Allotments and Cottage Gardens Compensation for Crops Act, 1887, and in the Market Gardeners Compensation Act, 1895 ; to remove the defects shown to exist in the Agricultural Holdings Act, 1883, by cases in the courts ; to prevent loss to tenants by capricious eviction ; to abolish the right to distrain for rent ; to simplify and cheapen the present procedure by the appointment of agricultural arbitrators with local jurisdiction to decide all matters in dispute between landlord and tenant, including rent ; and to place landlord and tenant on the same footing as regards making claims.

The Bill makes compensation payable for all improvements, checks the renting of tenants on their own improvements, provides that the improving tenant shall be fully compensated for the value added to his holding by continuous good farming, and by giving greater freedom both to make improvements and as to cropping and the sale of produce, is intended to give increased inducements to the application of capital and labour to the soil.

The Agricultural Holdings Act, 1883, the Tenants' Compensation Act, 1890, and the Market Gardeners' Compensation Act, 1895, are repealed, and such parts of those Acts as are to be retained, and which have not been modified by subsequent legislation, are re-enacted with amendments and additional provisions, the whole constituting a complete code determining the rights of landlords and tenants of agricultural holdings of all sizes at the present time.

The chief alterations made in the Agricultural Holdings Act 1883, are as follows :—

(1.) In section 1, the words "on quitting his holding" are struck out, with the object of securing compensation for improvements to a tenant who remains in his holding at the determination of his tenancy. *"Sitting tenant."*

(2.) The tenant is enabled to carry out and to get compensation for any improvements suitable to his holding, but in the case of buildings and a few other permanent improvements and drainage, notice is required, and the landlord may carry out the improvement in his own way, the terms of interest and repayment being modified. *First-class improvements.*

(3.) Improvements made prior to the Act, and not dissented from by the landlord at the time they are made, are to be compensated for, if found to be suitable to the holding. *Improvements prior to the Act.*

(4.) The right of the landlord to make a claim under the Act, in respect of hay or other produce removed from a holding, or in respect of any permissive waste by the tenant, will be strictly limited to the express covenants of the contract of tenancy (*see* section 6); and no penal rent will be recoverable for a larger amount than the damage actually caused (*see* section 7). *Landlord's claims.*

(5.) The tenant will be enabled to claim for damage to crops by game during the last year of the tenancy (section 6, subsection (*g*)). *Damage by game.*

(6.) Compensation is given for any loss a tenant may suffer from quitting his holding by a capricious or unreasonable notice to quit. *Compensation for disturbance.*

(7.) Section 7 of the Act of 1883 is amended so that the landlord as well as the tenant may make a claim under the Act, and that both claims be made twenty-eight days before the determination of the tenancy. *Notices of claim.*

(8.) Provision is made for a record of the condition of holdings at the commencement of tenancies and in awards. (*See* sections 5 and 17, subsection (2.).) *Record of condition.*

(9.) Agricultural arbitrators, who shall be practical men with local knowledge, are to be appointed by the *Agricultural arbitrators.*

Note. The corresponding sections of the Agricultural Holdings Act, 1883 (46 & 47 Vict. c. 61.), are placed in the margin of each section, in brackets thus [Act 1883, s. 1]—to facilitate comparison.

References are also given to cases in the Law Reports which are made the ground for amendments of the existing Acts.

Board of Agriculture, and the Board shall fix the area of jurisdiction of each arbitrator and, with the assent of the Treasury, the remuneration to be paid to him by the Treasury.

No appeal on facts. (10.) With the object of reducing expense, no appeal on the facts or valuation is allowed, but an appeal will lie to the county court judge on any question of law.

Parish valuers for allotments. (11.) For the settlement of compensation in respect of allotments or of holdings of less than ten acres, special parish valuers are to be appointed, with reduced scale of fees. References may be made by the county or parish valuers as the tenant may prefer.

Abolition of the law of distress. (12.) The right to distrain for rent is abolished.

Freedom of cropping and sale. (13.) Freedom of cropping and of selling off produce from the holding is given to the tenant where an adequate return of manures has been or is to be made to the holding. (*See* section 53.)

Omission of proviso in s. 1 Act 1883. (14.) The proviso in section 1, "that in estimating "the value of any improvement there shall not be "taken into account as part of the improvement "made by the tenant what is justly due to the "inherent capabilities of the soil," is omitted. (*See* section 1.)

Extension as to tenancies. (15.) The provisions of the Act of 1883 are extended to agricultural holdings held for a shorter period than one year, and to allotments and cottage gardens not previously included under the Act. (*See* section 46 (2), and observe addition of words "or for any other period" in section 55, paragraph 2.)

Protection to tenants of mortgaged holdings. (16.) The Tenants' Compensation Act, 1890, giving protection to the tenants of mortgaged holdings, is embodied in this Bill with amendments rendering the recovery of compensation by the tenant more simple, and omitting the special protection to tithe (section 40); also recovery of compensation by the tenant is rendered more simple where the landlord is a trustee, etc. (section 30).

Extension of Act to matters under customs or agreement. (17.) The tenant will be enabled to claim and recover under the Act compensation for all matters or things for which he is entitled to claim compensation either under the custom of the country or under any special agreement. (*See* Farquharson *v.* Morgan.)

ARRANGEMENT OF CLAUSES

PART I.

IMPROVEMENTS.

Compensation for Improvements.

Clause
1. General right of tenant to compensation.
2. Notice to landlord as to improvements in Schedule, Part I.
3. Improvements made prior to this Act.
4. Compensation under agreement.

Record of Condition of Holding.

5. Record of condition of holding.

Regulations as to Compensation for Improvements.

6. Regulations as to compensation for improvements.
7. Penal rents to be limited to actual damage.

Compensation for Disturbance.

8. Compensation for disturbance.

Procedure.

9. Statement of claims.
10. Compensation agreed or settled by reference.
11. Mode of submission to reference.
12. Power for referee, &c. to require production of documents, administer oaths, &c.
13. Power to proceed in absence.
14. Form of award.
15. Awards where tenancy is determined at different periods.
16. Decision of arbitrator to be final.
17. Award to give particulars.
18. Costs of reference.
19. Day for payment.

Fair Rent.

Clause
20. Fair rent.
21. Appointment of guardian.
22. Provisions respecting married women.
23. Costs in county court.
24. Service of notice, &c.
25. Official agricultural arbitrators.
26. Parish valuers.
27. Fees for referees, &c.

Charge of Tenant's Compensation.

28. Power for landlord on paying compensation to obtain charge.
29. Incidence of charge.
30. Provision in case of trustee.
31. Advance made by a company.

Notice to Quit.

32. Time of notice to quit.

Fixtures.

33. Tenant's property in fixtures, machinery, &c.

Crown and Duchy Lands.

34. Application of Act to Crown lands.
35. Application of Act to land of Duchy of Lancaster.
36. Application of Act to land of Duchy of Cornwall.

Ecclesiastical and Charity Lands.

37. Landlord, archbishop or bishop.
38. Landlord, incumbent of benefice.
39. Landlord, charity trustees, &c.

Land in Mortgage.

40. Compensation to tenant when mortgagee is in possession.

Resumption for Improvements, and Miscellaneous.

41. Resumption of possession for cottages, &c.

Clause
42. Provision as to limited owners.
43. Provision in case of reservation of rent.

PART II.

Abolition of the Law of Distress for Rent.

44. No distress may be taken in respect of rent.

PART III.

General Provisions.

45. Commencement of Act.
46. Holdings to which this Act applies.
47. Avoidance of agreement inconsistent with Act.
48. Right of tenant in respect of improvement purchased from outgoing tenant.
49. Compensation under this Act to be exclusive in some cases.
50. Compensation under custom to come within the Act.
51. Provision as to change of tenancy.
52. Restriction in respect of improvements by tenant about to quit.
53. Freedom of cropping and disposal of produce.
54. General saving of rights.
55. Interpretation.
56. Repeal of Acts.
57. Short title of Act.
58. Limits of Act.

SCHEDULE.

A.D. 1897.

BILL TO AMEND THE LAW RELATING TO AGRICULTURAL HOLDINGS IN ENGLAND, AND FOR OTHER PURPOSES.

Be it enacted by the Queen's most Excellent Majesty, by and with the advice and consent of the Lord's Spiritual and Temporal, and Commons, in this present Parliament assembled, and by the authority of the same, as follows :

PART I.

IMPROVEMENTS.

Compensation for Improvements.

General right of tenant to compensation. [Act 1883. s. 1.]

1. Subject as in this Act mentioned, where a tenant has made on his holding any improvement, he shall, on and after the commencement of this Act, be entitled at the determination of a tenancy to obtain from the landlord as compensation under this Act for such improvement such sum as fairly represents the value of the improvement to an incoming tenant.

Notice to landlord as to improvement in Schedule. Part I. [Act 1883. ss. 3, 4.]

2. A tenant may execute on his holding any improvement, but compensation under this Act shall not be payable in respect of any improvement mentioned in the First Part of the Schedule hereto, and executed after the commencement of this Act, unless the tenant has, not more than *three months* and not less than *two months* before beginning to execute such improvement, given to the landlord, or his agent duly authorised in that behalf, notice in writing of his intention so to do, and of the manner in which he proposes to do the intended work, and of the estimated cost thereof, and upon such notice being given, the landlord and tenant may agree on the terms as to compensation on which the improvement is to be executed, and any such agreement shall be deemed to be an agreement within the

meaning of and subject to the provisions of section four of this Act, or the landlord may, unless the notice of the tenant is previously withdrawn, undertake to execute the improvement himself, and may execute the same in any reasonable and proper manner which he thinks fit, and charge the tenant with a sum not exceeding *three pounds* per centum per annum on the outlay incurred in executing the improvement, or not exceeding such annual sum payable for a period of *twenty-five years* as will repay such outlay in the said period, with interest at the rate of *two and a half* per centum per annum, such annual sum to be recoverable as rent. In default of any such agreement or undertaking, and also in the event of the landlord failing to comply with his undertaking, within *three months*, the tenant may execute the improvement himself, and shall in respect thereof be entitled to compensation under this Act subject to the provisions of section three of this Act.

3. Where a tenant has executed on his holding prior to the commencement of this Act, whether under a contract of tenancy then current or not, any of the improvements mentioned in Part I of the Schedule, without having received previously to the execution thereof any written notice of dissent by the landlord, he shall be entitled to compensation in respect of such improvement, unless on a reference under this Act, the arbitrator shall be of opinion that the improvement was not suitable to the holding as an agricultural holding. Improvements made prior to this Act. *See* Smith *v.* Pocock (1885, 53 L. T., 230). Woodward *v.* Clark (Market Gardeners' Compensation Act), county court case.

4. (1.) Where an agreement in writing secures to the tenant for any improvement other than the improvements mentioned in the First Part of the Schedule to this Act, or for any tillages, crops, or other matters or things in respect of which he is entitled to claim compensation under any custom, fair and reasonable compensation, having regard to the circumstances existing at the time of making such agreement, then in such case the compensation in respect of such improvement, or of such tillages, crops, or other matters or things shall be payable in pursuance of the particular agreement, and shall be deemed to be substituted for compensation under this Act, and in case of dispute, the question whether any such compensation is fair or reasonable shall be determined by a reference under this Act. Compensation under agreement 46 & 47 Vict. c. 61. s. 53. Morgan *v.* Farquharson (1894, 1 Q.B., 532).

(2.) The amount of any compensation so substituted under this section and section two may be included in any notice of claim and in any award, and recovered under the provisions of this Act.

Record of Condition of Holding.

Record of condition of holding.

5. Every contract of tenancy entered into after the commencement of this Act shall contain a scheduled record of the agricultural condition of the holding and its several parts, and of the buildings, fences, roads, and drains at the beginning of the contract of tenancy. At any time during a tenancy existing at the commencement of this Act, either party may require a record in similar form to be made by an arbitrator appointed by the county court. Copies of all such records shall be deposited in the office of the registrar of the county court, and either party shall be entitled to inspect same at all reasonable times, and to take copies thereof.

Regulations as to Compensation for Improvements.

Regulations as to compensation for improvements. [Act 1883, s. 6.]

6. In the ascertainment of the amount of the compensation under this Act payable to the tenant in respect of any improvement there shall be taken into account in reduction thereof :

(*a.*) Any benefit which the landlord has given or allowed to the tenant in consideration of the tenant executing the improvement; and

Schofield v. Hincks (1888. 60 L.T., 573).

(*b.*) In the case of compensation for manures, the value of the manure that would have been produced by the consumption on the holding of any hay, straw, roots, or green crops sold off or removed, contrary to the written terms of the tenancy, from the holding within the last year of the tenancy, or other less time for which the tenancy has endured, except as far as a proper return of manure to the holding has been made in respect of such produce so sold off or removed therefrom; and

(*c.*) Any sums due to the landlord in respect of rent, and any taxes and rates due or becoming due in respect of the holding to which the tenant is liable as between him and the landlord ;

(*d.*) Any sums due to the landlord in respect of any waste committed by the tenant, or in respect of any breach of covenant or other agreement connected with the contract of tenancy committed by the tenant :

There shall be taken into account in augmentation of the tenant's compensation—

(*e.*) Any sum due to the tenant for compensation in respect of a breach of covenant or other agreement connected with a contract of tenancy, and committed by the landlord ;

(*f.*) Any sum due to the tenant under section eight of this Act ;

(*g.*) Any sum which may be found by a reference under this Act to be due to the tenant in respect of damage to crops by winged or ground game during the last year of the tenancy.

Nothing in this section shall enable a landlord to obtain under this Act compensation in respect of waste by the tenant, or of breach of covenant by the tenant, committed or permitted in relation to a matter of husbandry more than *two years* before the determination of the tenancy, or shall authorise the taking into account of permissive waste by any tenant from year to year, except so far as such tenant may be under an express covenant to repair.

7. (1.) Where any claim is made by the landlord, either in pursuance of the preceding section, or by action or otherwise, for any penal or additional rent or payment (and whether expressed to be liquidated damages or not) in respect of any breach or non-performance of any covenant or other agreement connected with the contract of tenancy, the sum taken into account in reduction of compensation, or recoverable by action or otherwise, shall be limited to the damages actually suffered by the landlord from any such default, notwithstanding any provision in the contract or tenancy. *Penal rents to be limited to actual damage.*

(2.) Where any action is brought, or proceeding taken by the landlord for rent, or any other matters mentioned in section six of this Act, it shall be lawful for the tenant to counter claim for any matters for which he is entitled to *See* Gas Light and Coke Co. *v.* Holloway (1885, 52 L.T., 434).

claim compensation under this Act, instead of proceeding to a reference hereunder.

Compensation for Disturbance.

Compensation for disturbance.

8. Where a tenant is compelled to quit his holding by the act of his landlord for any cause other than the following, that is to say:—
(1.) That he has not paid the rent due to his landlord within any period agreed by the contract of tenancy or otherwise; or
(2.) That he has persisted in committing or permitting waste, to the prejudice of his landlord, by the dilapidation of buildings or fences, or by the deterioration of the soil, after notice has been given by the landlord to such tenant not to commit, or permit, or to desist from the particular waste specified in such notice;

the tenant shall be entitled on quitting his holding to obtain from the landlord, in addition to the compensation if any, due to him under this Act, further compensation in respect of the loss sustained by reason of quitting his holding; and any question under this section, if in dispute, and the amount of such compensation, if the parties do not agree, shall be determined by a reference under this Act, and such compensation shall be separately specified in the award, and shall be recoverable under the provisions of this Act.

Procedure.

Statement of claims [Act 1883, s. 7.]

9. A tenant claiming compensation under this Act shall, *twenty-eight days* at least before the determination of the tenancy, send in writing to the landlord a statement of the particulars and amount of such claim.

See Holmes and Formby (1895) 1 Q.B., 174.

A landlord may make a claim under this Act in respect of any waste or breach of covenant or other agreement, and in any such case shall, twenty-eight days at least before the determination of the tenancy, send in writing to the tenant a statement of the particulars and amount of such claim.

No such statement whether by tenant or landlord shall be invalid for want of particularity.

10. The landlord and the tenant may agree on the amount and mode and time of payment of compensation to be paid under this Act. If in any case they do not so agree the difference shall be settled by a reference of the question in dispute to the agricultural arbitrator. Compensation agreed or settled by reference [Act 1883, s. 8.]

11. The delivery to the agricultural arbitrator of a certified copy of the statement of claim or of the question in dispute shall be deemed to be a submission to reference by the party delivering it; and neither party shall have power to revoke a submission without the consent of the other. Mode of submission to reference.

12. The arbitrator may call for the production of any sample, or voucher, or other document, or other evidence which is in the possession or power of either party, or which either party can produce, and which to the arbitrator seems necessary for determination of the matters referred and may take the examination of the parties and witnesses on oath, and may administer oaths and take affirmations; and if any person so sworn or affirming wilfully and corruptly gives false evidence he shall be guilty of perjury. Power for referee, &c. to require production of documents, administer oaths, &c. [Act 1883, s. 13.]

13. The arbitrator may proceed in the absence of either party where the same appears to him or them expedient, after notice given to the parties. Power to proceed in absence. [Act 1883, s. 14.]

14. The award shall be in writing, signed by the arbitrator. Form of award. [Act 1883, s. 15.]

15. Where the tenancy of a holding is determined at different periods in respect of the land and of the buildings, the arbitrator may make, at the proper time, separate awards in respect of the several parts of the holding the tenancy whereof is so determined.[1] Awards where tenancy is determined at different periods. See *ex parte* Earl of Portarlington. *In re* Paul (1889, 24 Q.B.D., 247).

16. The decision of the arbitrator in regard to any of the matters referred to him shall be final, and shall have the effect of a judgment of the county court; provided always that the arbitrator, if a point of law shall arise before him, may, and upon the application of either party, shall submit a case raising such point of law for the decision of the county court judge in whose district the holding or the Decision of arbitrator to be final.

---

[1] See also Q.B. Act 29, 1897, Morley *v* Carter.

greater part thereof is situate, and the decision of the county court judge shall be final.

<small>Award to give particulars. [Act 1883, s. 19.] See Shrubb v. Lee (1888, 59, L.T., 376).</small>

17. (1.) The award shall not award a sum generally for compensation, but shall, so far as possible, specify—
(*a.*) The several improvements, acts, and things in respect whereof compensation is awarded, and the several matters and things taken into account under the provisions of this Act in reduction or augmentation of such compensation ;
(*b.*) The time at which each improvement, act, or thing was executed, done, committed, or permitted ;
(*c.*) The sum awarded in respect of each improvement, act, matter, and thing ; and
(*d.*) Where the landlord desires to charge his estate with the amount of compensation found due to the tenant, or in the case of a sitting tenant to pay the same by a reduction of rent, the time at which, for the purposes of such charge, each improvement, act, or thing in respect of which compensation is awarded is to be deemed to be exhausted.

(2.) The award shall contain a schedule recording the condition of the holding and its several parts, and of the buildings, fences, drains, and roads at the determination of the tenancy.

<small>Costs of reference, s. 32.</small>

<small>[Act 1883, s. 20.]</small>

18. The costs of and attending the reference, including the remuneration of the arbitrator, and including other proper expenses (such remuneration and expenses not to exceed the scale hereinafter provided), shall be borne and paid by the parties in such proportion as to the arbitrator appears just, regard being had to the reasonableness or unreasonableness of the claim of either party in respect of amount, or otherwise, and to all the circumstances of the case.

The award may direct the payment of the whole or any part of the costs aforesaid by the one party to the other.

The costs aforesaid shall be subject to taxation by the registrar of the county court, on the application of either party, but that taxation shall be subject to review by the judge of the county court.

<small>Day for payment. [Act 1883, s. 21.]</small>

19. The award shall fix a day, not sooner than *one month* and not later than *two months* after the delivery of the

award, for the payment of money awarded for compensation, costs, or otherwise.

Fair Rent.

20. (1.) Either party to a contract of tenancy may apply to the arbitrator to determine what is a fair rent to be paid by the tenant to the landlord for the holding. Fair rent.

In determining what is a fair rent the arbitrator shall take into account—
  1. The earning capacity of the holding.
  2. The special circumstances or character of the holding, including the effect, if any, of restrictive covenants or stipulations.
  3. All special circumstances affecting farming operations in the district in which the holding is situate.
  4. The value, if any, of unexhausted improvements made by the tenant or his predecessors.
  5. The value of the tenant's own labour as superintendent or otherwise.

(2.) The rent so determined (in this Act referred to as the arbitration rent) shall be deemed to be the rent payable by the tenant as from the period commencing at the rent day next succeeding the decision of the arbitrator, and shall come in place of the existing rent, and, save by mutual agreement, the arbitration rent shall not be altered for a period of *three years* from such term.

(3.) Where the arbitrator shall decide that the fair rent shall be a sum more or less in amount than the existing rent, the tenant shall be bound or entitled, as the case may be, at the next payment of rent, to add to or deduct from the amount of the arbitration rent such sum or sums as will bring the amounts paid to the amount due under the arbitration rent in respect of the period between the date of the notice of application to fix the fair rent and the date when such rent was fixed.

(4.) When an application is lodged with the arbitrator to fix a fair rent it shall be in the power of the arbitrator, either under the same or under another application of the tenant, to stay all proceedings for the removal of the tenant in respect of non-payment of rent till the said application is finally determined, upon such terms as to payment of rent or otherwise as the arbitrator shall think fit.

Appointment of guardian.
[Act 1883, s. 25.]

21. Where a landlord or tenant is an infant without a guardian, or is of unsound mind, not so found by inquisition, the county court, on the application of any person interested, may appoint a guardian of the infant or person of unsound mind for the purposes of this Act, and may change the guardian if and as occasion requires.

Provisions respecting married women.
45 & 46 Vict. s. 75.
[Act 1883, s. 26.]

22. Where any woman married before the commencement of the Married Women's Property Act, 1882, is desirous of doing any act under this Act in respect of land, her title to which accrued before such commencement as aforesaid, her husband's concurrence shall be requisite. Except as aforesaid a married woman shall for all the purposes of this Act be in respect of land as if she was unmarried.

Costs in county court.
[Act 1883, s. 27.]

23. The costs of proceedings in the county court under this Act shall be in the discretion of the court.

The Lord Chancellor shall from time to time prescribe a scale of costs for those proceedings, and of costs to be taxed by the registrar of the court, other than those provided for by section thirty-two of this Act.

Service of notice, &c.
[Act 1883, s. 28.]
See Schofield v. Hincks (1888, 60 L.T., 573).

24. Any notice, request, demand, or other instrument under this Act may be served on the person to whom it is to be given, either personally or by leaving it for him at his last known place of abode in England or Wales, or by sending it through the post in a registered letter addressed to him there; and if so sent by post it shall be deemed to have been served at the time when the letter containing it was registered; and in order to prove service by letter it shall be sufficient to prove that the letter was properly addressed and posted, and that it contained the notice, request, demand, or other instrument to be served; and for such purpose a receipt bearing the post office stamp shall be evidence of the same until the contrary has been proved.

Official Agricultural arbitrators.

25. The Board of Agriculture shall appoint for every county (other than the metropolis or a county borough) or, where it is in their opinion advisable, for any group of counties one or more fit persons to be agricultural arbitrators, who shall have a practical knowledge of the agriculture of the county or counties, and shall assign to each such arbitrator the district within which he shall act, and for such appointment and assignment of districts shall have due regard to

representations, if any, made by the county council or councils concerned.

The remuneration, other than fees, of agricultural arbitrators shall be fixed from time to time by the Board of Agriculture, and approved by the Lords of the Treasury, *and such remuneration shall be paid out of moneys provided by Parliament for that purpose.*

If any agricultural arbitrator shall be proved to the satisfaction of the Board of Agriculture to be incompetent, or guilty of any misconduct in the execution of any duty under this Act, he shall be liable to have his appointment summarily cancelled by the Board.

26. The council of every parish or the councils of adjoining parishes containing together a population not exceeding two thousand, where they so agree, or where there is no parish council, the district council, shall from time to time appoint one or more fit persons at their discretion to be parish valuers in the case of allotments or holdings of less than ten acres within such parish or parishes, and any claim under this Act in the case of an allotment or holding of less than ten acres may be referred either to the agricultural arbitrator for the county, or to the parish valuer, as the tenant in any case may prefer. Provided that nothing in this sub-section shall apply to any tenancy created by compulsory hiring under the tenth section of the Local Government Act, 1894. *Parish valuers*

27. Arbitrators appointed under this Act shall be paid according to a rate of charges fixed by the Board of Agriculture, and the said Board may from time to time revise and alter such rate, and shall in any such rate of charges provide a special rate for allotments or holdings of less than ten acres. *Fees for referees, &c.*

Charge of Tenant's Compensation.

28. A landlord, on paying to the tenant the amount due to him in respect of compensation under this Act, or in respect of compensation authorised by this Act to be substituted for compensation under this Act or on expending such amount, as may be necessary to execute an improvement under the First Part of the Schedule hereto, after notice given by the tenant of his intention to execute such improvement in *Power for landlord on paying compensation to obtain charge. [Act 1883, s. 29.] See Gough v. Gough (1891 2 Q.B., 665).*

accordance with this Act, shall be entitled to obtain from the county court a charge on the holding, or any part thereof, to the amount of the sum so paid or expended.

The court shall, on proof of the payment or expenditure, and on being satisfied of the observance in good faith by the parties of the conditions imposed by this Act, make an order charging the holding, or any part thereof, with repayment of the amount paid or expended, with such interest, and by such instalments, and with such directions for giving effect to the charge, as the court thinks fit.

But where the landlord obtaining the charge is not absolute owner of the holding for his own benefit, no instalment or interest shall be made payable after the time when the improvement in respect whereof compensation is paid will, where an award has been made, be taken to have been exhausted according to the declaration of the award, and in any other case after the time when any such improvement will, in the opinion of the court, after hearing such evidence, if any, as it thinks expedient, have become exhausted.

The instalments and interest shall be charged in favour of the landlord, his executors, administrators, and assigns.

The estate or interest of any landlord holding for an estate or interest determinable or liable to forfeiture by reason of his creating or suffering any charge thereon, or disentitling himself to receive the income thereof, shall not be determined or forfeited by reason of his obtaining or giving a charge or agreeing for any reduction of rent under this Act, anything in any deed, will, or other instrument to the contrary thereof notwithstanding.

_{45 & 46 Vict. c. 38.} Capital money arising under the Settled Land Act, 1882, may be applied in payment of any moneys expended and costs incurred by a landlord under or in pursuance of this Act in or about the execution of any improvement mentioned in the First Part of the Schedule hereto, as for an improvement authorised by the said Settled Land Act ; and such money may also be applied in discharge of any charge created on a holding under or in pursuance of this Act in respect of any such improvement as aforesaid, as in discharge of an incumbrance authorised by the said Settled Land Act to be discharged out of such capital money.

_{Incidence of charge.} 29. The sum charged by the order of a county court

under this Act shall be a charge on the holding or the part [Act. 1883, thereof charged for the landlord's interest therein, and for s. 30.] all interests therein subsequent to that of the landlord; but so that the charge shall not extend beyond the interest of the landlord, his executors, administrators, and assigns, in the tenancy where the landlord is himself a tenant of the holding.

30. Where the landlord is a person entitled to receive the rents and profits of any holding as trustee, or in any character otherwise than for his own benefit, the amount due from such landlord in respect of compensation under this Act, or in respect of compensation authorised by this Act to be substituted for compensation under this Act, shall be recoverable personally against such landlord, but :— *Provision in case of trustee.* [Act 1883, s. 31.]

(1.) Such landlord shall, either before or after having paid to the tenant the amount due to him, be entitled to obtain from the county court a charge on the holding to the amount of the sum required to be paid or which has been paid, as the case may be, to the tenant.

(2.) If such landlord neglect or fail within one month after the determination of the tenancy or the amount has become due, whichever shall last happen, to pay to the tenant the amount due to him, then after the expiration of such *one month* the tenant shall be entitled to obtain from the county court in favour of himself, his executors, administrators, and assigns, a charge on the holding to the amount of the sum due to him, and of all costs properly incurred by him in obtaining the charge or in raising the amount due thereunder.

(3.) The court shall on proof of the tenant's title to have a charge made in his favour make an order charging the holding with payment of the amount of the charge, including costs, in like manner and form as in case of a charge which a landlord is entitled to obtain.

(4.) A charge under this section or under section thirty of this Act shall be a land charge within the meaning of the Land Charges Registration and Searches Act, 1888, and shall be registered accordingly. 53 & 54 Vict. c. 57. s. 3.

31. Any company now or hereafter incorporated by Par- *Advance made by a company.*

liament, and having power to advance money for the improvement of land, may take an assignment of any charge made by a county court under the provisions of this Act, upon such terms and conditions as may be agreed upon between such company and the person entitled to such charge ; and such company may assign any charge so acquired by them to any person or persons whomsoever.

[Act 1883, s. 32.]

Notice to Quit.

Time of notice to quit
[Act 1883, s. 33.]
See Beddoe *v.* Rees, March 12th, 1885, "Times" Legal Report. Barlow *v.* Teal (1885, Q.B.D., 501).

32. Where a half year's notice, expiring with a year of tenancy is by law necessary and sufficient for determination of a tenancy from year to year, in the case of any such tenancy under a contract of tenancy made either before or after the commencement of this Act, a year's notice so expiring shall by virtue of this Act be necessary and sufficient for the same, unless the landlord and tenant of the holding, by writing under their hands, agree that this section shall not apply, in which case a half year's notice shall continue to be sufficient ; but nothing in this section shall extend to a case where the tenant is adjudged bankrupt, or has filed a petition for a composition or arrangement with his creditors.

Fixtures.

Tenant's property in fixtures, machinery, &c.
[Act 1883, s. 34.]
See Meux *v.* Cobley (1892, 2 Ch., 253).

33. Where after the first day of January, one thousand eight hundred and eighty-four, a tenant has affixed, or shall hereafter affix, to his holding any engine, machinery, fencing, or other fixture, or erects any building for which he is not under this Act or otherwise entitled to compensation, and which is not so affixed or erected in pursuance of some obligation in that behalf or instead of some fixture or building belonging to the landlord, or where a tenant has acquired any such engine, machinery, fencing, or other fixture or building by purchase or by inheritance, then such fixture or building shall be the property of and be removable by the tenant before or within twenty-one days after the termination of the tenancy.

Provided as follows :—

1. Before the removal of any fixture or building the tenant shall pay all rent owing by him, and shall perform

or satisfy all other his obligations to the landlord in respect to the holding ;

2. In the removal of any fixture or building the tenant shall not do any avoidable damage to any other building or other part of the holding ;

3. Immediately after the removal of any fixture or building the tenant shall make good all damage occasioned to any other building or other part of the holding by the removal ;

4. The tenant shall not remove any fixture or building without giving *one month's* previous notice in writing to the landlord of the intention of the tenant to remove it ;

5. At any time before the expiration of the notice of removal the landlord, by notice in writing given by him to the tenant, may elect to purchase any fixture or building comprised in the notice of removal, and any fixture or building thus elected to be purchased shall be left by the tenant, and shall become the property of the landlord, who shall pay the tenant the fair value thereof to an incoming tenant of the holding ; and any difference as to the value shall be settled by a reference under this Act, as in case of compensation (but without appeal).

6. A landlord shall not recover more damages for a breach of this section than he shall prove that he has actually suffered.

Crown and Duchy Lands.

34. This Act shall extend and apply to land belonging to Her Majesty the Queen, Her heirs and successors, in right of the Crown. [Application of Act to Crown lands. [Act 1883, s. 35.]

With respect to such land, for the purposes of this Act, the Commissioners of Woods and Forests, or one of them, or other the proper officer or body having charge of such land for the time being, or in case there is no such officer or body, then such person as Her Majesty, Her heirs or successors, may appoint in writing under the Royal Sign Manual, shall represent Her Majesty, Her heirs and successors, and shall be deemed to be the landlord.

Any compensation payable under this Act by the Commissioners of Woods and Forests, or either of them, in respect of an improvement mentioned in the First or Second Part of the Schedule hereto, shall be deemed to be payable in respect of an improvement of land within section one of the Crown Lands Act, 1866, and the amount thereof shall be charged and repaid as in that section provided with respect to the costs, charges and expenses therein mentioned.

Any compensation payable under this Act by those Commissioners, or either of them, in respect of any other improvement, shall be deemed to be part of the expenses of the management of the Land Revenues of the Crown, and shall be payable to those Commissioners out of such money and in such manner as the last-mentioned expenses are by law payable.

Application of Act to land of Duchy of Lancaster. [Act 1883, s. 36.]

35. This Act shall extend and apply to land belonging to Her Majesty, Her heirs and successors, in right of the Duchy of Lancaster.

With respect to such land for the purposes of this Act, the Chancellor for the time being of the Duchy shall represent Her Majesty, Her heirs and successors, and shall be deemed to be the landlord.

The amount of any compensation payable under this Act by the Chancellor of the Duchy in respect of an improvement mentioned in the First or Second Part of the Schedule to this Act shall be deemed to be an expense incurred in improvement of land belonging to Her Majesty, Her heirs or successors, in right of the Duchy within section twenty-five of the Act of the fifty-seventh year of King George the Third, chapter ninety-seven, and shall be raised and paid as in that section provided with respect to the expenses therein mentioned.

The amount of any compensation payable under this Act by the Chancellor of the Duchy in respect of any other improvement shall be paid out of the annual revenues of the Duchy.

Application of Act to land of Duchy of Cornwall. [Act 1883, s. 37.]

36. This Act shall extend and apply to land belonging to the Duchy of Cornwall.

With respect to such land, for the purposes of this Act, such person as the Duke of Cornwall for the time being, or other the personage for the time being entitled to the revenues and possessions of the Duchy of Cornwall, from time to time, by sign manual, warrant, or otherwise, appoints, shall represent the Duke of Cornwall or other the personage aforesaid, and be deemed to be the landlord, and may do any act or thing under this Act which a landlord is authorised or required to do thereunder.

Any compensation payable under this Act by the Duke of Cornwall, or other the personage aforesaid, in respect of an improvement mentioned in the First or Second Part of the Schedule to this Act shall be deemed to be payable in respect of an improvement of land within section eight of the Duchy of Cornwall Management Act, 1863, as amended by the Duchy of Cornwall Management Act, 1868, and the amount thereof may be advanced and paid from the money mentioned in that section, subject to the provision therein made for repayment of sums advanced for improvements.

Ecclesiastical and Charity Lands.

37. Where lands are assigned or secured as the endowment of a see the powers by this Act conferred on a landlord shall not be exercised by the archbishop or bishop, in respect of those lands, except with the previous approval in writing of the Estates Committee of the Ecclesiastical Commissioners. Landlord, archbishop or bishop. [Act 1883, s. 38.]

38. Where a landlord is incumbent of an ecclesiastical benefice, the powers by this Act conferred on a landlord shall not be exercised by him in respect of the glebe land or other land belonging to the benefice, except with the previous approval in writing of the patron of the benefice, that is, the person, officer, or authority who, in case the benefice were vacant, would be entitled to present thereto, or of Queen Anne's Bounty. Landlord incumbent of benefice. [Act 1883, s. 39.] 52 & 53 Vict. c. 63. s. 12 (16).

In every such case Queen Anne's Bounty may, if they think fit, on behalf of the incumbent, out of any money in their hands, pay to the tenant the amount of compensation due to him under this Act; and thereupon they may, instead of the incumbent, obtain from the county court a charge on the holding, in respect thereof, in favour of themselves.

Every such charge shall be effectual, notwithstanding any change of the incumbent.

39. The powers by this Act conferred on a landlord in respect of charging the land shall not be exercised by Landlord, charity trustees, &c. [Act 1883, s. 40.]

trustees for ecclesiastical or charitable purposes, except with the previous approval in writing of the Charity Commissioners.

Land in Mortgage.

Compensation to tenants when mortgagee is in possession.
[*See* Tenants' Compensation Act, 1890.]
50 & 51 Vict. c. 26.

40. Where a person occupies land under a contract of tenancy with the mortgagor, whether made before or after the passing of this Act, which is not binding on the mortgagee of such land, then—

(1.) The occupier shall, as against the mortgagee who takes possession, be entitled to any compensation which is, or would but for the mortgagee taking possession be due to the occupier from the mortgagor as respects crops, improvements, tillages, or other matters connected with the land, whether under this Act, or the Market Gardeners' Compensation Act, 1895, or the Allotments and Cottage Gardens Compensation for Crops Act, 1887, or the custom of the country, or agreements sanctioned by this Act or the last-mentioned Act of 1887.

(2.) Any sum ascertained to be due to the occupier for such compensation or for any costs connected therewith may be set off against any rent or other sum due from him in respect of the land, and recovered as compensation under this Act or the said Act of 1887, and may, as against the mortgagee, be recovered as if the mortgagee were the landlord, and any sum so paid by the mortgagee may be added by him to his security.

(3.) Before the mortgagee deprives the occupier of possession of the land otherwise than in accordance with the said contract, he shall give to the occupier *six months'* notice in writing of his intention so to deprive him, and if he so deprives him compensation shall be due to the occupier for his crops, and for any expenditure upon the land which he has made in the expectation of holding the land for the full term of his contract of tenancy, in so far as any improvement resulting therefrom is not exhausted at the time of his being so deprived, and for any other loss sustained by him by reason of quitting his holding, and such compensation shall be determined in like manner as compensation under this Act, and shall be set off and recovered in manner before provided in this section. This sub-section shall only apply where the said contract is for a tenancy from year to year, or for a year or any less term or for a term of years not exceeding *twenty-one*, at a rack-rent.

Resumption for Improvements and Miscellaneous.

41. Where on a tenancy from year to year a notice to quit is given by the landlord with a view to the use of land for any of the following purposes :— {Resumption of possession for cottages, &c. [Act 1883, s. 41.]}

The erection of farm labourers' cottages or other houses, with or without gardens ;

The providing of gardens for existing farm labourers' cottages or other houses ;

The allotment for labourers of land for gardens or other purposes ;

The planting of trees ;

The opening or working of any coal, ironstone, limestone, or other mineral, or of a stone quarry, clay, sand, or gravel pit, or the construction of any works or buildings to be used in connection therewith ;

The obtaining of brick, earth, gravel, or sand ;

The making of a watercourse, or reservoir, or providing water supply ;

The making of any road, railway, tramroad, siding, canal, or basin, or any wharf, pier, or other work connected therewith, or any sanitary works or improvements ;

and the notice to quit so states, then it shall, by virtue of this Act, be no objection to the notice that it relates to part only of the holding.

In every such case the provisions of this Act respecting compensation shall apply as on determination of a tenancy in respect of an entire holding.

The tenant shall also be entitled to a proportionate reduction of rent in respect of the land comprised in the notice to quit, and in respect of any depreciation of the value to him of the residue of the holding, caused by the withdrawal of that land from the holding or by the use to be made thereof, and the amount of that reduction shall be ascertained by agreement or settled by a reference under this Act. And the tenant shall also be entitled to recover fair and reasonable compensation for any damage which he may suffer by the construction or carrying out of any of the works in this section mentioned.

The tenant shall further be entitled, at any time within *one month* after service of the notice to quit, to serve on the landlord a notice in writing to the effect that he (the tenant) accepts the same as a notice to quit the entire holding, to take effect at the expiration of the then current year of tenancy; and the notice to quit shall have effect accordingly.

<small>Provision as to limited owners. [Act 1883, s. 42.]</small>

42. Subject to the provisions of this Act in relation to Crown, duchy, ecclesiastical, and charity lands, a landlord, whatever may be his estate or interest in his holding, may give any consent, make and vary any agreement, or do or have done to him any act in relation to improvements in respect of which compensation is payable under this Act which he might give or make or do or have done to him if he were in the case of an estate of inheritance owner thereof in fee, and in the case of a leasehold possessed of the whole estate in the leasehold.

<small>Provision in case of reservation of rent. [Act 1883, s. 43.]</small>

43. When, by any Act of Parliament, deed, or other instrument, a lease of a holding is authorised to be made, provided that the best rent, or reservation in the nature of rent, is by such lease reserved, then, whenever any lease of a holding is, under such authority, made to the tenant of the same, it shall not be necessary, in estimating such rent or reservation, to take into account against the tenant the increase, if any, in the value of such holding arising from any improvements made or paid for by him on such holding.

PART II.

Abolition of the Law of Distress for Rent.

<small>No distress may be taken in respect of rent.</small>

44. After the commencement of this Act, it shall not be lawful for any landlord or other person entitled heretofore to take distress for rent due in respect of any holding to so take or cause to be taken any distress for rent due in respect of any such holding, and any agreement in contravention of this section, whether entered into before or after the passing of this Act, shall be null and void.

PART III.

General Provisions.

45. This Act shall come into force on the *first day of January* next after the passing of this Act, which day is in this Act referred to as the commencement of this Act. Commencement of Act. [Act 1883, s. 53.]

46. (1.) This Act shall apply to every holding that is either wholly agricultural or wholly pastoral, or in part agricultural and as to the residue pastoral, or in whole or in part cultivated as a market garden. Holdings to which this Act applies. [Act 1883, s. 54.] *See* Godfrey *v.* Jacobs 1888, June 10th, "Times" Legal Report.

(2.) This Act shall also apply to every holding which is a holding within the meaning of the Allotments and Cottage Gardens Compensation for Crops Act, 1887, and the tenant of every such holding shall be entitled to compensation under this Act, in accordance with the procedure of this Act, and every such tenant may, with reference to such matters and things for which a claim may be made under both this Act and the last-mentioned Act of 1887, elect to claim under either of them.

47. Every contract, agreement, or covenant, condition or arrangement which purports to take away or modify, or which in fact does take away or modify the right of a tenant to claim compensation under this Act in respect of any improvement or any other right of the tenant as declared given or reserved by this Act (except as is expressly provided for by this Act), or imposes upon him any disadvantage in consequence of his exercising such rights, shall be void both at law and in equity so far as it takes away or modifies his rights or gives him any disadvantage as aforesaid ; and the arbitrator may declare the same to be void accordingly, and proceed in the reference as though the same were non-existent. Avoidance of agreement inconsistent with Act. [Act 1883, s. 55.]

48. Where an incoming tenant has paid to an outgoing tenant any compensation payable under or in pursuance of this Act in respect of the whole or part of any improvement, such incoming tenant shall be entitled on the determination of his tenancy to claim compensation in respect of such improvement or part in like manner, if at all, as the outgoing tenant would have been entitled if he had remained tenant of the holding, and his tenancy had Right of tenant in respect of improvement purchased from outgoing tenant. [Act 1883, s. 56. *See* Shrubb *v.* Lee (1888, 59 L.T., 376.)

determined at the time at which the tenancy of the incoming tenant determines

Compensation under this Act to be exclusive in some cases. [Act 1883, s. 57.] *See* Branskill *v.* Atkinson, "Times" Legal Report, November 1st, 1884.

49. A tenant shall not be entitled to claim compensation by custom or otherwise than in manner authorized by this Act in respect of any improvements for which he is entitled to compensation under or in pursuance of this Act, except as provided in section seven sub-section (2).

Compensation under custom to come within the Act.

50. Where a tenant is entitled to claim compensation by custom or otherwise than in manner authorised by this Act, in respect of tillages, crops, fruit trees or bushes, underwood, seeds, straw, hay, or manure left on the holding, or for cartage, or in respect of a proportion of rent, rates, or tithes for any period, or for any other matter or thing connected with the holding, he may claim and obtain compensation therefor under this Act, as though all or any of such matters or things were improvements specified in this Act.

Provision as to change of tenancy. [Act 1883, s. 58.]

51. (1.) A tenant who has remained in his holding during a change or changes of tenancy, and has not thereupon received compensation for improvements, shall not thereafter at the determination of a tenancy be deprived of his right to claim compensation in respect of improvements by reason only that such improvements were made during a former tenancy or tenancies, and not during the tenancy which is then determining, but may claim for them as if made during such last-mentioned tenancy.

(2.) Where the tenant has so remained in any part of his holding, then this section shall have effect in respect of such part of the holding.

Restriction in respect of improvements by tenant about to quit. [Act 1883, s. 59.]

52. Subject as in this section mentioned, a tenant shall not be entitled to compensation in respect of any improvements (other than the use of fertilisers and feeding stuffs or continuous good farming or tillages and crops, including fruit and vegetables) begun by him, if he holds from year to year, within one year before he quits his holding, or at any time after he has given or received final notice to quit, and, if he holds as a lessee, within one year before the expiration of his lease.

A final notice to quit means a notice to quit which has

not been waived or withdrawn, but has resulted in the tenant quitting his holding.

The foregoing provisions of this section shall not apply in the case of any such improvement as aforesaid—
(1.) Where a tenant from year to year has begun such improvement during the last year of his tenancy, and, in pursuance of a notice to quit thereafter given by landlord, has quitted his holding at the expiration of that year ; and
(2.) Where a tenant, whether a tenant from year to year or a lessee, previously to beginning any such improvement, has served notice on his landlord of his intention to begin the same, and the landlord has either assented or has failed for a month after the receipt of the notice to object to the making of the improvemet.

53. (1.) Where by any contract of tenancy it is stipulated that the tenancy shall cease or determine, or that the landlord shall have the right to re-enter on the holding, or that a forfeiture shall accrue, or that any penal or additional rent shall become due or payable by the tenant, or that the tenant shall incur any liability or suffer any other disadvantage, on the breach or non-performance by such tenant of any covenant, or agreement, connected with the tenancy, in respect of the mode of cultivation, or cropping, or disposal of produce (other than a covenant, or agreement, or stipulation not to break up or convert into tillage any permanent pasture or meadow land included in the holding, or not to remove manure), such stipulation shall be void and of none effect if the tenant shall have made previously to the time when it is sought to enforce or take advantage of such stipulation, a return of natural or artificial manure, proper and adequate in respect of the mode of cultivation, or cropping, or disposal of produce adopted, to his holding, or shall offer and give sufficient security that he will, at the proper season, make such proper and adequate return of manure to the holding. *Freedom of cropping and disposal of produce.*

(2.) For the purposes of this section, a lease limited to continue so long only as the tenant abstains from committing a breach of, or performs some, covenant, shall be and take effect as a lease to continue for any longer term for which it would subsist, but determinable by a proviso for re-entry on such a breach or non-performance. *See 44 & 45 Vict. c. 41. s. 14 (3).*

> General saving of rights.
> [Act 1883, s. 60.]

54. Except as in this Act expressed, nothing in this Act shall take away, abridge, or prejudicially affect any power, right, or remedy of a landlord, tenant, or other person vested in or exerciseable by him by virtue of any other Act or law, or under any custom of the country or otherwise, in respect of a contract of tenancy or other contract, or of any improvements, waste, emblements, tillages, away-going crops, fixtures, tax, rate, tithe rent-charge, rent, or other thing.

> Interpretation
> [Act 1883, s. 61.]
> [*See* 46 & 47 Vict. c. 61. s. 61.]

55. In this Act—

"Improvement" means any act or thing whereby the letting value of the holding is increased, and shall include increased fertility and cleanliness due to continuous good farming:

"Contract of tenancy" means a letting of or agreement for the letting land for a term of years, or for lives, or for lives and years, or from year to year, or for any other period:

A tenancy from year to year under a contract of tenancy current on the first day of January, one thousand eight hundred and eighty-four, shall for the purposes of this Act be deemed to be a tenancy under a contract of tenancy beginning after that date:

"Determination of tenancy" means the cesser of a contract of tenancy by reason of effluxion of time, or from any other cause:

> *See* Gough *v.* Gough.

"Landlord" in relation to a holding means any person for the time being entitled to receive the rents and profits of any holding:

"Landlord" includes the executors, administrators, assigns, legatee, devisee, or next-of-kin, husband, guardian, committee of the estate, or trustees in bankruptcy of a landlord, or the mortgagee who takes possession of any holding in respect of that holding:

"Tenant" means the holder of land under a landlord for a term of years, or for lives, or for lives and years, or from year to year, or for any other period:

"Tenant" includes the executors, administrators, assigns, legatee, devisee, or next-of-kin, husband, guardian, committee of the estate, or trustees in bankruptcy of a tenant, or any person deriving title from a tenant; and the right to receive compensation in respect of any improvement made by a tenant shall enure to the benefit of such executors, administrators, assigns, and other persons as aforesaid :

"Holding" means any parcel of land held by a tenant :

"County court," in relation to a holding, means the county court within the district whereof the holding or the larger part thereof is situate :

"Person" includes a body of persons and a corporation aggregate or sole :

The designations of landlord and tenant shall continue to apply to the parties until the conclusion of any proceedings taken under or in pursuance of this Act in respect of compensation for improvements, or under any agreement made in pursuance of this Act or otherwise.

56. On and after the commencement of this Act, the Agricultural Holdings (England) Act, 1883, the Tenants' Compensation Act, 1890, and the Market Gardeners' Compensation Act, 1895 shall be repealed. Repeal of Act of 1883 and Tenants' Compensation Act 1890. [Act 1883, s. 62.]

Provided that such repeal shall not affect—

(*a*) any thing duly done or suffered, or any proceedings pending under or in pursuance of any enactment hereby repealed ; or

(*b*) any right to compensation in respect of improvements to which either of the Agricultural Holdings (England) Acts, 1875, 1883, applies, and which were executed before the commencement of this Act, or any right to fixtures or other right by either of the said Acts given to the tenant ; or See s. 4.

(*c*) any right to compensation in respect of any improvement to which the Agricultural Holdings (England) Act, 1875, applies although executed by a tenant after the commencement of this Act if made under a contract of tenancy current on the first day of January, one thousand eight hundred and eighty-four ; or

(*d*) any right of any occupier given or reserved to him under the Tenants' Compensation Act, 1890, or the Market Gardeners' Compensation Act, 1895 ;

and any right reserved by this section may be enforced after the commencement of this Act in the same manner in all respects as if no such repeal had taken place ; but it shall be competent for the tenant, if he shall think fit, to claim and enforce rights to compensation arising or which could have been enforced under the Act of 1883 by the precedure given by this Act.

Short title of Act.
[Act 1883 s. 63.]

57. This Act may be cited for all purposes as the Agricultural Holdings (England) Act, 1897.

Limits of Act.
[Act, 1883, s. 64.]

58. This Act shall not apply to Scotland or Ireland.

SCHEDULE.

PART I.

IMPROVEMENTS IN RESPECT OF WHICH NOTICE TO LANDLORD IS REQUIRED.

(1.) Erection, or enlargement of buildings, including labourers' cottages; making of drains or other sanitary accommodation or works.
(2.) Formation or enlargement of silos.
(3.) Making of water meadows, or works of irrigation.
(4.) Making of roads or bridges.
(5.) Making of watercourses, ponds, wells, or reservoirs, or of works for the application of water power, or for supply of water for agricultural or domestic purposes.
(6.) Making or removing of permanent fences.
(7.) Reclaiming of waste land.
(8.) Embankments and sluices against floods.
(9.) Drainage.

PART II.

IMPROVEMENTS IN RESPECT OF WHICH NOTICE TO LANDLORD IS NOT REQUIRED.

(10.) Erection or enlargement of buildings for the purposes of the trade or business of a market garden.
(11.) Repairing of buildings.
(12.) Improving of roads.
(13.) Improving of watercourses, ponds, wells or reservoirs, or of works for the application of water power, or for supply of water for agricultural or domestic purposes.
(14.) Making or planting of osier beds.

(15.) Making or enlarging of gardens.
(16.) Planting of hops.
(17.) Planting of orchards, or fruit trees, or fruit bushes.
(18.) Planting of strawberry plants and asparagus.
(19.) Warping of land.
(20.) Laying down of permanent pasture.
(21.) Laying down of seeds or other temporary pasture for not less than two years.
(22.) Boning of land with undissolved bones.
(23.) Chalking of land.
(24.) Clay-burning.
(25.) Claying of land.
(26.) Liming of land.
(27.) Marling of land.
(28.) Application to land of purchased artificial or other purchased manure.
(29.) Consumption on the holding by horses exclusively engaged or kept on the holding, cattle, sheep, or pigs, of cake or other feeding stuff not produced on the holding.
(30.) Consumption on the holding by horses exclusively engaged or kept on the holding, cattle, sheep, or pigs, of corn grown on the holding.
(31.) Continuous good farming and cultivation or good husbandry in excess of the standard of cultivation or good husbandry which the tenant was bound to maintain.
(32.) Any other improvement increasing the value of the holding as an agricultural holding.

J. Miller and Son, Printers, Edinburgh.

www.ingramcontent.com/pod-product-compliance
Lightning Source LLC
Chambersburg PA
CBHW030423300426
44112CB00009B/819